PRIVATE INTERESTS
Women, Portraiture, and the Visual Culture
of the English Novel, 1709–1791

This ambitious interdisciplinary study undertakes a new definition of the eighteenth-century novel's investment in vision and visual culture, tracing the relationship between the development of the novel and that of the equally contentious genre of the portrait, particularly as represented in the novel itself. Working with the novels of Richardson, Fielding, Haywood, Manley, Sterne, Wollstonecraft, and Inchbald, and the portraits of Reynolds, Gainsborough, Highmore, Hudson, Hogarth, and others, *Private Interests* points to the intimate connections between the literary works and the paintings. Arguing that the novel's representation of the portrait sustains a tension between competing definitions of private interests, Conway shows how private interests are figured as simultaneously decorous and illicit in the novel, with the portrait at once an instrument of propriety and of scandal. Examining women's roles as both authors of and characters in the novel and the novel's encounters with the portrait, the author provides a new definition of private interests, one which highlights the development of women's agency as both spectacles and spectators.

ALISON CONWAY is Associate Professor of English at the University of Western Ontario.

Private Interests

Women, Portraiture, and the Visual Culture of the English Novel, 1709–1791

ALISON CONWAY

UNIVERSITY OF TORONTO PRESS
Toronto Buffalo London

© University of Toronto Press 2001
Toronto Buffalo London
utorontopress.com

Reprinted in paperback 2019

ISBN 0-8020-3526-4 (cloth)
ISBN 978-1-4875-2544-6 (paper)   ISBN 978-1-4426-7876-7 (PDF)

Library and Archives Canada Cataloguing in Publication

Title: Private interests : women, portraiture, and the visual culture of the
   English novel, 1709–1791 / Alison Margaret Conway.
Names: Conway, Alison, author.
Description: Paperback reprint. Originally published 2001. | Includes
   bibliographical references and index.
Identifiers: Canadiana 20190190329 | ISBN 9781487525446 (softcover)
Subjects: LCSH: English fiction—18th century—History and criticism. | LCSH:
   Art and literature—England—History—18th century. | LCSH: Women and
   literature—England—History—18th century. | LCSH: Visual perception in
   literature. | LCSH: Portraits in literature. | LCSH: Women in literature.
Classification: LCC PR858.A74 C66 2019 | DDC 823/.509357—dc23

University of Toronto Press acknowledges the financial assistance to its
publishing program of the Canada Council for the Arts and the Ontario Arts
Council, an agency of the Government of Ontario.

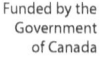

for Bryce

Contents

List of Illustrations ix
Acknowledgments xi

Introduction   3

1 The Novel and the Portrait in Eighteenth-Century England   14

2 Envisioning Literary Interest:
   Manley's *The New Atalantis*   50

3 'Ravished Sight': Picturing *Clarissa*   78

4 Refiguring Virtue:
   The History of Miss Betsy Thoughtless and *Amelia*   115

5 'Paint her to your own mind':
   Sterne's Concupiscible Narratives   150

6 Portraits of the Woman Artist:
   Kauffman, Wollstonecraft, and Inchbald   178

Afterword   210
Notes   215
Bibliography   265
Index   287

Illustrations follow p. 132

Illustrations

1. Joshua Reynolds, *Kitty Fisher as Cleopatra Dissolving the Pearl*, 1759.
2. Thomas Gainsborough, *Grace Dalrymple Elliot*, 1782.
3. Thomas Gainsborough, *Grace Dalrymple Elliot*, 1778.
4. Joseph Highmore, *Elizabeth Harris*, 1748.
5. Thomas Hudson, *Mary, Lady Wray* (d. 1751), date unknown.
6. George Romney, *Lady McLeod*, 1788.
7. Thomas Gainsborough, *Lady with a Spaniel*, ca. 1750.
8. Joshua Reynolds, *Emily, Countess of Kildare*, 1763.
9. John Russell, *Miss Chambers*, 1792.
10. Joshua Reynolds, *A Girl Reading*, 1771.
11. George Romney, *Serena*, date unknown.
12. Joseph Wright of Derby, *A Girl Reading a Letter by Candlelight, with a Young Man Peering Over Her Shoulder*, ca. 1760-2.
13. Joseph Wright of Derby, *A Girl Reading a Letter by Candlelight, with an Old Man Peering Over Her Shoulder*, ca. 1767-70.
14. Joshua Reynolds, *Kitty Fisher*, 1759.
15. William Hogarth, *Miss Mary Edwards*, 1742.
16. Peter Lely, *Portrait of Louise de Keroualle, Duchess of Portsmouth*, ca. 1672.
17. Peter Lely, *Nell Gwyn and Her Infant Son the Duke of St. Albans* (sometimes known as *Venus and Cupid*), ca. 1665.
18. Simon Verelst, *Nell Gwyn*, ca. 1690.
19. Artist unknown: possibly Hogarth, *Peg Woffington*, c. 1730-40.
20. Edward Haytley, *Miss E. Wandesford*, 1753.
21. Edward Haytley, *Sir Roger and Lady Bradshaigh*, 1746.
22. Thomas Hudson, *Anne Bouverie*, 1749.
23 Philip Mercier, *Peg Woffington*, ca.1735.

x   Illustrations

24. Thomas Gainsborough, *Mary 'Perdita' Robinson*, 1781.
25. Joshua Reynolds, *Laurence Sterne*, 1760.
26. Caricature of Elizabeth Lumley Sterne, wife of Laurence Sterne (putative).
27. Angelica Kauffman, *Self-Portrait*, ca. 1770–5.
28. Angelica Kauffman, *Self-Portrait in the Character of Painting Embraced by Poetry*, 1782.
29. Angelica Kauffman, *Self-Portrait: Hesitating between the Arts of Music and Painting*, 1791.

Acknowledgments

This study's first debt is to my family. My children, Hannah and Matthew, lived through the worst of times as I struggled to finish *Private Interests*. Bryce Traister has proven himself the best of partners: generous, loving, and committed. My extended family also endured years of my preoccupied nerviness, and I thank the members of this support group for their patience. Friends far and near listened to endless worries; particular thanks are due to Katherine Binhammer, who has lived with the book from its inception as a dissertation project years ago and who has provided me with emotional and intellectual support for more than a decade, to Dawn McGoey, neighbour and friend *par excellence*, and to Anne Bailey. I am also thankful to the undergraduate and graduate students who served as research assistants on this project. David Pennington deserves special thanks for his work in helping to prepare the manuscript submitted to the University of Toronto Press. At William and Mary College, Sandra Burr smoothed many, many wrinkles from the manuscript's brow before the book went to press. My colleagues Elizabeth Harvey and Mark Cheetham served as mentors in my early years as a teacher and scholar and always encouraged me to extend the reach of my research interests deeper into the worlds of theory and art history. Senior colleagues in the American Society for Eighteenth-Century Studies have been supportive since I first attended the society's annual conference in 1993; I am especially grateful to Bertrand Goldgar, Thomas Lockwood, Ruth Perry, Peter Sabor, Rusty Shteir, Peter Walmsley, and John O'Neill. And, finally, my dissertation readers proved allies long after I left the University of California, Berkeley. In particular, James Turner and Catherine Gallagher paced me through revisions of the project and, most importantly, repeatedly reminded me that I would, in fact, survive the whole ordeal.

My thanks to librarians and staff at the British Library, the National Portrait Gallery, the Paul Mellon Centre for the Arts, and the Courtauld Institute of Art. The early stages of research for this study were supported by SSHRCC. A Mellon dissertation fellowship from the Andrew M. Mellon Foundation funded my writing year as a graduate student. More recently, research grants from the University of Western Ontario, supported by SSHRCC funding, have enabled the archival work that turned the dissertation into a book.

A portion of chapter 1 first appeared in *Eighteenth-Century Life* 21, n.s., 3 (November 1997): 1–15, and a part of chapter 4 was published in *Eighteenth-Century Fiction* 8.1 (October 1995): 35–50.

PRIVATE INTERESTS

Introduction

It is not good that he who makes the laws execute them, nor that the body of the people turn its attention away from general considerations to devote it to particular objects. Nothing is more dangerous than the influence of private interests on public affairs.

Rousseau, *The Social Contract* (1761), Book III, Chapter 4

Ian Watt's famous definition of Richardson's *Pamela* as 'a work that gratified the reading public with the combined attractions of a sermon and a striptease'[1] reveals the extent to which the eighteenth-century novel's 'display' is always a display of the private, here figured as soul-making and sexual gratification. *Private Interests* argues that the interrelationships between the sermon and the striptease create new modes of seeing and being in the eighteenth-century novel and, most importantly, enable women to use the idea of the spectacle to their own advantage. In particular, I claim that the eighteenth-century English novel uses the painted portrait to analyse the meaning of women's relation to private interests, and that it places the idea of the spectacle and the aesthetics of beholding at the centre of its discussion. I examine how women's roles as both authors and characters in the novel's visual field inform eighteenth-century understandings of the acts of novel writing and novel reading. The portrait's frequent appearance in the novel renders the issue of visual agency – in relation to both display and beholding – an important means of assessing how the eighteenth century understood women's connection to the cultural power that was associated with those activities.

The term 'private interests' appears as the marker of a particular

4   Private Interests

interpretive conflict that informed discussions of women's role in eighteenth-century English cultural life. Within the framework of progressive – i.e., Whig – ideology, the term defined a new commitment to the domestic and personal life as the origin of social unity and cooperation, a doctrine of sentimental affiliation that looks to women to guarantee the integrity of the private sphere. But as the epigraph to this study reveals, an anxiety remained that private interests could threaten the integrity of the public sphere.[2] Rousseau's warning – 'nothing is more dangerous than the influence of private interests on public affairs' – signals a concern that was never completely overcome in discussions of the idea's cultural implications. 'It is not good ... that the body of the people turn its attention away from general considerations to devote it to particular objects,' Rousseau argues;[3] in England, novels and portraits became the 'particular objects' around which the public debated the idea of private interests. In its representation of the portrait, I argue, the novel entertains the idea of private interests as both decorous and illicit, and creates its literary interest through sustaining a tension between these competing definitions of the idea. Out of this dialectic a third definition of private interests emerges, one that highlights women's capacity to claim agency as spectacles and spectators, as subjects figured as both embodied and critical within the visual moment created by the novel's representation of the portrait.

In the past fifteen years, the shape of the novel's visual dimensions has been most frequently viewed through the lens of Michel Foucault's analysis of vision and spectatorship. In *Discipline and Punish*, Foucault traces a shift from 'the spectacle of the scaffold' to the disciplinary mechanisms of 'panopticism,' a move toward a social order that 'fabricates' individuals through the disciplinary operations of an authorial gaze that is both nowhere and everywhere. The social order of modernity, Foucault argues, avoids the 'sensual proximity' afforded by public spectacles in favour of decorporealized and diffused visual modes of surveillance.[4] The eighteenth century marks a transitional moment in which the omniscient eye capable of occupying multiple visual sites replaces the embodied subject of the spectacle. Following Foucault, Nancy Armstrong's *Desire and Domestic Fiction* locates the struggle for spectatorial authority at the heart of the eighteenth-century novel. Armstrong's analysis of spectatorship in *Pamela* confirms her understanding of the eighteenth-century novel's transformation from 'semi-scandalous tale-telling to demonstrations of exemplary behavior,' a transformation that allows domestic ideology to shape women as subjects, rather than objects, of the gaze.⁵ In his analysis of the relationship between the eighteenth-century penitentiary and the early modern novel, John Bender traces a similar trajectory toward the creation of Foucault's subject.⁶ Bender's recent work suggests that the later eighteenth-century novel's representation of sympathetic spectatorship exposes a degree of violence latent in sentiment's narrative operations and highlights the workings of a dissecting gaze that 'cuts open the body in the act of mapping its functions.'⁷

Bender, Armstrong, and other critics following Foucault echo the suspicion of the visual that informs Foucault's study of the Enlightenment.⁸ While this suspicion has had the wholly positive effect of opening up the field of eighteenth-century studies to new considerations of the ideological systems that underpin the modern novel, it also has had the effect of straightening, somewhat, a road filled with unexpected curves.⁹ Most immediately, the totalizing impulses of Foucault's paradigms tend to transform a highly contested set of ideas into a series of middle-class social imperatives, a reconceptualization that empties out the eighteenth century of both its counter-discourses and moments of resistance. In embracing Foucault's compelling analysis of the Panopticon, we have imposed our own disciplinary gaze on the eighteenth-century novel, leaving in our blindspot the novel's dialectics and the possibility that women might emerge from the period in any other guise than that of the 'proper lady' Mary Poovey describes in her study of the late eighteenth and early nineteenth century.¹⁰

The question of vision stands at the center of the novel's discussion of private interests. In the third Earl of Shaftesbury's account of the benefits of reading classical literature, we find that

> We might ... as in a looking-glass, discover ourselves, and see our minutest features nicely delineated, and suited to our own apprehension and cognizance ... And, what was of singular note in these magical glasses, it would happen that, by constant and long inspection, the parties accustomed to the practice would acquire a peculiar speculative habit, so as virtually to carry about with them a sort of pocket-mirror, always ready and in use.¹¹

The reader, who looks at a mirror located in a text and then internalizes that mirror, remains continually divided, as one part of the self monitors the individual as a whole. In Shaftesbury this monitoring takes on an authoritarian judiciary force: 'As cruel a court as the Inquisition appears, there must, it seems, be full as formidable a one erected in ourselves, if we would pretend to that uniformity of opinion which is necessary to hold us to one will, and preserve us in the same mind from one day to another' (p. 122). Self-surveillance through reading helps the individual to avoid the trap of solipsism and its dangerous cousin, enthusiasm.

Shaftesbury's ideas on reading find expression in the eighteenth-century novel, where the exercise of spectatorial sympathy manifests the subject's commitment to fostering community. In the demonstrations of sympathy elicited by particular objects, characters in novels reveal their ability to establish the intersubjective relations that ensure the integrity of sentiment, maintaining its distance from solipsism and delusion by establishing an empirical marker by which the reader can gauge his or her own response.[12] The sincerity of the sentimental response to the portrait is guaranteed by the transparency of the visual moment. In *The Portrait*, for example, we find the heroine surprised by a portrait of her father: 'Maria had not gone many steps, when a full length portrait of her father caught her eye; the resemblance it seems was striking, a thousand interesting reflections instantly occurred to her imagination ... She faintly exclaimed, while her eyes, filled with tears, were fixed on it, oh! My father, my revered, my beloved father, and instantly sunk to the floor in a swoon.'[13]

If the portrait can confirm the benevolence of spectatorial sympathy, it can also reveal its latent violence; Leo Bersani has noted 'a certain risk in all sympathetic projections: the pleasure that accompanies them promotes a secret attachment to scenes of suffering or violence.'[14] Sentimental violence and violent sentimentality often appear in conjunction with the figure of the portrait, which has the ability to expose the voyeurism, sadism, and masochism at work in the visual field of the novel.[15] However, the import of the portrait is not limited to its revelations of the violence at work in the aesthetics of sympathy, and its dual aspect takes as its 'other' not the flip-side of the sentimental coin, but rather an alternative spectatorial dynamic, one that grants the spectacle an agency of its own. This agency finds its starting point in a number of different places. The portrait's materiality – the conditions of its making and consumption, and its status as an object of exchange and possession – complicates the sentimental ethos, as well as the violence, that its representation maintains. The portrait can refuse revelation and limit access to the person it represents by insisting on one aspect of the sitter's identity. The portrait may overwhelm its beholders, functioning as a sublime object, or establish competing responses to its representation. With the power of the spectacle it represents, the portrait may embolden its beholder. Signifying a range of positions and ideas, the portrait sustains an interpretive crisis around the idea of spectatorship in the novel, emerging as the '*punctum*,' to quote Roland Barthes, in the visual plane. Barthes uses the idea of the *punctum*, a wound or mark made by a pointed instrument, to designate how a photograph affects him: 'It is this element which rises from the scene, shoots out of it like an arrow, and pierces me.'[16] I use the term to emphasize the disruptive force of the portrait in the novel's field of vision, a violence that originates, not in the spectatorial gaze, but in the object itself. More generally, the *punctum* created by the portrait's appearance marks the place where competing visual agencies clash in the novel.[17]

Questions of women's cultural agency stand at the centre of eighteenth-century social and political discourses, and the ascendence of domestic ideology allowed the idea of private interests to link the sermon to the secular world in which private interests played an increasingly important role. In the framework of domestic ideology, as Harriet Guest has observed, the heightened importance granted to women's retirement and commitment to spiritual devotion allowed the nonaristocratic woman to become a moral yardstick for the culture as a whole.[18] Nancy Armstrong puts novel reading at the heart of eighteenth-century domestic ideology, arguing that the novel became the accepted means of inculcating 'a specific form of political unconscious' in women.[19] In describing the visual agency that appears in the novel, Armstrong emphasizes the extent to which women were encouraged to relinquish their desire to become part of a public spectacle as they assumed authority over the visual space of the home, over their own private interests.

The impetus toward disciplining the female spectacle appears early in the century in Joseph Addison's *The Spectator*. Although Addison relishes the sensual gratifications afforded by vision in his essays on the imagination, he confines these gratifications to the polite men of letters to whom his aesthetic commentary is directed. In the social realm, the embodied subject so crucial to aesthetic judgment becomes a liability. The attachment of women to display and spectatorial gratification renders them always already 'interested' individuals:

> I have often reflected with my self on this unaccountable Humour in Woman-kind, of being smitten with every thing that is showy and superficial; and on the numberless Evils that befall the Sex, from this light, fantastical Disposition ... When Women are thus perpetually dazling one anothers Imaginations, and filling their Heads with nothing but Colours, it is no

8   Private Interests

> Wonder that they are more attentive to the superficial Parts of Life, than the solid and substantial Blessings of it.

Addison assumes that women's visual agency in the public sphere, unlike men's, remains fundamentally divorced from intellectual insight, and he objects to women's greater interest in looking at each other, in 'perpetually dazling one anothers Imaginations,' than in pursuing a moral subjectivity. Addison and Steele encourage women to become inconspicuous by remaining in the private sphere and by cultivating a moral ethic with a self-critical eye. One of the *The Spectator*'s female correspondents writes: 'Dear Sir, be pleased to put such Books in our Hands, as may make our Virtue more inward.'[20]

The Spectator returns several times to the idea of the portrait to advance their moral agenda for women. John Hughes sets his understanding of women's value against that advanced by the banality of portraiture:

> It is, methinks, a low and degrading Idea of that Sex, which was created to refine the Joys, and soften the Cares of Humanity, by the most agreeable Participation, to consider them meerly as Objects of Sight. This is abridging them of their natural Extent of Power, to put them upon a Level with their Pictures at Kneller's. How much nobler is the Contemplation of Beauty heighten'd by Virtue, and commanding our Esteem and Love, while it draws our Observation?[21]

Hughes attacks the reduction of women to mere surfaces or 'pictures' and asks the viewer to develop an eye capable of discerning women's interiority. The scrutiny of women shifts from their physical presence (here associated with the eroticism of beauty as opposed to the beauty of virtue) to their moral integrity. In describing *The Spectator*'s socializing project, Addison represents himself as a portrait painter: 'As I would fain give some finishing Touches to those which are already the most beautiful Pieces in humane Nature, I shall endeavour to point out all those Imperfections that are the Blemishes, as well as those Virtues which are the Embellishments, of the Sex.' In a later number, he criticizes women's desire to speak in the public sphere from a similar vantage point: 'As I would fain contribute to make Woman-kind, which is the most beautiful Part of the Creation, entirely amiable, and wear out all those little Spots and Blemishes that are apt to rise among the Charms which Nature has poured out upon them, I shall dedicate this Paper to their Service. The Spot which I would here endeavour to clear them of, is that Party Rage which of late Years is very much crept into their Conversation.'²² In each of these moments, *The Spectator* seeks to remove the 'Spots and Blemishes' that tarnish women, especially when they fashion themselves political subjects in the public sphere. Women who appear in public as 'Objects of Sight' only arouse disrespect in men, who understand them as they would a Kneller portrait – that is to say, as erotic objects. If women align their gaze with the moral agenda that helps to 'refine the Joys, and soften the Cares of Humanity,' they can gain an alternative form of power.²³

For Addison and Steele, women's attachment to the aesthetics of the spectacle perverts the natural order of gender relations: 'For my own part, as I do not love to be insulted by Women who are taller than my self,' writes Addison in his commentary on women's hair fashions, 'I admire the Sex much more in their present Humiliation, which has reduced them to their natural Dimensions, than when they had extended their Persons, and lengthened themselves out into formidable and gigantick Figures.'²⁴ Addison's flippancy masks an anxiety that women might intimidate men such as Mr Spectator. The woman who fashions herself through a commissioned portrait endangers her entire family: 'Why should the lovely *Camilla* deceive us in more Shapes than her own, and affect to be represented in her Picture with a Gun and a Spaniel, while her elder Brother, the Heir of a worthy Family, is drawn in Silks like his Sister? The Dress and Air of a Man are not well to be divided.'²⁵ The name 'Camilla' evokes the Virgilian model of the Amazon, a figure that the male observer could only fear; here, Camilla's desire to pose with 'a Gun and a Spaniel,' in betraying naturalized standards of gender, threatens the family structure, most immediately by emasculating the heir. Camilla's self-representation 'in more Shapes than her own' puts men in a precarious relation to their patrimony. In claiming that the 'Dress and Air of a Man are not well to be divided,' *The Spectator* acknowledges the element of masquerade in the performance of social codes – that is to say, acknowledges the potential for self-division – but only to argue for the regulation of gender roles. Presumably either the painter or the family should have objected to the costumes and props of the portrait's subjects. Instead, Camilla threatens the viewer as he gazes upon her image, refusing his desire to bring women into the fold of the domestic and the moral. She interrupts the fantasy of visual omnipotence and omniscience that *The Spectator* strives to maintain, insisting on a visual perspective and agency different from those of Mr Spectator.²⁶

The portrait brings Camilla's visual impetus to the eighteenth-century novel. It would be easy to suggest that the novel gratifies male readers' erotic fantasies in formulating models of spectatorial pleasure while serving women a disciplinary lesson in the sentimental gaze it offers them. But such a reading simplifies the effect the moment of display achieves in narratives where the portrait appears. The representation of the portrait in the novel is most remarkable for the extent to which, as a spectacle, the portrait becomes an object that, to return to Barthes, marks and wounds its beholder. Epistemologically the portrait, as a 'particular object' that holds the reader's attention, disables the move toward the general standpoint that a disinterested subject is required to assume. The threat of scepticism appears in this moment when the beholder is unmoored, seduced away, from a stable vantage point. The discourses of political, philosophical, and cultural agency meet and merge in the female figure, which, in the dynamics surrounding the portrait's representation and beholding, remains a site of pleasure and power, and an instigator of epistemological uncertainty, throughout the eighteenth century.[27]

In the novel, the persistence of the female body and its connection to the trope of the portrait signal a discourse that runs counter to that of domestic ideology.[28] The eighteenth-century novel inherited its attachment to the spectacle from Restoration and early eighteenth-century scandal writers, especially Aphra Behn, Delarivier Manley, and Eliza Haywood.[29] Despite protestations to the contrary, novelists like Richardson repeatedly take their cue, in representing vision and visual aesthetics, from the licentious texts of these authors. I begin my reading of the eighteenth-century novel with Delarivier Manley's *New Atalantis*, whose portrait narrative articulates a scandalous approach to questions of female agency most graphically, demonstrating the principles against which later authors would claim to write. Manley's scandalous fiction, I argue, embodies a novelistic aesthetic that locates the female body within the public domain, and asserts the woman author's status through its spectatorial control. I then jump forward a generation to Richardson's *Clarissa*. While, in its representation of a disembodied female virtue, *Clarissa* may seem to promote an aesthetic far removed from the erotically charged Restoration ideal of Manley's novel, in fact it draws extensively on elements of Manley's fiction in representing women's relation to vision and visual culture. I am particularly interested in the portrayal of Clarissa in a 'Vandyke style' dress, popular in the eighteenth century both for the self-display that signalled status and privilege in a portrait, and as a masquerade costume. The chapter maps the ambiguity of the Vandyke portrait onto two competing hermeneutical strands in *Clarissa*.

Rather than oppose libertine and sentimental modes of beholding in the novel, I link the voyeurism of Lovelace's gaze to Richardson's most explicitly 'pious' moments of visual revelation. The novel resists the exposure of its heroine, not by contrasting the brightness of Clarissa's translucent body with the darkness of Lovelace's relentless corporeality, as has been argued, but by granting the heroine a visual opacity that blocks the gaze of both the reader and the libertine. That opacity takes us back to the element of masquerade in the portrait, which figures Clarissa's, and *Clarissa's*, material properties – both literal and figural – in the novel's concluding pages. The chapters that follow discuss authors writing in response both to *Clarissa* and the tremendous authority it claimed as a novel, and to the aesthetics of Delarivier Manley embedded in Richardson's narrative.

Starting with the trope of the portrait, each chapter of this study more generally considers the novel's engagement with visual culture and questions of beholding. I have chosen to write on Manley, Haywood, Richardson, Fielding, Sterne, Wollstonecraft, and Inchbald because these writers bring together a range of perspectives and also seem to speak to each other in very concrete ways in their analysis of women's relation to visual power. This study stresses, in other words, the connections, rather than differences, between the members of a group that, at first glance, may appear to cover all possible points of literary dispute. The fourth chapter, for example, discusses how Haywood and Fielding attempted to respond positively to *Clarissa*, though each of these authors had a history of writing against Richardson's cultural imperatives before 1748. Fielding's *Amelia* and Haywood's *The History of Miss Betsy Thoughtless*, both published in 1751, create narratives that resurrect the female body from Clarissa's coffin, and both novels turn to the miniature portrait to define female spectatorial agency; in doing so, they enable a comic vision to emerge from a Richardsonian aesthetic. These novels reflect the difficulty of articulating the representation registered in Richardson's text outside a tragic framework at a moment when the novel was still grasping the mantle of cultural propriety tenuously. Writing only ten years later, Sterne could count on the novel's enormous popularity in cheerfully and sceptically recounting how sentiment fosters community around objects such as the portrait.[30] In countering any semblance of a disinterested aesthetic perspective, the portrait defines the novel in the terms that govern women's relation to private interests in *Tristram Shandy*. In my concluding chapter, Wollstonecraft and Inchbald mark the crossroads where women writers found themselves at the end of the century, when the idea of private interests threatened to relegate women entirely to a domestic sphere of influence. Each of these writers provides a different response to portraiture, and their various representations establish a continuum of possible responses to women's relation to the visual in the 1790s. In analysing this range of responses in my final chapter, I signal the extent to which my study maps out, not so much a lineage, as a mosaic of ideas concerning portraiture and the visual culture of the eighteenth-century novel.

Finally, I want to address the issue of methodology, for although my focus is literary, this book also makes claims about the history of art, and about particular eighteenth-century paintings. In claiming that the critical reception histories of the portrait and the novel shared a common vocabulary, I argue that eighteenth-century critics of art and literature together shaped a particular language in their discussions of the nature and value of aesthetics.[31] This overlap resulted from strong links between the writing and painting communities that were based on shared interests and on personal friendships. Moreover, although I do not try to establish a one-to-one correspondence between the novel's and the portrait's understanding of each other, I believe that the novel's interest in the portrait was reciprocated. In chapter 1, I analyse the portrait's representation of novel reading to demonstrate the depth of the connection between the two genres. Their reciprocity heightens the sense that the novel drew on a well-developed cultural understanding of the portrait-novel connection. Furthermore, while 'private interests' could and did refer to a range of ideas in the novel and the portrait, the recurrence of the female figure at the centre of these genres' discussions provides a useful comparative framework.[32] Finally, unlike Richard Wendorf's illuminating study of the connections between portrait painting and biography in Stuart and Georgian England, this book makes no attempt to link specific works of art and any given novel's representation of the portrait.[33] The discussions of particular paintings that appear serve to illuminate the element of portraiture with which each novel frames its *ekphrastic* hermeneutics.[34] My goal is to recreate, as fully as possible, the visual immediacy of the eighteenth-century English portrait and its significance as a cultural presence in the lives of eighteenth-century readers and writers.

The focus of this book allows me to fold into my examination of the portrait the pleasure that art historians take in the study of visual objects.[35] In tracing the outline of a pleasure that is not solely tied to the imperatives of either domestic ideology or a libertine gaze, I hope to encourage a reexamination of the looks that we have directed, in recent years, at the eighteenth-century novel. Any reading of the portrait trope, and of vision and spectatorial modes, comments not only on the eighteenth-century novel and its readers, but on the early twenty-first-century reader and her own investment in the idea of the visual. Martin Jay's recent claim that antivisual discourse 'is a pervasive but generally ignored phenomenon of twentieth-century Western thought' invites a reconsideration of this investment.[36] My reading of the novel takes a step in this direction.

Chapter One

The Novel and the Portrait in Eighteenth-Century England

The novel and the portrait appear at the centre of eighteenth-century debates in England about the nature of private interests and about women's relation to those interests. The critical reception histories of the portrait and the novel reflect the divisions that organized factions for and against private interests as a social imperative, and a comparison of the commentaries surrounding each genre reveals a series of striking parallels. The first half of this chapter will analyse how competing understandings of private interests structured two radically different notions of the novel and the portrait in eighteenth-century art and literary criticism. Critics hostile to the novel viewed the intimate world it created as a breeding ground for illicit behaviour, while the portrait's detractors pointed to its relationship to solipsistic states of vanity and narcissism; advocates for the novel praised its ability to inculcate principles of morality and sympathy in its readers, and supporters of the portrait celebrated its role in establishing affective relations between individuals. The extent to which a set of common terms governs evaluations of these genres indicates the imbrication of art and literary critical practices, and it suggests, as well, that reading and beholding were considered related activities. In the second half of the chapter, I will turn to the painting practices that were both inspired by, and contributed to, eighteenth-century accounts of portraiture, in order to identify the visual material upon which novelists drew as they shaped the contours of eighteenth-century prose fiction. In particular, I will discuss how female portraiture became the focal point for critical commentary as a result of its ability to incite both desire and virtue – to represent, in other words, the divided aspect of private interests. Both novels and portraits of the period were able to exploit the debates surrounding the idea of private interests by highlighting the gendered aspect of the debates and the competing interpretations of female character that they produced. The genres were able to turn the idea of private interests into a principle of aesthetic pleasure by sustaining a paradoxical vision of female character as both an idealized object of virtue and an erotic icon.

This study's engagement in a particular set of interpretive problems stemming from the idea of 'private interests' and its focus on the extent to which early eighteenth-century narrative practices – especially those related to amatory fiction – continue to exert their influence throughout the century make my argument less chronologically than thematically focused. My intention is not to underestimate the innovations that occurred in both novel and portrait techniques, nor to blur the very different motivations driving the diverse group of authors I will study in the chapters that follow, but rather to highlight a particular set of questions that evolve over the course of the eighteenth century in relation to visual culture, women's cultural status, and the moral and aesthetic questions linked to two genres that failed – for a variety of reasons – to overcome fully critical disapproval. This book argues against the critical tradition that, in literary studies, witnesses the novel's 'rise' as a form of escalating powers of discipline, and that, in art historical accounts, views Joshua Reynolds's achievement at the end of the eighteenth century as a happy assimilation of history painting and portrait practices. In this chapter, I will set up some of the terms that organize both positive and negative accounts of the novel and the portrait, moving back and forth through the period in order to study the connections that link different historical moments. The terms I have chosen to make central to my discussion serve as common denominators in the novels I examine in the chapters that follow, appearing in a range of configurations and contexts. So, for example, the portrait's association with sexual misconduct remains a constant theme from 1660 to 1800, even though the specific nature of the misconduct and the object of criticism – from the Restoration court's promiscuity to the advertisement of middle-class self-importance – changes in the commentary. Similarly, if the novel was able to achieve some cultural authority after the works of Fielding and Richardson appeared, it never escaped its association with the scandal narratives of Manley, Haywood, and Behn; John Tinnon Taylor has documented the immense volume of negative criticism directed toward the novel between 1760 and 1830.[1] What becomes clear as one reads the period's assessments of the portrait and the novel is that even as writers and painters reinvent the traditions within which they are working, they also recognize the power embedded in the discourses that surround them – both negative and positive – and draw on that power to further their aesthetic goals.

The Novel, the Portrait, and the 'Extravagance of the Passions'

John Barrell's *The Political Theory of Painting from Reynolds to Hazlitt: 'The Body of the Public'* (1986) defines the hierarchy of genres maintained by eighteenth-century art critics, a hierarchy that placed history painting at the top of the ladder, portraiture near the bottom.[2] Despite the portrait's ascendence in practice, the idea of history painting's value 'took an intolerable time to die.'[3] In a wide range of meditations on art practices and philosophy, the portrait painter – 'the mere face-painter' – and portraiture – 'the wretched business of face painting' – were attacked as socially and artistically detrimental.[4] The portrait was viewed as incapable of instructing the viewer in high moral principles, as promoting only sensual appetite as a universal experience. The status of the portrait as a commissioned object created the suspicion that the paintings reflected little else besides the vanity of the sitter, and that the habit of producing portraits for this end was destroying the talent of England's preeminent painters. Writing of his friend Sir Godfrey Kneller, Dryden complains, 'They who pay the taxes bear the rule: / Thus thou sometimes art forced to draw a fool; / ... You only paint to live, not live to paint.'[5] A generation later, the third Earl of Shaftesbury phrases Dryden's vaguely insulting comments more aggressively, denying the portrait painter any artistitic status: '[Portraiture is] not so much as a liberal art nor to be so esteemed; as requiring no liberal knowledge, genius, education, converse, manners, moral-science, mathematics, optics, but merely practical and vulgar.'[6] Fifty years later, a critic for the *London Chronicle* complains that Joshua Reynolds has been forced into a career of portrait painting by the appetite of his clients for images of themselves:

> It is indeed to be lamented, that Sir Joshua Reynolds, who, by some former specimens, has demonstrated his talents as well for historical as for other species of painting, should be confined entirely to the drawing of portraits; but such is the mean vanity and selfishness of the age, that most of our great personages would rather give two or three hundred pounds for their own dear likeness, than one half, or even one third of that sum for the noblest historical picture that ever was produced.[7]

Another critic, unsure whether to blame the portrait painters or those that commission their paintings, asks, 'Are the sons of *Apollo* lost in the world's dissipation, that we have so few in history? or are our nobles satiated with chaste pursuits?' (*Morning Post*, 1 May 1777). The *St. James Chronicle* argues that, in the absence of history painting, the visual arts sink to an 'ornamental Occupation,' a description that aptly summarizes the conflation of the portrait's status as mere decoration and the portrait painter's low status as a hack artificer (29 April 1781). According to the *Morning Star*, portraiture must necessarily usurp history painting because it speaks to the common corruption of human nature:

> The [portrait], in general the most frivolous branch of the art, is that however from which the brothers of the brush reap the greatest profit, and on which their existence must for ever depend. *Riches, liberality*, and *taste*, are fluctuating, local, and temporary – *Vanity* is immutable, universal, and eternal.
>
> Ten thousand fat and greasy citizens would not give Sir Joshua a tester for his *Scipio*, or his *Robin Goodfellow*, but every one of them would give him fifty guineas for the representation of their own unmeaning phizes.
>
> (30 April 1789)

Each of these comments reflects the fear that private interest has usurped civic purpose as the standard governing art's appreciation. All who participate in portraiture's consumption must necessarily be tainted: the portrait's sitter initiates the corrupting process by valuing self-representation over history painting; the painter participates in the degradation by abdicating his role as a cultural leader for the sake of profit; and the portrait completes the cycle in its display of the triumph of self-interest over the public good.

At stake is the idea of the aesthetic.[8] The *Morning Star*'s reference to the 'unmeaning phizes' speaks to the fear that portraits can convey no useful message to their beholders due to the relative anonymity of the vast majority of sitters, and that their very materiality is tainted by the terms of their circulation. Samuel Johnson's 'The Vanity of Human Wishes' (1749) articulates this idea forcefully in its description of the courtier's fall from power to obscurity:

> From every room descends the painted face,
> That hung the bright Palladium of the place,
> And smok'd in kitchens, or in auctions sold,
> To better features yields the frame of gold.[9]

The portrait is always expendable as a result of its content – one human face, subject to fate and mortality. A reviewer for the *London Chronicle* makes the same objection thirty years later:

> Those who employ their pencil on the portraits of great men, or on history-pieces, may say, with the painter of old, *in æternitatem pingimus*, we paint to all ages and all nations. But those who continue their talents to the portraits of persons illustrious for nothing but their rank or opulence (both of them perishable qualities or possessions), must content themselves with the humbler praise of acknowledging, that they do not paint to all ages or all nations, nor even to any whole age or any whole nation, but merely to one particular family.[10]   (25 April 1778)

Rather than projecting a universal standard summed up by the style and content of its representation, the portrait, in the eyes of its critics, remains opaque by virtue of its refusal to gesture toward any recognizable civic values. The interpretive community extends only to 'one family,' rendering its function merely private. The idea of rank and opulence as 'perishable ... possessions' suggests, as it does in Johnson's poem, that the goods – including portraits – consumed by the vain sensualist are unstable as objects. In the later eighteenth century, Joshua Reynolds defines the problem in idealist terms, opposing the local and the universal attributes of art in portraiture and history painting, respectively: 'An History-painter paints man in general; a Portrait-Painter, a particular man, and consequently a defective model.'[11] Portraiture may be destroyed as an insignificant art object, or destroy itself in its own narcissism; most fundamentally, as Reynolds's comment makes clear, it can never represent any moral *exempla* – and by extension any aesthetic ideals – because of its attachment to particularity.

Paradoxically, the same singularity that renders the portrait weak and inadequate also makes it potentially dangerous. In particular, critics fear that the singularities of various portraits will blur into a large and chaotic mass of images. The critic for the *Morning Star* who points to the enduring standard of vanity emphasizes the numbers of portraits that the English public is consuming – 'ten thousand fat and greasy citizens' would rather spend their money on portraits than on history paintings. Another critic complains of 'the superabundant number of portraits, which, like dominos at a modern masquerade, crowd every corner of the rooms' (*Morning Chronicle and London Advertiser*, 30 April 1777). The idea of the domino suggests not only a devotion to masquerade fashion, but also a more disturbing quality of disguise and mechanical reproduction, whereby all of the faces of various portraits converge into a collection of identical masks, all equally impenetrable.[12]

Thus portraits, for all of their apparent simplicity, produce an aura of discord and stubborn materiality in the eyes of their detractors. They blur categories that ought to remain distinct so that we are no longer able to discriminate between commodities and art. Shaftesbury issues a warning about the corrupting effect of viewing art that does not meet the aesthetic standards set by history painting:

> It is evident however from reason itself, as well as from history and experience, that nothing is more fatal, either to painting, architecture, or the other arts, than this false relish, which is governed rather by what immediately strikes the sense, than by what consequentially and by reflection pleases the mind, and satisfies the thought and reason. So that whilst we look on painting with the same eye, as we view commonly the rich stuffs, and coloured silks worn by our ladies, and admired in dress, equipage, or furniture; we must of necessity be effeminate in our taste, and utterly set wrong as to all judgment and knowledge in the kind.[13]

For Shaftesbury, the central challenge faced by art critics centres around the stability of a beholding eye that can differentiate between aesthetic and materialist pleasure. The luxury that has been created by England's new wealth places the nation at risk, according to Shaftesbury, for now 'rich stuffs' can compete with the liberal arts for the viewer's attention. The visual landscape, in other words, is full of potential diversions. The temporal logic of Shaftesbury's ideas is important – 'nothing is more fatal ... than ... what *immediately* strikes the sense.' Judgment must take precedence over the immediacy of vision – an idea which Reynolds reiterated later in the century: 'It is not the eye, it is the mind which the painter of genius desires to address.'[14] Within this frame of reference, the portrait cannot possibly compete with history painting, since it lacks a narrative that might engage the beholder in a dialogue.

Shaftesbury's denunciation of false taste reflects a concern for the state of the nation in a time of conspicuous consumption. J.G.A. Pocock has argued that women were often metaphorically associated with the worst features of commercial culture in the eighteenth century, an association that appears, unsurprisingly, in the attack on the portrait.[15] Roger de Piles, whose *Cours de Peinture par Principes* (1708) influenced many English art critics, went so far as to claim that women's taste was facilitates the seduction of the viewer, who in turn corrupts himself by participating in a transaction sexually and financially controlled by a woman. Here Somerset Place and the brothel become indistinguishable in a conflation of the spaces that other critics attempt to keep separate. The cynical view of the portrait's preeminence suggests that as long as vanity rules the exhibition's productions, no public space is safe from sexual corruption. This nightmarish scenario sums up the terms of the critical reception that greeted the portrait's ascendence in the eighteenth century. The portrait's status as a material object that fosters vanity in its sitter, a luxury item that corrupts both its subject and the painter, and a work that renders its spectator a victim of sexual appetite – all of these indictments secured portraiture's low place in the hierarchy of painting genres.

The critical reception that greeted the novel reflects a similar degree of hostility, as many critics have demonstrated.[20] John Moore, writing in 1797, confirmed that earlier in the century 'the very words Romance or Novel conveyed the idea of a frivolous or pernicious book.'[21] William Beatty Warner, following Ioan Williams, has observed how the success of the novel after Fielding's and Richardson's mid-century successes paradoxically made novel reading 'a more pressing cultural issue' than it had been earlier in the century.[22] Warner stresses the disjunction between the early eighteenth century's concern with questions of fact and fiction and the later period's moral anxieties about novel-reading, but I would like to focus on the terms of mid- and later eighteenth-century criticism that connect the novel's concerns to the subject matter and phenomenology, rather than the formal principles, of the scandal narratives and amatory fiction labelled as 'romances' at the time of their publication and later.

Like portraits, novels were viewed as mass-produced commodities; Henry Mackenzie refers to the 'common herd of novels (the wretched offspring of circulating libraries),' and the *Analytical Review* argues a similar logic: 'The generality of them ... are so near akin to each other, that with a few very trifling alterations, the same review would serve for almost all of them.'[23] The cynical bookseller created in one of Elizabeth Montagu's dialogues claims, 'I assure you these Books were very useful to Authors and their Booksellers: and for whose Benefit besides should a man write?'[24] In the *Gentleman's Magazine*, another critic refers to novels as 'the offspring ... of the managers of the circulating libraries, or their venal authors.'[25] The image of the books' origins in peripatetic libraries, themselves objects of suspicion, contributes to the sense that the novels are spreading a disease throughout the nation, a disease that cannot be regulated because its host body is both everywhere and nowhere. As Warner elegantly notes, circulating libraries allowed novels to become 'an ambient presence' in eighteenth-century England.[26]

Like the portrait, the novel was characterized by critics as puny on the artistic scale and monstrous on the cultural register. One critic describes the vast assortment of novels available in a given month as 'an horrible mass of hurtful insignificance,' a theme expanded upon by the *Monthly Review*: 'So long as our British Ladies continue to encourage our hackney Scriblers, by reading every Romance that appears, we need not wonder that the Press should swarm with such poor insignificant productions.'[27] In an attempt to distance himself from other novelists, Henry Fielding warns in Book IX of *Tom Jones* that, should the lessons of his prefaces go unheeded, 'a Swarm of foolish Novels, and monstrous Romances will be produced, either to the great impoverishing of Booksellers, or to the great Loss of Time, and Depravation of Morals in the Reader.'[28] Fielding's concern about the 'Loss of Time' encountered in the reading of novels echoes Shaftesbury's fear that false painting (i.e., portraiture) will bring the viewer to a spectatorial halt, unable to discern a historical meaning in the object. Here the 'foolish' novel takes the reader out of a progressive time, productive and moral, and leads him or her into an empty time of random fantasy. The Earl of Chesterfield refers to 'the reading of Romances' as 'time merely thrown away' and Vicesimus Knox argues that 'the futility of the modern Novel precludes its power of causing any other mischief, than the consumption of time that might be more usefully employed.' The emptiness of the temporal moment in turn creates vacuity in the minds of the novel's readers: Owen Ruffhead claims that readers peruse novels, 'not for the sake of thinking, but for want of thought.'[29]

Even more dangerously, novels seem to unmoor their readers from ethical ties. According to their detractors, novels are designed to produce an appetite for pleasurable reading divorced from morality: 'Can it be imagined,' Oliver Goldsmith writes of the novel, 'that the art with which the author inspires the love of virtue, can overcome that crowd of thoughts which sway them to licentiousness. To be able to inculcate virtue by so leaky a vehicle, the author must be a philosopher of the first rank.'[30] Bemoaning the bad attitudes that novels inspire in women, Richard Berenger asks, 'Why do we suffer those hearts, which ought to be appropriated to the various affections of social life, to be alienated by the mere creatures of the imagination?' John and Anna Laetitia Aikin complain that the reading of 'pathetic' fiction produces 'apathy and indifference' toward real suffering in young people.[31] Attacking the sentimental novel in particular, Henry Mackenzie argues that 'in the enthusiasm of sentiment there is much the same danger as in the enthusiasm of religion, of substituting certain impulses and feelings of what may be called a visionary kind, in the place of real practical duties.' In each of these examples, the critic fears that the affective experience created by the novel will allow its readers to remove themselves from the world they ought to inhabit: 'I know several unmarried ladies, who in all probability had been long ago good wives and good mothers, if their imaginations had not been early perverted with the chimerical ideas of romantic love.'[32]

Like the portrait, the novel often was characterized as a debilitating form undermining the health both of individual readers and of society in general. In the eyes of its detractors, the novel appears pedagogically unsound because it turns the reader inward rather than outward, encouraging narcissism and self-indulgence; 'Our readers must be amused, flattered, soothed,' claims Montagu's cynical bookseller. The feelings created by novels never transcend the realm of the merely sensual, according to Richard Hurd, who complains of 'our rage for incessant gratification,' which encourages us to 'take up with half-formed pleasures' such as the novel provides.[33] The novel can only create an interpretive community by appealing to our basest appetites: 'Were brutes but suddenly gifted with speech and reason, they would express their *instinct*, in the very stile of modern Novelists.'[34] These attacks mirror the art critics' apprehensions concerning the appeal of the portrait and its attendant sensuality and irrationality.

As in the hostile reviews of portraits exhibited at the Royal Academy, literary criticism frequently describes this perversion of the reader's character as a form of seduction, whereby the text's dubious subject matter and formal technique incite sexual fantasies in its readers.[35] In 'Advice to an Author,' Shaftesbury complains of modern literature's tendency to ensnare its readers in a 'pretty amour and intercourse of caresses' with the writer.[36] Shaftesbury's corrective to this problem is revealing, especially as it returns us to the terms of the attack on the portrait Shaftesbury launches elsewhere. In order to control the potential damage that novels might cause, Shaftesbury redirects his audience to dialogues written in the classical mode: 'For here the author is annihilated, and the reader, being no way applied to, stands for nobody.'[37] By limiting the personification of either the reader or the writer, as well as that of the characters producing the sexual charge, neoclassical dialogues will prevent the text from eliciting any kind of response other than the rational. They will also encourage a civic perspective, by emptying out personality of any private interests that may divert it from a rational perspective. Interestingly, Shaftesbury elsewhere objects to portraits because they represent, for the most part, nobodies, but advocates a literature of nameless representatives. Presumably the canvas fails to impart any moral meaning in its representation of blank faces, whereas the literary text can fill in all the virtuous details without linking them to a historical figure. A portrait must have an identity if it is to mean anything, for only in recalling the history of the figure in front of them will spectators be able to learn from it.

Knox argues that 'the languishing and affectedly sentimental compositions formed on the pattern of Sterne, or of other less original Novelists, not only tend to give the mind a degree of weakness, which renders it unable to resist the slightest impulse of passion, but also indirectly insinuate, that the attempt is unnecessary self-denial.'[38] The sensuality of the novel-reading experience, like that of portrait viewing, corrupts the mind's integrity, filling the mind, according to another critic, 'with criminal propensities.' The *London Magazine and Monthly Chronologer* goes as far as to suggest that novels encourage 'unlawful Commerce between the Sexes,' adding that it hopes 'the Ladies, the young ones especially, will shun them, as they wou'd a more dangerous and destructive Sort of Poison.'[39]

As many of the above examples reveal, the female reader often appears as the prototype for the 'bad' reader.[40] As in the case of the portrait, the novel's popularity was identified in the writing of the period with a particularly female appetite. In 1788, Henry James Pye commented on the dangerous patterns of behaviour arising out of novel reading: 'The general effect of novel-reading on the gentler sex is too obvious to be doubted; it excites and enflames the passion which is the principal subject of the tale, and the susceptibility of the female votary of the circulating library, is proverbial.'[41] Not only female readers, but female characters in novels, came under attack; the *Gentleman's Magazine* claims that novels acquaint their readers 'with the worst part of the female sex ... and thus send them into the world debauched.'[42] This fear resembles the anxiety that female subjects in portraits may corrupt their viewers, enabling the representation to manipulate its beholder in a particularly feminine and sexual fashion. Moreover, as Laura L. Runge points out, the novel itself was identified as feminine in relation to its more masculine neoclassical counterparts, leading to a circular logic that connected women and novels, whereby 'citing one of these inferiorities reinforced belief in the other.'[43] The various terms associated with the novel's allure – sensuality, appetite, irrationality, immediate gratification – corresponded to standard misogynist conceptions of women, and so, as in the case of the portrait, it is perhaps unsurprising that the link between women and prose narrative was forged as strongly as it was.

What is more surprising is the extent to which these same characteristics of the novel and of the portrait informed positive responses to both genres. That is to say, there appears in eighteenth-century criticism a parallel universe to the one governing negative accounts of the portrait and the novel, one in which sensuality and materialism are reframed as sentimental experience. The critical comments that praise these genres have been overshadowed by our interest in their hostile counterparts, but they are nonetheless important if we are to assess what opportunities painters and writers perceived in their productions of these 'particular objects.' Furthermore, the immense popularity of the novel and the portrait speak to the fact that the hostile criticism directed toward the genres did little to dam the rising tide of their consumption, and the positive comments about the novel and the portrait reveal some of the features (besides the titillation of scandal) that a larger audience may have found compelling in the literature and paintings despised by so many cultural critics. Finally, it is also important to assess the positive responses in order to recognize the paradoxical nature of the interpretive experiences created by the novel and the portrait.

Influenced by Continental theories and practices, eighteenth-century art critics were reluctant to acknowledge the artistic merits of portrait painting, to the extent that Joshua Reynolds seems to have written his *Discourses* with almost no regard for the most notable achievements of his portrait-painting career.[44] One exception to this rule appears in the writing of Jonathan Richardson Sr, who attempts to unite his theory and practice in a defence of portraiture in *An Essay on the Theory of Painting* (1715).[45] Richardson challenges the conventional understanding of the portrait's relation to vanity, not by stripping portraiture of its association with narcissism but rather by revaluing that association:

> And why should we not also believe, that considering the violent Thirst for Praise which is natural, especially in the noblest Minds, and the better sort of People, they that see their Pictures ... are often secretly admonish'd by

the faithful Friend in their own Breasts to add new Graces to them by Praise-worthy Actions, and to avoid Blemishes, or deface what may have happen'd, as much as possible, by a Future good Conduct.[46]

By this account the portrait creates incentive for the sitter to modify his or her behaviour, setting in motion a mechanism of self-surveillance in the form of the 'faithful Friend'; the portrait enables this process because it represents an objective correlative of the individual, encouraging the split that makes the conscience audible. The sitter becomes, in a sense, his own portrait painter, capable of adding 'new Graces' and avoiding 'Blemishes' by meditating on the relation between the original painting and his daily character, itself a walking portrait. In this passage Richardson echoes a view also expressed in the Renaissance; in a letter of Claudio Tolomei to Sebastiano del Piombo (1543), Tolomei calls his portrait 'a mirror ... because in it I shall see you and me together ... a continual stimulus to purge my soul of its many defects.'[47]

Confronting all of portraiture's negative associations directly, Richardson goes on to celebrate the status of the portrait as a commodity. 'This Nation is many Thousands of Pounds the richer for *Van-Dyck*'s Hand, and which is as current Money as Gold in most parts of *Europe*, and this with an inconsiderable Expence of the Productions of Nature; what a Treasure then have all the Great Masters here, and elsewhere given to the World!'[48] The idea of the portrait as an object that can be circulated like an expensive part of an equipage here becomes part of a national economy, one that links luxury to power, artists to national strength. Portraits are valuable because of their proximity to, rather than their distance from, gold, a proximity that effectively stabilizes their meaning by rendering the objects part of an international currency.

In theorizing what a portrait does, Richardson focuses on the relationship that the portrait establishes between the mind and the face: 'to sit for one's Picture, is to have an Abstract of one's Life written, and published.' The portrait is capable of projecting a general and public knowledge of the individual, and rather than remaining entrenched within a solipsistic universe of self-gratification, the portrait takes the individual into the arena of public judgment, much like a biography.[49] The portrait painter's skill is demonstrated by his ability to create the abstract meaning in the particular representation: 'A Portrait-Painter must understand Mankind, and enter into their Characters, and express their Minds as well as their Faces.'[50] The success of a portrait depends on its movement between the question of physical resemblance and the larger truths manifested by the sitter's character, a movement that defines the portrait as both private and public, particular and general.

The particularity of the portrait (which in the eyes of hostile critics renders it meaningful to nobody but one family) becomes, in Richardson's mind, the grounds for its ability to generate sympathy. Portraits, Richardson argues, 'may be instrumental to Maintain and sometimes to Augment Friendship, and Paternal, Filial and Conjugal Love, and Duty.' Richardson's understanding of the portrait depends on its power to organize a family around the affect its representation creates, rather than on any abstract moral principle. Thirty years after Richardson, Samuel Johnson used the same idea to praise Reynolds's portraits over the painter's idealization of history painting: 'I should grieve to see Reynolds transfer to heroes and to goddesses, to empty splendour and to airy fiction, that art which is now employed in diffusing friendship, in reviving tenderness, in quickening the affections of the absent, and continuing the presence of the dead.'[51] Johnson reverses the usual association of history painting with substance, portraiture with vacuity, infusing the particularity of the portrait with the power to hold its viewer in a sympathetic moment. Johnson relegates history painting to the realm of 'airy fiction,' signalling the historical irrelevance to a painting tradition that draws its strength from its contemporary specificity and realism. History painting's public narratives no longer take precedence over the very private accounts of human history that portraits provide. Instead, the privacy of the portrait ensures a stable ground for sympathetic relations among individuals, relations that in turn form the bedrock of social stability and historical continuity. The idea that Reynolds's art is now 'employed' in portrait painting becomes a positive, rather than a pejorative, comment in this context, for rather than highlighting a mechanical or rote performance that aims only to guarantee profit, the idea of utility serves to emphasize a social efficacy more frequently attributed to history painting.

The private emotions that a portrait can elicit also serve, according to Richardson, to promote social ethics through the modification of the beholder's feelings. Meditating on Vandyke's portrait of the Countess Dowager of Exeter, Richardson exclaims that 'there is such a Benignity, such a Gentile, Becoming Behaviour, such a Decent Sorrow, and Resignation Express'd here, that a Man must be very Insensible that is not the Better for considering it.'[52] The portrait seems animated in this account, supporting Marcia Pointon's claim that 'portraits may be understood ... not only as representations of individuals but as representative of individual bodily presences.'[53] In a letter written in 1768, Laurence Sterne describes the effect of a Benjamin West portrait of his friend Mrs James: 'Such goodness is painted in that face, that when one looks at it, let the soul be ever so much un-harmonized, it is impossible it should remain so.'[54] In these accounts, the representation's force resides in the immediate gratification provided by a face, rather than in the narrative of a historical event, and the goodness of the face stands for a universal standard that can reestablish harmony in the viewer's soul. Far from fading into a blank anonymity, the portrait's individuality humanizes the viewer by virtue of, rather than despite, its particularity. Beholding the face enables the reorganization of the viewer's soul in much the same manner that the spectator of the portrait, in the negative account of various paintings, is seduced by the image of a beautiful woman. The agency of the portrait takes on an entirely benign aspect, and the passivity of the beholder enables moral restoration rather than corruption. The privacy of the anonymous face – its unique claim to a particular kind of goodness – becomes the very grounds for its translatability into a universal aesthetic.

In a similar defence of private experience as the grounds for cultural integrity, Edmund Burke writes of Reynolds's famous portrait of Lord Keppel: 'It was but the other day that ... I looked over a number of fine portraits, most of them of persons now dead, but whose society, in my better days, made this a proud and happy place. Amongst these was the picture of Lord Keppel. It was painted by an artist worthy of the subject, the excellent friend of that excellent man from their earliest youth, and a common friend of us both.'[55] While Burke's response to the portrait depends in part on his fame, as well as that of Keppel and Reynolds, it also emphasizes the feelings of private friendship that the portrait evokes. Reynolds's painting of Keppel is grounded in their personal relationship, rather than in a desire for profit or fame, so that the portrait, both in its production history and in its representation, stands as a testimony to the transcendent principle of sympathy. At a moment when he could have meditated on the public men that Reynolds and Keppel became, Burke focuses on their childhood association and the pleasure he has derived from participating in their friendship, rather than in their public lives.[56]

The limited critical acclaim that the novel managed to garner in the eighteenth century defined its terms according to the same idea – that the affective moment could be understood as useful, and that the particular formal qualities of the novel rendered it an ideal form for the creation of feeling. Early in the eighteenth century, Delarivier Manley celebrated the immediacy of the gratifications afforded by novel reading in her preface to *The Secret History of Queen Zarah*, defining the brevity of novels as characteristically English: 'These little pieces which have banished romances are much more agreeable to the brisk and impetuous humor of the English, who have naturally no Taste for long-winded performances, for they have no sooner begun a book but they desire to see the end of it.'[57] Rather than challenging the novel's relation to appetite, Manley promotes the formal attributes of the new genre in relation to an English impatience for plot. Within this context, the 'little Pieces' bear a natural affinity to a temperament already formed, rather than corrupting the reader's sensibility.

The idea that the sensual pleasures provided by novels might grip the mind worried many literary critics, but others viewed the heightened emotion novels afforded as a pedagogical opportunity. In his praise of Fielding's *Amelia*, published in the *Monthly Review*, John Cleland draws attention to the 'colours' of fiction:

> By the attractions of pleasure he puts morality into action; it is alive, and insinuates its greatest truths into the mind, under the colours of amusement and fiction. Readers are, by the magic of this association, made to retain what has at once instructed and diverted them, when they would be apt to forget what has perhaps no more than wearied, or *dulled* them.

Amusement and fiction create the 'attractions of pleasure,' which in turn animate morality so that it can engage with the mind, a mind that otherwise resists precepts and regulation. The sensuality of fiction advances, rather than retards, moral virtue, and the seduction of the reader by the pleasures of the text constitutes a necessary part of the pedagogical moment, as Cleland himself proposes at the close of *Memoirs of a Woman of Pleasure*. Another critic suggests that Romances, 'when conducted by a Writer of fine talents and elegant taste, may be rendered as beneficial as delectable. They have this peculiar advantage, that, by making a forcible impression on the imagination, they answer the purposes of conviction and persuasion, with the generality of mankind, much better than a direct appeal to the judgment.'[58] Delectability ensures, rather than undermines, the beneficial qualities of novel reading by opening up the mind to the reception of moral lessons. Sensuality, in other words, creates a strong enough response in the reader to render him or her vulnerable to the text's moral lesson. Samuel Richardson identifies the development of this readerly vulnerability as a central tenet of *Pamela*'s agenda, which aims to '*engage the Passions of every sensible Reader, and strongly interest them in the edifying Story.*'[59] Expanding on this idea, one critic celebrates the novel's ability to seduce the credulous: 'How many readers may be taught to pursue good, and to avoid evil, to refine their morals, and to detest vice, who are profitably decoyed into the perusal of these writings by the pleasure they expect to be paid with for their attention.'[60]

The critics who assess the novel's potential gratifications in positive terms reconceptualize the private interests that the novel promotes as part of a new public ethic, one that links the interiority of the reading experience to a world that uses sympathy such as the novel produces to cement social relations. By embracing, rather than resisting, the idea of private interests, critics are able to approach the particularity of the novel's representation as a virtue rather than a vice. For example, one critic describes Richardson's characterization of the Harlowe family as a masterful illusion: 'When I read *Clarissa*, I am of the family of the Harlowes. I am interested for one, I hate another, I am indifferent for a third.' Unlike the critic we encountered above who attacks the portrait's ability to speak only to 'a particular family,' this critic believes that the specificity of the portrait guarantees its affective power, bringing the reader into the circle of the family that the novel represents. The representation of the Harlowes as a unique family, rather than detracting from the novel's aesthetic status, ensures *Clarissa*'s success: 'What art must he have had to produce it!'[61] The critic praises the individuality of the novel in much the same way that Richardson, Burke, and Sterne praise the sentiment created by the subjectivity of the portrait, a subjectivity that seems to bring the representation to life. Maria Edgeworth, writing to Elizabeth Inchbald about her impressions of *A Simple Story*, exclaims, 'I never read any novel that affected me so strongly, or that so completely possessed me with the belief in the real existence of all the people it represents.'[62]

The same interest in private experience allows Clara Reeve to claim that even a human vice such as vanity can be put to good use by the novel: 'Mankind are naturally pleased with what gratifies their vanity; and vanity, like all other passions of the human heart, may be rendered subservient to good and useful purposes.'[63] Echoing Jonathan Richardson's celebration of the portrait, Reeve's statement represents the view that challenges Shaftesbury's and others' fear of private interests as debilitating, creating an alternative idea of individual passions as a common unifying principle. Richard Griffith confirms Reeve's view in his discussion of the novel's potential for the creation of a community governed by a benign self-interest:

> Here passions may be refined, pointed to their proper objects, and produce their warrantable, or admonitory effects.
> For in passion are sown all our virtues, which bear fruit, according to their culture. Ambition may be restrained to emulation, avarice rendered oeconomy, extravagance exercised in benevolence, and courage exerted in the vindication of our honour, or the defence of our country, only.

The potential for oscillation – between sentiment and sensuality, virtue and eroticism – produced the divided responses that I have analysed here. Two examples from critical commentary of the period indicate a cultural awareness of the novel's ability to move in either direction:

> *Novels* are either exceedingly useful or dangerous, according to the Nature of their Composition: For the Reader, under the Notion of Entertainment, comes open and unguarded to them; our good Humour disposes us to be affected; and Love and Pity, the tenderest of all the Passions, being the only ones that are generally addressed to in these Performances, the Impression strikes deeply, and has a lasting good or bad Influence upon the Mind and Temper, in Proportion as the Images are more or less pure and just.
> The effects of that coarse taste introduced in the reign of Charles the Second, have scarcely yet decreased. The sentimental manner seems, however, likely to supplant it. But it is matter of doubt, whether even this manner is not equally dangerous. It has given an amiable name to vice, and has obliquely excused the extravagance of the passions, by representing them as the effect of lovely sensibility.[64]

The first account of the novel's operations focuses on the process by which the novel 'strikes' the mind, defining the reader's vulnerability as a necessary condition for literary interest, for better or worse. The second passage highlights the licentious ideas that the novel has inherited from the literature of the Restoration, focusing on the 'extravagance of the passions' that both erotic and sentimental narratives feed. The fashionable understanding of heightened aesthetic response as the product of 'sensibility' veils the appetitive desire created by the novel. In both of these accounts, the critics' awareness of the novel's commitment to the passions mirrors the art critics' concern with the portrait's investment in private desires.

While positive accounts of the portrait and the novel do not stress the importance of women's relation to sentiment and the world of private interests to the same extent as the negative accounts we have reviewed, the frequent turn to the representation of women as the source of affect – whether in *Clarissa* or the portrait of the Countess Dowager of Essex – highlights the degree to which female character became the example that proved the theory of the novel's and portraiture's affective value. As we shall see, both the portrait and the novel translated the critical concerns about the genres into interpretive opportunities, sustaining a divided view of their female subjects that constituted, to a large extent, the pleasure of each of these visual and literary practices.

'Mimic Harlots': Women, Portraits, Texts[65]

> While Hands obscene, at vicious Grandeur's call,
> With mimic Harlots clothe th'indignant Wall,
> Destructive Snares for youthful Passion spread,
> The slacken'd Bosom, and the faithless Bed,
> Thy pencil, *Reynolds*, innocently gay,
> To Virtue leads by Pleasure's flowery Way.
> 'To Sir Joshua Reynolds, on his Portrait of Miss Kemble, in the Exhibition at the Royal Academy,' *Public Advertiser*, 28 April 1784

Portrait painters responded to the debates about women's relation to private interests both by exploiting the idea of scandal and by encouraging the foundation of a new social ethic through the depiction of sympathy in the female sitter. The competing interpretations of female character circulating in eighteenth-century discourses became part of the portrait's comment on its own function as an aesthetic object, a comment that found its most explicit representation in the figure of the female reader. In what follows I will look first at the portraits that celebrate women's relation to erotic and material desire before turning to representations of women as readers, representations that comment on the hermeneutics of beholding, just as novels of the period allegorize reading as a form of spectatorship. In particular, I am interested in the degree to which the scandalous elements of female portraiture became an integral aspect of the moment of beholding the female reader, rendering the oppositions between scandal and virtue, voyeurism and disinterested spectatorship, more tenuous than they appear in art criticism of the period.

The celebration of Reynolds's representation of virtue in 'To Sir Joshua Reynolds' demonstrates the degree of anxiety that often was attached to female portraiture in the eighteenth century. In this case, the poet identifies the hack portrait painters' works as products of both ambition and lust, reducing the painters' creations to the works of 'Hands obscene,' the servants of 'Grandeur.' The idea of 'mimic Harlots' identifies female portraiture as a form of prostitution, linking women's desire to display themselves to sexual transgression. The Royal Academy's 'indignant Wall' stands as a virginal space molested by the painter and forced to wear the drapery of illicit portraiture – the wall itself is a tableau, the artist suggests, that now depicts a scene of debauchery. The corruption of the viewing space extends into society as a whole in the image of the youth whose moment of beholding leads to the disintegration of cultural values. The state of social chaos is registered first in the idea of the female body's 'slacken'd Bosom' – the breast that could be either uncorseted, or lacking a mother's milk, or both – and then in the 'faithless Bed'; inferior female portraiture, in other words, is anathema to domestic harmony. Reynolds's 'pencil,' by contrast, encourages domestic, and by extension, social cohesion in its yoking of pleasure and virtue for the beholder through the representation of a virtuous woman.

The concern that this poem registers around the idea of female display was not unique to the eighteenth century, but it took on an added dimension in relation to the recent past of the Restoration court's aesthetic, which relied heavily on the display of its famous female beauties, often the courtesans of the king. In response to the perceived excess of this display, as well as the sexual activities surrounding it, the eighteenth century formulated a new standard of visual reticence for women. As Nancy Armstrong has observed, the conduct books of the period argue that 'a woman's participation in public spectacle ... injures her, for as an object of display, she always loses value as a subject.'[66] One example of the disciplining of the female spectacle that occurred in eighteenth-century discourses appears in Joseph Addison's admonishment of 'Fulvia.' Describing a woman who seeks to draw attention to her appearance, Addison writes: 'What a Mortification would it be to *Fulvia*, if she knew that her setting her-self to View is but exposing her-self, and that she grows Contemptible by being Conspicuous.'[67]

And yet for all the talk of visual reticence, painters seemed to have delighted in indulging the public's desires for the opposite – for the representation of women as erotic spectacles. Not only mimic harlots found their way onto the walls of the Royal Academy's exhibition space, and one critic for the *Morning Herald* exclaimed:

The Novel and the Portrait in Eighteenth-Century England   35

> The French, who visit our exhibitions, are shocked at the indelicacy of placing the portraits of notorious prostitutes, triumphing as it were in vice, close to the pictures of women of rank and virtue. In Paris, such portraits would, on no account, be admitted; the name of the King is a sufficient check upon them to keep a just decorum in *his* academy; and it is no small reflection upon our academicians here to have as little regard for the dignity of their master, as they seemingly have for their own.[68]

The critic worries that the public viewing space has been tainted by the portraits of prostitutes, whose display constitutes in itself a 'triumph'; the painters have conferred status on the scandalous women by deeming their representations worthy of the Royal Academy's aesthetic standard. The critic also seems concerned that these representations will taint the reputations of the women 'of rank and virtue' – that it may become difficult to distinguish between the various women seen hanging together, a recurring motif in a variety of cultural commentaries of the period, all of which worried about the ability of prostitutes to 'pass' in the public domain. The passage conflates moral and aesthetic value, and extends the commentary to include a political critique of the Royal Academy's failure to consider its obligation to its patron, the king, linking, as in the poem addressed to Reynolds, the illicit nature of the representations to the personal failings of their creators – in particular, to their appetite for private, rather than public, gratifications. At stake again is political stability, for as long as the painters act like libertines in their pursuit of pleasure, the Royal Academy's mandate to serve the country cannot be fulfilled.

It is important to assess the extent to which the representation of dubious women in portraits came to affect how female portraiture was perceived categorically, and there is no better subject with which to begin this assessment than the notorious Kitty Fisher. Kitty Fisher entered into the fashionable world at the age of eighteen, around 1759, and accumulated a vast fortune before she married and, soon after, died (in either 1767 or 1769, as a result of lead poisoning from her make-up). She became one of Reynolds's favourite models, sitting to him on numerous occasions, to the extent that one critic insinuated that Reynolds and Fisher were lovers. When Reynolds received his knighthood in 1769, 'Fresnoy' wrote:

> Why should you have exchanged your honour for a title? ... Have you received a frown from salacious Catherine, the tailor's maid, or is the

affection of the fair creature alienated from you entirely since her elevation to matrimony – from you, alas! and many others? Have you lost any of your friends, that might induce you to fly into the toils of infamy? No, all your friends, your amiable friends, are still about you; and Catherine has sat to you in the most graceful, the most natural, attitudes, and indeed I must do you the justice to say that you have come as near the original as possible.[69]

Reynolds's ambition is interpreted first as the rechannelling of the sexual desire once gratified by Kitty Fisher into the arena of political patronage. But then the critic transforms Reynolds's desire for a 'title' into an extension, rather than a sublimation, of his illicit sexual conduct, conduct that also becomes intimately related to the painter's artistic practices: 'Catherine has sat to you in the most graceful, the most natural, attitudes.' Sarcastically noting Kitty's 'formal' name as an extension of Reynolds's 'Sir,' the critic suggests that Reynolds's representations of Fisher on canvas are turned into a reenactment of their affair, and verisimilitude – coming near to the original – takes on the meaning of both sexual contact and moral decay. Reynolds's desire for his knighthood links him to the figure of the prostitute, for he is willing to compromise his 'honour' and to flatter his political masters in order to capitalize on the reputation he achieves with 'Sir' added to his name.

It appears that, regardless of whether or not he was sexually involved with his model, Reynolds was willing to translate Kitty Fisher's status as a courtesan into an aesthetic and material opportunity for himself, to respond to a popular demand for scandalous images. His 1759 portrait, *Kitty Fisher as Cleopatra Dissolving the Pearl* (figure 1) appeared before the founding of the Royal Academy, but was widely circulated in print form to a public that eagerly purchased prints of Fisher's portraits. The portrait recalls Cleopatra impressing Mark Anthony by dropping a pearl into a glass of wine and drinking it at their first banquet, a scene that was more commonly represented as a historical painting, as in Tiepolo's and Trevisani's renditions. Reynolds most certainly saw Tiepolo's fresco, *The Banquet of Cleopatra*, as he took a sketch from the fresco, *The Meeting of Anthony and Cleopatra*, also at the Pallazo Labia in Venice, in 1752. He also must have seen Trevesani's painting, *The Banquet of Anthony and Cleopatra*, as Kitty Fisher's dress and pose are almost identical to those depicted in the painting. Reynolds's choice of this scene is particularly apt as a comment on Kitty Fisher's status as a courtesan, for it serves to refigure the famous story of Fisher's registering her disgust at the Duke of York's parsimony by placing the £50 banknote he had given her between two slices of bread and eating it.[70]

Reynolds's choice of the historical allusion for his representation of Fisher is significant in two ways. First, the dissolving of the pearl would have highlighted the gap between the idea of the jewel as a traditional sign of fecundity, and Kitty Fisher's attack on that sign. In a reading of Pliny's attack on Cleopatra, Marcia Pointon notes that the story strikes a particular nerve in the author as he narrates Cleopatra's destruction 'not only of one of the largest pearls ever found, but also of one of the greatest men ever known ... The female subject's claim to status through her reproductive organs is cancelled out by her key role in the processes of depredation and excess.'[71] Reynolds's decision to represent Kitty Fisher as Cleopatra speaks to the eighteenth century's increasing obsession with the idea of maternal duty; in its wilful refusal to march to the tune of marriage plots and maternal demands, the courtesan's body, in principle, flouts social expectations. Kitty Fisher never attempted to claim status through her reproductive capacity, and her failure to produce children, even within the confines of her illicit relationships, especially offended 'Simon Trusty,' who used Fisher's apparent refusal to become a mother as a central feature of his attack on the courtesan: 'You are wholly averse to the State [of maternity], and often perhaps, by horrid Means, deprive yourself of one of the most natural and tender Pleasures a Woman can possess.'[72] Fisher's apparent disregard for the pleasures of motherhood challenges the authority of 'nature's' calling and, by extension, of society's new investment in the maternal body as a site of moral agency and education. This depravity is connected, in Trusty's mind, to the depravity of Kitty's visual exhibitionism, which simultaneously reveals and conceals the prostitute's body. Fisher is willing to render her body's exterior surface – including her genitals – available to all who can pay even as she maintains an opacity around her body's interior workings. Fisher's perversity, according to her critic, resides in her refusal to allow the gaze of the public to move beyond the surface into the depths of the female body.

Cleopatra refuses the fetishization of the pearl – and of her sexuality – or rather, she internalizes the fetishized object, transforming her body into a sign of a desire that transcends the limits of the biological. The fact that Kitty's dress is covered in pearls, and that her pale skin and the white of the gown blend in with the ivory colour of the pearl, strengthens the connection between the woman's body and the jewel she holds. The symbolism of Kitty's gesture would also have registered as a comment on women's legal right to circulate, exchange, bequeath, or sell their personal jewellery, a right that also entitled women to claim portraits of themselves as personal, rather than family, property.[73] Here the instance of private and intimate exchange that might occur around a piece of jewellery becomes, in the scandalous sense of the jewel's status as a sign of female genitalia, *les bijoux indiscrets*, a public spectacle of female sexual agency.

The allusion to Fisher's consumption of the Duke of York's bank note effectively restages Cleopatra's gesture at a moment when paper currency was becoming established as the financial authority governing social relations in England. Fisher demonstrates her control over that new authority by internalizing its representative, highlighting her proximity to sums of money much larger than £50. Her body constructs a positive value around the association of the female body with new forms of currency, an association often defined as hysterical and uncontrollable, as in Addison's caricature of Credit earlier in the century. Fisher's gesture reminds us of the association of women, commerce, and culture that Pocock has outlined as a central aspect of Enlightenment discourses, an association that established women 'in the role of cultural entrepreneurs, encouraging the exchange of politeness and refinement in a variety of forms.'[74] This idea is reinforced by the manipulation of genre that Reynolds's painting effects, whereby it both refers to and draws upon the idea of history painting, a genre conventionally defined as the domain of masculine civic values, even as it feminizes the history painting and celebrates the portrait in its depiction of one private individual whose identity was nevertheless highly public. Reynolds's decision to move away from a representation of the historical drama toward the more immediate gratifications afforded by a portrait serves at once to unmoor the scene from its usual preoccupation with the downfall of Mark Anthony and to draw attention to the sitter – in this case, a courtesan. Rather than moving the beholder through a moral historical narrative, the portrait enraptures the spectator with the spectacle of female sexual allure, creating a moment of temporal suspension figured in the painting by the pearl held – for a fleeting moment – over the cup. That the courtesan should stand for the cultural entrepreneur capable of modernizing the history painting, of bringing it into conformity with the public taste for portraiture, adds to the scandal quotient of the image.

Many of the portraits that Reynolds painted of Kitty Fisher remained in his studio, a fact that one critic takes to mean that 'Kitty's liaisons lasted less time than it took Reynolds to paint her, and her jilted lovers did not want to be reminded of her.'[75] But it seems more likely that

The Novel and the Portrait in Eighteenth-Century England 39

Reynolds and Fisher collaborated in the creation of portraits that could be profitably reproduced as prints: an advertisement for a print of the Cleopatra painting appeared in the *London Chronicle* in July of 1759, and it indicates that the painting was owned by Kitty Fisher herself at that time, and that she must have authorized the prints' creation and sale.[76] The print was so popular that, at one point, it was miniaturized to decorate a watchcase.[77] The circulation of the portrait as a print links the painting to the courtesan as an object of exchange, figured in the painting through the association of the pearl and the woman. The portrait's proximity to the prostitute's world of commodification and exchange in turn feminizes the portrait painter – indeed, later in the century one critic referred to Thomas Lawrence as 'a man-milliner painter – a meteor of fashion.'[78] Rather than attempting to establish a masculine aesthetic to compensate for this kind of association, Reynolds appears to have capitalized on the scandal that his association with dubious women such as Kitty Fisher created. One critic claimed that Reynolds was 'as injurious to the true principles of painting as a fine prostitute to the establishment of morals.'[79] Indeed, the structural similarities between Fisher's and Reynolds's relationship with the aristocracy – their dependency on its patronage, their hold over its imagination, and their ability to mimic, in their own acts of self-display, its ostentation – allow us to imagine Kitty Fisher as a figure of Reynolds himself and of the authority his painting – like the spectacle of the courtesan's body – commanded over its beholder.

Kitty Fisher's ability to transfix those who beheld her was not lost on various social commentators, one of whom directly linked Fisher to the decline of the English nation:

> Now, while the weaken'd Pride of *Gaul*
> Is drawing nearer to its Fall,
> And only waits, from *British* Foe,
> The last, but great, decisive Blow:
> Where shall the Genius of our Lands
> Find Chiefs to lead her Martial Bands?
>
> ....
>
> Are all her friends, that well shou'd wish her,
> Now turn'd the Dupes of K— F—?
>
> ....

40   Private Interests

> Think then, ye Fair, so neat and pretty,
> Whether you would not all be *Kitty?*
> What would you give to have a Tribe
> Of D—s and L—ds, from each a Bribe;
> To see'em bow and cringe before ye;
> Sigh, fawn, and flatter, and adore ye:
> As now this envied *Kitty* reigns,
> While powder'd C——rs wear her Chains. [80]

The poem laments English noblemen's willingness to shift their attention away from England's military interests to Kitty Fisher's sexual enticements, declaring the nation's genius bereft of support. Instead of ruling the world, England is ruled by a whore – 'now this envied *Kitty* reigns' – and this perversion threatens not only England's status abroad, but also her social stability at home (as it did, according to Pope, in the Restoration, when '*Jilts* rul'd the State').[81] The speaker fears an England filled with a nation of women mimicking Kitty, a woman capable of collecting a 'Tribe' of men and of draining their wealth. As in the art criticism of the period, the concern about the illicit woman – in reality or in representation – centres as much on her effect on other women as on her possible corruption of male admirers. 'Simon Trusty' begs Fisher to join the ranks of virtuous women, a rhetorical strategy that seems less designed to encourage the prostitute to reform her ways than to convince English women of the courtesan's depravity: 'In the cool Moments of Recollection, when we view you, we see nothing but what creates our Aversion, and gives Disgust.' Indeed, the subtitle of the pamphlet recommends the piece '*to the Perusal of the LADIES of GREAT BRITAIN.*'[82]

A decade after Fisher and Reynolds profited from the sale of prints made from Fisher's portraits, Gainsborough created a scandal by exhibiting portraits of various notorious women at the Royal Academy: 'It should seem from this artist's female portraits, that he is a favourite among the demireps. He has, it is plain, been visited by Miss Dalrymple; Clara Haywood, and another well-known character of the same stamp.'[83] One portrait of Grace Dalrymple Elliot, exhibited by Gainsborough in 1782 (figure 2), provoked a critic to remark: '*Dally* ... is *not* a good moral Likeness ... the *Eyes* are too characteristic of her Vocation.'[84] This statement highlights the concern that female portraiture must represent an abstraction of virtue in order to become eligible for public display, for the critic objects, not to a lack of verisimilitude between the subject and the representation, but to the closeness of the likeness – Gainsborough's accurate portrayal of Elliot's eyes reveals his sitter's 'Vocation' as a mistress. The idea of 'a good moral Likeness' indicates the painter's duty to represent virtue in all female sitters as a way of establishing the social efficacy of the representation.

In the case of Grace Elliot, however, the reputation of the sitter makes the representation of virtue unlikely, if not impossible. Having divorced her husband, Sir John Elliot, 'Dolly the Tall' became the lover of Lord Cholmondely, whose wife raised his and Elliot's illegitimate daughter. The interpretive problems caused by Elliot's portraits stem both from the idea that her status may reveal itself in her representation, and from the idea that it may not. For, when placed alongside other portraits of the period, there is nothing to distinguish Gainsborough's portraits of Elliot from those of more reputable women (see figure 3). In a review of Alice Browne's work on eighteenth-century gender codes, James Grantham Turner observes that 'eighteenth-century costume did not mark any distinction between prostitutes, upper-servants and "ladies," who followed precisely the same fashion codes,' and Marcia Pointon notes that this confusion was exacerbated by women like Emma Hart, who began her career as a mistress but went on to marry extremely well.[85] The critics' objections to the portraits of 'demireps' take us back to the comments about the exhibition rooms full of 'dominos'; the representations have an element of opacity that clouds the viewing experience. For without the knowledge of Grace Elliot's exploits, the viewer may admire her image, becoming an unwitting dupe to the charms that have incited divorce and adultery.

We can infer, from the critical reception that greeted scandalous portraits, that painters were well aware of the type of anxieties representations of women like Kitty Fisher and Grace Elliot could create. It is also likely that they recognized the potential for such women to generate a market for the paintings, just as portraits of respectable women became the bread and butter of their trade. Indeed, it appears that painters were willing to represent virtue and vice alongside one another, and in doing so they placed the period's two understandings of private interests – as potentially destructive or beneficial – on a visual continuum.[86]

The uncertainties surrounding the meaning of female portraiture provided eighteenth-century novelists with a visual trope with which to explore the nature of female character, private interests, and their relation to novel reading and writing. The portrait's interest in representing women with texts adds to the visual intrigue surrounding female portraiture, and – to the extent that women readers were often associated with the novel – it confirms the idea that the portrait and the novel inhabited parallel lives in the eighteenth century's cultural imagination.[87] The visual interest created by the images of women with texts stems from the diversity of the representations that surrounds the subject of women readers. On the one hand, many portraits of women holding books idealize the female reader as a figure of domestic retirement and leisure. On the other hand, the representation of women with private letters – the letters that, compiled, became the epistolary novel – represents female reading as a potentially illicit activity, one that allows female agency to undermine, rather than confirm, cultural values. These two modes of representation speak to each other, of course, as well as to the ideas of virtue and scandal raised by female portraiture more generally.[88]

In many eighteenth-century portraits (see figures 4–7), the presence of a book – which may or may not be a novel – seems to confirm the sitter's respectability.[89] The book announces the sitter's relation to a culture of leisure, a culture often marked also by the presence of a natural landscape that provides, we assume, a setting for the sitter's recreation. The book stands as a symbol of privacy and retirement, of civility and education, and as such announces the sitter's wealth and status. The prominent displays of the book in Joseph Highmore's portrait of Elizabeth Harris and Thomas Hudson's portrait of Mary, Lady Wray (figures 4, 5) equate the book and the women's expensive clothing, both of which contribute to the women's worthiness as objects of aesthetic representation. The book stands as the sign of wealth and of the leisure time that the women enjoy, as well as the respectability of the activities the women pursue in that time – they are not holding a deck of cards. In George Romney's less formal portrait of Lady Macleod (figure 6), the representation sets the reader in a rural landscape, signalling the virtues of retirement and privacy associated with the country seat. Gainsborough places the female reader in a similar landscape in his *Lady with a Spaniel* (figure 7), where the young woman's entitlement displays itself in the connection that the painting establishes between the park, the girl, and her book. In each of these cases, the beholder is invited to interpret the book's presence as benign, reinforcing positive accounts of women readers that were available in the period. The emphasis on the sitters' interest in books also comments on the women's purchasing power, exercised in the accumulation of books, and also in the commissioning of portraits; both the book – in particular, the novel – and the portrait formed part of the constellation of objects defining women's cultural and financial agency in the period.[90]

The Novel and the Portrait in Eighteenth-Century England   43

The book may also be used to signal a state of absorption such as Michael Fried elucidates in his analysis of eighteenth-century French painting practices. This state represents, according to Fried, the ideal of 'a new, nonvoyeuristic, intensely empathic' idea of representation and beholding that emerged in France in the second half of the eighteenth century. In a Reynolds portrait of 1763 and a John Russell portrait of 1792, for example, the women seem to be reflecting on what they have read in the books they are holding, oblivious to the presence of the beholder (figures 8, 9). Insofar as the women turn away from the world of the spectacle in their disavowal of the beholder, they establish a means by which the portrait painter can '*detheatricalize beholding* and so make it once again a mode of access to truth and conviction.'[91] This turn away from the spectator would appear a very useful way of counteracting charges of self-promotion and the anxieties surrounding the question of female display, enabling the portrait painter to respond to attacks on both his character and those of his sitters. Instead of registering a state of narcissism and a love of flattery, these portraits promote the ideals of moral integrity and unselfconsciousness.[92]

Two representations of young women absorbed in novels highlight the portrait's ability to idealize the female reader, an idealization that in turn allows the portrait to elevate itself as a genre. Reynolds's portrait of his niece, titled *A Girl Reading*, exhibited at the Royal Academy exhibition of 1771, represents a young woman deeply absorbed in Richardson's *Clarissa* (figure 10). Theophila Palmer's face registers the distress caused by the novel's unfolding tragedy, displaying the sentimental moment that the novel was famous for sustaining. Reynolds's explicit reference to *Clarissa* (the title of the novel is visible on the spine of the book) announces his desire to contain any damaging associations that the novel could denote for the viewers of the painting, for the moral integrity of the sitter – and, by extension, of the painting – is guaranteed by the evocation of a novel whose moral intent few questioned. Theophila's engagement with the novel effectively blocks out the beholder, and at the same time elevates the portrait to the status of a moral discourse that contributes, like Richardson's novel, to the education of young women. Unlike the portrait of Kitty Fisher, this representation alludes to a narrative that aligns women with moral integrity and religious piety, summed up in Richardson's idealization of his sentimental novel as a Christian tragedy.[93] We are encouraged to engage in the same moment of absorption that the portrait represents by recalling the religious ethic that *Clarissa* imparts, an ethic closely linked to the heroine's agency as a reader and a writer – and also, significantly, as a spectator.

A similar hermeneutics of beholding appears in George Romney's *Serena* (figure 11).[94] The portrait represents a young lady in the character of Serena from W. Hayley's 'The Triumph of Temper.' In its epigraph, J.R. Smith's engraving of the portrait names *Evelina* as the novel that 'Serena' reads:

> Sweet Evelina's fascinating power
> Had first beguil'd of sleep her midnight hour,
> Possesst by Sympathy's enchanting sway,
> She read, unconscious of the dawning day.

Like Reynolds, Romney represents the young woman as sympathetically engaged in the text she reads, creating a state that the poem explicitly identifies as 'unconscious.' The young woman, through her association with the novel, is able to escape the system of display and self-aggrandizement associated with portraiture. Like Richardson's novel, Burney's *Evelina* creates a pedagogical imperative for its female readers in the representation of its young heroine's conduct, and the portrait encourages a similar ideal in its desire to create an absorptive aesthetic that will remove the portrait from the system of self-aggrandizement and female narcissism associated with the genre.

The aesthetic promoted by these portraits establishes a viewing experience that encourages the beholder to empathize with the subject of the painting even as it maintains a distance between the representation and the spectator by stressing the sitter's absolute absorption. In this double movement the portraits seem to mirror the dynamic that Catherine Gallagher has defined as the work of the novel, whereby the genre encourages 'an affective pulsation between identification with fictional characters and withdrawal from them, between emotional investment and divestment.'[95] But an alternative account of women's relation to texts also appears in eighteenth-century painting, one that takes us back to the scandalous elements of female portraiture that I described above, insisting on the voyeurism that emerges in response to the idea of women's agency as readers and writers.

Even in the portraits I have just examined, traces of the novel's scandal appear. Richardson's novel did come under scrutiny for some of its representations – the fire scene, for example – and we might ask which volume, exactly, is Miss Palmer reading? As Laclos makes clear in *Les Liaisons Dangereuses*, the early volumes of the novel could very well lead a vulnerable young woman astray. In Romney's portrait of Serena, we are

The Novel and the Portrait in Eighteenth-Century England 45

granted access, as viewers, to the privacy of the girl's reading alone, 'fascinated' and 'possessed,' late at night, a scene that in Manley's world would develop into a seduction narrative. The complexity surrounding the figure of the woman reader is writ large in three mid-eighteenth-century genre paintings that make the female letter reader their subject of investigation. These paintings, completed by Joseph Wright of Derby between 1760 and 1772, reflect the period's preoccupation with women's reading activities and suggest how the portrait's imaging of the female reader might have been experienced by an eighteenth-century audience. In each of the three paintings, a woman is represented as an absorbed reader of a letter. But rather than evoking an antitheatrical moment that eradicates the beholder, each of the paintings represents a male onlooker as part of the reading scene. By depicting this onlooker, the painter explicitly addresses the spectator's voyeurism in relation to the female subject.

In the earliest of these three paintings (figure 12), a young man peers over a girl's shoulder as she reads. The letter beside the girl begins, 'Dere Jack,' and next to it a book titled *The Art or Guide of Writing a Letter* rests open. The letter the girl is reading is addressed to 'Mrs Eliza Jeltem,' a name which has led one critic to suggest that Wright 'could ... have intended to signify a jilt.'[96] Whether or not Eliza is in the process of distancing herself from Jack, she is clearly involved in writing, as well as reading, her way into or out of the relationship. The reference to the girl's authorial activity qualifies the idea that reading necessarily signals a state of absorption, insofar as it presumes a heightened, rather than diminished, self-awareness on the part of the reader – her letter reading is intimately tied to her letter writing. The anxious look of the young man trying to read the contents of the letter seems provoked by the degree of control the young woman has over the moment. Her absorption signals, not the pious sympathy of Theophila Palmer, but authorial and sexual agency.

This heightened consciousness of the female reader also appears integrated into the reading scene in the second painting (figure 13), in which the male onlooker appears not only as a figure for the beholder, but as part of the girl's reading experience. The man's hand rests on the young woman's shoulder, signalling her awareness of his presence. His presence does not seem to qualify her engagement with the letter, a fact which suggests that the female figure may understand her reading to constitute, in part, a theatrical moment of display paradoxically staged in a private moment, the intimacy of which is highlighted by the use of candlelight to illuminate the scene. As in the first painting, the young woman's reading appears directly related to her own authorship – a letter and quill rest on the desk. These factors contribute to a sense that the female reader controls the display orchestrated around her reading activity. Unlike the Reynolds portrait of Palmer, this painting invites the beholder to become part of the painting's spectatorial activities, rather than establishing an absorptive mode through the idea of reading.

In the latest of the three paintings, yet another spectatorial configuration appears, in which the complicity between the male onlooker and the beholder is explicitly addressed.[97] In the foreground, a woman reads a letter, a letter that she has authored herself; the letter reads, 'Dear Roger – The many hours and days that have elapsed since I was blest with thy composition.' Behind her a young man holds onto the back of the woman's chair with one hand, and gestures to the spectator to remain still with the other. The stillness of the spectator presumably establishes the conditions of voyeurism by allowing the woman to read her letter uninterrupted, creating the spectacle that incites male desire. But, as in the other two paintings, the female subject seems in control of the spectacle her reading creates. If the woman's pleasure resides in the act of reading her own letter, then the male spectator must also appreciate the subject's self-gratification as the suitable object of his voyeurism. The male spectator's position depends on an identification with the man who addresses him. But who is this man? Is it Roger, enjoying the spectacle of his lover's desire for him, or is it a third party, interested in exploring a woman's secret life? The woman may be aware of his presence, happy to indulge the man's desires. Most importantly, it does not matter whether she knows or not: her pleasure relates to her letter writing and reading only. Paradoxically, the painting simultaneously insists upon and disregards the theatricality of its representation. Wright of Derby's engagement with the figure of the female reader becomes, ultimately, a meditation on the conditions for the aesthetic appreciation of these genre paintings, whereby the painter signals his awareness of the beholder without allowing him to define the meaning or integrity of the representation.

In each of these paintings, the figure of the female reader takes on sexual characteristics as a result of her engagement with the love-letter, an engagement that eroticizes the acts of reading and writing. These representations speak to cultural concerns about women's activities in the private sphere, concerns that also find expression in eighteenth-century portraits. I would like to conclude this chapter with an examina-

The Novel and the Portrait in Eighteenth-Century England   47

tion of two very different paintings: Reynolds's portrait of Kitty Fisher holding a letter (figure 14) and Hogarth's portrait of Miss Mary Edwards (figure 15). The Reynolds portrait of Kitty Fisher, now at Petworth, registers a set of associations around a text that mark women's relation to spectacle and eroticism. Fisher's status as an object of display is marked in the large amount of wealth signalled by her clothes and jewelry, and the letter in front of her becomes part of that system of display. The letter reads 'My dearest Kit,' although, based on prints after the painting, Nicholas Penny speculates that the painting originally read 'My dearest Life.'[98] In the case of the anonymous address, 'My dearest Life,' the portrait comments simultaneously on women's relation to letters in general and on the specific circumstances of Kitty Fisher's career. The letter indicates a world of intimacy placed on display, and the sitter's direct look at the beholder suggests women's awareness of the dynamic involved in this interaction between the private and the public. In this sense, the presence of the letter confirms the stance claimed by the women in Wright of Derby's genre paintings – it identifies the sitter as an active, rather than a passive, spectacle. In its comment on Kitty Fisher, the letter stands as the sign of the courtesan's desirability, of the universal demand for her company, just as her expensive clothes and jewels reflect the enormous personal wealth that Fisher was able to generate from her appeal. Fisher can approach the letter as she does a bank note; she can read it or dismiss it, according to her sense of its value. The letter represents Fisher herself: private, yet available for exchange, but only within an arena governed by Fisher – and, by extension, by Reynolds.

The letter also emblematizes the profitability of the portrait itself, signalling the idea of wealth created through an appeal to private interests, and it is significant that this portrait of Kitty Fisher quickly became 'public property: the earliest mezzotint was copied by four other engravers and so must have been one of the bestsellers in the print shops of the period.'[99] The prints' status as public property does not place them outside of the control of Kitty Fisher and Joshua Reynolds, however. Rather, it enhances the personal wealth they already enjoy and furthers both of their careers.

Hogarth's painting, at first glance, formulates a rather different understanding of one woman's relation to a letter, and its aesthetic resembles that of traditional male portraiture, rather than either Wright's or Reynolds's eroticized paintings. Most notably, Edwards's text quotes an address by Queen Elizabeth I to her troops: 'Remember Englishmen, the Laws, the Rights / The generous Plan of Power deliver'd down /

From age to age by your renown'd Forefathers.'[100] The strong colour of Edwards's dress marks her privilege and wealth, wealth also registered in the spectacular display of jewels. To the left of the painting we see a globe and busts of Queen Elizabeth and King Alfred, icons that link Edwards to a world of education and imperial enterprise, as well as establishing the importance of her lineage as the heir to her father, who had no sons. Hogarth, it would first appear, has defined Edwards's gender in relation to the public sphere of English monarchical authority only.

And yet upon closer examination, the representation also provides its viewer with an alternative narrative, one very closely tied to questions of female sexual conduct. In 1731, Mary Edwards – whose income came to approximately £50,000–60,000 a year – secretly married Lord Anne Hamilton, son of the fourth Duke of Hamilton. A son was born to the couple a year later. By 1733, however, Mary Edwards was aware that her husband was in the process of ruining her fortune, and in a bold stroke eradicated all evidence of her marriage, publicly claiming her son to be a bastard. She went on to recover her fortune from Lord Anne and was a faithful patron of Hogarth until her death in 1743.[101] Within this context, the text that declares her allegiance to the political values of constitutional tradition also announces Edwards's ability to transform the law and her willingness to protect the tradition that her child represents by forsaking the 'plan of Power' signified by marriage. The edifice of jewels displayed on Edwards, like Kitty Fisher's pearl, creates a spectacle of wealth controlled by a woman, a financial power that translates into a sexual and social authority. Edwards's red dress marks not only her control over money, but also over her sexuality and its meaning. For far from becoming marked as a harlot, she has transformed herself into a bastion of society, drawing on the authority of Elizabeth I's legacy in much the same way that Lely's courtesans drew on the king's. Within this context, the text presented in the painting, like the letter in Reynolds's portrait of Fisher, appears integrally bound both to the idea of female agency and to the portrait's command over its beholders – and this idea of the female spectacle's control, with its origins in Restoration portraiture (which I will discuss in the next chapter), reappears over and over again in the vast range of images produced of female readers in the eighteenth century.[102]

The eighteenth-century novel has its roots in the hermeneutics of the private letter placed on display, a display that extends to include the female authors and readers of letters.[103] Portrait painters were able to capitalize on cultural fantasies of women's relation to texts as virtuous and erotic, placing in their frames images that confirmed either or both versions of the female reader. In the chapters that follow, I will show how the eighteenth-century novel united the competing accounts of portraiture that I have discussed here in order to create a particular kind of literary interest, an interest that found its mirror image in the figure of the portrait.

Chapter Two

Envisioning Literary Interest: Manley's *The New Atalantis*

Curiosity is an early and dangerous enemy to virtue.[1]

Delarivier Manley approached the idea of literary interest – and its connection to the private – from a position defined almost entirely by the politics of scandal. Her most infamous work, *Secret Memoirs and Manners of several Persons of Quality, of both Sexes. From the New Atalantis, an Island in the Mediteranean* (1709), sustains a vast machinery of gossip and intrigue, allowing readers in the know access to the most salacious details of various politicians' private lives. In its preoccupation with the social and political ramifications of individual actions, Manley's novel resembles what Peter Brooks has described as 'the novel of worldliness,' a form dedicated to engaging the reader in 'epistemology (finding people out)' and 'social ideology (judging the extravagant or mistaken).'[2] A novel concerned primarily with satirically and ironically representing the aristocracy and its corrupt behaviour, *The New Atalantis* seems only remotely related to later eighteenth-century novels and the language of sincerity and sympathetic identification they promote. But it is worth reconsidering Manley's contribution to the novel's evolution in eighteenth-century England: first, to identify the features of Manley's work that distinguish it from the type of aesthetic upheld in the French works that Brooks analyses, in order to nuance the aristocratic/middle-class opposition often used to separate early and later eighteenth-century prose fiction practices in England; second, to suggest how the most scandalous features of Manley's prose remain a defining presence, rather than a ghostly trace, in later narratives.[3]

The continuum this study traces begins with Manley's representation of the portrait. Both Brooks and, more recently, April Alliston have identified the centrality of the verbal portrait to seventeenth- and eighteenth-century French prose narratives, noting the centrality of *portrait moral* to the representation of character. For Brooks, this portrait trope defines a moment of 'complete and final representation'; for Alliston, it signifies the authority of 'heritable exemplary histories' organizing women's relation to patrilineal and matrilineal structures.[4] In Manley, we find the portrait typical of this tradition rewritten to reveal patterns of circulation and consumption that anticipate modes of knowing and being developed by later eighteenth-century authors. Manley also recalls England's recent history in order to capitalize on the iconophilia of the courtiers, both men and women, that she represents, drawing on the power of the spectacle that emerged in the figure of the restored monarch and the art works that he commissioned. She further delineates the novel's visual imperative by triangulating the representation of the gaze through the narrative's female narrators, who figure as spectators of various illicit scenes and who assume a critical distance from their moments of beholding, refusing any easy identification with the women who appear before them. The spectatorial pragmatism of these female narrators creates a defamiliarized visual perspective, effectively unmooring the gendering of the gaze from any fixed vantage point.

The idea of visual pleasure appears tightly linked to the practices of fiction reading and fiction making in *The New Atalantis*, and this chapter will define how this pleasure, and these practices, appear distinct from the novel's engagement with politics. The portrait serves as the place where this distinction appears most clearly, where the text establishes different modes of beholding that isolate, rather than unite, notions of political and literary interest. In its satirical mode, the text advocates a Tory interpretive framework that draws on sentimental understandings of women's character. In its fictional mode, the novel undermines the sentimental by exposing our attachment to the violence embedded in the voyeurism of the sentimental gaze, and representing an authority in the spectacle that establishes a potential for conflict between subjects and objects of the gaze, rather than an easy or necessary domination of the object. Within this configuration of subject and object relations, the portrait appears as the place where the complexity of reading and viewing come to the foreground, and where the stubborn materiality of representation asserts itself. In this sense the portrait's logic anticipates Reynolds's portrait of Kitty Fisher as Cleopatra, which, even while it emphasizes the material pleasures afforded by the portrait and the prostitute's body as the stimulus to voyeuristic pleasure, grants the spectacle a voice of its own. As we shall see, Manley's representation of the portrait works, like Kitty Fisher's moments of self-fashioning, to locate a place from which the female reader and writer can speak.[5]

Visual Ethics and Political Observations

Manley's novel sets up its opposition of politics and fiction by establishing, in general terms, two modes of portraiture, one that draws on the conventions of male, state portraiture, and one that takes the female portraiture of the Restoration as its model for the principles governing the creation of narrative pleasure. In its commentary on English politics, *The New Atalantis* functions as a 'gallery of portraits and scenes,' a public display of an array of Whig politicians whose personal lives Manley exposes in all of their sordid glory.[6] In displaying these 'portraits,' Manley manipulates the idea of male portraiture as a form of history painting, exploiting the portrait's proximity to the private individual in order to expose the intimate details of various noblemen's personal lives. The representations she provides challenge the idealizing tendency of state portraiture and insist on the significance of the details of private lives conventionally concealed by a public mask. The understanding that portraiture allows the state to celebrate the individual's personal charms in relation to his heroic actions allows Manley to represent the personal as political.[7] Indeed, Manley's scandalous revelations ensure that the weight of personal corruption will become significant enough to transform public understandings of certain politicians and their role in England's national affairs.

Manley's manipulation of the conventions informing the creation and consumption of public portraiture is framed by a more general discussion of spectatorial agency and visual revelation that places ways of seeing at the heart of the text's satiric technique. The narrative presents Manley's political perspective in the text in the guise of divine beings who circulate through society, observing its behaviour and mores. As Virtue suggests to Astrea upon her arrival on earth, the world's corruption is everywhere visible to the careful observer: 'You will by this visit only furnish your self with matter of complaint to Jupiter, from ocular proof; when you have seen how abandoned they are, it will excite your desire to destroy the race' (8). The authority of Manley's narrators is marked by their ability to move invisibly through the world, a talent that, as Ros Ballaster has noted, transforms the 'enforced invisibility of women in the world of politics ... [into] a supernatural gift.'[8] The narrators' ability to see all without being seen themselves grants them autonomy as well as anonymity and calls attention to Manley's powerful position as an insider to the political scene.[9] While none of the narrators possesses omniscient powers, together they pool their respective resources, drawing also on the information proffered by the women they meet on their journeys. These acts of unseen seeing and information exchange establish a line of communication among the women whose knowledge society conventionally deems irrelevant, creating a female community that Cynthia Richards has defined as a 'locus of resistance' in women's amatory fiction of the early eighteenth century.[10] Furthermore, the deities' ability to render themselves invisible at will facilitates their progress through society by allowing them to escape aggressive men at any moment: 'All the arguments they could use would not hinder him from following them, till, by virtue of their divinity, having made themselves invisible, they left him to wonder at their disappearing' (86).

The visual acumen of the text's narrators stands in sharp relief to the impaired vision of the corrupt Whig politicians populating Manley's narrative. Indeed, the novel presents a series of unveilings that distinguish those capable of virtuous responses to the scenes that unfold around them (the few) from those unable to perceive moral truths (the many). Complaining of the weak minds of the debauched, i.e., Whig, noblemen, Intelligence observes:

> Hence they rejoice, they mourn, they weep, they laugh, they look, but they scarcely see ... They seldom go to the head of the spring, rarely ever examine into the true motive, and throw out either tears or smiles, either joy or grief, not as they are in reason and reality affected, but as they are infected by custom and swayed by decency. (215)

The surface/depth dichotomy Manley establishes here points to her critique of modern culture and politics. To 'look' is only to perceive the surface of things, to neglect the truths revealed by the investigation of inner causes and effects. Like Swift's knaves and fools, Manley's Whigs are incapable of the reflection required for perception that extends beyond a merely superficial understanding of the world, one based on appearances.

In the world of Machiavellian Whig politics, the text argues, most responses are impostures and insight an almost impossible goal. Manley defines the noblemen's inability to experience genuine emotion as blindness – 'they scarcely see' – and implies that the lack of insight corresponds to a character that lacks agency. The politicians are 'infected by custom and swayed by decency,' rendered passive by their appetite for power, an appetite that effectively prevents 'reason and reality' from informing their private and public actions. Like marionettes, the Whigs 'throw out' their emotions, creating illusions that conceal their true feelings, or lack thereof. To look and be looked at in this facile manner destroys an ethics of seeing that requires a moral agent capable of establishing a correspondence between surface and depth, one that allows appearances to signal virtue or corruption in a transparent fashion. The Whigs' ability to simulate insincere responses enables them to pillage the nation while pretending to advance its causes.

The Whigs' particular form of blindness not only ensures their own failure to perceive reality but, more dangerously, it prevents the queen from perceiving the true condition of nation:

> Were she but to judge all things by her own eyes and ears, all things would be administered with the same impartiality and justice as if your self [Astrea] had held the balance, but alas! what defence is there against the corruption of favourites and the by-interests of ministers? 'Tis impossible a prince can come to the knowledge of things but by representation, and they are always represented according to the sense of the representator. Either avarice, revenge, or favour, are their motive, and yet how is it possible to prevent it? A prince knows not how to distinguish by the out, and are [sic] seldom let into the inside. (110)

Here the Whigs are characterized by their ability to corrupt the monarch's view of the nation, a corruption determined by the smokescreen of representations the queen's ministers establish around her. The queen's 'knowledge of things' is jeopardized by the politicians' ability to replace her sight with their own modes of seeing, which, as I have noted, are governed by an appetite for 'avarice, revenge, or favour.' In this passage the Whigs' vision takes on a more active character in its desire to refuse the monarch access to 'the inside.' The queen, rather than her ministers, appears passive in relation to the world, incapable of distinguishing the truth 'by the out,' unable to see through the representations carefully orchestrated to convey a Whig vision of England's political reality.[11] Within this corrupt political context, representation itself appears guilty of obscuring the truth and serving the political interests of the Whigs. Were the queen able to escape the gallery of representations presented to her by the Whigs and to judge the world 'by her own eyes,' truth would reveal itself to her in a transparent and unmediated fashion, and the queen would be able to serve the public good more effectively. Representation draws her inexorably into the world of the private interests of her ministers, interests that ensure that the ministers appear at court only 'in prospect of making, advancing, or preserving their fortunes' (110).

In using this language of blindness and insight, surface and depth, representation and reality, Manley evokes a civic notion of personal and public virtue uncorrupted by private interests.[12] The two opposing modes of spectatorship that the text defines as the alternative visual hermeneutics of political life correspond to eighteenth-century art criticism's valorization of the disinterested, apolitical beholder of painting, one whose own integrity is confirmed in his rational response to an art object, on the one hand, and its denigration of the embodied, self-interested spectator, on the other.[13] Within the framework of this visual epistemology, the integrity of the beholder corresponds to the worthiness of the object that the viewer confronts. In his analysis of Shaftesbury's treatise on *The Judgment of Hercules*, John Barrell notes Shaftesbury's insistence upon the clarity of a painting's representation: 'The painting must ... be as unambiguous as possible.'[14] This insistence, Barrell argues, speaks to Shaftesbury's concern 'with the integrity of the personality of the citizen, achieved by a subordination of private to general interests.'[15] Manley represents the sincerity of her political mode of beholding in her celebration of the spectacle created in the figure of the Duke de Beaumond (Beaufort), who shines by virtue of his independence and distance from the debauchery of a Whiggish culture. Anticipating his rise at court, Intelligence exclaims, 'He will show what it is to be a prince, that is, what a prince ought to be – magnificent, humane, sedate, free from all those vices that ruffle the calm of youth and cost the best part of their time to reform from, if ever they reform' (97). 'Showing' here becomes a matter of demonstrating a correspondence between external appearances and inner virtue. This virtue, in its physical manifestation, will far exceed the paltry trappings of the Whig gentlemen; Beaumond will be magnificent, a visual beacon for the rest of the nation. His aristocratic body will transcend the merely corporeal, becoming an abstract principle capable of holding the attention of the public and demonstrating how real leaders must act. Beaumond serves as a localized example of how the monarch's body has the potential, ideally, to close the gap between representation and the self, leaving no room for the type of fragmented agency that the Whigs' perverted vision and political life engenders.[16] The Tory aristocrat's singularity, like that of the monarch, separates him from the herd of corrupt politicians.

In her dedication of the second volume of *The New Atalantis* to the Duke of Beaufort, Manley aligns her literary ambition and the greatness of 'Beaumond' in her discussion of the success that greeted the first volume of the novel: 'I scarce believe the conquest but, still trembling, look back with wonder at my own ambition, how it durst put it self to that imminent trial: which was mightiest, your Grace's unequalled goodness or my unequalled presumption!' (131). Here the ambition of the female author is associated with the moral agency of the Tory aristocrat. The spectacle he represents and the literary star she has become are aligned in a common political purpose, and Manley is able to inhabit a world conventionally defined by male prerogative, while shielding herself against accusations of self-promotion behind the figure of the duke. Through this Tory perspective, Manley disengages her political text from the world of self-interested intrigue that she has defined as Whig terrain.

This moral understanding of the political efficacy of satire also informs the text's sentimental aesthetic. Women, in particular, are invited to recognize the commonality of women's shared experiences, producing what Cynthia Richards has defined as a 'model of alliance,' established through the public retelling of private stories of betrayal and deception.[17] Intelligence links the idea of visual revelation and political justice to stories of female seduction, declaring, 'Did I wrong the good! accuse the innocent! that indeed would be blameable, but the libertine in practice, the devotee in profession, those that with the mask of hypocrisy undo the reputation of thousands, ought pitilessly, by a sort of retaliation, to be exposed themselves' (137). When read as real stories about real women, the tales of rape and seduction that Manley recounts confirm the visual epistemology premised on sincerity and transparency that the text aligns with its Tory politics. Men disguise their intentions behind a screen of representations, and women, believing what they see on the surface, fall prey to the libertines' advances. In retelling her own tale of woe in the figure of Delia, Manley rails against the system of appearances that allow corrupt men to move throughout society unscathed while their victims, 'though oftentimes guilty but in appearance,' find themselves socially ostracized, condemned to obscurity and poverty (227). Within an allegorical frame of reference, the self-interest governing the actions of corrupt Whig players is, as John Richetti has argued, 'the sign of sin' in *The New Atalantis*.[18] In Delia's narrative, the sentimental tale of female abjection becomes a spectacle worthy of Beaumond's pity; the duke's 'Grand Druid' (Thomas Yalden, chaplain to Beaufort) assures her, 'A penitence so sincere as yours, a distress so moving, has pleaded powerfully for you ... I will even engage his Eminence to compassionate your suffering and know you not that in so great, so true a hero, to compassionate is to redress?' (227–8). The figure of an abject woman moves into the field of vision established around the Tory aristocrat, and, in the alignment of these two figures, an opening appears for Manley's social and political advancement.

'Animated Canvas': Manley's Erotic Tableaux

In the final instance, however, the seduction narratives that Manley tells do not create their literary pleasure by insisting on the reader's sympathetic identification with the female victims of Whig appetite, and even as the tales unfold, 'honour and virtue obtain no transcendental meaning.'[19] Paulson has argued that Manley's erotic narratives function as 'a come-on to lure neutral readers into her labyrinth of anti-Whiggery,'[20] but I would like to suggest, in what follows, that *The New Atalantis* goes a long way toward opposing moral virtue (as defined by the terms of the novel's Tory agenda) and narrative pleasure, toward juxtaposing, rather than conflating, its political and literary interests. In the field of vision, this separation pits a visual hermeneutics of sincerity and transparency – a hermeneutic explicitly identified as Tory – against a mode of beholding that celebrates the materiality of representation that finds its most cogent expression in the trope of female portraiture. This materiality heightens the novel's voyeuristic tendencies, but it also becomes the starting point for a consideration of the way that objects may be able to talk back to those that seek to appropriate their meaning. In turning away from the visual perspective defined by a Tory model of disinterested civic duty, Manley seeks to complicate the oppositions sustained by her political perspective, oppositions that only provisionally grant women a speaking place. Manley does not want to depend on aristocratic patronage for her protection and self-definition. In order to claim an alternative space from which to speak, Manley traces the roots of the visual mysteries grown in the hothouse of Whig intrigue and scandal.

The narrative's opening moments reveal the central role that visual hermeneutics will play in the text's definition of literary pleasure:

> [Astrea] wondered at the raptures of the stranger; therefore repelling her eager caresses, she ran over her form to see if she could recollect who this dejected beauty was. Her habit obsolete and torn, almost degenerated to tatters, but her native charms, that needed not the help of art, gave to Astrea's returning remembrance that it could be no other than her beautiful mother Virtue. (5)

The fact that the daughter does not recognize her mother immediately allows the narrative to dwell on the 'native charms' of Virtue as a 'dejected beauty' whose momentary anonymity incites the curiosity of the reader.[21] Manley's representation of the pleasures of interpretation created by allowing eyes to 'run over' the various forms that appear in her text corresponds with Addison's formulation of visual pleasure in *The Spectator*: 'A spacious Horison is an Image of Liberty, where the Eye has Room to range abroad.'[22] The motion of the eye constitutes, for both Addison and Manley, the sensual pleasure afforded by nature and art.[23] Within this framework, the eye becomes larger than the sum of its perceptual parts, serving in and of itself as an object of pleasure. Manley describes the 'glittering eyes' (260) of Astrea and Virtue in *The New Atalantis*; in *The Adventures of Rivella*, her fictional biographer refers to Manley's eyes as 'the best feature in her face ... Nothing can be more tender, ingenious and brilliant with a mixture so languishing and sweet, when love is the subject of the discourse, that without being severe, we may very well conclude, the softer passions have their predominancy in her soul.'[24] The narrator associates Manley with the world of private interests through this description of her eyes, in part to distance Manley from attacks on her political inclinations, and in part to identify the 'truth' revealed by the expressive eyes with her status as an author capable of creating narrative pleasure in the representation of the 'softer passions.' Manley's eyes are both perceptive – capable of interpreting information accurately – and gestural – capable of transmitting knowledge and feeling to those that behold them.

The status of the scandal narrative as a representation requiring an active visual imagination is signalled by Lady Intelligence's appearance in garments that are 'all hieroglyphics' (13). The materiality of the signs she displays marks the degree of mystery surrounding the scandalous stories she narrates, and the extent to which the stories are constructed so as to incite a readerly desire to uncover their truths. Indeed, the text presents to its readers one erotic tableau after another, creating a series of visual displays that, unlike the rhetoric of visual revelation and unmasking that informs the text's Tory political satire, invite us to dwell on the surface of appearances even as we attempt to penetrate them. As Ruth Perry observes in her discussion of early eighteenth-century fiction, 'again and again ... there are scenes which do not advance the plot but seem especially prepared, garnished, and served as inducements to fantasy.'[25] In this sense the images oppose, in their celebration of ambiguity and shifting visual indices, the representations idealized by Shaftesbury and other art critics of the early eighteenth century.

The scenes that Manley's narrative describes more often than not centre around a female figure, as in the description of young Charlot (Stuarta Werberge Howard), one of the many hapless virgins populating *The New Atalantis*:

> Charlot no sooner arrived but, the weather being very hot, she ordered a bath to be prepared for her. Soon as she was refreshed with that, she threw her self down upon a bed with only one thin petticoat and a loose nightgown, the bosom of her gown and shift open, her nightclothes tied carelessly together with a cherry-coloured ribbon, which answered well to the yellow and silver stuff of her gown. She lay uncovered in a melancholy careless posture, her head resting upon one of her hands; the other held a handkerchief that she employed to dry those tears that sometimes fell from her eyes. (39)

The detailed description of the fabrics and the body's stylization as a 'posture' render Charlot a luxurious object to be enjoyed, with rich drapery and a nubile young body working together to heighten the sensuality of the image. Here the representation corresponds to the spectacle that Paula Backscheider, following Roland Barthes, has described as a 'classical (or ideological) beauty,' whereby a woman is defined in wholly passive terms by the man assessing her appeal. As Backscheider points out, early women writers were alert to the implications of this ideal: 'In the novels by women, the control of the body and its presentation is of paramount importance, and loss of control inevitably leads to judgment.' In her assessment of Manley's mode of self-representation in *Rivella*, Backscheider claims that the autobiography 'gives us a depressingly detailed picture of the extent to which women had internalized the patriarchy's hierarchy of assessment.'[26] Such an evaluation of Manley's interest in the ideal of female beauty underestimates the degree of critical awareness Manley brings to her discussions of this ideal and men's and women's responses to it. While women like

Charlot may appear the objects of a predatory gaze, they are not necessarily destined to assume a passive role within the visual field they inhabit.

In particular, Manley draws on a tradition of female portraiture in the Restoration that complicates the idea of the spectacle as always already passive. The works of Peter Lely, the Restoration's most famous portrait painter, represent women as objects of pleasure, but they also signal these women's authority within the court circle. The women are powerful because they are beautiful, but they are also beautiful – i.e., suitable objects of Lely's attention – because they are powerful. Lely's portraits achieve a heightened sense of a particular court aesthetic in the making, to which each woman contributes a particular element. Pepys refers to Lely's portrait of Lady Castlemaine over and over again in his diary, and to its circulation in print form: 'By coach home in the evening, calling at Faythornes and buying three of my Lady Castlemaynes heads, printed this day; which endeed is, as to the head, I think a very fine picture, and like her.'[27] The proximity of the royal mistresses to the king establishes a metonymic relation to the powerful spectacle exerted by the monarch's body, a body most powerful, as Louis Marin has pointed out, when circulating as an object of representation.[28] The women's public status as courtesans whose sexual skills are 'professional' in the service they render the king elevates the portraits to the level of state portraits, even as their meaning remains fully encoded within the world of private interests.

Lely's female portraits serve as a model for the aesthetic that Manley creates in her erotic tableaux, not only in the authority wielded by their sitters, but also in the formal attributes of the paintings and the poses assumed by their subjects. One of the most striking features of his work is the liveliness Lely depicts in his subjects. As Ellis Waterhouse has observed, Lely's sitters 'tend to be restless, the figures are often in movement, and the hands are eloquent.'[29] In one portrait of Charles II's mistress, Louise de Kerouaille (figure 16), the sitter toys with the drapery of her *déshabillé*, and even the fabric of her dress seems animated; her hair falls loosely over one shoulder. In a portrait that represents either Nell Gwyn or the Duchess of Cleveland (figure 17), both the woman and her child (the king's son) finger the drapery upon which she reclines.[30] The women's restlessness seems to speak to the particularity of the moment they inhabit, rather than gesturing toward a timeless abstraction of beauty, and the presence of the child in the 'Nell Gwyn' portrait speaks even more concretely to an isolated moment in the history of one woman's relation to the king's body. That King Charles was considered to have jeopardized his 'immortal' king's body by indulging the demands of an appetitive 'natural' body heightens the sense of this portrait's immediate historical significance.

Our eyes are kept in perpetual motion by these portraits, and the idea of movement is heightened by the baroque emphasis on chiaroscuro that appears throughout Lely's portraiture, an emphasis that enables the 'richly atmospheric' effect that Oliver Millar has noted in the landscape backgrounds of Lely's portraits. The Beale family commented on Lely's use of '"a more conceled misterious scanty way of painting then the way he used formerly"'[31] in the late stages of his career. Their intriguing description sums up the effects of a technique apparent throughout Lely's work, one that both reveals and veils its subjects through a brushwork that gestures toward an object rather than laboriously filling in the details of each representation. This kind of technique defines the landscape that serves as the backdrop to Nell Gwyn's portrait, casting a brooding, sublime, and shadowy tone over the painting as a whole.[32] The shadows invite visual curiosity in the portrait's beholder, while blocking the viewer's entry into the obscure corners that the painting represents.

A generation later, Pope singled out the animated aspect of Lely's female portraits in his attack on Restoration culture and politics:

In Days of Ease, when now the weary Sword
Was sheath'd, and *Luxury* with *Charles* restor'd;

....

Lely on animated Canvas stole
The sleepy Eye, that spoke the melting soul.
No wonder then, when all was Love and Sport,
The willing Muses were debauch'd at Court.[33]

Two ideas governing Pope's characterization of female portraiture interest me here. First, it is significant that all of Lely's portraits of women blur together in Pope's allusion, a blurring that reiterates a common complaint made even by Lely's contemporaries, that the painter's portraits rarely achieved a significant degree of resemblance to the sitter. After Lely's death in 1680, Dryden wrote that 'It was objected against a late noble Painter, that he drew many graceful Pictures, but few of them were like.'[34] Even as each women's particular character as the king's mistress remains crucial to understanding the image, the courtesan's body is subsumed into a larger aesthetic ideal, a transformation that Ann Plogsterth has commented upon in her discussion of sixteenth-century French courtesan portraiture: 'In the end, we are left with a paradox: these paintings were at the same time both portraits and stereotypes, suggesting a specific identity while simultaneously submerging that identity to depict a more general erotic ideal.'[35] Pope highlights the extent to which the power of this ideal is not merely personal and private, but immediately political. For Pope, the cumulative effect of so much female beauty in one place is the overpowering of the monarch's sense of duty and obligation. The desire of the king's body, always present even in its absence, marks the women's agency as political actors, and allows the portraits to bridge the public and private divide.

The creation of an aesthetic ideal around the subject of female portraiture informs our understanding of another feature of Lely's portraits to which Pope draws our attention. The 'sleepy Eye' refers to the 'melting soul' of the sitter and of the individual who beholds the image, to the extent that the eyes seem to interpellate, to 'speak,' the beholder's response, which Lely orchestrates in 'stealing' the real and transforming it into the aesthetic. On the one hand, the direct gaze of Nell Gwyn and Louise de Keroualle can be read as part of an erotic come-on, in which the subjects confront the beholder with 'the enticement of a coyly inviting or contemptuously cool glance' (see figure 18).[36] On the other hand, the gaze seems to confront the beholder, demanding that the painting be viewed from a position defined by the portrait subject. Michael Fried has defined the significance of 'the alienating, distancing character' of the female gaze in Manet's *Olympia*, and its ability to stand for the effect sustained by the painting as a whole, which creates the sense that the '*painting itself* looks or gazes or stares at one – it is as though it confronts, fixes, even *freezes* one.'[37] The authoritative aesthetic that Lely's portraits produce allows the female sitters to assume a visual agency of their own, speaking from within the frame as private, public, and aesthetic subjects simultaneously.

In her creation of stylized tableaux of female beauty, Manley uses some of Lely's techniques as a way of theorizing the pleasures of reading outside of a strictly allegorical, political framework. The more stylized Charlot becomes, the less likely we are to read her rape as a public crime for which the man who has violated her should be held accountable – the demands of the literary supersede those of the political. Instead, Charlot appears as part of a seduction narrative that encourages our complicity in the duke's lascivious gaze, rather than inciting moral outrage at the duke's ability to destroy a woman's life. Indeed, when Virtue and Astrea lament the world's moral corruption, Intelligence diverts our attention: 'Whilst your Eminences are declaiming a length beyond my understanding, give me leave to get what information I can of that new adventure before us' (136). Adventure replaces sentiment and politics as the locus of readerly and narrative engagement.

As in the Lely portraits of the women of the Restoration court, Manley's descriptions of female beauty create an interpretive community governed by a pleasure principle. The erotic tableaux appear one after another, like a gallery of Lely beauties, confirming the pleasure of sexual corruption. In her reading of *The New Atalantis*, Janet Todd has observed how 'the sheer number and variety of the sexual scenes Manley describes makes physical enslavement a soothingly uniting predicament.'[38] The question that remains is: given that the women in the tableaux do not, as do Lely's sitters, usually confront the male spectator's look with their own, how do they gain the degree of spectatorial authority that I have attributed to Lely's subjects? Furthermore, as Ros Ballaster has asked, 'What "interest" does the woman spectator and, by extension, the female audience have in watching this spectacle of the man amorously contemplating the inviting female body?'[39] How can we suggest that women are able to gain any degree of agency within this configuration of spectatorial roles?

The answer to the first of these questions lies in the definition of the subject of the spectacle as an artist capable of transfixing the spectators who behold her: 'The Duke, awed and trembling with his passion, approached [Charlot] as a goddess, conscious of his and her own desires' (38).[40] Women may not look out at their male beholder in the initial spectatorial moment, but they are soon alerted to his presence and to the power they wield in the visual field; as painterly tableaux, they have the power to freeze those who approach them. In turn, Manley's descriptions of the women become opportunities for the author to figure her own ability to hold our attention. In *Rivella*, the author's boudoir appears at the end of the narrative as an invitation to male fantasy:

I should have brought you to ... a bed nicely sheeted and strowed with *roses*, *jessamins* or *orange-flowers*, suited to the variety of the Season; her Pillows neatly trimmed with lace or muslin, stuck round with *junquils*, or other natural garden sweets, for she uses no perfumes, and there have given you leave to fancy your self the happy man, with whom she chose to repose her self.[41]

Reading *The New Atalantis* through the erotics of authorship that this passage represents allows us to mingle the figure of the hapless heroine with that of the powerful author. Manley replaces the king's political body, so crucial to our understanding of Restoration portraiture, with the female author's body as the sign of social and literary authority.

The hapless heroine is not the only woman present in the scenes that unfold around the narrative's erotic tableaux, and the narrators' commentary on the descriptions they hear or represent themselves grants the possibility of a female visual agency insofar as they provide insight into the level of awareness that the spectacle can achieve. Their presence also answers, in part, my second question – where does the female spectator reside in relation to this scene? The narrators' presence effectively triangulates the moment of beholding, breaking the monopoly of the male gaze. The female narrators become commentators on the visual dynamic that unfolds before them, providing a gloss of the author's intended meaning of the image.

Finally, in assessing the novel's desire to transform moments of violence into aestheticized accounts of pleasure, it is worth noting that the narrators typically assume the subject position of both the male and female participants in the scene. The pleasure arises out of the assumption of a gaze typically reserved for men, as the women describe with obvious sensual delight the spectacle of the women inhabiting the narratives they tell. In doing so they create a shifting ground of visual perspectives, a spectatorial dynamic that Teresa de Lauretis has theorized: 'The analogy that links identification-with-the-look to masculinity and identification-with-the-image to femininity breaks down precisely when we think of a spectator alternating between the two ... This manner of identification ... uphold[s] both positionalities of desire, both active and passive aims.'[42] At the same time, the narrators recognize the import of this gaze for the women towards whom it is directed, often anticipating the sexual encounter that follows. This form of worldliness is highly pragmatic; in response to illicit sexual conduct, the narrators more often than not are concerned with the practical responses that victims of seduction and violence take to their situation, a concern that asserts that women can control, to some degree, the outcome of their various narratives. This pragmatism challenges the idea of sentimental outrage as a universally appropriate response to the various scenes that unfold. The literary focus insists on the particularity of each moment, balancing the generalized erotic and violent impulses with a careful assessment of the narrative potential embedded in each episode.

Nowhere is the distancing of the female spectator from the sentimentalization of a woman's violation more apparent than when *The New Atalantis* tells Manley's own story. Upon hearing the story of Delia, a figure for Manley herself, Astrea declares, 'I am weary of being entertained with the fopperies of the fair ... The penalty must be there and something of a quicker sense (if possible) than that of honour lost! Since we see the tender sex with all their native timorousness, modesty and shame-faced education, when stung by love, can trample under foot the consideration of virtue and glory, though by the loss they are reduced to be the despicablest part of the creation' (228). Astrea's remark rejects a sympathetic reading of female destruction at the hands of a male predator, refusing to read the erotic narratives as necessarily controlled by men, rather than women. By extension, the woman author appears capable of exerting control over the events of her life by assuming the role of the critical spectator of her own past.

In this context we return to the figure of Charlot as an erotic tableau that cannot necessarily be subsumed into a previously established interpretive framework, either sentimental or libertine. Instead, the image points to the restlessness of Manley's own authorial persona, lurking in the shadows of the images and signalling the presence of a female voice that is engaged in the creation of a literary eye governing the vision of both the subjects and the objects of a desiring gaze.

'Dangerous commerce': Reading Portraits

Throughout *The New Atalantis*, Manley creates moments of beholding that are filtered through a variety of perspectives, including those of the female narrators and the readers, both male and female, that the spectacles address. The Tory mode of seeing, which depends on an ethics of transparency and sincerity, gives way to a divided spectatorial perspective at the moments when the narrative becomes more interested in story telling than political satire. I have described the tableaux that Manley builds into the narratives she recounts as a form of erotic portraiture that bridges the divide between the private and the public, the particular and the general, through its commitment to the exigencies of the narrative. The trope of the portrait functions even more concretely in the text, however, appearing as an object that defines the spectatorial authority – or lack thereof – of women. The beholder's agency, as well as that of the spectacle, is defined by a spectatorial pragmatism, by an ability to manipulate the visual moment created by the painting. This pragmatism looks suspiciously like the Whig way of seeing that the novel's political satire decries, suggesting the extent to which Manley was willing to draw on her political enemies' discourses in her quest to grant women an identity that could escape the constraints of the gender hierarchy maintained by the Tory *Weltanschauung*.[43] But Manley's interest in the portrait creates, in effect, a third term, one that enables a vision of private interests not controlled only by the self-seeking ambition characteristic of the Whigs who populate *The New Atalantis*, but that allows private interests to promote the careers of women traditionally denied access to political, social, and literary authority.

The trope of the portrait appears as part of the text's terrain of character analysis, but rather than resolving interpretive anxiety surrounding the representation of character, it confirms the sense that individuals can manipulate relationships through their use of masks. As one heroine laments of her deceiver: 'Whoever would draw a true resemblance of the gentleman ought to have more skill in painting that [sic] I have, his person excepted; there 'tis easy to represent him, but his mind! his mind a complication of seeming good and real evil is impenetrable!' (163). Here the idea of the portrait appears to indicate, not visual revelation, but inscrutability and the difficulty of ascertaining the true feelings and motives of a professed lover. The transparent body – 'there 'tis easy to represent him' – stands in opposition to the opaque and 'impenetrable' mind of the seducer. The disadvantage at which women find themselves in conventional seduction narratives appears here as the speaker's lack of painterly skill. The inadequacy of this female 'painter' is addressed by the text's ability to fill in the details of the male libertine character through its various female spectators, who can penetrate the surface in order to delineate the workings of 'real evil' in the men they encounter. However, the narrators are not necessarily devoted to the principles of truth governing the Tory way of seeing. As Intelligence notes, 'I take Truth with me when I can get her. Sometimes, indeed, she's so hard to recover that Fame grows impatient and will not suffer me to wait for her slow approach' (162). Rather, the scandalous narratives Intelligence recounts play one notion of the portrait's function off against another, allowing competing modes of beholding and representation to emerge simultaneously.

As a physical object the portrait creates narratives that situate modes of spectatorship within a logic of exchange. In the case of young Charlot and the duke, the program of seduction and betrayal begins when the duke takes Charlot from his pornographic library, itself a kind of picture gallery, to his cabinet, where he offers her jewels, including a miniature portrait:

> He told her she was now of an age to expect the ornaments, as well as pleasures, of a woman. He was pleased to see her look down with a seeming contempt upon what most other girls would have been transported with. He had taught her other joys, those of the mind and body ... Charlot, as tender and gallant as the Duke, seeing his picture in little set round with diamonds, begged that he would only honour her with that mark of his esteem. The ravished Duke consented, conditionally that she would give him hers in return. (37)

The miniature portrait appears in a web of competing modes of beholding.[44] Both Charlot and the duke value the miniature's ability to exceed the value of mere 'ornament,' its ability to signal a particularly private form of affect. But how each character understands that affect differs drastically. The duke is delighted with the refined sensibility that he has cultivated in Charlot, one that refuses the material appeal of jewelry. In the eyes of the duke, the maturity of this sensibility is defined by its ability to anticipate pleasures 'of the mind and body' that exceed the gratifications afforded through the display of ornament, and that can compete with the promise of reputation secured only through marriage. The duke defines Charlot as a woman in order to sexualize her body, to situate it within the pornographic narratives that he has been encouraging his ward to read. In the duke's eyes, Charlot, and by extension her miniature, represent a singular pleasure, but that singularity is defined by the terms of a libertine appetite for new, 'unique' conquests, rather than by the integrity of the relationship that the exchange of the miniatures ostensibly signifies. The duke is able to exploit the idea of the miniature's sentimental singularity even as his plot confirms its effectiveness as a tool of seduction. He understands the power of the visual register to displace moral ideas, and the degree to which having an image of himself held before Charlot's eyes or pressed close to her body as a piece of jewelry may facilitate the sexual conquest he is planning. His own possession of Charlot's miniature confirms her status as a passive object of his gaze and, by extension, of his sexual advances.

In contrast, Charlot views the duke's love for her – signalled by his desire for her miniature and by his willingness to part with his own – as a mark of a singularity that places their relationship outside of systems of exchange: 'With pride and pleasure, she saw her self necessary to the happiness of one that she had hitherto esteemed so much above her' (36). Charlot views her entry into womanhood as a personal triumph, rather than as the starting point for her destruction as a woman viewed as one trophy among many. She defines the exchange of the miniature portraits as the seal of intimacy between herself and the duke as 'that mark of his esteem,' that separates their exchange of gifts from the crass bartering that governs both marriage plots and the purchase of sexual favours from mistresses. For Charlot, the miniature maintains the familial relationship that has defined her status as the foster daughter of the duke, and fixes the paternal eye upon her. The particularity of the portrait, for Charlot, elevates her relationship with the duke above the public spheres of exchange that a marriage would inhabit, and so she refuses to place herself on the footing of bride-to-be by accepting the rest of the family jewels. Charlot believes in the sanctity of the private moment of exchange that the miniature enables, investing all of her emotional assets in the integrity of that moment, and, by extension, in the promise that the duke's feelings – like his portrait – will never undergo a transformation.

The duke, of course, recognizes the extent to which Charlot's desire for the miniature promotes, rather than thwarts, an illicit sexual narrative. And indeed, the exchange of portraits achieves the effect the duke anticipates: 'After this tender, dangerous commerce, Charlot found every thing insipid' (37). Significantly, the narrative goes on to describe the reading addiction Charlot develops in the days that follow as visual obsession, to the extent that one wonders if the girl is reading illustrated pornography. The duke leaves her texts that explain 'the nature, manner and raptures of enjoyment ... She was indefatigable in reading ... She had too well informed her self of the speculative joys of love' (37). Charlot moves away from the moral imperatives presented by various amatory fictions – morals that depend on an attention to narrative constructions of cause and effect – into a purely 'speculative' trance of visual pleasure. The attachment Charlot forms to the scenes of sexual intercourse she imagines with the duke renders her incapable of resisting his advances, and even the warnings she receives in reading tales of female self-immolation cannot compete with the fantasy life his image has inspired: 'These admonitions were too feeble' (38).

In recounting the predictable destruction of Charlot at the hands of the duke, the narrative is careful to avoid attributing her decline to the idea that a visual register necessarily places women in the position of passive spectacle. Indeed, the text provides a foil to Charlot in the figure of the countess, who counsels Charlot in her management of the duke, encouraging the young woman to force him into marriage: 'Charlot told her, she found all she desired in the Duke's love and her friendship; she had nothing further to wish ... The Countess pitied the lovesick maid but, finding she was incorrigible, resolved to speak to her no more of her marrying the Duke' (42). Charlot cannot renegotiate the fixed terms of her relationship with the duke without revising her understanding of the principles that governed the relationship from the outset; she is 'incorrigible,' fixed in her belief that their feelings, like the miniature, occupy a realm uncorrupted by the vagaries and duplicity of conventional social relations. Unlike Charlot, the countess is able to control the visual register she inhabits. The countess also appears to the duke in her 'genteel *dishabile*, even to the very nightclothes that she intended to lie in,' assuming a gaze from within the frame of the portrait she creates, like Lely's female sitters (44). She turns her status as a spectacle to her advantage so as to transform her objectification into a larger aesthetic principle – she becomes, in effect, an 'animated Canvas.' Meanwhile Charlot becomes trapped in a passively iconic role: 'She died a true landmark to warn all believing virgins from shipwracking their honour upon (that dangerous coast of rocks) the vows and pretended passion of mankind' (45).

Astrea provides only an acerbic comment on Charlot's lack of judgment, and the narrative as a whole, while it offers its sympathy to the young woman, grants its respect to the countess. The sentimental meaning that Charlot attaches to the miniature portrait of the duke can only be read as an indication of her inability to interpret visual signs, both in her own person and in the objects and characters that surround her. In refusing Charlot's visual hermeneutics, the narrative assumes the knowingness of the countess's gaze, itself a version of the male libertine's. Women have an opportunity to control the field of vision, but only if they understand that field within a larger context of exchange relations and the material conditions informing their status as women.

The portrait appears again as the weathervane of women's ability to negotiate social relations and the field of vision in Manley's representation of a powerful cabal of Whig women. The cabal itself represents an interpretive crux within the narrative as a whole. On the one hand,

Manley satirizes society's refusal to acknowledge lesbian sexuality: 'For how can they be guilty? They vow eternal tenderness, they exclude the men, and condition that they will always do so. What irregularity can there be in this?' (154). On the other hand, Manley fears the Whig power collected in the hands of the cabal women, and identifies the women as lesbians in order to link their political claims to a particular form of social powerlessness.[45]

The portrait narrative begins when a widow in the cabal attempts to seduce an actress after she finds herself aroused by the actress's appearance as a male libertine on the stage, an appearance that appeals to the widow's appetite for 'the representation of men in women' (235). The objective correlative of the actress's performance appears in a portrait that the widow commissions: 'The widow sent for the girl and made her very considerable presents, ordered her picture in that dress to be taken at length by one of the best hands, and carried her to remain with her during the season at her villa' (235). The complexity surrounding the representation is heightened by the idea of the comedian's 'dress en cavaliere' (235), presumably recreated in the portrait. Libertinism usually denotes an attitude rather than a physical appearance, a presence that manifests its identity in particular kinds of acts. Indeed, the fop, not the libertine, exposes himself to ridicule with his overnice attention to dress. Manley's evocation of a type of dress that in fact does not exist represents the concretization of the libertine attitude, a physical manifestation of a particular form of desire. The widow's obsession with 'seeing' the libertine also indicates that the portrait serves as a screen onto which desires are projected. But the ambiguity surrounding the idea of a libertine costume points to the difficulty of stabilizing this screen, which may find ways to assert its own understanding of the image it portrays, establishing an interpretive conflict that the widow soon is forced to confront.

The widow's social privilege is marked by her ability to pay for a full-length portrait – a very expensive commodity – and by her ability to demand that the actress sit for the portrait. By purchasing the portrait and placing it in her home for her own viewing pleasure, the widow assumes both the material and the spectatorial power usually reserved for the libertine that the painting represents. She participates in a fantasy that allows women to assume male attributes and to transform, Pygmalion-like, other women into objects of their own creation. The widow hopes that she can project her own desiring gaze onto the subject of the portrait's representation, in order to have the actress respond to her amorous advances. Like the duke, the widow looks to the visual register as a means of advancing her amorous plot. Unlike the duke, she cannot force her narrative upon the actress, but must depend rather on the comedian's willing collusion in the fiction created by the portrait. Of course, this fantasy is only made possible by the comedian's inferior class status, which, like Charlot's youth and inexperience, places her at a social disadvantage.

The actress, at this point, appears powerless, and is passively 'carried' to the widow's villa. The widow imagines, in bringing the actress and the portrait home, that she has established the grounds for transforming fantasy into a reality governed by the fiction established in the portrait's representation. The portrait, in other words, introduces the theatrical into the home, where the widow hopes to have the actress act out a cabal script. However, the narrative that unfolds at the villa provides competing understandings of that script:

> The comedian was dazzled at those endearments and advances from a lady of fortune and did not know how to behave herself in a manner regular enough (for her conversation had been pretty much at large) ... The widow redoubled her kindness and caresses, assured her of her tenderness and amity; she even proceeded to gentle squeezes and embraces. Nothing could be more innocently endearing than her transports! The comedian was at a loss to know not only how to merit so many favours, but of the meaning of 'em. She was also weary of the solitude and splendour of the widow's family and wanted to return to the amorous hurry and theatrical littleness she had been used to and therefore received those honours with no new Cabal air, but, as if rather disgusted at such amiable proofs of amity, told the lady she did not like those hugs and endearments from her own sex, they seemed unnatural: did they come from a man, she should be able to guess at his design, but here she was at a loss. (235–6)

The conflict in this scene is summed up by the contrast between the two worlds that the women inhabit. The widow believes that the 'splendour' of her villa will elicit in the comedian a desire for the material rewards a relationship with the widow will ensure, but the actress longs for other forms of sensual gratifications – those afforded by her fellow actors and their world of 'amorous hurry and theatrical littleness.' The clash of these two sources of identification results in the comedian's refusal to occupy her theatrical role off-stage, to allow the image her portrait has idealized to serve the needs of its owner. She refuses, in other words, to conflate representation and the real, to assume the amorous gaze projected onto the portrait by the widow. Her sexual promiscuity finds expression not in the aristocracy's libertine register, but in a world remote from the portrait's command, one that fails to recognize the significance of a singular passion such as the widow's feelings reveal.

As Catherine Gallagher has observed, the actress's refusal of the widow's advances is made possible by the fact that the terms of the relationship with her benefactor are left somewhat vague: 'The ambiguous monetary relationship with the actress fails to seal off the realm of fantasy from that of reality.'[46] The portrait embodies this ambiguity by inhabiting two different real worlds, and one fantasy world, simultaneously. As a commodity, it represents the widow's financial power, but as a representation, it 'belongs' to the sitter, who here attaches herself to the theatrical world in which the 'libertine' is merely one fiction among many that she has inhabited on the stage. The comedian's refusal to take the role beyond the stage marks her refusal of both the real power the widow possesses and the power the widow wishes to confer upon her as a libertine male. The portrait stands as the actress's marker of resistance insofar as its status as a 'likeness' grants the actress a proprietary relation to the representation. She can claim the transparency of this likeness against the theatrical role that her costume, in the portrait, represents, and which the widow hopes she will maintain as a sexual role.

But such claims to authenticity appear more forceful as rhetorical strategies rather than guaranteed truths. While the actress uses the discourse of the 'real' versus the 'unnatural' in her confrontation with the widow – 'here she was at a loss' – the text also reveals that she may be using this language of 'natural' heterosexuality provisionally, as a means of escaping her life with her patron. She receives the widow's advances '*as if* rather disgusted at such amiable proofs of amity' (my emphasis), and her desire to return to her theatrical life appears as the motivating factor in her refusal to acknowledge the meaning of the widow's advances. Having played the part of the male libertine on stage, the actress could participate in the widow's fantasy if she chose to – she is familiar with the terms of the illusion the widow hopes to sustain, having seduced, presumably, a fellow actress in her libertine role on the stage. And indeed, the narrative's dénouement suggests that the actress is well aware of the nature of the widow's desires, and that she has used the cabal's secrecy against itself by claiming her ignorance of the sexual relations the widow hopes to enjoy. In other words, she outperforms the widow, drawing on the powers conventionally conferred on the libertine in the interpretation of sexual relations.

The portrait appears as the object around which the actress and the widow work out their conflict:

> When [the widow] was returned to her house in town, to show the lurkings of her malice, or rather her detestation to vice, though but in effigy, she caused the comedian's picture to be let down and with her own hand cut out the face, so stamped upon and abused sent it back to her whom it represented, at the same time causing her to be told she had by her loose libertine life made it a scandal to her house to have such a picture seen in it. The poor comedian fell a crying and said she might have let her alone: she did not for her part seek nor covet the acquaintance: she was no worse now than when 'twas first drawn, neither could her manner of life be a secret to the virtuous widow: she should have objected it to her then, before she gave her the trouble of sitting not to affront her picture so, but she guessed the reason, and would leave her Ladyship to be punished by the reflection of it. (236)

In an interesting reversal of interpretive positions, the widow uses the idea of the portrait's status as a 'likeness' of the actress to enact her revenge and attributes her violence against the painting to her moral objection to the 'loose libertine life' that the comedian leads off the stage. The widow's claim to a disinterested and moral view of the painting appears in stark relief to the mode of beholding – governed by private desires and sexual longing – that initially governed her appreciation of the portrait. The widow enjoyed beholding the representation as long as she believed she had complete power over its sitter, and her 'moral' mode of spectatorship only appears when the widow's pursuit of personal gratification has been thwarted. As a response to her disappointment, the widow is able to insult the actress by demoting the painting from its status as an art object to a mere piece of canvas, an item of her personal property, that she can destroy. The violence that the widow metes out on the portrait speaks to the malice lurking below the surface of her moral pronouncement. It also confirms her desire to assume a masculine position in relation to the actress, now that the actress has refused to play the libertine to her feminine self. Her use of the knife imitates the male practice of humiliating prostitutes by scarring their faces, and it also performs a symbolic rape of the picture, acting out a desire that otherwise cannot be forced upon another woman.[47] Having been refused her own desire to sexually and socially seduce a woman, the widow symbolically castrates the 'libertine' by cutting out her face, the only aspect of the painting which actually 'belongs' to the comedian. By destroying the face, the widow denies the comedian the subjectivity she has claimed for herself by refusing to stay in character long enough to satisfy her benefactor.

But because the portrait is not merely a piece of property, but also an object governed by social codes of propriety, the actress is able to challenge the widow's destruction of the painting. Gallagher has noted how the faceless canvas forces the comedian to acknowledge 'the blankness of representation,' but that destruction of the painting also allows the comedian to respond to the widow's violence by insisting on the materiality of the representation, a materiality governed by conditions that made the representation possible.[48] She draws attention to the labour she has contributed in the creation of the portrait, complaining that the widow 'should have objected it to her then, before she gave her the trouble of sitting.' Whereas she previously insisted on the disjunction between her identity and that of the representation, in her response to the widow she conflates the two in order to protest the assault. She allows the idea of her own brand of libertinism – now that it is defined outside of her relationship with the widow – to extend to the portrait's representation of her: 'She was no worse now than when 'twas first drawn.' The actress points out that it is the widow's wilful blindness, rather than any fault in the portrait or herself, that has created the conflict around the representation. She can claim a more authentic understanding of the portrait because her life has been transparent to all: 'Neither could her manner of life be a secret to the virtuous widow.' The actress exposes the hypocrisy of the widow's moral disapprobation by reconstructing the historical circumstances surrounding the portrait's creation, consumption, and destruction.

In exposing the private interests governing the widow's relation to the portrait, the comedian successfully challenges the authority that the widow, by virtue of her class, wields. Her attention to the illusions governing the widow's perspective also allows the actress to throw the final stone. She hints that she understands the widow's sexuality and its demeaned social status, and reverses the moral tables on the widow in her response: 'She guessed the reason, and would leave her Ladyship to be punished by the reflection of it.' The comedian's heterosexuality enables her to trump the widow's class privilege by asserting a normative standard against which the widow is found lacking. The widow's imaginary phallus is here stripped of its power in the actress's condemnation of her patron's lesbian desire – it is now the widow who is figured, symbolically, to be 'at a loss.' The widow may have the money to commission a large portrait and the power to destroy it, but she must always be doomed to read the painting as society will have her read it, regardless of her fantasies.

In pitting the comedian's understanding of her portrait against the widow's desire to appropriate the painting as part of her fantasy life, Manley does not oppose an idea of transparent, abstract, and public account of beholding against an obfuscating, particularizing, and private mode of spectatorship. Rather, she exploits the portrait's ambiguous relationship to its owner and the subject of its representation in order to define two versions of private interests. In the case of the Whig woman, private interests allow her to assume that privilege and wealth create, in and of themselves, spectatorial authority within her world of sexual fantasy, an authority that poses disingenuously as disinterested, once the seduction attempt has failed. In detailing the actress's claim to the portrait, both in terms of the labour she contributes to its creation and the painting's proximity to the property she has in her self, Manley provides an alternative account of private interests, one that allows those most frequently disenfranchised a certain degree of access to power. Private interests allow the integrity of the comedian's personal circumstances to take precedence over the social dictates authorized by the Whig cabal. Insofar as the comedian claims her right to her own pleasure over those of her benefactor, the idea of private interests represents not only a pleasure principle, but also a spirit of integrity and resistance that allows an alternative understanding of what is moral to contest the widow's sanctimonious claims.

The difference between the two women's approach to the idea of their personal rights finds expression in Manley's treatment of the question of cross-dressing and women's modes of self-fashioning:

> Hence it is that those ladies are so fond of the dress en cavaliere, though it is extremely against my liking, I would have the sex distinguished as well by their garb as by their manner. That bewitching modesty which is so becoming to the opening veil is against kind in the confirmed, bold and agreeable air of the hat, feather and peruke. If in this dress you retain the shamefacedness of the other, you lose the native charm that recommends it. If you dismiss it, you dismiss the highest beauty of the sex, for, without regard to that much-in-fashion virtue assurance, next to real innate modesty in ladies (which indeed never fails of giving the appearance), I think the outward blush and seeming habitude of it one of the greatest ornaments they can wear. (235)

Ballaster has argued that Manley excuses the cabal's practice of cross-dressing, claiming that because many of the members of the cabal are artists and writers, Manley supports their practices: 'If ... the power of fiction lies with men, then it is perhaps appropriate that the woman artist should be addicted to male disguise.'[49] But I would argue that rather than idealizing the cabal world against the public sphere controlled by men, Manley establishes a third alternative. In the above description of the cabal's cross-dressing habits, the opposition between the 'bewitching modesty' of the 'opening veil' and the revealing habit of the 'hat, feather and peruke' suggests that the veil grants women agency by controlling the extent to which they expose themselves to a public obsessed with the spectacle of female denigration. Manley is not concerned with the correlation between virtue and appearances, as 'the outward blush and seeming habitude' of modesty serve as usefully as 'real innate modesty' in women. Modesty becomes an 'ornament' that women put on in order to move more freely, and in order, most importantly, to assume a gaze within the visual field without fear of reprisal. In April of 1717, Lady Mary Wortley Montagu would make a similar observation to her sister, the Countess of Mar, about women's use of the veil in Turkish society: 'This perpetual masquerade gives them entire liberty of following their inclinations without danger of discovery.'[50] As screens upon which culture projects its fantasies, women's bodies need to maintain a degree of opacity if they are to remain subjects, as well as objects, in the field of vision. Paradoxically, then, the illusion of privacy provides women with access to public life. 'Seeming habitude' becomes the performative moment of identity, the costume which, like the comedian's libertine attire, allows the surface to hold the spectator's attention, without allowing the beholder a degree of visual access that would render the spectacle passive. Manley positions herself as far as possible from the aesthetic governing Addison's understanding of the cross-dressed 'Camilla,' whose masquerade challenges his naturalized standard of female beauty, according to which any departure from the norm initiates a social disruption requiring immediate regulation.

The portrait's representation in *The New Atalantis* confirms the scandalous content attributed to portraiture as a genre throughout the eighteenth century. Working as an agent of seduction, the portrait incites voyeuristic desires that find expression in the sentimental gaze of the later eighteenth-century novel. It also frames the possibility of female spectatorship, figured in the women who behold and those who look out from the portrait. Female beholding appears both as a form of social agency and as an attribute of the spectacle. At the centre of the field of vision stands the figure of the woman author, herself both the subject and the object of public and private gazes. Her activity as informant and interpreter of the visual tableaux that appear in the novel link her authority to that manifested in the figures of the Restoration's most powerful courtesans, allowing her to govern because of her simultaneous attachment to private and public spheres.[51] For Manley, the presence of the female authorial mind marks the possibility of the retrieval of women from the position of social and spectatorial passivity to which the machinations of Whig corruption and the gendering of Tory discourses consign them, and the portrait appears as the place where that mind makes, or, as in the case of young Charlot, fails to make, its appearance.

Critics have suggested that the kind of authorial power Manley asserts in *The New Atalantis* became increasingly difficult to claim for women later in the eighteenth century. Susan Sniader Lanser paints a particularly bleak picture in her reading of the rise of the female character in the eighteenth-century novel: 'Negotiating the tension between patriarchal imperatives and Enlightenment politics, between individual desire and collective control, the narrating voice became a fiction of authority beneath which historical women and their public power could be erased.'[52] This assessment underestimates, I believe, the extent to which writers following Manley were compelled by the vision of female authority her representations provided, and the extent to which women writers remained, like Manley, a public spectacle throughout the century, a status that was not necessarily, as the following chapters will suggest, a liability for the promotion of women's interests.

Chapter Three

'Ravished Sight': Picturing *Clarissa*

And is not the mind indicated strongly by its outward dress?

My beloved only revenges herself upon her clothes.[1]

A portrait of the actress Peg Woffington (1714–60), now owned by the Garrick Club, depicts its subject reclined on a red damask sofa, with a green curtain behind her (figure 19). Woffington, dressed in gold with red and black embroidery, holds a book in her lap. The painting establishes a rich and luxurious aesthetic and is reminiscent of Lely's female portraits in the knowing female gaze it represents. Woffington's notoriety as a woman involved in various illicit affairs ensured that her private life would be put on display, and it appears, in this portrait, that Woffington has taken control of the viewing experience that her scandalous reputation creates. In particular, the presence of the book signals her agency as a reader – not only of scripts for the stage, but also of the scripts governing social and sexual relations. The text could be a script, or it could be an amatory fiction of Haywood, Manley, or Behn, serving as a link between fiction and reality – a link that allows Woffington's lived experience, summed up in the portrait's celebration of her beauty, to become part of the larger moment of literary interest writ large in the *chronique scandaleuse*. Woffington's success as an actress, which ensures public recognition of her face, seems to expand into a more general statement about her success off, as well as on, the stage. Rather than attempting to escape the association of women with 'bad' reading practices, Woffington's representation encourages us to read her acting, reading, and scandalous sexual activities as part of a master narrative of which she is both the author and the reader.

This painting echoes the configuration of authorial agency established by Manley in her use of the portrait in *The New Atalantis*, and the appearance of Woffington's portrait in the 1730s or 1740s suggests the enduring power of the ideas that Manley's work articulates, and brings us forward to the moment of Samuel Richardson's meteoric rise to fame in the wake of *Pamela*'s publication in 1740. This chapter takes Richardson's greatest literary success, *Clarissa*, back to the aesthetics of beholding Manley represents so as to keep the image of women like Peg Woffington active in our thinking about a moment that so often seems defined by strict moral and domestic imperatives. At first glance, such a move appears, at the very least, counterintuitive. Manley's celebration of the power that techniques of concealment and revelation grant the heroines of her tales would seem to stand in direct contrast to the aesthetics of visual sincerity that Richardson promotes in *Clarissa*. Richardson's avowed detestation of the century's early writers of amatory fiction and scandal narratives and his commitment to a narrative excess measured by voluminous textual detail, rather than salacious pictorial tableaux, would seem to establish the author's greatest work as representative of a paradigmatic shift, a rupture between early and late developments in the eighteenth-century novel's evolution. But just as Manley's novel self-consciously interrogates the conventions it adopts in order to imagine ways of escaping social restrictions, so too Richardson's novel entertains all the discourses of story telling it can imagine, and not only in order to assert the superiority of the most moral of these discourses.[2]

Richardson develops a narrative world that richly complicates both amatory and sentimental conventions; the idea of private interests plays a central role in his reconsideration of these conventions. In a recent essay, Scott Paul Gordon suggests that, repelled by the idea that universal self-interest was taking hold of the English public's imagination, Richardson set out to create a heroine capable of transcending its limits; in particular, Gordon notes how the pathetic response the novel elicits in its readers breaks down the structures of judgment linked to private interests: 'By making readers weep, the novel enables them to disprove the denial of disinterested behavior.'[3] Two issues, I believe, complicate Gordon's claims: first, by focusing only on the economic and philosophical discourses of private interests – most notably those expounded by Mandeville – Gordon fails to notice the idea's prevalence in, and rewritings by, earlier narratives; second, by insisting on upholding the opposition between judgment/private interests and feeling/disinterestedness, Gordon makes it impossible to uphold the integrity of an intellectual enquiry into Clarissa's motivations and behavior: 'Richardson relies, then, on a *physical* solution to the problem of Mandevillian (mis)reading ... Richardson weights the interpretive contest in Clarissa's favor by enlisting each reader's body on her side.'[4] Gordon's insistence that the novel opposes those invested in private interests to a community of unthinking, weeping readers ignores a fact that the novel returns to repeatedly: however devastated by our own or others' experiences, eventually we all dry our tears and the faculty of judgment reasserts itself, for better and worse: which is why a reader as sympathetic as Johnson to Richardson's heroine could note, 'You may observe there is always something which she prefers to truth.'[5] The novel is so exciting to read precisely because it moves away from the opposition of body and mind toward a more textured integration of the faculties of feeling and reason.

Clarissa does not promote disinterestedness, I argue here, but rather a version of private interests that claims a personal and ethical integrity missing in Mandeville's and others' accounts of their social and political efficacy. Richardson's heroine is self-interested and ought to be; as Leopold Damrosch Jr has argued, 'Clarissa ... has her narcissistic aspect (who does not?) but her story is an attempt to redirect it and make it healthy.'[6] Richardson's representation of private interests requires both a rethinking of the kinds of sentimental conventions that Gordon sees the novel upholding and the libertine attack on those conventions. The struggle between sentiment and libertinism finds its most cogent expression in the novel's visual poetics. Most critics argue that Richardson achieves his moral purpose in part by associating his heroine with the principles of transparency and light, by creating in Clarissa an ethereal subject struggling to escape the sordid world that destroys her. For William Beatty Warner, Clarissa appears as 'a figure in a Vermeer painting – bathed in the holy light that streams through the window on the left, but imprisoned in the mundane actuality of an ordinary room and prosaic activity'; Margaret Anne Doody asserts that the conclusion of *Clarissa* is dominated by 'a bright picture in which virtue explicitly triumphs over darkness and evil in an affirmation of limitless space and glowing light'; and these pictorial allusions support other critics' more general claims about the visual hermeneutics of *Clarissa*, which define the sentimental novel in terms of its ability to maintain an aura of visual truth-telling around the figure of the heroine.[7] An alternative reading of the novel highlights Richardson's suspicion of vision as a tool of libertine oppression and emphasizes the extent to which the novel seeks to escape the world's visual regimes entirely. By this account Richardson would not so much be providing an alternative visual register to the amatory models constructed by Manley and other predecessors, but refusing the register's allure altogether. Thus Leo Braudy asserts that 'Clarissa's refusal of physicality parallels the almost non-visual world of Richardson's novel.'[8] Although these two assessments seem completely opposite, they are both, surprisingly, correct in identifying a central aspect of Richardson's response to the question of the visual and his heroine's relation to its materiality. His response, in other words, is divided: on the one hand he wants to represent his heroine's transcendence with the intensity afforded by pictorial language, while on the other hand he wants to avoid betraying her body to a voyeuristic gaze that pictorial language can invite – a gaze that starkly aligns sentimental and libertine interests.[9]

This chapter will argue that Manley's techniques of veiling and unveiling reappear in *Clarissa* as the means by which Richardson negotiates this interpretive dilemma. That is, Richardson draws on the idea of doubling, in terms of both narrative time and space, as the means by which he can draw the threads of competing visual discourses together to create a third term. Manley's association of the theatrics of appearance with women's ability to claim social authority, furthermore, serves as the lynchpin in Richardson's configuration of Clarissa's final triumph over Lovelace, one that neither washes its heroine in translucent light, nor shrouds her body in eternal darkness. Rather, we are confronted again with the figure of the 'opening veil' so central to the workings of *The New Atalantis* and its representation of the female body in the visual field. In what follows, I will use the portrait as a starting point for a reading of the novel's visual hermeneutics, tracing a path from the portrait's initial treatment, through the novel's understanding – in the largest sense – of its aesthetic relation to Clarissa's character, to Richardson's account of the female body's place in the visual field both in relation to the libertine gaze of Lovelace and to the reader's own curiosity. The portrait, insofar as it disappears from view for almost a thousand pages, serves as a trope that echoes through the narrative until it finally reappears, not in a singular form, but as a series of portraits that configure the heroine's aestheticization of her death and final will.

Public and Private Selves: Clarissa's Portrait

Clarissa's portrait appears in the novel's third volume, after Clarissa's elopement with Lovelace, as the icon of the daughter's fall from grace.[10]

82 Private Interests

The Harlowes' treatment of the painting signals the dissolution of Clarissa's identity, previously defined by a close fit between public reputation and private good, and incites the reader to formulate a new identity that will place Clarissa above the humiliation her family inflicts on her. We learn of the portrait's existence in the same letter that informs Clarissa of her father's curse. While the curse condemns Clarissa to punishment 'both *here* and *hereafter*,' Arabella focuses on the present moment of her sister's disgrace:

> Your drawings and your pieces are all taken down; as is also your own whole-length picture in the Vandyke taste, from your late parlour: they are taken down and thrown into your closet, which will be nailed up as if it were not a part of the house; there to perish together: for who can bear to see them? Yet, how did they use to be shown to everybody: the former for the magnifying of your dainty fingerworks; the latter for the imputed dignity (dignity now in the dust!) of your boasted figure. (509)

Clarissa's private space – her 'late parlour' – has served as the exhibition hall for both her own work and for the portrait that celebrates her status as a young woman of privilege. Clarissa's works have gained a reputation despite their seclusion in a home – 'how did they use to be shown to everybody' – suggesting that Clarissa's private interests had been able to bridge the private-public divide, a crossover implied by the 'magnifying' of the 'dainty' art, the elevation of the merely domestic to the level of the aesthetic, while also suggesting the scrutiny to which Clarissa's performances are subjected. The passage brings together the portrait of Clarissa, Clarissa's own art work, and the young woman herself together in the idea of the 'boasted figure,' a characterization that suggests how firmly Clarissa has been understood as a representation, a term that could guarantee a particular response in the public sphere. As Mrs Harlowe later writes, 'It was enough for those who knew who she was, to cry, *Why, it is Miss Clarissa Harlowe!* – As if everybody were obliged to know, or to have heard of Miss Clarissa Harlowe, and of her excellencies' (584). Clarissa participates in her status as a representation as both a subject and an object, a relationship figured in the spatial arrangement of works in the parlour, where the portrait has celebrated the talents announced in the framed needlepoint next to it. In other words, the works of art, collectively, have celebrated the fit between Clarissa as icon and agent. Clarissa's own works of art bring her portrait to life, demonstrating the abilities of the young woman the static portrait represents, so that we are confronted with another version of the animated canvas that Manley creates in *The New Atalantis*.

The significance of the 'Vandyke taste' governing Clarissa's portrait resides, at first glance, in its stunning lack of originality. Janet Aikins observes that this type of portraiture 'is exactly the sort of work to be commissioned by the socially aggressive Harlowes.'[11] The Vandyke style implies a representation of Clarissa in seventeenth-century costume, whose ostensible purpose is to link Clarissa to an earlier moment in the history of the Harlowe family. But, of course, there is no earlier moment in Harlowe history. As Lovelace sneeringly notes, 'Everybody knows Harlowe Place – for, like Versailles, it is sprung up from a dunghill within every elderly person's remembrance' (161). It is the Harlowes' desire for a powerful genealogy, figured in the social attitude the costume represents, that creates the conditions that enable Lovelace to abduct Clarissa. James Jr is determined to keep all of the family's wealth for himself, and so banishes Lovelace from Harlowe Place, fearing that a union between Clarissa and Lovelace would require money that he wants to inherit. Clarissa also believes in the idea of aristocracy to which portraits in the Vandyke style allude, and, indeed, her abduction results in part from her attachment to the idea that aristocratic birth guarantees personal integrity. In thinking about Lovelace before she flees Harlowe Place, Clarissa repeatedly returns to Lovelace's pedigree as the source of his hoped-for reformation: 'We shall conclude in his favour, that he knows what sort of behaviour is to be expected from persons of birth, whether he act up to it or not. Conviction is half way to amendment' (182).[12] The difference between Clarissa's and James Jr's approach to the aristocracy, however, marks the competing things that the portrait can mean. For Clarissa, the aristocracy represents an ideal standard of politeness and civility, whose moral integrity she hopes to revitalize, while for James, a peerage only stands for a further exercise of his power, defined in economic terms through his greed for property. Clarissa's portrait, for James, signals his family's ability to exchange its daughter in order to enhance its wealth, while for Clarissa, it speaks to the integrity of her family and its worthiness to become part of a higher social caste.[13]

As Doody observes, 'The association of [Richardson's] heroine and a Vandyke subject conveys an impression of the Clarissa of the world, in her health and beauty, with all her worldly prospects before her.'[14] While prized by her family, Clarissa can claim property, as a potential bride, both in her own abilities and in the Harlowes' wealth, which has enabled the commissioning of an expensive work of art. Aileen Ribeiro

84   Private Interests

notes the extent to which eighteenth-century female portraiture most often represents a young woman at 'the height of [her] beauty,' in order to signal the power she commands, momentarily, as she negotiates the marriage market.[15] Clarissa's appearance in the Vandyke costume not only heightens Clarissa's beauty through artifice, but also, in its reference to the past, draws on the Vandyke style's reference to the sitter's cultural literacy in both history and art, as well as her ability to transcend the transience of contemporary fashion; Ribeiro notes that women appear far more often in Vandyke clothing than men do, and speculates that for women, 'wearing such costume ... for a portrait provided an escape from the everyday world, a chance to engage in another role – however vicariously – of Time Past.'[16] This account of women's desire for the costume speaks directly to Clarissa's nostalgia for an aristocratic code that Lovelace is meant to signify, and for her projection of her own identity into a model of selfhood that transcends the particularity and the relentlessly present moment of the Harlowe family.

The Vandyke style's place as a signifier of a larger engagement in historical narratives appears starkly in an Edward Haytley portrait of 1753, in which the young woman appears posed next to an obelisk covered in hieroglyphs (figure 20). She gestures toward the signs on the obelisk, while looking out at the beholder, as if to signal her understanding of and interest in the secrets of the hieroglyphs. Her studious aspect is confirmed by the restraint of the dress and her hair, and her authority is marked by the setting of the portrait – the vast park grounds of her family's estate, which is wealthy enough to import an Egyptian relic and to build the neoclassical structure represented in the distant background of the painting. The association of women with hieroglyphics that we traced in Manley's allusion to the interpretive problems of determining character appears, in this canvas, submerged by the confidence of the portrait's imperial command. Nevertheless, the young woman's distance from the public sphere, and the fact that the beholder is unlikely to be capable of reading the hieroglyphs imaged on the canvas intimate the difficulty of translation, a challenge also connected – as we shall see – to the Vandyke dress.

In another Haytley portrait of the period, one of Richardson's most assertive critics and admirers, Lady Bradshaigh, appears with her husband; both are dressed in Vandyke costume (figure 21). Lady Bradshaigh holds a text in her hands – *Clarissa*, perhaps – while her husband grasps a telescope. The landscape represents their stately home and its park, and the scene as a whole speaks to the Bradshaigh family's wealth and culture. The Vandyke costume suggests that the family is both learned and appreciative of history, and at the same time contemporary and progressive. Richardson admired this portrait so much that he requested a copy for himself, and it appears in the background of one portrait of the author.

The Vandyke style of costume was enormously popular among eighteenth-century portrait painters and their sitters. Ribeiro describes the costume and its appeal:

> For women the dress usually comprised a tight bodice and a skirt with fullness over the hips (it was close to the eighteenth-century aesthetic in costume) ... It was a type of costume that attracted Rococo artists; they liked its asymmetry and the three-dimensional effects created by such details as ruffs, ribbon lacing and slashed sleeves.[17]

An interesting paradox emerges from Ribeiro's account, for if the Vandyke costume was meant to allude to a historical past, it as surely spoke to the immediate present of eighteenth-century fashion, thus appearing both timeless and historically over-determined as a set piece in eighteenth-century portrait practices. An example of the style described by Ribeiro appears in a Thomas Hudson portrait of Anne Bouverie (figure 22). The confidence in the girl's face and pose matches the authority of the gleaming dress, which appears to announce itself as both an expensive costume, linked to world of art making and art buying, and an integral component of the sitter's identity, one occasional piece among others in her wardrobe. The girl's jewelry, in her hair and over her bodice, celebrates the luxury enjoyed by the girl's family, a luxury also marked in the lush growth of the landscape that serves as the portrait's backdrop.

The Vandyke dress's ability to speak to a particular moment of appearance, a public staging of identity in a dress both connected to, and separated from, the daily routines of social fashion, takes on added significance in light of the fact that the Vandyke costume served as a staple uniform for masquerade goers throughout the period, as both Terry Castle and Ribeiro have observed. Ribeiro notes that many women used the Vandyke costume as an opportunity to cross-dress. While Clarissa, of course, is not pictured as one who would attend a masquerade or cross-dress, the idea of masquerade casts its shadow across her narrative in the figure of Lovelace, who is always taking on new disguises – and having his henchmen do the same – to achieve his nefarious ends. Castle refers to the 'hermeneutic disequilibrium' created by the masquerade spectacle, and it is this experience of disruption, dislocation, and violation that Lovelace comes to instill in Clarissa.[18] But the Vandyke portrait marks Clarissa's ability to create the same experience in her beholders, including the libertine voyeur. The association of Clarissa with the workings of masquerade appears, early in the narrative, not only impossible but intensely undesirable. The unfolding of Clarissa's narrative will entail, nonetheless, the realization of this potential, and takes us back to the problem of the potential for a gap to appear between private and public understandings of its heroine.

More immediately, the Vandyke dress takes us back to the significance of Clarissa's needlework, and the extent to which it comes to mark the gap between the Harlowes' understanding of their daughter and Clarissa's understanding of her own worth. The delicacy of the lace and appliqué of the Vandyke dress mirror the intricacy of Clarissa's own designs, which Lovelace later describes as 'an Abraham offering up Isaac, a Samson and the Philistines, and flowers, and knots, and trees, and the sun and the moon, and the seven stars' (971). Needlework, we discover after Clarissa's death, formed an integral part of her life at Harlowe Place, to the extent that her appearance among her neighbours often found Clarissa with a piece in her hand: 'She used to converse as she worked: and it was a custom she had introduced among her acquaintance,' Anna Howe writes (1471). The rich design of the Vandyke demonstrates the practices that have made Clarissa famous, connecting the costume to an integral aspect of Clarissa's identity. Indeed, it is possible that Clarissa herself has contributed to the design.[19]

The needlework stands as Clarissa's signature, both of the portrait and of her identity more generally, against which her father asserts his force. In anticipation of a wedding between his daughter and the odious Solmes, James Harlowe orders Clarissa's trousseau: 'Your papa intends you six suits (three of them dressed) at his own expense. You have an entire new suit; and one besides, which I think you never wore but twice. As the new suit is rich, if you choose to make that one of the six, your papa will present you with a hundred guineas in lieu' (188). The patterns that her father orders come to define Clarissa's antagonism toward Solmes: 'Must not the very richness of the patterns add to my disgusts? – Great encouragement indeed, to think of adorning one's self to be the wife of Mr. *Solmes!*' (190). The patterns are offensive both because they would reduce Clarissa to a passive spectacle, and because they announce the end of Clarissa's participation in the domestic economy of Harlowe Place, where she has always patterned her clothes with her own needlework.[20] The needlework on her clothing represents the linking of the work of the hand and the mind to the body that appears in the world as an object of admiration, not an object that can be traded at will. In *Gender and the Poetics of Excess: Moments of Brocade*, Karen Jackson Ford traces the image of women as needle-workers back to Ovid's Philomela, who weaves her story of rape and mutilation into a tapestry that she sends to her sister Procne. In her analysis of nineteenth- and twentieth-century authors, Ford analyses the appropriation of Philomela's gesture as 'an aesthetics of excess' that finds expression in female literary characters from the classical period, as well as in the women writers whose works Ford studies.[21] I am particularly interested in this definition of needlework as a form of female literary authority because it is precisely such a connection that ultimately will enable Clarissa to author her own fate, like Philomela. The idea of extravagance allows us to link Clarissa's needlework to her later baroque coffin, the final visual display of her artistic talents and authorial power; it also takes us back to Manley's narrative decadence, which Warner has recently described as 'a baroque aesthetics of excess.'[22]

Clarissa's beauty, as well as her wealth, has made the match appealing to Solmes, but it also serves as the starting point of her resistance to him; even Mrs Harlowe observes that the 'sightliness' of Clarissa's person speaks to the incongruence of the match (189). Clarissa associates her visual integrity with her mind in her argument against marrying Solmes, by whom, she imagines, 'my eye is to be disgusted and my reason not convinced' (95). The Harlowes have failed to realize that women cannot be reduced to commodities in any simple fashion, for, as Eve Kosofsky Sedgwick observes, they are 'at the same time objects of symbolic exchange and also, at least potentially, users of symbols and subjects in themselves.'[23] The Harlowes, in other words, have not recognized the significance of the close fit between the needlework that Clarissa has produced and the portrait that celebrates her value.

Formerly useful as a public display of the Harlowes' most valued family member, Clarissa's art loses all meaning in light of the daughter's transgression. The Harlowes refuse the objects any intrinsic aesthetic value, a value that depends on viewing Clarissa as inherently exemplary. The Harlowes' appreciation of Clarissa has rested entirely on the conformity of their daughter to familial designs. Once the icon of family potential in all of its virginal purity, Clarissa's body is defined as loathsome – 'dignity now in the dust' (509) – when it moves outside of the confines of familial exchange relations. Clarissa's virtue is meaningful only in its ability to secure profitable marriage settlements. Now, in an attempt to contain the damage the daughter has done to the family name, the Harlowes take the first step toward placing Clarissa in her grave by symbolically shutting the door upon her representation, refusing her a familial identity; the closet will be 'nailed up as if it were not a part of the house' (509). The public no longer has access to the private realm that represented Clarissa's domain, and now both the daughter and her works are obscured from view, although curiously preserved, perhaps in recognition of their value as commodities, rather than simply destroyed. The art's isolation marks the first stage of the fulfilment of Clarissa's earlier prophetic remarks to her uncle: 'I will undergo the cruellest death: I will even consent to enter into the awful vault of my ancestors, and to have that bricked up upon me, than consent to be miserable for life' (305). The excessiveness of the Harlowes' actions belies a certain fear that Clarissa will continue to haunt the family after her departure, so that only nailing the portrait away can contain the danger she represents. Nailing the closet door as though it were a coffin and leaving Clarissa's portrait to perish fetishizes the father's curse, to which Clarissa later will attribute, in part, her decline into death. The Harlowes assume that by disowning Clarissa and her representations they can reestablish their public reputation, though their excessive behaviour will in fact guarantee their social ostracization. The family, which James Harlowe and his son believe they can rule autocratically as private citizens, constitutes part of a larger social contract, the rules of which the Harlowes break in their treatment of Clarissa.

The novel provides a direct challenge to the Harlowes' view of Clarissa's portrait in a footnote to Arabella's letter: 'This picture is drawn as big as the life by Mr Highmore and is in his possession' (509). By granting the painting a 'real' status, Richardson invites the reading public to imagine the portrait as something that it 'owns' (insofar as the painter has not sold it to a private buyer) and that it might view. In relocating the portrait outside of the Harlowe home, Richardson implies that the Harlowes have been overruled in their denigration of its value. The portrait, by the time the letters of *Clarissa* have been gathered, has been removed from the Harlowes' closet and returned to its creator. The footnote provides an odd temporal perspective, as we are encouraged to believe both that the portrait is in the closet and that the portrait is on display elsewhere at the moment of our reading the epistolary narrative.[24] Even as the narrative unfolds, Richardson encourages the public to become the alternative family to the Harlowes, who repeatedly fail in their duty to Clarissa.

The idea that Joseph Highmore has the painting in his possession incites a readerly desire to visit the painter's studio and view the portrait. Lady Bradshaigh wrote to Richardson, 'May I ask, if there is any such painter as Mr. Highmore, or has he any picture in his possession which we are to suppose was taken for Clarissa?'[25] By heightening the illusion of Clarissa's existence, Richardson encourages the reader to respond to his heroine as though she were a person whom they might know. As Clarissa suggests, 'In my opinion, the world is but one great family; originally it was so; what then is this narrow selfishness that reigns in us, but relationship remembered against relationship forgot?' (62). Richardson's evocation of Clarissa's portrait asks us to reconstitute the originary bonds of sympathy which link the readers both to the novel and to each other. To appreciate Clarissa's portrait, to accept its 'essential' meaning, is to generate the social virtue that Clarissa both desires and represents.

The banishment of Clarissa's portrait signals a stripping away of the status Clarissa has always enjoyed as a member of the Harlowe family. Clarissa's battle to regain her status is rendered graphically in the struggle for possession of her clothes. 'I shall take it for a very great favour to have my clothes directly sent me,' Clarissa writes to her sister in her first letter home (411). The issue of Clarissa's clothes – and the control over their possession – takes us back to the portrait and its status as a representation tied both to Clarissa's ideal understanding of herself, and to the Harlowes' understanding of Clarissa as an object created for display and exchange. Clarissa insists on viewing her clothing as an integral aspect of her self-possession, and refuses all attempts to make her enter into the world of costume, either literal or metaphorical. Thus when Anna Howe encourages Clarissa to 'throw off a little more of the veil' in her interactions with Lovelace, Clarissa can only respond, 'I never knew that I wore one' (432, 433). Clarissa's fall into experience will involve an increasing recognition of the power of the veil that she does, indeed, wear. The idea of clothing, as we shall see, becomes the means by which Clarissa returns to the portrait with an altered understanding of the meaning of her representation.

The visual hermeneutics underpinning the narrative's unfolding confirm the sense of self that informs Clarissa's approach to the 'rich patterns' and to the idea of costume more generally. Clarissa's belief in the transparency of the relation between her virtue and her actions enables her to declare, early in the narrative: 'I am sometimes tempted to think that we may make the world allow for and respect us as we please, if we can but be sturdy in our wills, and set out accordingly' (54).[26] Clarissa believes that the world will view her as she sees herself if she can maintain a consistency of character. Indeed, she has no reason to believe otherwise. Clarissa has always been assured of the interchangeability of private and public domains; 'everybody [is] obliged to know' what she means, because her meaning is self-evident (584). She has never encountered a discrepancy between her vision and the eyes of the world, and she trusts both perspectives. But the complacency that accompanies such a confidence blinds Clarissa to the possibility that Anna's first letter intimates, that the world might speak of her in a language other than her own. 'Every eye' is upon Clarissa 'as an example' (40); the general standard has been set, and Clarissa must now conform to its rules. Clarissa thinks of the spectatorial relationship she enjoys with the world as dialectical, but in fact the world judges her actions without regard to Clarissa's understanding of them. The novel's trajectory is defined by its desire to reverse this power dynamic in order that Clarissa's vision can assume control over the public's perspective.

This process involves rendering the private public, not in the Harlowe manner, but in such a way as to have virtue manifest itself as an attribute that transcends familial law. The problem Anna identifies is that the private interests of the individual often remain inscrutable to the public: 'I long to have the particulars from yourself,' she writes, in the hopes that Clarissa's account will challenge appearances (39). Clarissa's letters begin to unravel the various interwoven threads of the situation for Anna, and in doing so establish Clarissa's innocence. In focusing more and more narrowly on the special circumstances its heroine faces (circumstances that will ultimately explain, if not justify, Clarissa's rash meeting with Lovelace), the text paradoxically begins to render the particular example of Clarissa a general ideal. But Clarissa's exemplarity will not have an opportunity to reveal itself, in the context of the narrative, for a long while; we are left, perversely, with only Lovelace to espouse Clarissa's status: 'Is not then the whole sex concerned that this trial should be made? – and who is it that knows her, that would not stake upon her head the honour of the whole?' he writes (429). Clarissa's isolation, her involuntary exclusion from the public sphere, marks the acceleration of her *telos* toward death, the only state that will incorporate her into the body of the public once more, taking it out of the living incarceration imposed on it by the Harlowe's closet and Lovelace's brothel.

'Ravished Sight': Picturing *Clarissa*   91

The Libertine Gaze

Lovelace, more than any other character in the novel, invests his interpretive energies in an epistemology of the visual. It is Lovelace who provides us with the first description of Clarissa, a description that relies heavily on the details of the heroine's dress patterns:

> Her wax-like flesh ... by its delicacy and firmness, answers for the soundness of her health ... I never in my life beheld a skin so *illustriously* fair. The lily and the driven snow it is nonsense to talk of ... This lady is all alive, all glowing, all charming flesh and blood, yet so clear, that every meandering vein is to be seen in all the lovely parts of her which custom permits to be visible ...
>
> Her morning gown was a pale primrose-coloured paduasoy: the cuffs and robings curiously embroidered by the fingers of this ever charming Arachne in a running pattern of violets and their leaves ... A white handkerchief, wrought by the same inimitable fingers, concealed – Oh Belford! what still more inimitable beauties did it not conceal! – And I saw, all the way we rode, the bounding heart; by its throbbing motions I saw it! dancing beneath the charming umbrage. (399, 400)

In his analysis of this scene, James Grantham Turner stresses Lovelace's attention to the fabrics covering Clarissa's body: 'The details of her dress crowd onto the page and take over the authorial persona, transforming him into a breathless fashion editor.' He goes on to argue that Lovelace's preoccupation with 'Brussels lace and primrose-coloured paduasoy' undermines the libertine's claim to masculine power,[27] and notes the extent to which Lovelace – like Richardson – claims an intimate knowledge of femininity and women's culture, taking us back to the terms of Shaftesbury's attack on a female world defined by 'rich stuffs, and coloured silks.'[28] Lovelace's interest in the details of fabric design also links him to the heroine's preoccupation with clothes as an aspect of selfhood. Like Clarissa, Lovelace iterates an understanding of Clarissa's clothing that marks an unbroken continuum between the dress and the body it covers. As Janet Aikins has noted, the '"running pattern of violets and their leaves" ... not only seems startlingly real to him but enables him to view her internal organs as if, like a powerful Tiresias, he had a superhuman vision.'[29] The pattern, in other words, provides Lovelace access to Clarissa's body; most immediately, the needlework repeats the pattern of 'every meandering vein' that Lovelace visually traces. Lovelace enjoys the spectacle that Clarissa's distressed body affords, and Clarissa's own artifice, rather than countering his encroachment with the substance of her person, only heightens the voyeuristic titillation. While Clarissa insists on a transparent correlation between her work and her virtue, Lovelace finds her embroidery 'curious,' a mystery he must unravel. If Lovelace's fascination with Clarissa's dress links the libertine to a language of display, the preoccupation with unknotting the threads that bind Clarissa's identity connects the rake to the violence of penetrating surfaces in order to explore depths. Paradoxically, Lovelace's refusal to admit of a disparity between inner and outer matches Clarissa's similar refusal, only the trajectories move in different directions – the one toward eroticization of the whole person, the other toward revealing the integrity of virtue lived as identity rather than reputation.

The extent of the libertine's power can be measured by his ability to transform Clarissa's own interpretive rubric into the means by which the plot is forwarded. Lovelace comes back to the figure of Arachne first used to describe Clarissa as a metaphor of his own plot-weaving persona:

> A silly fly, that has neither courage nor strength to resist, no sooner gives notice by its buzz and its struggle, of its being entangled, but out steps the self-circumscribed tyrant, winds round and round the poor insect, till he covers it with his bowel spun toils; and when so fully secured, that it can neither move leg nor wing, suspends it, as if for a spectacle to be exulted over ... and sometimes advancing, sometimes retiring, preys at leisure upon its vitals. (418–19)

Clarissa's diligence with a needle becomes the metaphor governing the weaving of Lovelace's violent plots, here figured again as a means of accessing the 'vitals' of his victims. Ford notes how often 'the *processes* of weaving and unweaving tend to be invoked to describe the processes of writing and reading privileged works, while the *products* of weaving tend to be invoked to describe the works of marginalized writers,' an opposition that defines Lovelace's and Clarissa's relationship for the first two-thirds of Richardson's novel.[30] Lovelace assumes the agency Clarissa has always taken for granted, leaving Clarissa almost completely passive. As Braudy observes, Clarissa and Lovelace seem locked in a battle for selfhood: 'Both Lovelace and Clarissa act out of fear that they will themselves disintegrate if they do not first annihilate or by dying obviate the existence of others.'[31] For Lovelace, the annihilation of Clarissa requires access to her female body, about which he fantasizes in relation to the clothes she designs, patterns, and wears. Significantly, his fantasy life pictures the rake dressed in women's clothing. Imagining a world of sex-segregated church communities, Lovelace dreams of passing for a woman: 'Yet, were it so, and life to be the forfeiture of being found at the female churches, I believe I should, like a second Clodius, change my dress to come at my Portia or Calpurnia' (419–20).

The idea of cross-dressing enables Lovelace's invasive strategies of surveillance, which form part of a continuum of violence figured in visual terms. Anna Howe recognizes early that Lovelace's vision is superior to Clarissa's in the context of the cat-and-mouse game they are playing: 'It is my opinion ... that he has seen more than *I* have seen; more than you think *could* be seen – more than I believe you *yourself* know' (71). Lovelace's experience enables him to see more clearly than Clarissa, whose innocence renders the rake's designs unfathomable to her, and he dominates the narrative up to the rape as a result, as Castle has noted: 'Clarissa is deceived by those visual systems that only appear to hold out meanings.'[32] Clarissa feels his gaze as a form of penetration: 'He confidently seemed to enjoy my confusion ... and gazed upon me as if he would have looked me through' (489). Clarissa's only protection appears to reside in the clothes she wears: 'Full dress creates dignity, augments consciousness, and compels distance,' Lovelace notes, complaining of his inability to catch Clarissa in her dishabille, but even this barrier seems to inspire, rather than thwart, the rake's plots: 'How must all this distance stimulate!' (619). Clarissa's clothing comes to signify, literally and metaphorically, the self that precludes the possibility of a seduction. As he approaches his final 'success,' Lovelace imagines his achievement in removing Clarissa's protective veil – 'I have no doubt but I shall either *shine* or *smuggle* her out of her cloak' (663). In fact, Lovelace will only find access to Clarissa's body after he has drugged her unconscious, and only with the help of the prostitutes.

The novel demonstrates the extent to which Lovelace's viewpoint organizes social relations and, more specifically, Clarissa's narrative. Its encroaching presence is everywhere apparent, most markedly in the representation of Lovelace at the keyhole. Having come close to raping Clarissa under the pretence of saving her from a fire, Lovelace witnesses her distress the next morning:

> I looked through the keyhole, and saw her on her knees, her face, though not towards me, lifted up, as well as hands, and these folded, deprecating I suppose that gloomy tyrant's [James Harlowe, Sr's] curse.
> I could not help being moved. (729)

Later, after he has raped her, Lovelace watches Clarissa sleep: 'I looked through the keyhole of my beloved's door ... There I beheld her in a sweet slumber ... See the difference in our cases, thought I!' (904). In both cases, a tension emerges between the violence involved in Lovelace's intrusion into Clarissa's space, and the exemplarity of the spectacle he produces for the reader. We are meant to be moved by Clarissa's posture and to admire her repose after the rape, and to visualize the difference between Lovelace's distraction and torment and Clarissa's calm resolve. And yet the text produces a spectatorial double-bind by having Lovelace teach us its lessons; one can only learn by participating in his unsavoury actions. To see what Lovelace sees, one must assume the libertine's posture by the door.[33]

Richardson's investment in Lovelace's ability to see and to write some version of the truth – in his power as an author, in other words – led him to defend his rake's admiring descriptions of Clarissa. When it was protested that the fire scene borders on the pornographic, Richardson wrote:

> Shall not a *Lovelace*, having the Object of his Attempt at such Disadvantage to herself, exalt the admirable Creature for a *personal* as well as for a mental Purity *so exemplary*? Are his Descriptions, the Character and Delicacy of the Lady considered, above the Life? Are they so hyperbolically inflaming as those of the Poets, where they pretend to describe personal Graces?[34]

Richardson argues that the detailed presentation of Clarissa's body before the reader heightens the realism informing her characterization. Lovelace acts as Richardson would by refusing to indulge in 'hyperbolically inflaming' accounts of Clarissa's beauty, presenting to us instead a vision which exemplifies both her physical and mental 'Purity.' Clarissa's degradation at Lovelace's hands thus paradoxically heightens our sense of her excellence. The heroine excels in her suffering, which, according to Richardson, ought to carry no erotic charge. Clarissa's idealized status means that her body cannot serve as a degraded sexual object, even at the hands of the libertine, but rather always furthers public edification.

In exalting Clarissa to the point where she cannot be linked to the commonality of other women, Richardson insists that she can never be understood as sexual by the right-minded reader.[35]

The authority Lovelace wields as a viewer links his eye to the public perspective that his aristocratic privilege assumes. Clarissa stands in the novel just as *Clarissa* stands in the world – exposed to intense scrutiny by those who determine social convention. While Lovelace's fantasies pervert Clarissa's 'true' meaning, one looks in vain for a vision of Clarissa that clearly distinguishes itself from the images the rake generates outside of Clarissa's own private imagination. Indeed, the social attitudes that the text represents confirm Lovelace's assumptions. This absence of alternative ways of seeing Clarissa enables a veiled social critique to appear in the text.

I would like to illustrate one moment when the novel explicitly defines the ways in which the libertine mentality and social regulation work hand-in-glove, a concord that Richardson confirms in a letter. Lovelace's recurring fantasy that Clarissa will bear his children – 'Let me perish, Belford, if I would not forgo the brightest diadem in the world for the pleasure of seeing a twin Lovelace at each charming breast' – echoes the language of the marriage licence that Lovelace reads to Clarissa: 'I suppose she did not care to hear of so many children, first, second, third, fourth, fifth, sixth, and seventh sons, and as many daughters, *to be begotten upon the body of the said Clarissa Harlowe*' (706, 701, emphasis in text). Richardson, writing to Lady Bradshaigh, uses this language and implies its degrading effects: 'Let us attend Clarissa in the Issue of her supposed Nuptials. We will imagine her to have repeatedly escaped the Perils of Child birth. How many Children shall we give her? Five? Six? Seven? How many, Madam? Not less I hope.'[36] Richardson's ironic 'Not less I hope' suggests the way that women are valued only for their childbearing capacity. The marriage licence effectively eradicates female agency – the children will simply be begotten 'upon the body' of Clarissa. In this light Lovelace's anticipation of the gratification he will receive from Clarissa's reproductive abilities places him firmly within the realm of social assumptions. More generally, Lovelace's dreams of stripping Clarissa of both her mental and physical agency articulate what eighteenth-century society enacted in upholding the sanctity of patriarchal law in marriage. Even the violence Lovelace is willing to use in order to bring his dreams to fruition does not contravene the law, as a result of the social apparatus Lovelace has set up around Clarissa's abduction, including her consensual cohabitation with him and her willingness to let them pass as a married couple. Society will exonerate the rape of Clarissa, and Lovelace knows it.

Within this framework it is possible to reverse Richardson's defence of the fire scene to produce another meaning, one that works against all of Richardson's pronouncements regarding the purity of his representations. Rather than arguing that Lovelace's gaze is efficacious because of its alignment with the public eye, which views Clarissa as exemplary, I would assert that the public eye's connection to the libertine's renders the public viewpoint exploitative. The violence inherent in the public body reveals itself in the threat the mob poses to the brothel where Clarissa is imprisoned; the prostitutes fear that the public will smash in their windows if it discovers the true nature of the house.[37] Lovelace's vision does not reveal Clarissa's perfection, but the violence that attends the demand for that perfection. Richardson's text both exposes the workings of, and itself enacts, the violence of the Lovelacian gaze.[38]

Rather than providing an escape hatch either by proving Lovelace's irredeemable baseness or by serving as the moment of Clarissa's metamorphosis, the rape forces us to consider the extent to which our own desire to objectify and idealize Clarissa – to have her prove something, as Lovelace wants her to do – entails a kind of epistemological violence. Warner acknowledges this violence, claiming that 'the rape is ... to be a moment of knowing – the moment when Clarissa will be undressed, seen, penetrated, and known. These are activities which engage every reader.'[39] Warner defends the novel's representation of rape by pointing out its distance from a 'real' rape – *Clarissa* belongs to the realm of fiction, after all, not social fact. This critique is useful, I believe, insofar as it warns against assuming a moralizing posture vis-à-vis Lovelace. We are implicated in Clarissa's rape, Warner argues, 'as it unfolds inside and around us all.'[40]

Warner's comments highlight the spectatorial role *Clarissa*'s reader must assume. Lovelace's domination, both thematically and formally, in terms of the amount of writing he produces in the middle of the novel, implies that no interpretation of Clarissa is completely free of his influence. And it is Lovelace, more than anyone, who generates a visual aesthetic around Clarissa. Lovelace imagines Clarissa in a series of tableaux, usually nursing a child, always exemplifying some kind of sexuality brought to life by her rapist. Lovelace's power resides in his ability to place Clarissa in a variety of artistic frames. For example, when Lovelace revels at the thought of a twin at each of Clarissa's breasts, he aestheticizes her as a lower-class woman, almost a peasant figure, as it is unlikely that an upper-class woman would breast-feed two children together. In his fantasy Clarissa is stylized into the figure of a rustic wetnurse, a corrupted vision of *madonna con bambino*.

Lovelace recognizes the extent to which the desire to turn his antagonist into a living testimony to transformative powers of the imagination reflects an impulse shared by Clarissa:

> She [Clarissa] had formed pretty notions how charmingly it would look to have a penitent of her own making dangling at her side to church, through an applauding neighbourhood ... And then, what a comely sight, all kneeling down together in one pew, according to eldership, as we have seen in effigy, a whole family upon some old monument. (970)[41]

The monument Lovelace goes on to describe in detail appears less a product of Lovelace's imagination than a realistic representation of the kind of aesthetic Clarissa hopes to achieve in her life and to circulate in the public realm. After her rape Clarissa writes of the distance she has fallen, imagining her lost wedding day: 'Who now shall provide the nuptial ornaments? ... No court now to be paid to my smiles! ... No elevation now for conscious merit, and applauded purity, to look down from on a prostrate adorer, and an admiring world, and up to pleased and rejoicing parents and relations!' (892). The energy of Clarissa's vision here outstrips even Lovelace's, as Clarissa evokes the vertical movement of a baroque painting, alternately looking down, like God, on her 'adorer' and up, as a supplicant, to her family.[42] Clarissa takes seriously the emblematization of her purity and the value of public reputation that her rapist mocks. What Lovelace acknowledges is the extent to which this monumentalizing tendency idealizes the institution of marriage, obscuring what he describes as its usual 'brawl and contradiction' (970). As Doody argues, 'What he chooses to see in the memorial is not sweet domestic piety but an image for the rigidity and hypocrisy of marriage and family life.'[43] Perhaps Clarissa also recognizes the flaws in the institution she refuses to enter into with Lovelace, despite her elegy to the celebration she will never enjoy. For Clarissa had refused several offers of marriage before Solmes precipitated her flight from the realm of 'pleased and rejoicing parents and relations,' a fact which suggests her awareness that the wedded state may not be all sweetness and light. Clarissa's vision, then, contains elements of Lovelace's, however suppressed they appear.

When Belford writes that he 'cannot but look upon her [Clarissa] as one just entering into a companionship with saints and angels' (1275), Lovelace responds with a description of a monument in Westminster Abbey that represents a female figure being drawn up to heaven by a cupid: 'Thou wilt say perhaps that the dame's figure in *stone* may do credit in the comparison to thine, both in grain and shape, *wooden* as thou art all over. But that the lady ... is but sorrily represented by the fat flanked cupid' (1302-3). The comparison of Clarissa to the cupid undermines all of Belford's idealizing visions of Clarissa, which appear, in this slight, bathetic. Of course, by this point in the narrative, Lovelace's perspective plays a more limited role, as Clarissa gains the upper hand in their hermeneutical struggle. Nonetheless, his timely satirization of the iconography that is accumulating around Clarissa demonstrates that the voyeurism that colours *his* descriptions of the heroine differs only in intent from the spectatorial posture informing Belford's effusive portraiture.[44] Furthermore, the idea of Clarissa as a fat cupid highlights the extent to which Clarissa's aesthetic depends on an emaciated body for success. I will return to this idea below; for now it is enough to state that Lovelace's need to eroticize and satirize Clarissa's emblem-desire challenges the terms that govern Clarissa's status as an aesthetic object. Not only does Lovelace's gaze implicate us in his view of Clarissa, then, but it also refuses to allow Clarissa her other-worldly transcendence, by repeatedly pointing to the religious and social values informing her idealization.

Lovelace's mastery over the field of vision appears most forcefully after the rape, when he makes a public appearance at Colonel Ambrose's ball. Anna recounts his ability to attract every eye as a form of mastery: 'He entered with an air so hateful to me, but so agreeable to every other eye, that I could have looked him dead for that too' (1133). But Anna's gaze is no match for Lovelace's power as a spectacle: 'Nobody was regarded but him. So little of the fop, yet so elegant and rich in his dress' (1137). Lovelace's authority over the effect that his clothing will have on his audience signals his command of visual codes and the modes of beholding that his presence elicits. The scene that unfolds between Anna and Lovelace is governed entirely by a sense of surveillance, and the phrase 'everybody's eyes upon us' is repeated over and over again as Anna describes Lovelace's successful attempt to gain an interview (1135-6). Lovelace himself draws attention to the witnesses who surround them – 'We are so much observed' – to force Anna to listen to his case (1135). Drawing on the Restoration heritage of the libertine's status as a spectacle, Lovelace experiences no sense of shame or humiliation in this public space, even in the knowledge that all know of his crimes against Clarissa. Rather, he rests assured that his mere presence will transform detractors into admirers: 'He had something in his specious manner to say to everybody: and this too soon quieted the disgust each person had at his entrance' (1134).

Lovelace's implication in the world of visual oppression leads Braudy to claim that *Clarissa* indicts 'the treasonous nature of the visual world.'[45] And yet, despite the potential for vision to deceive, the novel maintains a belief in the power of the eye to communicate what language will not reveal. More than just an organ of sight, the eye is gestural, sending signals and messages to others. As John Preston argues, 'It is the eyes, communicating with disturbing immediacy and in unguarded encounters, that tell a story which cannot get onto the pages of a letter or a book.'[46] Lovelace claims what the text as a whole confirms, that 'the *eye*... is the *casement* at which the *heart* generally looks out' (1099). Lovelace's comment appears ironic in the context in which it is pronounced, for the destruction of Clarissa depends on the opacity of the literal casements of her prison-house; the brothel hides behind a respectable facade, revealing nothing through its windows that might belie its true function. The text contrasts the purity of Clarissa's vision with the corruption of Lovelace's, and by the end of her story Clarissa is able to transform her blindness into an insight that far transcends Lovelace's deceptive looks. This transformation starts in the brothel, where Clarissa half-realizes that the women around her are not who they pretend to be.[47] Lovelace recounts Clarissa's quoting of the Bible: 'The whoredom of a woman may be known in her haughty looks and eye-lids. Watch over an impudent eye, and marvel not if it trespass against thee' (876a). Lovelace goes on to note that Dorcas's eyes 'were found guilty of treason the first moment she saw her' (876). Clarissa writes to Anna that 'Mrs Sinclair ... has an odd winking eye' (525). But all of Clarissa's intuitive distrust of the Lovelacian eyes watching her cannot save her from the violence they conspire to enact; within Lovelace's world, as John Mullan has argued, the visual is stripped of sentiment and its attendant sociability.[48] It is only after the rape that Clarissa's superior vision, bolstered by the revelation of the evil around her, becomes capable of influencing action. The inner eye of virtue then controls the narrative, and Clarissa can finally free herself from the bondage to which Lovelace's gaze has subjected her.

Clarissa's vision establishes its power when Lovelace threatens to rape

Clarissa for a second time: 'She cast her eye towards me [Lovelace] ... God's eye is upon us! [she said] – His more *immediate* eye; and looked wildly. But the women looked up to the ceiling and trembled, as if *afraid* of God's eye' (951). Clarissa identifies two eyes of God, presumably differentiating between the eye that looks over the world in a general way and the eye that she feels is now watching *with* her. Her 'wild' look suggests a prophetic knowledge and power, which the prostitutes fear will translate into a literal ability to call God's wrath down upon them. At the moment that Clarissa assumes mastery over her vision, she also claims a self-defined aesthetic. As Tassie Gwilliam has argued, 'Clarissa wrests the power to create spectacles from Lovelace at the moment she grasps the penknife.'[49] Just as earlier in her life Clarissa's portrait and her own artwork served as companion pieces, now Clarissa's handiwork with the penknife aligns itself with her new aesthetic status as a Lucretian heroine. She is both a subject and an object, capable of action even as the aestheticization of her body illustrates its exemplarity as the sign of private virtue. The knife indicates Clarissa's willingness to sculpt herself into a new form, one that transcends the painting medium that earlier represented her.

In contrast to the chilling paralysis that Lovelace's designs earlier imposed on Clarissa, rendering her, finally, a mute, unconscious object to be raped, now Clarissa's moral vitality appears in her form. 'The LAW shall be all my resource,' Clarissa asserts while holding the penknife to her breast (950). As several critics have pointed out, Clarissa's invocation of the law at this moment strikes a curious note, for it is clear, in threatening to kill herself, that Clarissa is not referring to secular law, and yet suicide would seem to deny her access to heaven's law as well.[50] Clarissa nonetheless claims God's authority as her standard, suggesting that God will understand that her threatened destruction of the body is preferable to the rape that Lovelace might attempt. Only Clarissa's willingness to do violence to herself frees her from the threat of Lovelace's violations. The opposition that emerges in this scene pits an allegorical understanding of death and the law, which aligns God's eye with Clarissa's, against the material realism of Lovelace's menace and the prostitutes' corrupt eyes. Clarissa's vision is linked securely to the fate of her body, but that fate is now in her hands, and she understands her new power as metaphysical rather than corporeal. In locating Clarissa's power outside of the social nexus which Lovelace controls, Richardson acknowledges Clarissa's defeat in the world while preparing her for a victory that will trump the social entirely. When Lovelace remarks that the world does not need to know of her downfall, Clarissa replies, '[You have] ruined me in my *own* eyes, and that is the same to me, as if *all the world* knew it' (909). The novel does not, however, finally come to reassert a visual aesthetics premised on transparency and clarity. Clarissa's status as a 'ruin,' a fallen spectacle, requires an alternative way of seeing.

'The grave's a fine and private place'

So far I have described two modes of spectatorship at work in *Clarissa*. The idealized version of the gaze that the novel presents situates the readers as a community of sympathetic onlookers who watch the narrative unfold with a firm belief in Clarissa's moral exemplarity. This perspective emerges in various characters' representation of Clarissa as a public icon, mistreated by her family and manipulated by Lovelace, but singular and transparent in meaning. The portrait stands as the aesthetic embodiment of Clarissa's innate excellence, an object that has the potential to train the spectator in the appropriate ways of seeing. Within this framework Clarissa's own vision emerges as the standard of excellence, a model to which the reader must aspire. The second spectatorial regime that the novel represents complicates the first by insisting on Lovelace's role in the visual construction of Clarissa's meaning. Lovelace's gaze dominates the narrative to the extent that it is almost impossible to separate our own viewpoint from the rake's, since Lovelace provides our only visual access to the heroine for much of the story. Lovelace's eyes, however, reduce all issues of representation to questions of power and undermine the novel's spiritual agenda by insisting on the empirical materiality of vision – understood erotically by the rake – and aesthetic representations. Lovelace's gaze complicates the novel's didactic agenda in part because the text at times seems to grant it an authorial role, allowing Lovelace to present many of Clarissa's most exemplary moments without distancing itself from the voyeurism that organizes the libertine's viewpoint. But while Richardson invests in Lovelace's visual energy to sustain the narrative momentum and pleasure of the novel's central volumes, it is to Clarissa, and her ontological crisis, that the book is finally dedicated.[51] The novel's concluding volumes reveal how Clarissa learns to thwart the workings of the Lovelacian gaze, even while she highlights its effects in order to heighten the sense of victory the deathbed narrative grants her. In order to formulate a third term that can challenge the have/have-nots theory of the gaze promoted by Lovelace and others, Richardson draws on the dynamic described in Manley's *New*

Atalantis, one that both invites and blocks the desires of the voyeur. In what follows, I will trace *Clarissa*'s attempt to disengage its own and the reader's gaze from that of the libertine in its concluding volumes. Finally, I will argue that it is not this purging gesture which defeats the Lovelacian perspective, but a more subtle contest that Clarissa's dying sets in motion, a contest organized around the introduction of a hieroglyphic opacity into the visual field.[52]

In the heat of the fire scene, in which Lovelace finds himself overwhelmed by Clarissa's desperation in the face of rape, the libertine describes his sight as 'ravished,' a condition that speaks to his failure to dominate her in the moment (725). Later, in a letter begging for her forgiveness after the rape and her escape, Lovelace refers to Clarissa as 'the visible anchor' of his hopes (1185). Clarissa's revenge on Lovelace centres around her ability to avoid becoming visible to him ever again, either literally or metaphorically – even as she keeps herself at the centre of his visual imagination. Clarissa's escape from the visual world governed by the rake is enabled by her ability to use the conventions at work in her Vandyke-style portrait – by her ability to masquerade. Indeed, her escape from the brothel is made possible only through the donning of someone else's clothes, a costume that provides her with the cloak that Lovelace symbolically has stripped from her. Clarissa no longer assumes an identical relation between herself and her clothes and, in the larger sense, becomes adept at manipulating appearances to evade Lovelace. In the days following her arrival at Smith's, she assumes a variety of names – Mrs Rachel Clark, Mrs Dorothy Salcomb, for example – which she asks her correspondents to use in addressing their letters to her, letters that are likewise directed to a range of addresses, a range that demonstrates Clarissa's increasing knowledge of the urban landscape of London. The divided aspect of Clarissa's identity appears most forcibly when she decides to part with her clothes – the same clothes that originally signalled her commitment to the identity she had enjoyed when she lived at Harlowe Place: 'Her reason for so doing,' Belford recounts, 'was that she should never live to wear them: that her sister, and other relations were above wearing them: that her mother would not endure in her sight anything that was hers: that she wanted the money' (1082–3). The clothes become the sign of Clarissa's new power – 'I have all my clothes in my own possession' – even as she sells them; or rather, her selling of the clothes paradoxically returns to her the social status she enjoyed as their owner at Harlowe Place, when she could choose among them as part of her moment of self-fashioning (1122). Clarissa is willing to alienate what once seemed inalienable to her. Interestingly, she transforms clothing into cash, just as her father had offered to do when he presented Clarissa with the rich patterns intended to adorn her for Solmes. Clarissa returns to the crasser elements of the Harlowe interest in clothing as property in order to guarantee her absolute independence from that family.

The sale of Clarissa's clothes now becomes part of the means of reestablishing the integrity of her body. Clarissa deciphers Belford's innocent deception – 'she mistrusted that I was the advancer of the money; and would not let the clothes go' – and only allows the clothes to circulate in an economy entirely governed by the new female community she assembles at Mrs Smith's (1090). The sale of the clothes heightens the sense of crisis surrounding Clarissa, adding interest to the investment they originally represented. Clarissa treats her clothes as she once treated her money: 'It *is* ... out at interest! – And I hope it will bring me interest upon interest! – Better than to lie rusting in my cabinet' (195). Clarissa's clothes circulate in order to generate value for their owner, becoming, like her letters, part of Clarissa's new public persona, a persona that increasingly gains authority without having to present the body of its subject for scrutiny by the public or the rake, whose interests are uncomfortably similar. The private interests represented by the clothes take on the significance of a public voice, gaining sympathy among the purchasers, who will see the clothes on other bodies only to remember Clarissa's status as a woman and an artist, a status writ large in the skilful needlepoint that adorns the clothing.

Lovelace senses the degree of violence that attends the sale of Clarissa's clothes: 'What then is there in the parting with her apparel but female perverseness? – And I am not sure, whether I ought not to be glad if she does this out of *spite to me* – Some disappointed fair ones would have hanged, some drowned, themselves. My beloved only revenges herself upon her clothes' (1099). Lovelace, of course, can only read Clarissa's gesture as directed toward him and imagines that he can easily compensate for the loss that Clarissa sustains by parting with her clothes: 'Dost think I shall grudge to replace, to three times the value, what she disposes of?' (1099). But the removal of the clothing constitutes part of a larger plan by which Clarissa intends to escape the body altogether. Distressed by Anna Howe's description of the 'Clarissa' to whom her letter was delivered in Hampstead, she writes: 'Were you to see your poor Clarissa *now* ... you would not think her *bloated*, or *flush-coloured*: indeed you would not' (997). Emaciation frees the body from the surveillance imposed on it by social standards, by returning it to the status of a child's body.[53]

As Clarissa dies the flesh of her body is replaced by the accoutrements of death – first her shroud, which Clarissa describes as her 'wedding garments' (1339), and finally her coffin. Gwilliam writes that 'although her body has become an encumbrance to [Clarissa], her preparations of it for deathbed and coffin have the aura of an artistic self-memorialization that parallels her careful preparation of the text of *Clarissa*: she transcends her body, but she retains its use as a representation of herself.'[54] Most significantly, for my purposes, Clarissa's coffin comes to represent the new place where her needlepoint skills may be placed on display: 'She excused herself to the women, on the score of her youth, and being used to draw for her needleworks, for having shown more fancy than would perhaps be thought suitable on so solemn an occasion' (1306). The coffin becomes the means by which Clarissa symbolically retrieves her needlepoints from the closet at Harlowe Place: 'She did not know but her father would permit it, when furnished, to be carried down to be deposited with her ancestors; and in that case she ought not to discredit them in her *last appearance*' (1306). Serving as her '*last appearance*' the coffin reminds the Harlowes of their treatment of her portrait and needlepoint works, still nailed up, we presume. The coffin now replaces the art objects that originally functioned as family icons. The coffin assumes the dignity lost earlier by the portrait; in death Clarissa will regain a place 'with her ancestors,' forming part of the genealogical design the portrait first articulated. By leaving only her coffin to be viewed after her death, Clarissa undermines Lovelace's satirization of her aesthetic impulses, for she becomes inseparable from the aesthetic itself. As Ian Watt notes of the coffin, 'We, perhaps, can only try to regard it in the same light as we do a good deal of baroque memorial sculpture – forget the crushing banality of the symbolism and notice only the elaborate assurance of its presentation.'[55] The 'elaborate assurance' Watt identifies signals the correlation between Clarissa's coffin and Clarissa's voice, which manages to speak, finally, without a body – at least, without a live one. In the last of Lovelace's dreams Clarissa's body disappears into heaven like an ascending Virgin Mary in a baroque painting: 'I lost sight of *her*, and of the *bright form* together, and found wrapped in my arms her azure robe' (1218). Clarissa, like the angel, becomes nothing but 'bright form' as she shrinks beneath her dazzling white shroud. But the portrait, now in the form of the coffin, remains.

The bright form, however, is not transparent; nor is the coffin, as

Castle has observed: 'The coffin itself *says* nothing, but acts as a site for individual discoveries ... the process of interpretation is exposed as a form of solipsism, a mode of estrangement.'[56] Clarissa's monument, then, does not so much reveal her meaning as represent a resistance, however muted, against those who would read the heroine in any simple manner. This resistance finds its most powerful articulation in a hieroglyphic sign that never makes an appearance, discovering itself only as a trace.[57] In the novel's final volume, a controversy emerges around the idea that Clarissa's illness might be a result of a pregnancy. Lovelace's fantasies of Clarissa's reproductive 'consent' to his violation of her find expression in his interpretation of her illness: 'It would be the pride of my life to prove, in this charming frost-piece, the triumph of nature over principle, and to have a young Lovelace by such an angel: and then, for its sake, I am confident she will live, and will legitimate it' (1147). Returning to his penchant for visualizing Clarissa, here Lovelace imagines her resistance to him as one more pose, part of a 'frost-piece,' a winter scene in a painting. For Clarissa to be pregnant would sidestep the issue of her consent by invoking the higher law of nature. Lovelace's language echoes the marriage licence that he earlier quoted, implying the eradication of female agency in the legal understanding of pregnancy. A pregnancy would render Clarissa's will subservient to her body, which would ultimately back up both Lovelace and social law by forcing Clarissa to marry her rapist in order to legitimate the child. Lovelace recognizes in the idea of pregnancy his opportunity for a final triumph over his opponent, for a pregnancy would qualify Clarissa's separation from Lovelace and give credence to a relationship she has never entered into. Pregnancy would complete the cycle of humiliation that Lovelace began when he abducted Clarissa from her home, by rendering Clarissa a pawn in a familial drama once again. Worst of all, the familial drama would be of her own creation, something to which she would be tied at the level of a biological function.[58]

The separation of the workings of Clarissa's body from those of her mind – a separation that allows for a pregnancy to result from the rape – marks the distance between Clarissa's and Lovelace's understanding of female subjectivity.[59] Clarissa refuses to believe that her body might inform her actions, while Lovelace pins all of his hopes on the idea that Clarissa will agree to become his mistress – in effect, a new person – when introduced to her body as a sexed entity. Richardson breaks the continuum between the mind and the body in his refutation of the logic of libertinism. Clarissa's semi-conscious state during the rape supports this idea. Clarissa is in some sense 'there' for the rape, but not in any way that might compromise her status as a victim.

Lovelace's preoccupation with reproduction throughout the novel suggests that Richardson was thinking about the idea of Clarissa's maternal potential even before the question of her pregnancy arises. That she should be dying when pregnancy becomes an issue is particularly apropos in light of Richardson's personal experiences, which established a strong connection between death and reproduction. In the same letter in which he argues with Lady Bradshaigh about the possibility that Clarissa might have been happy married to Lovelace and raising his children, Richardson writes, 'Thus have I lost six Sons (all my Sons!) and two Daughters with every one of which ... I parted with great Regret.'[60] Richardson highlights the dangers of childbirth elsewhere in the letter, painting a dim picture of family life at the reproductive level.

Clarissa's transformation of her body's meaning depends on her ability to prevent occasion for further humiliation and to transform the degradation Lovelace has inflicted upon her into a moral triumph. When Clarissa finally escapes from the brothel, Mowbray writes to Lovelace: 'She is gone away with thy marks, I understand. A foolish little devil! Where will she mend herself? For nobody will look upon her' (963). Mowbray echoes Arabella's comments concerning Clarissa's art works earlier in the narrative – 'who can bear to see them?'(509) – suggesting a continuum between the violation and humiliation inflicted by Clarissa's family and the rape acted out by Lovelace. Clarissa accepts the assertion that by raping her Lovelace has somehow transformed her meaning, that he has left his marks upon her, and that he somehow inhabits her still: 'When all my doors are fast, and nothing but the keyhole open, and the key of late put into that, *to be where you are*, in a manner without opening any of them – Oh wretched, wretched Clarissa Harlowe!' (894, emphasis added). The keyhole image reminds us of the visual intrusion Lovelace's gaze first performed, an intrusion that the rape literalizes. Clarissa's challenge is to remove Lovelace from the keyhole and to block the space that has allowed for penetration. Mowbray argues that 'nobody will look upon her,' indicating the way that society may punish Clarissa by refusing her entry into its visual field, most literally by refusing to acknowledge her in public. Clarissa must find a way to reconstitute her social meaning without generating the scopic dynamic that has led to her rape. The task becomes, for Clarissa, to have the public see what she sees, that Lovelace has not changed her meaning to such an extent that she cannot reclaim a moral status. Clarissa needs both opacity and clarity to redefine herself.

The question of pregnancy goes to the heart of Clarissa's final challenge. For Lovelace is not the only one contemplating Clarissa's body as pregnant. The Harlowes are obsessed with the idea: 'Your mother *can't* ask, and your sister knows not in modesty *how* to ask; and so *I* ask you, if you have any reason to think yourself with child by this villain? – You *must* answer this, and answer it truly, before any thing can be resolved about you,' one uncle writes (1192). When Clarissa does not answer the question directly, the other uncle asserts: 'And yet it *must* be answered before you'll obtain from your father and mother, and us, the notice you hope for, I can tell you that' (1195). For both the Harlowes and Lovelace, Clarissa's supposed pregnancy determines the future of their relationships with her.

What exactly does the pregnant body signify in this novel?[61] Primarily, it establishes a singular meaning for Clarissa's body, and that meaning is biological. For Lovelace, a pregnancy will validate his libertine understanding of female subjectivity as determined by the body's sexual response.[62] Working with a similar logic, the Harlowes believe that Clarissa's pregnancy will manifest her sexual guilt: 'She may be with child! – This would perpetuate her stain,' declares Clarissa's mother (1156). Pregnancy divests the body of its privacy, rendering it not only a public spectacle, but public property. It refuses all of the body's other meanings, and it subordinates the will of the pregnant woman to the welfare of the fetus inside her; Lovelace believes that Clarissa will live 'for its sake' (1147). Should she be pregnant, her forgiveness is inevitable: 'Such is the natural course of things' (1143). Pregnancy initiates the impulse toward selflessness that controls the discourse of motherhood. Both the Harlowe family and Lovelace look forward to the spectacle of Clarissa's self-abnegation that pregnancy would force upon her. They know that pregnancy would generate the one obstacle that Clarissa could not overcome. The 'natural' will vindicate their oppressive attitude toward Clarissa, they believe. The Harlowes and Lovelace wait impatiently for the body to express visually what Clarissa will not admit.[63]

Clarissa never confirms or denies a pregnancy, declaring instead that 'a little, a very little time, will better answer than I can' (1193). As Jonathan Loesberg notes, 'Now, at first blush, this is a rather odd response. Clarissa could be pregnant and still die. And since she explicitly forbids an autopsy upon her ... there is no immediate reason to presume her death will answer anything.' Loesberg goes on to argue that the pregnancy is impossible because Clarissa's death must take on a 'supernaturally inexplicable quality' in order for it to participate in the allegorical impulse which controls the novel's conclusion. But the novel, it seems to me, makes a point of raising rather than answering the question. As Toni Bowers notes, 'Indeed, what is most important is not whether Clarissa is or is not pregnant, but the fact that the book never decides.'[64] I would like to explore the implications of Clarissa's refusal to clarify this point in relation to the issues of vision and self-portraiture I have discussed so far.

Clarissa replaces the idea of pregnancy with the idea of death, and in doing so challenges the authority which a pregnancy would grant Lovelace and her family. She is saying, in effect, that even if she were pregnant she would rather die than be roped back into a libertine or familial corral. Clarissa draws a veil around her body at the moment it might betray her, and she dies to ensure that the veil remains in place. The rhetorical force of this gesture, whatever its empirical grounds, effectively silences any attempt to render Clarissa's meaning socially determinable. Clarissa, and only Clarissa, establishes what her body will say in its final transfiguration. The silence that Clarissa maintains around the question of pregnancy does not allow the body to continue on its allegorical way, as Loesberg argues. Rather the silence, accompanied by death, leaves the body's meaning unclear. The body is not, finally, as transparent as both her detractors and admirers hope. Clarissa's refusal to answer questions about it marks a wilful denial of the authority her family would exert over her in her dying hours. She angrily rejects the question about pregnancy as 'a cruel question, put by him [Uncle John] in a shocking manner' (1193). Clarissa outmanoeuvres the family by claiming a delicacy which, in fact, her usual bluntness about her rape belies.

Lovelace's defeat is summed up in his response to Clarissa's famous allegorical letter, in which she promises Lovelace a future meeting. Clarissa is referring to a heavenly reconciliation, but Lovelace can only read her words as a confirmation of all his hopes. He uses the letter to transform the meaning of his dark dream into a wish-fulfilment, drawing on the ornate exuberance of the baroque tradition to celebrate the renewal of all his old fantasies: 'The bright form, lifting her up through [the ceiling] to another ceiling stuck round with golden Cherubims and Seraphims, indicates the charming little boys and girls that will be the fruits of this happy reconciliation' (1234). 'I verily believe,' he goes on, 'laying all circumstances together, that the dear creature unexpectedly finds herself in the way I have so ardently wished her to be in; and that this makes her at last incline to favour me, that she may set the better face upon her gestation when at her father's' (1239). But Lovelace's misreading of the letter is not only attributable to his egotism, for the reader knows as little as the libertine does about the real meaning of the letter, a meaning which remains undisclosed for another fifty pages. While hindsight reveals its place in the more general allegory governing Clarissa's death, Clarissa's letter initially jars that allegory by invoking, in both the reader's and Lovelace's mind, the idea that Clarissa's narrative is going to take a new turn.

The confusion between the workings of realism and allegory enables the implications of Clarissa's imminent death to emerge more starkly. Within this context death not only forecloses the possibility of any future children, but also, more immediately, insists on the death of any child Clarissa may be carrying. Clarissa only needs 'a little time, a very little time' to make her point (1193). Clarissa confronts Lovelace's vision of 'golden Cherubims and Seraphims' with a material body that can no longer be penetrated, either visually or literally; she invokes a gloomier version of the baroque, one that hides her body in shadow. The pregnancy, if there is one, remains covered by a body that will not facilitate a birth. In this way, Clarissa blocks Lovelace's movement toward her, and it is significant that Lovelace, in the agony of waiting to hear about Clarissa's death, compares himself to a body in labour: 'My grief, as my joy, is sharper-pointed than most other men's; and, like what Dolly Welby once told me, describing the parturient throes, if there were not lucid intervals – if they did not come and go – there would be no bearing them' (1310). Unlike Lovelace, Clarissa no longer dreams of 'lucid intervals,' and by refusing to answer the Harlowes' questions about a pregnancy, Clarissa also delays the arrival of their final letters of forgiveness, letters which would have mitigated, in part, their cruelty. Instead Clarissa dies, and the Harlowes are left to reflect on their contribution to her death. Where the reader is meant to position himself or herself at this junction is unclear. For we know as little as Lovelace and the Harlowes about the workings of Clarissa's body. Everyone, finally, is refused revelation.

In the final instance, it is Lovelace who dreams of the bright forms and light, while Clarissa manages to shroud both her language and her body in darkness even as she claims their transparency.[65] At the core of her body lies an opacity that nothing penetrates, and it is this opacity which generates a host of meanings outside of the emblematical framework governing the novel's ending. The spectacle the novel finally presents us with does not appear any more legible than the writing that has duped Clarissa, and that the heroine uses to trick Lovelace. Richardson redefines, finally, the public structures of sentiment that once organized his heroine's meaning: 'As to the *world*, and its *censures*, you know, my dear, that, however desirous I always was of a fair fame, yet I never thought it right to give more than a *second place* to the world's opinion ... What advantage would it be to me, were it retrievable, and were I to live long, if I could not acquit myself to *myself*?' (1139). Clarissa forgets that public opinion and her sense of self were identical before she ran away with Lovelace. Now that a rift has appeared, however, Clarissa reorients herself vis-à-vis the world, refusing to beg for its good opinion by recounting her story or taking Lovelace to court. The public must depend for its knowledge on whatever limited exposure of herself Clarissa grants it. It must identify, in other words, with the heroine's private interests.

The ambiguity surrounding Clarissa's body at the novel's conclusion disrupts both the model of accessibility and transparency that the novel's allegorical aspect endorses and the libertine's paradigm, which links vision to male power. In her will, the heroine exerts control over the gazes that circulate around her body: 'The occasion of my death not admitting of doubt, I will not on any account that it [the body] be opened; and it is my desire that it shall not be touched but by those of my own sex ... it is my desire that I may not be unnecessarily exposed to the view of anybody' (1413). Clarissa insists on guarding her dead body from the eyes of science, which might grant it a meaning that conflicts with her own, by refusing an autopsy. She recognizes the extent to which the scientific gaze, like that of the libertine, would exploit her body.[66] And indeed, Lovelace has designs on Clarissa's corpse: 'I THINK it absolutely right that my ever-dear and beloved lady should be opened and embalmed ... Her heart ... I *will* have. I will keep it in spirits. It shall never be out of my sight,' he writes (1383-4). Lovelace wants to place Clarissa's heart in a glass jar, as a surgeon would, so that he can continue to watch over the body that has escaped him in death. Clarissa refuses the consolation Lovelace seeks by keeping her body sealed; he can look but he can't touch. Clarissa can grant Lovelace visual rights knowing that only the kind of intrusion an autopsy involves would satisfy his desire: 'If, as he is a man very uncontrollable, and as I am nobody's, he insist upon viewing *her dead* whom he ONCE before saw in a manner dead, let his gay curiosity be gratified' (1413). What initially appears as another moment of abjection on Clarissa's part in fact contains a powerful gesture of repudiation. Lovelace can look at Clarissa because her body so adamantly refuses the terms he has tried to inscribe upon it. Clarissa reminds us of the rape as the moment when Lovelace tried to force her to mean one thing, and failed; as David Marshall notes, 'By comparing Lovelace's encounter with her corpse to the scene of the rape ... Clarissa makes the point that

Lovelace has not possessed her in possessing her body.'[67] Indeed, he has not even possessed her body, for, inert during the rape and in death, the body says nothing that Lovelace can understand.

Clarissa's will brings us back to the Vandyke-style portrait, both in general terms – the will stands as a written version of self-portraiture – and in the particular terms that allow Clarissa to bequeath her personal property to whom she chooses.[68] Interestingly, the will presents us with not just one portrait, but with three. Clarissa appears divided, a division that enables her to position herself in a particular relation to the members of her family – just as the self-division enabled by her earlier masquerade in a maid's clothes and the allegorical letter allowed her to define the terms governing her relation to Lovelace. The portraits function as epigraphs in the will, speaking through a face that is now emblematic as a death mask.[69] In this sense they assume the qualities that Paul de Man has theorized in relation to prosopopeia: 'Voice assumes mouth, eye, and finally face, a chain that is manifest in the etymology of the trope's name, *prosopon poien*, to confer a mask or a face (*prosopon*) ... By making the death speak, the symmetrical structure of the trope implies ... that the living are struck dumb, frozen in their own death.'[70] The punitive aspect of the bequests of Clarissa's portraits soon becomes apparent: 'I ... bequeath all the said family pictures to my said uncle John Harlowe. In these pictures, however, I include not one of my own, drawn when I was about fourteen years of age; which I shall hereafter in another article bequeath' (1414). This portrait, which originally hung in Clarissa's grandfather's closet, is presumably a small-scale portrait not intended for the type of display signalled by the Vandyke style. Aikins suggests that the grandfather's choice of this style 'reflects his more modest good taste and his affection for Clarissa.'[71] Clarissa's refusal to have this portrait hang in the family home signals the disintegration of the Harlowes' status, its premature demise occasioned by the death of its exemplary daughter, who bestows the affect the portrait represents to a member of the 'family' Clarissa has been forced to configure on her own: 'My picture at whole length ... I bequeath to that sister of my heart [Miss Howe]: of whose friendship, as well in adversity as prosperity, when I was deprived of all other comfort and comforters, I have had such instances as that our love can only be exceeded in that state of perfection in which I hope to rejoice with her hereafter to all eternity' (1415–16). Clarissa effectively carries Anna forward with her into death, leaving the living members of her family in the tomb of remembrance, without any visual markers of the daughter they have betrayed.[72]

If the portrait of Clarissa at fourteen enshrines a version of her identity that captures her early innocence and hopefulness, her miniature portrait signals a quite different identity. Clarissa bequeaths her miniature to her cousin Morden: 'I desire him likewise to accept of the little miniature picture set in gold, which his worthy father made me sit for to the famous Italian master whom he brought over with him; and which he presented to me that I might bestow it as he was pleased to say upon the man whom one day I should be most inclined to favour' (1415). The preciousness of the miniature is marked by its gold casing, as well as by the expense of its commission at the hands of a 'famous Italian master.' Clarissa recognizes the value she once had on the marriage market, and draws attention to that value in her bequest of the portrait – once intended to become a wedding gift – to Morden. As in her relationship with Belford, Clarissa finds in Morden an alternative male companion to Lovelace. Unlike her relationship with Lovelace's friend, however, Clarissa's understanding of Morden seems to place him closer to the rake that has defiled her, if only to set the two against each other. Here, the wedding gift that should have gone to Lovelace, goes to his rival, who, like Lovelace, is a libertine. Clarissa's will ensures that Morden will find reason for his eventual duel with Lovelace – as it is read, he reports later, 'vows or wishes of revenge, filled every mouth' (1420), and the miniature, intended as an intimate object to be carried with or worn by its owner guarantees that Morden will continually be reminded of his cousin's premature death. The appeal of Clarissa's adult beauty, appreciated best, as we have seen, by the libertine, can only serve to heighten Morden's desire for violence, just as it once encouraged Lovelace to proceed with his dangerous plots. Clarissa recognizes, perhaps, how her perfection has been used against her, and now rechannels the violence it has inspired back toward her aggressor.

Finally, the portrait in the Vandyke style appears again to be redeemed from its place in the closet, now that the family can exert no control over its meaning: 'My whole-length picture in the Vandyke taste, that used to hang in my own parlour ... I bequeath to my Aunt Hervey, except my mother shall think fit to keep it herself' (1416). Granting power to the mother who has never been able to claim agency for herself, Clarissa incites her to hang the daughter's portrait again, to identify with Clarissa openly as she previously did secretly. Clarissa effectively requires her mother to set herself against the Harlowe men, as she failed to do when Clarissa most needed her support – to prove that her alliances remain first with her daughter, and only secondly with the family that has sought to humiliate her. Clarissa also bequeaths to her mother one needlepoint, but makes a case against leaving her collection to the family based on its earlier treatment of the works: 'These pieces have all been taken down, as I have heard; and my relations will have no heart to put them up again' (1416). The Harlowes' original heartlessness is refigured as inevitable grief after Clarissa's death, to which Clarissa only responds by directing her works out of the closet and into the hands of Anna Howe and Morden.

Clarissa assumes, in her will, a magisterial voice that the Vandyke style confers upon its sitters, a voice that assumes social power and social privilege. Now that the power the Harlowes once enjoyed is located in the hands of the dead Clarissa, the heroine can occupy a performative position that her earlier reliance on the ideals of transparency and sincerity precluded. None of the portraits will ever function as they once did, as symbols of Clarissa's value as moveable property. Clarissa's comment, 'I am nobody's,' refuses the possession Lovelace has tried to claim over the meaning of Clarissa's identity. It also places a thorn in the side of the Harlowes, who were so busy trying to merge with the aristocracy that they lost the only daughter who could have enabled them to advance socially. They, too, are now nobodies.

In her request for the privacy conferred by death, Clarissa asks that her body not be touched 'but by those of my own sex' and that she not be 'unnecessarily exposed to the view of anybody,' once in her coffin (1413). Clarissa makes a similar request for her clothes: 'The trunks and boxes in which my clothes are sealed up, I desire may not be opened, but in presence of Mrs Norton ... and of Mrs Lovick' (1417). Clarissa's body, her coffin, and her trunks form part of a series of opaque surfaces that, in the final instance, grants us only partial access to the truth of the heroine. Terry Eagleton claims that 'in the prolonged detail of the death scenes the text unleashes upon Clarissa a sadistic violence which belongs with its Lovelacian unconscious.'[73] But Richardson chooses to grant the sadistic energies of the novel's concluding chapters not to his rake, but to his heroine, and this sadism takes more than Clarissa's body as its target. Clarissa revenges herself on her family, on Lovelace, on the public that has judged her, and on the reader who may have inadvertently, or even actively, enjoyed the spectacle of her humiliation. In the end Richardson's heroine proves her youthful ideal that 'We may make the world allow for us and respect us as we please, if we can be but sturdy in our wills' (54) in the defiant posture her body adopts. In death Clarissa paradoxically becomes, as Isobel Grundy has observed, 'what the feminist discourse of rape terms a survivor.'[74]

The ambiguity surrounding Clarissa's death takes us back to the world of Manley's hieroglyphs and veils, signs that allow women to write narratives of their lives that are not easily penetrated by social dictates. The Vandyke-style portrait emerges as a trope of masquerade that refuses any easy interpretation, emphasizing instead the theatrical elements of all social identities, and it confirms the extent to which the visual hermeneutics of the novel inhabit a terrain governed by both shadow and light, revelation and obscurity. While the portrait initially seems to create two mutually exclusive readings, Richardson eventually unites the ideas of integrity and masquerade that the painting upholds. In his *Journal of a Tour to the Hebrides,* James Boswell records a conversation with Johnson on the subject of portraiture and dress:

> I wished to know which he preferred, fine portraits, or those of which the merit was resemblance. – Johnson. 'Sir, their chief excellence is in being like.' – Boswell. 'Are you of that opinion, as to the portraits of ancestors whom one has never seen?' – Johnson. 'It then becomes of more consequence that they should be like; and I would have them in the dress of the times, which makes a piece of history ... Truth, sir, is of the greatest value in these things.'[75]

Clarissa discovers that various truths circulate in the culture she inhabits, and that her original understanding of the truth of her identity does not prevent its annihilation. It is rather by withholding knowledge from those who seek to claim it from her, by redefining the space between surface and depth – by inhabiting, in other words, the gap in historical meaning created by the Vandyke dress's status as a costume both about and removed from the eighteenth century – that Clarissa makes her own truth known, a truth that remains, necessarily, partial and private, complete and public.

Chapter Four

Refiguring Virtue:
The History of Miss Betsy Thoughtless and *Amelia*

We are reading Mr. Fielding's Amelia. Mrs. Don and I don't like it at all ... Our next important reading will be Betty [sic] Thoughtless; I wish Richardson would publish his good man, and put all these frivolous authors out of countenance.[1]

Two novels published in 1751 attest to the powerful influence *Clarissa* exerted over authors writing after its publication; Eliza Haywood's *The History of Miss Betsy Thoughtless* and Henry Fielding's *Amelia* both construct a novelistic practice of psychological realism around the figure of a woman dealing with a morally vexed and vexing world. That *Clarissa* should have such a pronounced impact on Haywood and Fielding takes on a particular significance insofar as these authors' earlier works were more likely to demonstrate an Augustan humour in their representations of female virtue than to engage in the contemplation of ethical catastrophes that Richardson undertakes in his representation of Lovelace's and Clarissa's relationship. Haywood had established her reputation in the 1720s by writing amatory tales filled with representations of illicit female sexuality untroubled by deep psychological reflection, and Fielding had displayed a similarly lighthearted streak in his ribald depictions of sexual intrigue throughout the 1740s. Fielding's and Haywood's attraction to *Clarissa* speaks to a recognition that Richardson's novel added a new dimension to the representation of sexuality and gender, not because it broke with the past traditions to which Manley and Haywood and Fielding belonged as Augustan writers, as some critics have argued, but rather because it added depth and structure to those traditions. *The History of Miss Betsy Thoughtless* and *Amelia* attempted to match the achievement that *Clarissa* represented, but despite their efforts, Haywood's and Fielding's last novels garnered only, at best, mixed reviews.²

The critical failure of *Amelia* and *Betsy Thoughtless* highlights the difficulty that mid-century novelists encountered in attempting to write 'legitimate' fiction. The aesthetics of tragedy governing *Clarissa* allowed Richardson to make claims that could only appear scandalous within a comic rubric, and neither Fielding nor Haywood had the desire to take their narratives the Richardsonian distance; neither wanted, in other words, to kill off the heroine to ensure her reputation. But their novels strikingly evoke both Richardson's moral imperatives and *Clarissa*'s complications of those imperatives in their portrait narratives. Of course, Fielding and Haywood approach the question of female embodiment, vision, and virtue from different perspectives; Fielding never grants his heroine a gaze of her own, focusing instead on the question of female visibility, while Haywood centres her attention on the relation between women's desire to act as both spectacles and spectators. Fielding endorses a domestic ideology that idealizes the virtuous wife as a public icon, an emblematic force capable of stabilizing social relations. Haywood advocates a more aggressive domesticity, whereby women will educate themselves to appreciate the virtues of retirement and family life. Fielding idealizes his heroine, while Haywood confronts the wayward desires of her teenage protagonist directly.³ And yet in both cases the authors' turn toward a Richardsonian narrative aesthetic does not so much involve a rejection of the more scandalous aspects of their past fictional practices, but rather a reconfiguration of the ideas central to those practices. As in *Clarissa*, the figure of the portrait defines the intensification of the terms that Fielding and Haywood, like Richardson, bring forward from the early eighteenth century.⁴

The portrait that appears in the narratives of both *Betsy Thoughtless* and *Amelia* is a miniature portrait, and this portrait, I believe, stands metonymically for a particular understanding of women's relation to private interests in the mid-eighteenth century. On the one hand, the miniature epitomizes the sentimental object that guarantees affect's dominion in the world of the mid-century novel. On the other hand, the miniature portrait represents the kind of new commodity that, as Deidre Shauna Lynch argues, 'put pressure on the norms and the categories that people had formerly invoked to explain the material world and to make its artifacts meaningful.'⁵ Richardson's most significant 'miniature,' Clarissa's diminutive corpse, comes to rest in the family crypt; but

Haywood's and Fielding's miniatures are more peripatetic, proving Lynch's claim that 'objects of sentimental value are surprisingly prone to wandering.'[6] In other words, the miniature portrait takes women's private interests out of the home, where domestic ideology – gaining strength as a discourse in this period – would keep them, breaking down the public/private divide as surely as Manley's engagement in boudoir politics and Richardson's obsession with Clarissa's public relations campaign. And like Richardson's and Manley's portraits, the miniature creates interpretive opportunities in its very materiality as an object, occasioned here by the image's smallness and the presence of the case that encloses it, itself an aesthetic object that shrouds in secrecy the portrait it contains.

Associated with intimacy in its representation of a loved one and connected to the body's private space as an object both held in the intimacy of the hand and worn against the body's surface as a piece of jewellery, the miniature portrait insists, first and foremost, on the private as the medium of its appreciation. Its celebration of familial and sentimental relations connects it to the world of the home, as well as with the aesthetics of the decorative and the rococo that Shaftesbury denigrated as effeminate earlier in the century. Both Susan Stewart and, in his discussion of *Amelia*, Steven J. Gores link the miniature to an aesthetics of containment; Stewart claims that the miniature 'presents a diminutive, and thereby manipulatable, version of experience, a version which is domesticated and protected from contamination,' while Gores argues that the miniature aesthetic reduces 'the inherent complexity of selfhood to a single note.'[7] This reading of the miniature, I believe, underestimates the complexity that surrounds the miniature's relation to both the private and the particular, and to the world at large. Richard Wendorf offers a compelling vision of the aesthetics of particularity intrinsic to the miniature's production: 'The miniaturist must suggest the entire figure by depicting its most telling features as searchingly as possible; and in the process, he will often isolate what is personally distinctive from what his subject shares with similar men and women ... The miniaturist, in other words, is perhaps more intensely aware than other painters of the fluctuations in the human countenance, and of what those fluctuations indicate about the character of the sitter.'[8] The miniature fetishizes the idea of the private associated with portraiture more generally, rendering precious what in negative accounts of portraiture is denigrated as the genre's necessary attachment to the merely local details of character. Even as it deepens the experience of private beholding, however, the miniature, as an object, represents women's increasingly public role as consumers, for the miniature could be purchased by women much more readily than a costly full-sized portrait. [9]

The miniature portrait's association with women's emotional and economic lives appears in a number of different portraits of the period. Two examples demonstrate the extent to which a gendered aesthetics of beholding appeared around the figure of the miniature. The first, Philip Mercier's portrait of Peg Woffington (figure 23), represents a woman looking pensively on a miniature, which was rumoured to represent David Garrick, Woffington's one-time lover.[10] That the woman is holding an image of a man who has abandoned her is suggested by the presence of the dog in the background, whose fidelity stands in contrast to the betrayal of the faithless lover. The sitter's absorption in the miniature incites our voyeuristic interest in the woman's sexual life and its vicissitudes. Sentiment and its libertine double, licentious solicitude, frame the moment of our viewing. A generation later, the same visual dynamic appears, with an added twist. In Thomas Gainsborough's 1781 portrait of Mary 'Perdita' Robinson (figure 24), a portrait commissioned by Robinson herself, the actress looks out at the viewer as she holds the miniature of the Prince of Wales on her lap; the miniature is positioned in such a way as to offer up the image to the portrait's beholder, but only just – we can only glimpse the blue garter that signals the presence of the prince. Also accompanied by a faithful dog, Mary Robinson publicly displays her abandonment, mirroring the role she has played as Perdita on stage. In Robinson's case, we can read the portrait's representation as part of a larger publicity campaign surrounding Robinson's bid to elicit a pension from the Prince of Wales, a campaign that she won. The beholder's sympathy and voyeurism are orchestrated by the subject of the representation, who uses her private life and the intimacy of her affairs to further her public career as an actress and a writer. The preciousness of the portrait, rather than idealizing character, highlights the miniature's status as a material and erotic object that contributes to a seduction narrative – a narrative we have seen unfold in Manley's *New Atalantis* around the miniature, and which *Clarissa* also taps into by using the miniature, after her death, to illicit feelings of jealousy and rage in her cousin Morden. This commentary in turn speaks to the larger portrait in which the smaller one appears; how does a woman's possession of a miniature speak to the issues of her own representation and to the staging of private desires in the public theatre?

Amelia and *Betsy Thoughtless* provide us with a contrast between how the dynamics surrounding the miniature portrait of a woman (*Amelia*) differ from those surrounding the miniature portrait of a man (*Betsy Thoughtless*). In both narratives, the preoccupation with the representation of female character governs the portrait's representation; in *Amelia*, the miniature stands in a synechdochic and metaphoric relation to the heroine, representing both a part of and a likeness of her whole body. As Wendorf has argued, it is this logic of compression that leads to an intensification of interest in the object's particularity.[11] In *Betsy Thoughtless*, however, the representation of Trueworth serves only as a means of accessing the spectacle of the heroine in her moments of private beholding. Because Trueworth, as a man, is not defined in relation to his objectness, his 'to-be-seen' aspect, his image is of little significance. In the sphere of private relations governing the miniature's circulation, Trueworth's power is limited, since outside the conventions of state portraits male portrait subjects do not command attention as spectacles. The miniature instead serves to establish a pedagogical standard for modes of beholding that are directly related to Betsy's status as both an object and subject of the social gaze. Betsy, we are led to believe, needs to learn the benefits of retirement, and the miniature draws her into a visual mode that initially seems to confirm this pedagogical imperative. Trueworth is not included in this impulse, except insofar as that, by learning how to retire, Betsy will prove herself worthy to be his wife; he stands only as a foil to the heroine's development. That his image should factor so little in the portrait narrative suggests the extent to which the spectacle of the body – associated in Restoration England with the king as much as with his courtesans – came to be predominantly associated with women's, rather than men's, social and familial identities in the world of the eighteenth-century novel.[12]

Betsy Thoughtless and the Privatization of Spectacle[13]

Eliza Haywood's early fiction depends on an explicit eroticization of a female body that exerts its power in its ability to signify without speech. The 'emotional inexpressibility' that John Richetti has highlighted in his reading of Haywood emerges out of the body's sexual character, which generates a plethora of symptoms guaranteed to stimulate desire.[14] One of Haywood's early heroines, Fantomina, manages to seduce her lover in a variety of disguises. While Fantomina must keep her identity private in order to seduce Beauplaisir, the kind of personalized and familial privacy that governs domestic ideology is entirely missing in Fantomina's theatrical performances, and the question of whether or not she is a virtuous individual is irrelevant. For Richardson such a formulation could only indicate the basest of moral positions, for the reader requires no delicacy of sentiment or ethical perspicuity to appreciate Haywood's scandalous texts, just an active sexual imagination. As we have seen, Richardson appreciates the idea of a body that can communicate without language, so that at times Clarissa looks suspiciously like one of Haywood's heroines: yet Richardson insists that a higher end is served by the spectacle his heroine creates.

In her attempt to follow in Richardson's footsteps and to sell fiction to the moralistic middle-class audience that had formed by the mid-century, Haywood turns away from the excesses of erotica and the pleasures of spectatorship they produce. *Betsy Thoughtless* denounces extravagant female visibility and warns against the dangers of a female gaze. The narrator constantly reminds readers that virtue demands the relinquishing of visual pleasure for domestic duty. But by dividing pleasure and duty, Haywood shoots her educational narrative in the foot. In the competition between the two models of vision in the text – the narrator's 'good' model versus Betsy's 'bad' one – readerly pleasure exerts a pull toward the immoral. As Janet Todd has observed, 'It is true that the heroine learns that she must be careful of her conduct and not enjoy power over suitors in the robust way of early eighteenth-century women, but in the process of learning she takes considerable liberties.'[15] In particular, the novel focuses its attention on the spectacle that Betsy provides both in her person and her actions, a tendency that the *Monthly Review* used to identify the sex of the author: 'Indeed, the minute detail of particulars, and circumstantial descriptions of every thing relating to dress and equipage, and other little exteriors that but too much attract the eye and heart of a woman, sufficiently confirm the voice of the public, as to the sex of our author.' The critic, sounding very much like Shaftesbury, uses the novel's attachment to 'little exteriors' as the lynchpin of its attack on the novel, which it describes as formally and thematically 'barren': 'Adventures thick sown, and amorous intrigues carried on by a numerous variety of persons (with but little variety of characters) compose all that the reader will find in these four volumes.' Superficiality imposes itself on the reader in search of a character with the depth of a Clarissa: 'A heroine like this, cannot but lay her historian under much disadvantage.'[16]

Without the absolutism that Richardson's tragic vision sustains, and without a strong cultural sense of the novel's formal and epistemological contours, a mid-eighteenth-century reader lacked a narrative register within which to place Haywood's complicated manoeuvres. In what follows, I will define the tension surrounding Betsy's status as a spectacle and suggest that Haywood prevents her text's meaning from imploding by working out a compromise. The text does not relinquish the visual altogether, finally, but in order to maintain a moral code governing the activity of spectatorship and the spectacle of the female body, Haywood modifies her earlier model of visual pleasure to accommodate a notion of privacy organized around domestic values that her more scandalous works lacked, even while maintaining women's public status.

The novel's debate about vision works itself out through the question of female education. The first sentence of *Betsy Thoughtless* announces the novel's pedagogical agenda: 'It was always my opinion, that fewer women were undone by love than vanity; and that those mistakes the sex are sometimes guilty of, proceed, for the most part, rather from inadvertency, than a vicious inclination.'[17] In opposing 'inadvertency' to 'inclination,' the narrator implies that women can be educated to appreciate morality over vanity, that nothing essential to the female mind inclines it toward a resistance to virtue. Betsy Thoughtless's participation in a *Bildungsroman* involves her movement away from narcissism toward a more enlarged understanding of her cultural role. But some of the contradictions informing the novel's understanding of vision colour its educational program, contradictions that can be summed up in the paradox of its title. How can 'Betsy Thoughtless' have a 'history'? That is to say, how can thoughtlessness, an ahistorical state of blankness, become either thoughtful – i.e., self-reflexive – or productive of a meaningful history? While the novel tells us that Betsy develops out of a state of thoughtlessness into an experienced understanding of the world based on reflection, the dynamic by which this transformation occurs never emerges very clearly. Similarly, the narrative announces Betsy's eventual adoption of a new visual perspective but, as we shall see, never demonstrates it outside of a context that seems to qualify its supposed virtues. The ideals of introspection and reflection – the antitheses of vanity and thoughtlessness – that the novel espouses never manage to determine the narrative's development, which relies instead on the visual and narratological dynamics of scandal.

The rather contorted plot of *Betsy Thoughtless* can be summed up briefly. Haywood's novel tells the story of a teenaged orphan poorly educated in a girl's boarding school who finds herself, upon the death of her father, living in London with one of her guardians and his family. Betsy immediately embarks on a pleasure-seeking career, refusing to take seriously the idea that she ought to marry to secure her somewhat precarious social position. She eventually alienates her most eligible suitor, Mr Trueworth, who goes on to marry a more sedate young woman, Harriot. Having jeopardized her reputation by entertaining a social imposter who tries to rape her, Betsy is finally persuaded to marry Mr Munden. Mr Munden proves himself an abusive and parsimonious husband and luckily suffers an early death. Conveniently Trueworth's wife also dies, leaving Trueworth free for a chastened and wiser young Betsy to marry at the novel's happy conclusion. At the centre of the narrative a miniature portrait serves as the device that exposes Betsy's changing feelings and organizes the novel's comic resolution.

Betsy's vanity constitutes her main flaw. Betsy's friend Mabel most astutely sums up the problem that Betsy must overcome if she is to win genuine respectability: '"It is however a great pity, methinks ... that so many rare and excellent qualities, as Miss Betsy is possessed of, should all be swallowed up and lost in the nonsensical vanity of being too generally admired"' (356). Betsy's desire for everybody's admiration, in other words, confirms her surname. She does not understand that she must curtail her powers of attraction in order to maintain her status and cannot rest content with the approbation of the few people she knows well, but rather continually ventures forth in search of public acclaim. Her reluctance to remain at home reinforces the idea that Betsy suffers from an intellectual vacuity. Betsy's mind seems incapable of holding onto thought (indeed, we are never sure what her 'rare and excellent qualities' consist of) and works only to generate desire: 'She had a great deal of wit, but was too volatile for reflection, and as a ship, without sufficient ballast, is tost about at the pleasure of every wind that blows, so was she hurried thro' the ocean of life, just as each predominant passion directed' (13). The pleasure Betsy takes in the responses she elicits motivates her to such an extent that while she can listen to the sage lectures given her by Lady Trusty and acknowledge their value, she cannot retain their message; the lectures are incapable of producing any noticeable change in her behaviour. Betsy always remains outside the home, both physically and mentally.

The desire to be too generally admired springs from the excessively public nature of Betsy's daily life. The narrator holds her guardian's wife, Lady Mellasin, responsible for the heroine's errant lifestyle: 'Never did the mistress of a private family indulge herself, and those about her, with such a continual round of publick diversions. The court, the play, the ball, and opera, with giving and receiving visits, engrossed all the time could be spared from the toilet' (18). The criticism leveled at Lady

Mellasin, and by association Betsy, echoes Addison's earlier chastisement of Fulvia, who, as we saw earlier, fails to realize that her self-promotion only encourages scandal. Like Addison, Haywood juxtaposes the pleasures of domestic tranquillity against the diversions afforded by London society, situating female virtue in the retirement of the home. The public sphere may be safe for a man like Mr Spectator, who refuses to participate in the spectacles he witnesses, but the temptation for women to gratify their vanity appears irresistible, Haywood and Addison suggest. The connection between Addison's and Haywood's ideas is not accidental; Haywood edited a journal entitled *The Female Spectator* in the 1740s, in which she used her own youth as an example of female frivolity: 'I should have thought the day lost, which did not present me with some new opportunity of shewing myself.'[18] The delight Betsy takes in watching the visually stimulating court, play, ball, and opera incites her to model herself as an object on display. The diversions created in the public sphere crowd out the private thoughts that alone can teach morality. The desire to look and be looked at are associated by their dependence on the eye, which in turn grounds the subject in a material, rather than an intellectual or spiritual, world.

Only scandal and guilt can result from Betsy's activities: 'There would be much less room either for the one or the other, were some part of that time, which is wasted at the toilet, in consulting what dress is most becoming to the face, employed in examining the heart, and what actions are most becoming of the character' (9). Her preference for a superficial, rather than introspective, form of vision stems from a desire to create pleasure in both her own eye and the eyes of others. She fails to develop an internalized eye, one that could regulate her behaviour or teach her moral lessons. Betsy refuses to fashion her gaze according to a domestic program, which expects actions, rather than faces, to be 'becoming.' Instead she continues to expand the domain both of her influence as a spectacle and of her gaze, establishing a regime of unchecked pleasure for herself in the vanity fair of London.

Betsy is particularly resistant to the idea that she should marry. As far as Betsy is concerned, marriage could only thwart her desires: '"They want to deprive us of all the pleasures of life, just when one begins to have a relish for them"' (431). When Trueworth attempts to offer his love an '"adoring and passionately devoted heart,"' Betsy responds by literalizing the language of love: '"A heart may be a pretty thing for ought I know to the contrary; but there is such an enclosure of flesh and bone about it, that it is utterly impossible for one to see into it, and consequently to know whether one likes it or not'" (116). She thinks of the heart just as she thinks of herself, in terms of its 'prettiness,' and she refuses to acknowledge what she cannot admire with her eyes. Betsy is able to sidestep the intention behind Trueworth's declaration by pitting her reliance on vision as a standard of judgment against his amorous discourse. Such rhetorical sleights of hand enable her to avoid marriage by refusing to enter into its discursive realm. Betsy's insistence on embodiment and the visual effectively blocks the attempts of those around her to have her think rather than look. She refuses to accept the marriage plot as the end to which her circulation in London society is the means. Rather, she insists on enjoying the means themselves, and courtship appears to her as merely one more diversion on her entertainment roster.

By juxtaposing Betsy's understanding of the world against a model of private virtue and duty, summed up in the idea of a suitable marriage, the text aligns the reader's gaze with the narrator's disciplinary eye. But this alignment cannot easily hold when all of the pleasure in the text resides in the heroine's visual perspective. She enjoys her spectatorial position in the world, and so do we. Why Betsy *ought* to change, beyond fulfilling a social mandate, is the question that the novel's representation of pleasure and duty raises. A similar problem appears in *The Female Spectator*. While the journal claims that it wants to warn young women against various dangers awaiting them, it fills its pages with exciting tales of intrigue and scandal, leaving the lessons it is supposed to be promoting to tacked-on introductions and conclusions. Similarly, the educational lessons that *Betsy Thoughtless* articulates cannot compete for narrative interest with its scandalous elements. Betsy's refusal to think, rather than hampering the novel's trajectory, motivates the narrative by creating a series of dangers and trials for the heroine to encounter. In its formal structure, the novel progresses not by witnessing the unfolding of a moral lesson but rather by moving anecdotally from one incident to the next. The term 'eclaircissement,' which the novel uses repeatedly, suggests the extent to which the plot relies on the logic of vision, even as the narrative condemns Betsy's participation in the spectacles it represents. The French origin of the word heightens its erotic connotation, as does its echoing of scandal texts, in which 'eclaircissement' also makes an appearance. Unlike Richardson, Haywood is unable to produce interest in the road to virtue, so that however much the narrator chastises Betsy's transgressions, she cannot convince us that saintliness is engaging. The virtue that appears challenging in Clarissa looks flat and unappealing in the insipid Harriot, the idealized woman whom *Betsy Thoughtless* presents as a foil to its heroine.

The tension between pleasure and duty appears most striking in the context of the marriage plot. While the narrator insists that Betsy's failure to consider marriage seriously represents a moral failing, the plot reveals the punitive aspect of marriage. Women must be disciplined to marry well, or they will be punished with a bad marriage, as Betsy is. Her marriage plot involves a degree of violence that belies the benevolent status of the institution, and Betsy finds her pleasure curtailed, finally, not by enlightened education but by brutality. The various violent episodes that punctuate the text appear in such a timely fashion that it seems as though the education that Betsy requires *necessarily* involves violence. Betsy only agrees to a marriage with Munden after she is very nearly raped by an imposter posing as a man of title. The threat such an attack represents coincides with the fear governing Betsy's brother's thoughts; like the men of the Harlowe family in *Clarissa*, Thomas Thoughtless only cares about his sister insofar as she reflects on the family name: 'He considered, that the honour of a family depended greatly on the female part of it, and therefore resolved to omit nothing in his power, to prevent Miss Betsy from being caught by any snares, that might be laid to entrap her innocence' (293). Both the brother and the imposter agree on the terms that grant Betsy meaning. The imposter knows that if he rapes Betsy he will 'ruin' her and by doing so place himself in a position to marry her as a means of reparation; the brother recognizes that maintaining Betsy's value depends on the avoidance of this kind of incident. Significantly, Betsy's response to the attempted rape instigates the first instance of her voluntary withdrawal from the public realm: 'She wished for nothing but to be unseen, unregarded, and utterly forgotten, by all that had ever known her' (390). The attack deprives Betsy of both her vision and the powers she has commanded as a spectacle and it precipitates her entrance into marriage, which also seems to preclude the possibility of visual pleasure.

But at the moment her brothers coerce their sister into a marriage with Munden, the heroine embarks on a new path of rebellion:

She made, for a great while, very little reply to all this [discussion of marriage]; – her head was now indeed very full of something else; – she sate in a kind of reverie, and had perfect absence of mind ... yet, at last, meerly

126   Private Interests

to get rid of their importunities and presence, that she might be alone to indulge her own meditations, she said as they said, and promised to do whatever they required of her. (393)

The imposter's attack on Betsy means that she can no longer avoid marriage, for the threat of a public humiliation now hangs over her head. Nonetheless, Betsy is able to retain her usual absence of mind by inventing an alternative plot, one that will compensate in part for the sacrifice of her freedom that marriage entails. Betsy's 'meditations' are occasioned by the mention of a miniature portrait of Trueworth, who by this time has broken ties with Betsy and is about to marry another woman. Betsy's brother Francis has seen the miniature at the painter's studio and remarks, '"I looked on it through my magnifier, and thought I saw his very self before me"' (392). Trueworth's portrait, for Betsy, becomes the new spectacle she must possess and enjoy, even as she marries someone else. No longer able to enjoy unlimited freedom in the visual excess of London society, Betsy narrows her field around an aesthetic object that recalls her earlier licence and that allows her, to a certain extent, to reenact it.[19]

Trueworth has wounded Betsy's pride, both by having thrown her over and by rescuing her from the imposter. Betsy's plan to obtain his portrait represents an attempt to restore control over the events unfolding around her. A list of reasons for a sleepless night signals the connection between two competing understandings of Trueworth that Betsy maintains: 'In the first, the shock of the insult she had sustained, and the shame of her receiving her protection from him, by whom, of all men living, she was least willing to be obliged, took up all her thoughts; – in the second, she was equally engrossed by the impatience of having something to preserve him eternally in her mind' (394). Betsy's feelings for Trueworth consist of a mixture of pride and sentimental affection, a mixture that complicates the meaning of the miniature Betsy is about to capture. On the one hand, we can read the portrait as the key to Betsy's late-discovered love for Trueworth, but on the other, as a token of her past ability to control men and their representations of themselves.

The fact that the portrait narrative begins in the moments following Betsy's escape from her rapist defines the abduction of the miniature as a response to the attack, as a gesture of defiance against those who would humiliate her. Betsy disguises herself and goes to the painter's studio, where she buys the miniature intended for Trueworth's fiancée: 'All her remorse, – all her vexation, for the base design laid against her at Mrs

Modely's, were dissipated the moment she took it into her head to get possession of this picture, and the success of her enterprize elated her beyond expression' (395). Several factors contribute to Betsy's elation: her renewed ability to move about in the public sphere without fear of reprisal, by virtue of her disguise; her successful execution of a plan filled with intrigue and scandal – a plan worthy of the theatre; the exercise of her purchasing power; and most of all, her triumph over Trueworth's lover: 'The thoughts of disappointing her rival's expectations, contributed greatly to the satisfaction she felt at what she had done' (396). The contrast between Betsy's earlier humiliation and her triumph in executing the theft of the portrait points toward Betsy's renewed control over the visual field and the social power attendant upon it. Betsy's appropriation of the portrait represents a type of theft, even though she buys the painting from the painter, because the portrait is not really for sale – it is a special order. Her action represents a socially taboo, if not strictly illegal, gesture. 'Theft' marks the attitude Betsy is adopting vis-à-vis Trueworth and Harriot, his fiancée.

Fooled once by the aristocratic posturings of a fake, now Betsy assumes the disguise. Betsy measures the success of her intrigue against the danger of being found out by Trueworth, a discovery that, writes the narrator, 'would have given her more lasting confusion, than even her late unlucky adventure with the mock baronet' (397). It is unclear what precisely would cause Betsy's 'confusion': would it be the discovery of feelings that Betsy has never acknowledged or the exposure of her social transgression? In either case, opacity grants Betsy a measure of power that she would lose were Trueworth to expose her plot. Disguise thus works literally to conceal Betsy's identity, and metaphorically to enable her resistance to Trueworth's understanding of her either as a sentimental heroine or as a social deviant.

The marriage that soon ensnares Betsy sustains none of the pleasures Betsy enjoys in disguise. Having reluctantly agreed to marry Munden, Betsy experiences a nightmare that points to the threat marriage poses to her freedom: 'Sometimes she imagined herself standing on the brink of muddy, troubled waters; – at others, that she was wandering through deserts, overgrown with thorns and briars; or seeking to find a passage through some ruin'd building, whose tottering roof seemed ready to fall upon her head, and crush her to pieces' (431). As Margaret Anne Doody observes, 'This dream results from an apprehension of the self under attack, and from a sense of severe loss which cannot be exactly defined.'[20] Both in its pictorial and emotional elements Betsy's dream resembles the macabre dream tableau that Clarissa's unconscious produces early in Richardson's text. The Gothic images of Betsy's dream, resembling those of a ruin painting or forest landscape, form a stark relief to the London that Betsy has enjoyed as a single woman; rather than circulating through the town in a coach, Betsy finds herself lost in a wilderness where nature – 'muddy, troubled waters' and 'thorns and briars' – encroaches upon her. The predominance of nature images suggests the sexual role that marriage dictates for Betsy, a role that, unchosen, reduces her to a body exchanged between men. The enclosure implied by the ruined building intimates the way that Betsy's marriage will become a prison for her, while the threat of destruction points to a violent streak in her future husband that Munden's courtship ritual conceals. The dark and gloomy Gothic atmosphere of the dream casts a shadow over the dazzling brightness of Betsy's daily life in the world. The confusion Betsy experiences in the dream portends the feelings that marriage will bring on; for Betsy, marriage will create a world whose signs she cannot read or manipulate.

The day after her nightmare Betsy looks at Trueworth's portrait again: '"I know not how it is, I did not then think him half so agreeable as I now find he is"' (432). Significantly, the text never refers to the magnifier that the brother used to view the miniature in its representations of Betsy's encounters with the painting. Trueworth's miniature takes on larger proportions in the eyes of its admiring beholder, even though it is the miniature format that enables easy access to the object. Looking at Trueworth's miniature, Betsy here begins to learn the value of her former suitor, the text implies, but in light of the dream it seems that Trueworth appears attractive less for any intrinsic value he may have than for the contrast he forms both to Munden and, insofar as he epitomizes Betsy's past, to marriage. If the portrait stands as a rebuke to Betsy's earlier dismissal of Trueworth, it also sustains Betsy's fantasy of desire and control. The representation appeals to her because the portrait's acquisition marked the pinnacle of her freedom from social restraint. Trueworth as a miniature painting does not represent the threat that Trueworth as a suitor once posed. Betsy was reluctant to marry Trueworth, just as she is reluctant to marry Munden. But now confronted with the inevitability of marriage, Betsy idealizes Trueworth, whose wealth could have generated a more fantasy-like marriage than the one into which she is about to enter. The description of Trueworth's opulent wedding procession reinforces this idea: 'There were three coaches and six ... with a great deal of luggage before and behind. – The ladies and gentlemen were all in extreme rich riding habits, and the footmen, eleven in number, being all in new liveries, and spruce fellows, the whole cavalcade altogether made a very genteel appearance' (419). Betsy projects onto the portrait all of her desires for a marriage that will somehow not entail her degradation, a humiliation that initially she sums up as the lack of a coach.

The marriage turns out to involve a series of much more serious degradations, brought on by Munden's understanding of a wife as 'an upper servant, bound to study and obey, in all things, the will of him to whom she had given her hand' (448). Betsy, who wants to continue enjoying the agency she possessed as a single woman, is unready for the violence Munden uses when his wife confronts him with resistance: 'The fondness she had always shewn of [her pet squirrel] put a sudden thought into Mr Munden's head ... He flew to the poor harmless animal, seized it by the neck, and throwing it with his whole force against the carved work of the marble chimney, its tender frame was dashed to pieces' (449). Munden acts out the symbolism of Betsy's dream in his crushing of the squirrel against the architecture of the house. The cruelty Munden shows to Betsy's pet takes on an added dimension in light of the fact that the squirrel was originally a gift from Trueworth. Munden can destroy both Betsy's former self and her fantasies in his acts of aggression; his 'whole force' stands behind his authority as a husband. Lest we think that Munden represents some kind of aberration, we only need to consider his name, a name which points to his mundane status, his averageness. The French connotation of the name – 'mondain' – further implies his worldliness and the privilege he enjoys in London, the city whose name rhymes with his. Indeed, Munden only confirms what other representations of men in the text imply – that men are authorized to deal with women in whatever manner they see fit. Betsy's imprisonment increasingly appears less a result of her poor judgment in choosing a husband than as a general phenomenon. Thomas Thoughtless keeps a mistress after having pressured Betsy into marriage in order to save the family name, and even Trueworth and his friend Sir Bazil indulge in libertine pleasures before marriage. The text never indicates how these men become virtuous subjects after marrying, and social custom does not appear forceful enough to ensure male obedience to marriage vows.

The social realism that characterizes the novel's representation of marriage reminds us of Lovelace's cynical remarks about 'the usual married life of brawl and contradiction.'[21] Betsy's *Bildungsroman* entails increasing degrees of humiliation, insisting on close ties between subjection and female subjectivity. Betsy's isolation in the marriage household prevents her from participating in the spectacles she enjoys, and in fact turns her visual pleasure into yet another scene of humiliation. Visiting a noble peer whose patronage her husband seeks, Betsy is attacked once again. Unlike the admiration that Betsy enjoyed as a single woman, which implied socially condoned courtship, now male praise only threatens her with a ruined social position. The peer's attack highlights the degree to which Betsy is unable to enjoy herself in the public realm without risk. While the home also represents a dangerous space for Betsy, it nonetheless remains the only place where she can avoid public censure.

The narrator chastises Betsy for courting the Lord's attention; the heroine becomes the blameworthy victim for the purpose of the novel's moralizing: 'It must be acknowledged, for it but too plainly appears from every circumstance of this lady's conduct both before and after marriage, that the unhappy propensity in her nature, for attracting universal admiration, rendered her little regardful either of the guilt, or the disquiets to which her beauty was accessory' (483). The peer's attempt on Betsy brings about the education the narrative suggests she needs because it forecloses, once and for all, Betsy's desire to act as a public spectacle. Now Betsy can become suitably 'regardful,' having learnt that the kind of vision she previously enjoyed now only means one thing: scandal. But the novel's attempt to assert the virtuous outcome of Betsy's humiliation is undermined by the social critique that the narrative's representations of male violence has produced. Given our sympathy for the heroine and the repulsiveness of the men who attack her, the text cannot sustain its alignment of Betsy's defeat with moral victory. The tension that emerges between the novel's pleasure and its instruction culminates in a release of the moral pressure valve, a release that allows the remainder of the narrative to serve as a type of wish-fulfilment for Betsy. While the dénouement appears to be generated by Betsy's newly developed virtue, in fact the narrative returns for its final impetus to the dynamics of vision and visibility that set the terms for its earlier representations of Betsy's scandalous behaviour.

The fantasy begins to unfold when Betsy separates from her abusive husband, a separation that coincides with the achievement of a new level of seriousness in Betsy's thought and manner. Contemplating her separation, Betsy reflects on its necessity in abstract terms: 'Yet she thought if she had acted otherwise, it would have been an injustice not only to herself, but to all wives in general, by setting them an example of submitting to things required of them neither by law nor nature' (531). In contrast to her earlier representation as a local specimen of vanity, Betsy now appears as a general ideal, a victim of injustice. Defined in this capacity Betsy's public status takes on a new meaning; Betsy is now exemplary rather than scandalous. The power Betsy gains from this position is summed up in her ability to turn the threat of scandal against her husband. Her lawyer warns Munden that '"when the affairs of a family are laid open, and every dispute between the husband and the wife exposed before a court of judicature, or even in a petition to a lord chancellor, the whole becomes a public talk, and furnishes a matter of ridicule for the unthinking scoffers of the Age,"' creating a singular moment when public surveillance appears to control a man (534). The language that the lawyer uses links public talk to public voyeurism, suggesting that Munden's refusal to settle his disputes with his wife out of court will automatically grant society visual access – his affairs will be 'laid open' – to his marriage, leaving him 'exposed' in the public domain. Having suffered her husband's abuse without retaliating, Betsy can now claim the moral upper hand and align the public gaze with her own. Betsy withdraws from the public realm, leaving her lawyer to claim her rights within it, a movement that further consolidates her virtuous status. In a private home in Surrey, Betsy believes herself to have escaped all of the dangers London represents, even as she publicly claims her rights.

It is not so much public scandal that Betsy fears as private embarrassment: 'This private recess seemed a certain defence against the sight of Mr Trueworth' (540). As when Betsy feared discovery in her theft of the portrait, the meaning of the threat Trueworth poses is ambivalent. Betsy wants to avoid having Trueworth see her in her socially embarrassed state. Does Betsy fear that Trueworth will consider her marriage crisis a reflection on her past behaviour? Or does Betsy imagine that the feelings she experienced upon hearing of Mrs. Trueworth's untimely death will resurface if Trueworth appears? In either case, Betsy seeks privacy as a means of maintaining control over the character she has constructed for herself, in both its rebellious and dutiful forms. The ambiguity of Betsy's fear is further heightened by the phrasing of the sentence: does Betsy fear seeing Trueworth and exposing her feelings in her looks, or does she fear that his 'sight' will penetrate the surface that, until now, she has managed to render opaque?

The fear of having her transgressive fantasies revealed appears the most salient feature of Betsy's avoidance of Trueworth, for it soon becomes evident that self-abasing remorse does not entirely govern Betsy's ruminations. Lamenting her failure to marry Trueworth when she had the chance, Betsy thinks, '"My reason – nay my very pride, might have influenced me to embrace a proposal, which would have rendered me the envy of my own sex, and excited the esteem and veneration of the other"' (538). While the narrator comments on this scene as constitutive of Betsy's new understanding of the merits of virtue, it more strikingly highlights the extent to which Betsy remains attached to her old dreams of glamour and universal admiration. The realization of Betsy's dreams of a marriage to Trueworth depends not so much on her ability to give up the pleasure she gains from attracting everybody's attention as on her ability to privatize the powers she commands as a spectacle. Betsy needs to incorporate a measure of privacy into her understanding of herself in order that she might appear suited, rather than hostile, to the domestic sphere. The domestic sphere, in turn, must be idealized so as to grant Betsy visual agency. Trueworth's portrait serves as the device that facilitates both transformations.[22] Standing in a garden in her nightclothes, Betsy contemplates Trueworth in miniature:[23]

> 'Though I no more must see himself,' said she, 'I may at least be allowed to pay the tribute of my gratitude to this dumb representative of the man to whom I have been so much obliged.' – At this instant, a thousand proofs of love given her by the original of the copy in her hand occurring all at once to her remembrance, tears filled her eyes, and her breast swelled with involuntary sighs.
>
> In this painfully pleasing amusement did she continue for some time, and had doubtless done so much longer, if a sudden rustling among the leaves behind her, had not made her turn her head to see what had occasioned it; – but where are the words that can express the surprize, the wild confusion she was in, when the first glance of her eyes presented her with the sight of the real object, whose image she had been thus tenderly contemplating. (542)

At first glance Betsy's sentimental effusions over the miniature appear to register her innocent appreciation of Trueworth's value. Her outburst of feeling indicates that Betsy can be moved by art in an appropriate fashion, rather than simply desiring to possess and consume it. Betsy has fallen into line with the ways of seeing Haywood advocates in *The Female Spectator:* 'These representations on the canvas, I say, will remain in our remembrance when the object is withdrawn, and cannot but inspire us

1. Joshua Reynolds, *Kitty Fisher as Cleopatra Dissolving the Pearl*, 1759. The Iveagh Bequest, London.

2. Thomas Gainsborough, *Grace Dalrymple Elliot*, 1782. Copyright the Frick Collection, New York.

3. Thomas Gainsborough, *Grace Dalrymple Elliot*, 1778. All rights reserved, The Metropolitan Museum of Art.

4. Joseph Highmore, *Elizabeth Harris*, 1748. Private Collection: photograph Courtauld Institute of Art.

5. Thomas Hudson, *Mary, Lady Wray* (d. 1751), date unknown. The Lady Braye. Photograph Courtauld Institute of Art.

6. George Romney, *Lady McLeod*, 1788. Photograph Sotheby's.

7. Thomas Gainsborough, *Lady with a Spaniel*, c. 1750. Courtesy of The Huntington Library, Art Galleries, and Botanical Gardens, San Marino, California.

8. Joshua Reynolds, *Emily, Countess of Kildare*, 1763. Private Collection: photograph Courtauld Institute of Art.

9. John Russell, *Miss Chambers*, 1792. The Viscount Cowdray. Photograph Courtauld Institute of Art.

10. Joshua Reynolds, *A Girl Reading*, 1771. Photograph The Paul Mellon Centre for Studies in British Art, London.

11. George Romney, *Serena*, date unknown. The Sutherland Trust.

12. Joseph Wright of Derby, *A Girl Reading a Letter by Candlelight, with a Young Man Peering Over Her Shoulder,* c. 1760–2. Lt. Col. R.S. Nelthorpe.

13. Joseph Wright of Derby, *A Girl Reading a Letter by Candlelight, with an Old Man Peering Over Her Shoulder*, c. 1767–70. Private Collection.

14. Joshua Reynolds, *Kitty Fisher*, 1759. Petworth House (The National Trust). Photograph Courtauld Institute of Art.

15. William Hogarth, *Miss Mary Edwards*, 1742. Copyright The Frick Collection, New York.

16. Peter Lely, *Portrait of Louise de Keroualle, Duchess of Portsmouth*, c. 1672. The J. Paul Getty Museum, Los Angeles, California.

17. Peter Lely, *Nell Gwyn and Her Infant Son the Duke of St Albans* (sometimes known as *Venus and Cupid*), c. 1665. By permission of the Trustees of the Denys Eyre Bower, Chiddingstone Castle, Kent.

18. Simon Verelst, *Nell Gwyn*, c. 1690. By courtesy of the National Portrait Gallery, London.

19. Artist unknown, possibly Hogarth, *Peg Woffington*, c. 1730–40. The Garrick Club. Photograph E.T. Archive, London.

20. Edward Haytley, *Miss E. Wandesford*, 1753. Photograph Sotheby's.

21. Edward Haytley, *Sir Roger and Lady Bradshaigh*, 1746. Courtesy of the Wigan Heritage Services.

22. Thomas Hudson, *Anne Bouverie*, 1749. Private Collection. Photograph Courtauld Institute of Art.

23. Philip Mercier, *Peg Woffington*, c. 1735. The Garrick Collection. Photograph E.T. Archive, London.

24. Thomas Gainsborough, *Mary 'Perdita' Robinson*, 1781. Reproduced by permission of the Trustees of the Wallace Collection.

25. Joshua Reynolds, *Laurence Sterne*, 1760. By courtesy of the National Portrait Gallery, London.

26. Caricature of Elizabeth Lumley Sterne, wife of Laurence Sterne (putative). All reasonable effort has been made to find the owner of this picture.

27. Angelica Kauffman, *Self-Portrait*, c. 1770–5. By courtesy of the National Portrait Gallery, London.

28. Angelica Kauffman, *Self-Portrait in the Character of Painting Embraced by Poetry*, 1782. Iveagh Bequest (National Trust).

29. Angelica Kauffman, *Self-Portrait: Hesitating between the Arts of Music and Painting*, 1791. Reproduced by kind permission of the Winn Family and the National Trust (Nostell Priory).

with ideas at once delightful and instructive: – they will afford us an agreeable entertainment within ourselves, and we shall no longer be under a necessity of seeking it elsewhere.'[24] The miniature stands as the lesson of all Betsy has learnt about pride and prejudice; a desire for contemplation and introspection has replaced a love of the superficial pleasures of London society. Betsy has learnt to 'read' the visual correctly as a result of her sufferings.

But the appearance of Trueworth dramatically undermines the moral model of spectatorship that the scene first presents, transforming the description into a scene from an amatory tale or even a pornographic text, and suggests that the miniature serves as the occasion for the framing of Betsy as an erotic tableau. The erotic elements that the scene already contains in its language of swelling breasts and involuntary sighs now come to the fore as the visual field triangulates itself around the points of the portrait, Betsy, and Trueworth. Not only do Trueworth's viewpoint and the reader's perspective merge into one eroticized spectatorial position, but the nature of Betsy's gaze radically alters as well. Having Trueworth step out of the hedge into the garden transforms Betsy's gaze into that of Pygmalion's, with an added dimension. Betsy both brings the representation that she loves to life and transforms her own identity as a static object of consumption into an active principle that establishes new social relations: Trueworth cannot resist the impulse to break into the moment of beholding. The representation becomes flesh and blood, and in doing so it makes manifest all of the erotic potential inherent in Betsy's spectatorial activities, as the description of Trueworth's response to the scene proves:

> But what was his amazement to find it was his own picture! that very picture, which had been taken from the painter's, was the object of her meditations! – he heard her sighs, he saw her lovely hand frequently put up to wipe away the tears that fell from her eyes while looking on it; – he also saw her more than once, though doubtless in those moments not knowing what she did, press the lifeless image to her bosom with the utmost tenderness. (543)

Trueworth's voyeurism transforms the meaning of Betsy's private meditation without robbing her of the virtue that accrues to her spectatorial activity, for she does not know Trueworth watches her. The body speaks unconsciously what virtue attempts to conceal. Only by presenting Trueworth's vision can the scene make manifest the double meaning of

Betsy's activities with the portrait. The portrait organizes a variety of perspectives, all of which complicate the sentimental tableau the passage initially presents.

The eroticism foregrounded in Trueworth's vision expands to encompass not only Betsy's spectatorial activities, but also Betsy herself: 'Though she was in the most negligent night-dress that could be, she seemed as lovely to him as ever; all his first flames rekindled in his heart, while gazing on her with this uninterrupted freedom' (543). The passage attempts to qualify the eroticism of the moment by implying that Betsy's state of undress renders her less, rather than more, attractive, but the effect of Betsy's half-naked appearance is unmistakable. Trueworth regresses to a state of infatuation as Betsy's earlier propensity to attract men with her physical charms reemerges in all of its force. Her virtue is guaranteed by the involuntary nature of the seduction, but the effect remains the same: Betsy wins back Trueworth's affection by demonstrating desire for him in the spectacle of her body. The spectacle, however, is private, and later, when a maid retrieves the miniature that Betsy has dropped in her confusion, Betsy is able to reclaim it without guilt: 'She was rejoiced indeed to have this picture once more in her possession ... because she thought she might indulge herself in looking on it, without any breach of that duty, to which she was resolved so strictly to adhere' (547).

Conveniently Betsy's husband dies at precisely the moment Betsy resolves on her new life of virtuous retirement. As a result, Betsy can reap the benefits of her garden encounter with Trueworth, who, himself recently widowed, declares himself as a suitor once again. At the same time, the narrative can hold up Betsy's transformation as the result of her new understanding of virtue and its rewards. Nonetheless, the marriage plot that soon unfolds takes a page from *Cinderella* rather than from *Clarissa*. The language of Trueworth's arrival at the country seat where Betsy spends her year of widowhood reminds us of Betsy's investment in the visual pleasures of an excessive spectacle: 'The first object that presented itself to them [Lady Trusty and Betsy], was a very neat running footman, who on the gate being opened, came tripping up towards the house, and was immediately followed by a coach with one gentleman in it, drawn by six prancing horses, and attended by two servants in rich liveries, and well mounted' (564). While the narrative asserts that Betsy is able to enter into a marriage with Trueworth as a result of her 'education,' it is obvious that marriage to Trueworth, by virtue of his wealth, will enable Betsy to reclaim the pleasures she enjoyed as a single woman.

Trueworth's value lies not so much in his moral character as in his financial ability to transform marriage into a less enslaving institution for Betsy. 'Trueworth' becomes as much a measure of material security as of sentimental attachment.

Much like Cleland's *Memoirs of a Woman of Pleasure*, Haywood's narrative creates a comic ending that undermines the moral of the story, despite its protestations to the contrary: 'Thus were the virtues of our heroine (those follies that had defaced them being fully corrected) at length rewarded with a happiness, retarded only till she had render'd herself wholly worthy of receiving it' (568). Haywood finally relinquishes the demands of didacticism when their cost appears too high for her heroine, and the conclusion of the novel overcomes the obtrusiveness of the narrator's moralizing tone by endorsing the type of fantasy that Betsy was originally condemned for indulging. Ros Ballaster argues that 'The ebullient resilience of Behn's and Manley's narcissistic self-representations is nowhere in evidence in the fiction of Haywood,'[25] but *Betsy Thoughtless* challenges this assertion. The kind of spectatorial role that Betsy assumes vis-à-vis Trueworth's portrait imitates the dynamics at work in the novels of Behn and Manley. *Betsy Thoughtless*'s flights into the realm of amatory fiction take on a particularly significant role in light of the context in which they first appeared, for Haywood's eroticized narrative renders the fit between fiction, discipline, and desire a difficult one. Mary Delany's comment concerning Haywood's status as a 'frivolous author' indicates the extent to which the imperatives of virtue and the comic vision Haywood upheld could not yet work together in 1751.

Amelia: The Miniature in the Public Sphere

The model of spectatorship that I have defined as central to the workings of *Betsy Thoughtless* establishes the visibility of the female body as a means of creating narrative coherence and resolution. This female body is not without a visual agency of its own; Betsy understands her own ability to see as linked to her power to represent herself in the world as a spectacle. Haywood's mitigation of the Richardsonian aesthetic emerges in part from her past career in amatory tales, and in part from a desire to avoid the tragic aspect of Richardson's moral code. Fielding's *Amelia*, while emulating *Clarissa* in many respects, also resists the totalizing force of Richardson's agenda and its advocacy of death as the guarantor of virtue, but this resistance emerges in a different form than in Haywood's novel. In particular, the realism that colours *Amelia* serves not only as a means of social critique but also as a means of granting Amelia more authority than her author may have intended she find in his narrative. Fielding's heroine is idealized, but she always remains firmly rooted in social practices, which in turn modify the idealizing impulses governing Amelia's representation. Rather than seeking solace from the harsh lessons of *Clarissa* by having fantasy come to the rescue, as in *Betsy Thoughtless*, *Amelia* allows the material world to work for its heroine.

The question of Fielding's relation to his heroine is vexed. My analyses of the works this study has analysed so far claim that Manley, Richardson, and Haywood explicitly support women's rights to both private and public autonomy. It is more difficult, I believe, to make such a claim for Henry Fielding.[26] As J. Paul Hunter has aptly observed, 'Given the guarded portrayals of women in the earlier novels, *Amelia* is for Fielding something of a risk, a challenge to his own double standard of morality and his own personal frets and fears,' and Jill Campbell has noted Fielding's anxiety that Amelia may 'take on a separate and even punishing authority of her own.'[27] Campbell reads the character as escaping, in part, her author's intentions, and I will likewise read Fielding's representation in a deconstructive vein.[28]

The differences between Fielding and Haywood appear in their representations of the heroine's body. In *Betsy Thoughtless*, the heroine's beauty produces the scandal of her body; in Fielding's novel, Amelia's broken nose, as well as her beauty, attracts attention. In 1751 this broken nose featured importantly in the novel's critical reception and demise. 'Beat all to pieces' early in the narrative,[29] the nose immediately became the target of Fielding's detractors, who pointed to the iconographic link it established between Amelia and the less reputable Blear-Eyed Moll. As Frederic T. Blanchard has suggested, 'The reputation of the pure and womanly Amelia, owing to the unfortunate slip about her nose, was reduced to that of a common strumpet.' Fielding attempted to defend his heroine by admitting his error in forgetting to repair her nose, but to no avail; the damage was done: 'As we take into account the incessant scurrility which was directed at the ill-starred heroine, Dr. Johnson's assertion to the effect that the sale of *Amelia* ... was spoiled by that "vile broken nose," is seen to be, in the main, a statement of actual fact.'[30]

Since the eighteenth century, Fielding's 'favourite Child' has fully recovered from the scandal that initially overwhelmed her.[31] In Fielding criticism Amelia has been identified as 'the ideal wife,' the embodiment of moral courage,' and 'the ethical center of the novel';[32] feminist critics have also viewed Amelia as singularly virtuous, though they are less enthusiastic about the ideas behind Fielding's characterization of his heroine. Patricia Meyer Spacks, for example, argues that Amelia represents a male fantasy of female subjectivity governed by 'unchanging structures of feeling'; 'Amelia in her fidelity and changelessness has a mythic aura, as though she existed outside of time.'[33] But the questions raised by the novel's early detractors are worth pursuing. Though Fielding took care to add a few sentences which repaired Amelia's nose in his preparation of the novel's second edition, its initial beating remains a curious component of the narrative. The battered nose generates an ambiguity of character which most critics are more inclined to grant to Mrs. Bennet/Atkinson and Miss Mathews. I will present here an answer to the riddle of Amelia's nose while addressing a larger question: in what terms does Fielding, author of *Shamela*, conceptualize a woman of virtue in the context of a moral universe which has become irredeemably compromised?

Jill Campbell has argued that 'there are a number of ways in which the character Amelia may slip the moorings of her safely "feminine" identity, as constructed for masculine ends, and raise at least the possibility of real female moral power.'[34] As we shall see, the question of Amelia's virtue is most intensely focused on a portrait of the broken-nosed heroine, a miniature Amelia that circulates in the world of the novel just as *Amelia* circulates in the world outside. The remainder of this chapter will analyse how the miniature portrait serves as the means by which Amelia is able to become unmoored from her narrative idealization. In particular, the miniature's intensification of the portrait viewing experience marks the pressure that is placed on the idea of private interests and their ability to sustain a coherent vision of women's social role. The miniature portrait of Amelia elicits not only the gaze of others, but stands for the possibility that Amelia may have a gaze of her own, an agency as a spectacle that she can exert, if only fitfully and sporadically, in her quest to establish a greater security for herself and her family in the dark underworld that the Booths inhabit in London. As in the images of women and their miniatures I examined earlier in this chapter, the representation of Amelia and her portrait creates a heightened sense of the theatricality of the visual moment that women inhabit. Amelia's miniature becomes the means by which Fielding's heroine, like Haywood's, is able to manipulate those theatrics to her advantage.

Fielding's anxious relation to the question of female visibility and subjectivity is apparent from the start of the novel. Two moments in the opening chapters establish the problematical nature of interpreting female character by 'reading' visual signs. The first scene takes place in the prison:

> A very pretty Girl then advanced towards them, whose Beauty Mr. *Booth* could not help admiring the Moment he saw her; declaring, at the same time, he thought she had great Innocence in her Countenance. *Robinson* said she was committed thither as an idle and disorderly Person, and a common Street-walker. (33)

The immediate difficulty facing Booth and the reader is that the beautiful face bears no relation to virtue – that it in fact serves as a mask, covering the disease and corruption inherent in the prostitute's body. Booth's cheerful optimism marks him not as a man of Good Heart but as dangerously naïve.[35] The interpretive community that in *Tom Jones* ensured an understanding between the narrator and the reader breaks down here, and we are forced to choose between Booth's innocent blindness and Robinson's cynical insight. The prison marks the absence of a moral context within which we might make an informed decision about the streetwalker, and it is unclear how we can discover for ourselves what Robinson already knows.

The potential for visual signs to act duplicitously reemerges even more menacingly a few pages later, when the narrator recounts a personal anecdote reminiscent of the scene that has just transpired between Booth and Robinson:

> One of the Ladies, I remember, said to the other – 'Did you ever see any thing look so modest and so innocent as that Girl over the way?' ... Now this Lady was no bad Physiognomist; for it was impossible to conceive a greater Appearance of Modesty, Innocence and Simplicity, than what Nature had displayed in the Countenance of that Girl; and yet, all Appearances notwithstanding, I myself (remember, Critic, it was in my Youth) had a few Mornings before seen that very identical Picture of all those ingaging Qualities in Bed with a Rake at a Bagnio, smoking Tobacco, drinking Punch, talking Obscenity, and swearing and cursing with all the Impudence and Impiety of the lowest and most abandoned Trull of a Soldier. (47)

This passage is meant to warn us against Miss Mathews (who is busy seducing Booth at the moment of this narrative intrusion) and, more generally, to act as a commentary on the opacity of women's nature: what you see is not necessarily what you get. In the above passage the narrator assumes the position which Robinson took up vis-à-vis Booth, confronting an idealistic belief in the correspondence between surface and depth with a profound suspicion of the posturing of innocence. Fielding offers the reader no advice but rather abandons the unwary to his gullibility; in fact, the only hope for knowledge seems to involve participation in the world's corruption – in this case, a visit to the bawdyhouse.[36]

The crux of the matter rests upon the 'identical Picture of all those ingaging Qualities.' Unlike the first scene, where Booth thought he saw innocence in the prostitute's face (and so perhaps had misinterpreted her look), here we are confronted with the certain knowledge that the look interpreted by 'no bad Physiognomist' *is* identical with the usual expression of the whore. The 'ingaging Qualities' can have no intrinsically moral meaning if they are the same at the opera and in the bagnio, and so the question of what, exactly, is engaging the viewer becomes the critical issue for the reader. Within this sceptical paradigm, Booth's 'admiration' for the young lady appears to be possibly tainted by lust. As Allan Wendt has argued, Fielding appreciates the fact that erotic desire can render moral ideals appealing, but when the object changes from Sophia Western to a prostitute, the happy marriage of desire and ethics is placed in jeopardy. The moral virtue which the viewer attributes to the prostitute is only a *trompe-l'œil*, a facade which renders the innocent gaze dubious if only by revealing its lack of discernment.[37]

Like Haywood's, part of Fielding's move toward a Richardsonian ideal involves reconfiguring female visibility in order to avoid the type of dilemmas produced by the prostitutes' bodies. But unlike Haywood, Fielding idealizes the spectacle that his heroine sustains, rather than attempting to remove it from the visual field. In her moralizing mode Haywood advocates that women remain inconspicuous, but Fielding hopes that the representation of an ideal woman will serve an iconographic function. Amelia's physical appearance is identical with her moral excellence, and her broken nose provides an important link in this chain of correspondence. Booth places the destruction of Amelia's nose at the centre of his courtship history: 'The Injury done to her Beauty by the overturning of a Chaise, by which, as you may well remember, her lovely Nose was beat all to pieces, gave me an Assurance that the Woman who had been so much adored for the Charms of her Person, deserved a much higher Adoration to be paid to her Mind' (66). Brian McCrea has argued that Amelia's broken nose advances Booth's suit by eliminating competitors of higher social rank: 'the injured nose places her within [Booth's reach].'[38] However, Amelia is never presented as a woman who would marry out of self-interest, and it is crucial we believe that her love match with Booth transcends material concerns. George E. Haggerty reads the broken nose as 'the ideological symptom of sensibility in Amelia,' and argues that her disfigurement stands as the sign of her husband's sexual guilt, projected onto the figure of woman as 'a form of contamination.'[39] The question remains, nonetheless: why does the narrative introduce such a loaded sign into its figuration of the heroine, given that Fielding was aware (as his representation of Blear-Eyed Moll indicates) of the popular understanding of a deformed nose as a sign of either syphilis or the remains of an attack usually made on prostitutes? This curious choice of site for the disfiguration of Amelia may have its roots in Fielding's willingness to make his heroines the butt of low-humour jokes and innuendos. But certainly this misogynist humour remains only as a vestigial trace in *Amelia*, for the novel tries tremendously hard to lift its heroine above the muck that Sophia falls into in *Tom Jones*.

It is significant that Amelia's battered nose links her to Charlotte Cradock, an allusion that Richardson caught in 1752: 'Amelia, even to her noselessness, is again [Fielding's] first wife.'[40] Fielding's decision to model Amelia after his deceased wife, even to the point of highlighting a physical flaw, adds to the novel's mimetic impulse and the atmosphere of individualized affect Fielding establishes around his heroine.[41] Most importantly, the nose marks Amelia, not as socially humiliated, but as morally superior, with a 'Mind' deserving 'a much higher Adoration.' The scene in which she unmasks herself after the accident suggests how the visual and the moral may work together:

> I begged her to indulge my Curiosity by shewing me her Face. She answered in a most obliging Manner, 'Perhaps, Mr. *Booth*, you will as little know me when my Mask is off as when it is on;' and at the same instant unmasked. – The Surgeon's Skill was the least I considered. A thousand tender Ideas rushed all at once on my Mind. I was unable to contain myself, and eagerly kissing her Hand, I cried – 'Upon my Soul, Madam, you never appeared to me so lovely as at this Instant.' (68)

Amelia's statement warns Booth against disappointment, but we never discover what the visual grounds for Booth's response might be. As Terry Castle points out, 'We are left only with the paradoxical assertion that disfigured, Amelia is not only still beautiful, but somehow more beautiful than before.'[42] This paradox defines Amelia's nature and separates her from the women Fielding fears most, women whose moral disfigurement coincides with a blameless countenance.[43]

Fielding is not simply stressing Booth's admiration of Amelia's mind in this scene, for the moment is narrated as an intensely visual revelation. On the one hand, the absence of description about Amelia's appearance and the presence of our awareness of Amelia's disfiguration effectively prevent us from imagining a conventional beauty who might arouse us. Fielding's silence at this crucial moment stands in sharp contrast to his intensely detailed and eroticized account of Sophia Western's beauty in *Tom Jones*.[44] This shift foregrounds Fielding's move toward an aesthetic Richardson also strives to achieve in the concluding pages of *Clarissa*. The *Spectator* formulated this aesthetic earlier in the century in almost exactly the same terms: 'When *Adam* is introduc'd by *Milton* describing *Eve* in Paradise ... he does not represent her like a *Grecian Venus* by her Shape or Features, but by the Lustre of her Mind which shone in them, and gave them their Power of charming.'[45] Instead of allowing us an erotic response as a means of ensuring our sympathy for the heroine, Fielding directs our attention toward Amelia's modesty. It is this modesty that, given the dearth of physical detail, seems in itself to inspire Booth's enthusiastic response.

On the other hand, we can guess (and later it is confirmed) that Amelia bears a scar on her nose. The scar grants Amelia a particularity, and it is this particularity that becomes linked to a moral standard. Unlike the allusion to the Venus de Medici which, in *Tom Jones*, establishes Sophia's appeal as universal, here the presence of a scar renders Amelia's beauty ideal. It does so because it identifies Amelia's beauty as unexchangeable; it cannot be compared to that of other women or be judged by traditional standards. In other words, Amelia's looks can be translated only in reference to Amelia's moral character. Thus the effect of *not* describing Amelia's beauty in conventional terms serves to render it singular. Castle suggests that the moment of Amelia's unmasking produces a type of 'dialectical confusion,'[46] but I would argue that it achieves the opposite effect. Amelia's beauty is unambiguous because her moral purity makes it so. Amelia's face cannot shock when unmasked because it is always identical with Amelia's self. Booth is rewarded for his ability to appreciate Amelia's new beauty with a wife truly singular in her virtue.

Amelia's beauty finds its only visual representation in a miniature portrait that is stolen early in the narrative. Just as Trueworth's portrait is meant to reveal the real worth of the individual it represents and incite a model of virtuous spectatorship, so Amelia's miniature appears to confirm the accessibility and transparency of the heroine's meaning, although we never discover whether the portrait depicts Amelia before or after the accident that scars her nose. Wendorf has observed that in the eighteenth century the miniature portrait constructed 'the cult of the private and carefully individuated subject, represented in a simple and direct manner that severed almost all ties with its iconic forebears.'[47] Given Fielding's interest in visual aesthetics, this observation casts light on the significance of the miniature portrait in *Amelia*. In earlier novels, Fielding was more likely to allude to Hogarth's satiric prints, as in his description of Bridget Allworthy as the figure represented in Hogarth's *Morning*. The turn towards the non-satiric Hogarth – Hogarth the portrait painter – marks the difference between the understanding of female character informing his representation of Sophia Western and the new ideas revealed in his characterization of Amelia.

In both *Betsy Thoughtless* and *Amelia*, the smallness of the miniatures indicates their preciousness and enables them to take on an intensely sentimental value as objects. Their visual impact, nonetheless, is always larger than one might expect, as the portraits come to stand for the individuals they represent. Despite their function as sentimental tropes, the portraits in both *Betsy Thoughtless* and *Amelia* inevitably raise more questions than they answer by virtue of the epistemological uncertainty they create in both their circulation as objects and in the moments of beholding that surround them. In *Amelia*, the act of replicating the visual experience the heroine creates seems to qualify the ideal of *non*-duplication that it initially represented. The theft of the portrait places even more stress on the paradigm of Amelia's unexchangeability that the narrative has so laboriously established. When Booth describes his departure for Gibraltar, he laments: 'What would I have then given for a little Picture of my dear Angel, which she had lost from her Chamber about a Month before? and which we had the highest Reason in the World to imagine her Sister had taken away' (108). Amelia's beauty, in replica, has now changed hands. Booth identifies the worth of the painting as residing, not in the jewels that surround it, but in its exact representation of Amelia: 'Next to *Amelia* herself, there was nothing which I valued so much as this little Picture: for such a Resemblance did it bear of the Original, that *Hogarth* himself did never, I believe, draw a stronger Likeness' (108–9). The miniature bears a relation both of similarity and contiguity to Amelia, its likeness generating a response so powerful that only the original has more worth in the catalogue of Booth's possessions. Booth's reference to Hogarth enlarges the miniature to the status of a full-sized portrait (since Hogarth did not paint miniatures), a gesture which further establishes the painting's verisimilitude and its proximity to Amelia's body.[48] Booth's description of the enormous worth he attaches to the miniature places Amelia and the visual representation of her face on a continuum of value, one which will take on a new significance in the context of London, where commerce and virtue meet and clash.

For Haywood London represents both a place of danger and a space where women can escape the seclusion imposed on them in the country; London is threatening but it is also immensely pleasurable. For Fielding London only enables violence and degradation. The London that the novel represents so darkly has become morally bankrupt as a result of its unwillingness to pursue any but financial goals. Fielding identifies the problem immediately in his characterization of Judge Thrasher: 'The Justice was never indifferent in a Cause, but when he could get nothing on either Side' (21). Far from establishing bonds between men as members of a newly prosperous commercial society, money only serves to intensify the victimization of those without sufficient funds.[49] William Booth is imprisoned for the first of many times almost immediately after he and his wife arrive in London, simply because he lacks the money to secure his release from the constable who arrests him on the street.

For Amelia, commercial vice takes on a particularly gendered and menacing aspect. In London a woman's beauty is always understood to be for sale. Indeed, almost all social and commercial transactions lead back to some kind of prostitution. The Booths' plight seems to originate in their unwillingness to barter Amelia's virtue, and their naïve trust in the benevolence of the noble peer, 'cousin' of their landlady, is placed in exact opposition to the rules of the city: 'Few Men, as I have observed, have such disinterested Generosity as to serve a Husband the better, because they are in Love with his Wife, unless she will condescend to pay a Price beyond the Reach of a virtuous Woman' (193). Almost all of the characters the Booths meet and befriend – the Trents, the Jameses, Miss Mathews, Mrs Ellison, and even Mrs Atkinson – have found ways to advance themselves by exchanging women's sexual favours. More generally, Fielding is echoing Swift and other Augustans, who frequently represent the sins of modernity, and particularly of modern capital, in metaphors of the sexually diseased, and usually female, body, a body that manages to hide its disgusting interior behind a veneer of social respectability. The disease of commercial culture seems embodied in corrupt sexual behaviour which circulates, like money, unseen and unnamed.[50]

A striking instance of this analogy appears in Fielding's representation of the noble peer, who remains nameless throughout the text, though he is the most politically and financially powerful figure in the novel. Only the lord's death reveals his 'true' nature, when his 'amours' finally leave him 'so rotten, that he stunk above Ground' (532).

The difficulty of establishing an icon of virtue whose meaning cannot be misunderstood emerges in Fielding's attempt to render Amelia an active heroine in a place where no one will recognize her moral value. Unlike Betsy Thoughtless, who willingly ventures into the public fray, Amelia remains confined within the home, as restricted as Clarissa imprisoned in Lovelace's brothel; there is certainly, as Hunter points out, the same 'claustrophobic, smothering sense of frustration, panic, and doom' as in Richardson's novel.[51] Amelia's broken nose, which guaranteed her singularity in the country, only adds to the sense of her vulnerability in London. Mrs Ellison is delighted by Amelia's appearance, and upon the occasion of the women's first meeting the narrator remarks, 'I know not whether the little Scar on her Nose did not rather add to, than diminish her Beauty' (184). Fielding added this remark to the second edition of the novel, in order to remind his readers that Amelia's broken nose did heal.[52] But the narrative intrusion only adds an ironic twist to the scene, in light of Mrs Ellison's plan to literalize the symbolic meaning of the scarred nose by selling Amelia to the noble peer. The frequency with which Amelia becomes an object of desire in London confuses the earlier narrative trajectory aimed at establishing an ethical, rather than an erotic, aura around the heroine. The intensity of the erotic responses Amelia elicits places the reader in a curious scopic position: her praises are sung again and again, but only in order to account for yet another illicit passion. It is unclear how Fielding's ideal reader, presumably male, is meant to separate himself from these adulterous admirers.[53] Indeed, the narrator comes dangerously close to situating himself and the reader in the position occupied by the novel's libertines.

Unlike Richardson's heroine, Amelia seems entirely passive in her efforts to achieve moral good. Cynthia Griffin Wolff argues that 'Amelia's virtue is private, and its influence can be felt only in personal interaction,'[54] but it seems that even privately Amelia can effect very little change; her husband repeatedly acts in a manner so irresponsible as to be immoral, and the men who seek her favours seem undaunted by her repeated demonstrations of moral excellence. Fielding's reluctance to transform Amelia into a more aggressive heroine, coupled with his hyperbolic and intrusive pronouncements on her innocence, marks the gap between his and Richardson's confidence in women's ability to effect the moral transformation of society.[55]

In the context of London society, the private sphere is incapable of exerting moral pressure on the world outside of it. Rather than identify the home as a site of social transformation, Fielding seeks to preserve it as a refuge. In public, Amelia is unable to prevent the attacks on her virtue that she wards off, in however bungling and naïve a fashion, in her own home. At Vauxhall Amelia is accosted by two aristocratic young men; the presence of a clergyman and her children does nothing to thwart their attack: '"D–n me," says he that spoke first, and whom they called Jack, "I will have a Brush at her, if she belonged to the whole Convocation"' (396). Amelia is saved only by the arrival of Captain Trent:

> 'It is impossible,' cries my Lord, 'to know everyone. – I am sure, if I had known the Lady to be a Woman of Fashion, and an Acquaintance of Captain Trent, I should have said nothing disagreeable to her; but if I have, I ask her Pardon, and the Company's.' (398)

The problem of 'knowing' everyone, or indeed anyone, in London is Fielding's central concern. The social codes which the aristocracy should guarantee disappear when noblemen choose to disregard them, as no one else has the power to enforce them. Even at the moment Amelia is rescued she is compromised yet again, for it is her husband's friendship with Captain Trent, a notorious pimp, that saves her. 'A Woman of Fashion' means very little when coupled with 'an Acquaintance of Captain *Trent*.' Amelia's meaning is necessarily altered when she enters the corrupt public domain, and neither her appearance nor her actions can rectify that slippage. Increasingly the novel implicates all of its characters in the realm of moral turpitude; as Fielding himself observed, 'No Man, I believe, ever removed great Quantities of Dirt from any Place, without finding some of it sticking to his Skirts.'[56]

In *Betsy Thoughtless*, the entrapment that the heroine faces at her lowest moment has the aspect of visual domination. Betsy, like Amelia, finds herself incapable of circulating without being threatened with an attack. Haywood, however, does not believe that the domestic space serves as any kind of haven, and so she returns to the tropes of amatory fiction to create an escape route for her heroine. Fielding attempts to overcome the realities Amelia faces, not by turning to fantasy, but by reinvoking the visual code he established earlier in the narrative, which insisted on the fit between Amelia's virtue and her visual representation. The bridging of the chasm that has opened up in Amelia's character begins with the reunion of the long-lost portrait and its owner. In a scene far removed from the crowds of dissolutes who torment the Booths, the narrative reestablishes the sentimental value of Amelia's face. Amelia visits Serjeant Atkinson when he becomes ill, and he confesses his earlier theft of the portrait:

> 'Here then, Madam,' said he, 'is your Picture, I stole it when I was eighteen Years of Age, and have kept it ever since. It is set in Gold, with three little Diamonds; and yet I can truly say, it was not the Gold nor the Diamonds which I stole – it was that Face which, if I had been the Emperor of the World –' (482)

The sergeant's assumed moral integrity, closely tied to his lower-class origins, differentiates his passion from that of the novel's multiple adulterers. And yet the child-like innocence which characterizes sentimental heroes seems oddly compromised in Serjeant Atkinson, insofar as he has retained a secret which links him to other, less well-intentioned, bearers of illicit knowledge. Most significantly, the language of the above passage, which aims to separate Atkinson's love for Amelia's particular beauty from the lust it has elicited in London society, does not entirely escape the commercial mores of the city. The 'three little Diamonds' are diminutive, almost endearing, like Amelia; '"if I had been the Emperor of the World,"' Atkinson begins, before Amelia interrupts him. Atkinson wishes he had been in a position socially advantageous enough to woo Amelia, to buy, in effect, her beautiful face. Even within the confines of the sentimental, marriage and prostitution, explicitly linked in London society, form part of the same continuum.

The scene becomes even more complex when Amelia responds in an ambiguous manner to the sergeant's declaration of love:

> To say the Truth, without any Injury to her Chastity, that Heart which had stood firm as a Rock to all the Attacks of Title and Equipage, of Finery and Flattery, and which all the Treasures of the Universe could not have purchased, was yet a little softened by the plain, honest, modest, involuntary, delicate, heroic Passion of this poor and humble Swain; for whom, in spite of herself, she felt a momentary Tenderness and Complacence, at which *Booth*, if he had known it, would perhaps have been displeased. (482–3)

Amelia's response to Atkinson seems in part motivated by the lack of any danger his love might pose, a lack guaranteed by his status as a 'poor and humble Swain.' The narrator can sympathize with Amelia's momentary lapse because he knows it will not lead to any real transgression. But the humility of Atkinson also has the effect of rendering Amelia's response powerful, insofar as she allows herself to indulge in feelings of 'Tenderness and Complacence' outside of the confines of marriage. This self-authorization fits in with the larger Richardsonian effect the novel has been striving to create – Castle notes that the scene reveals traits of 'a more exacting psychological realism' – and marks the moment when Amelia finally achieves some degree of autonomy as a heroine.[57]

The effect of the psychological realism that characterizes this scene is a certain amount of epistemological disruption. The moment is transgressive both in its origins – the theft of the portrait – and in its dénouement – the revelation of Amelia's potential for feelings not solely determined by a domestic agenda. While we are meant to view Atkinson's restraint as moral, his declaration echoes the many immoral addresses made to Amelia elsewhere in the narrative. Amelia's response, however sympathetically represented, compromises her righteous status if only by indicating a degree of female agency that in his representations of other women in the novel Fielding defines as dangerous. Thus the portrait, reintroduced after such a long hiatus, does not allow the visual and the moral to dovetail in quite the way that we might have expected. Most importantly, neither category seems able to escape the demands of an increasingly commercialized society.

What follows the scene between Atkinson and Amelia confirms this discovery. The sentimental tableau which is meant to secure meaning outside of the workings of exchange becomes firmly lodged within its confines when Amelia takes the miniature, the catalyst for her exchange with Atkinson, and sells it:

> She was scarce able to walk in her present Condition; for the Case of poor *Atkinson* had much affected her tender Heart, and her Eyes had overflown with many Tears.
>
> It occurred likwise [*sic*] to her at present, that she had not a single Shilling in her Pocket, or at home, to provide Food for herself and her Family. In this situation she resolved to go immediately to the Pawnbroker whither she had gone before, and to deposite [*sic*] her Picture for what she

could raise upon it. She then immediately took a Chair, and put her Design in Execution. (487)

At this point the strain of protecting virtue from the taint of commercial transactions becomes pronounced. The consequence of having the pawnshop scene follow the love scene so directly is that it appears as though Amelia is banking on the response that her looks have elicited in Atkinson when she takes her portrait to the pawnshop. The narrative reassures us that 'the prettiest Face in the World ... was deposited, as of no Value into the Bargain' (487), but the value Atkinson places in Amelia's face and the value residing in the gold and diamonds in which the picture is set are confused by their common status as precious objects (487). Recognizing, perhaps, the futility of an affective exchange as a means of social survival, Amelia redetermines her own value, in all senses of the term.[58]

Steven J. Gores reads this moment as an unequivocal sign of Amelia's moral stature and its powers of transformation: 'Because her gift of self is performed with no possible selfish motivation, and because her performance is seen by Robinson as a pathetic scene, it has the effect of mobilizing the miniature's ability to represent her whole, original self, unscathed by the trickeries of lawyers and the irresponsibilities of Booth.'[59] I would argue the opposite: that the portrait's ability to function both as a piece of jewellery, with a pretty face thrown into the bargain, and as a representation of ideal beauty and moral excellence is essential to the restoration of the Booths to their previous state of innocence. As in *Betsy Thoughtless*, the miniature's multiple valences meet and merge at a narrative crossroad that renders competing visual economies inextricable. The portrait is the means by which Amelia becomes rich; it takes the place of selling her favours to the noble peer. Because this exchange accomplishes the same end as prostitution, it links sentimentalism to a materialist eroticism, as well as to the creation of a female spectacle capable of exerting an authority from within its frame. Moreover, the pawnbroker's admiring response to the portrait – '*Upon my Word this is the handsomest Face I ever saw in my Life*' – serves as the moral catalyst of the narrative (516). Robinson's voyeuristic desire to view the object of the pawnbroker's admiration immediately becomes transformed into a sentimental feeling when he recognizes Amelia: 'My Guilt immediately flew in my Face, and told me I had been Accessary to this Lady's Undoing' (516–17). The term 'Undoing' echoes the pawnbroker's description of Amelia as 'some undone Wretch' (516); the face which was meant to represent all that differentiated Amelia from morally ruined women becomes identical with them for a brief but crucial narrative moment.

Ironically, the comic ending of Fielding's novel is premised on the fact that Amelia takes *herself* to the market. Unlike Clarissa, Fielding's heroine is able to compromise without destroying herself. In fact, because Amelia is able to divide herself, both by sending Mrs Atkinson to the masquerade in her stead, and by selling the portrait which Booth and Atkinson believe to be, in both its metonymical and metaphorical capacities, Amelia herself, she can retrieve the wealth which will allow her to retreat from the violence of London society and so ensure her family's domestic tranquility. As its meaning proliferates, the portrait trope imitates the figure of Amelia's broken nose and its ability to work both as a sign of a type of control claimed by prostitutes and of an ideal virtue; the doubling of both kinds of iconography finally becomes enabling, rather than crippling, for Fielding's narrative.

Fielding's characterization of Amelia does not situate her 'outside of time,' as Spacks asserts,[60] but rather places her within an intricate social and economic dynamic. Spacks correctly points to Fielding's desire to maintain Amelia's status as an emblem of virtue, but she fails to notice the way in which he also works to grant her control over the visual field in which she and her portrait circulate. In Haywood's text the 'real' stands as the sign of Betsy's degradation, and in Fielding's text, for the most part, it plays a similar role. But the miniature enables social realism to work another way in *Amelia*, to facilitate, rather than foreclose, women's ability to act. Fielding's idealization of Amelia is usurped by a more pragmatic and enabling conception of female virtue. Amelia never assumes an active look as Betsy does, but her portrait's ability to generate a particular visual response creates the same social effect. Both Betsy and Amelia gain an idealized form of domestic tranquillity as a result of the visual dynamics they set in motion. Rather than disciplining these women, the male gaze in Haywood's and Fielding's novels responds to the dictates determined by the texts' heroines, just as it does, though at greater cost, in *Clarissa*.

Chapter Five

'Paint her to your own mind': Sterne's Concupiscible Narratives

She has got your picture, and likes it: but Marriott, and some other judges, agree that mine is the better.[1]

It is tempting to read the success that greeted the publication of *Tristram Shandy*'s first two volumes in 1759 as a watershed in the literary history of the eighteenth-century novel, a moment that allowed the genre to claim its transgressive elements without fear of reprisal, confident that the reading public would understand the limits of literary pleasure and how to manage the emotional excesses represented by the genre. But, as I argued in chapter 1, antinovel rhetoric was as powerful in 1759 as it was earlier in the century, and continued to complain about the damage inflicted by novels on their readers – especially young female readers. Sterne's success was made possible not by the genre's stability within later eighteenth-century cultural discourses, but by *Tristram Shandy*'s atypicality, by its provision of the reassurance the text's singularity created: that the novel being brought forth was clever enough to escape the banality – and its attendant evils – of the more prosaic texts appearing in their multitudes around the country. Both the satiric and sentimental representations that *Tristram Shandy* sustain announce themselves the product of an imagination unbound, despite the fact that, as we shall see, the novel draws extensively on and repeats the refrains of a range of discourses familiar to novel readers by 1759. But by making no references to the novel's English tradition and by aligning himself with Cervantes, Rabelais, and the Scriblerian satirists, Sterne ensured, for the most part, his novel's escape from the usual attacks.[2]

'Paint her to your own mind': Sterne's Concupiscible Narratives   151

In this chapter I approach Sterne's exploitation of the novel's form and ideas as one element of *Tristram Shandy's* success, but I also want to lay claim to the text's indebtedness and commitment to its predecessors. *Tristram Shandy* brings to the fore the central concerns of the novels we have examined so far, delighting in the scandalous eroticism of *The New Atalantis*, exploring the ramification of *Clarissa*'s sentimental authority, lingering over the fetishized nose, and engaging with the power of a woman who, like Betsy Thoughtless, lives outside of the confines of marriage. An astute reader of the genre it wants to use as its vehicle to fame, *Tristram Shandy* takes up the conversation regarding women's relation to the novel and exploits, wherever it can, the pleasure that women bring to the text. At the same time, Sterne's novel articulates a profound distrust of this pleasure's capacity to grant women any kind of cultural status, a distrust that manifests itself most explicitly in Sterne's last work, *A Sentimental Journey*.[3]

The tension created by Sterne's novel/antinovel pendulum takes as its fulcrum the trope of the portrait, a figure both appropriated for satiric purposes and embraced as a powerful tool for the exploration of the human psyche. This chapter will investigate Sterne's engagement with the portrait and modes of beholding in relation to the narrative encounters with the visual arts that we have already traced from Manley to Fielding.[4] In particular, I will focus attention on how Sterne draws upon another innovative artist of the period, William Hogarth, in his representation of the portrait and of the visual more generally. Each of the novels studied in previous chapters implicitly challenges the tenets of neoclassical aesthetic theory and its celebration of the spectator emptied of desire, but Sterne makes this challenge explicit in his endorsement of Hogarth's aesthetic, echoing a commitment to the artist who also appears in Fielding's novels. But unlike Fielding, who was forced to temper his attachment to a Hogarthian world view in the writing of *Amelia*, Sterne is able to translate Hogarth into a language of the novel that takes as much from *Tom Jones* as it does from *Clarissa*. In particular, Sterne uses the language of art theory, including its understanding of the portrait and private interests, as a means of illuminating controversies surrounding the novel's relation to women's cultural status and activities; in doing so, Sterne not only draws on Hogarth, but substantially revises the artist's account of beholding by introducing the female spectator into the field of vision as a way of rendering Hogarth's aesthetic theory novel-friendly in a sentimental world.[5]

152   Private Interests

Tristram Shandy's Visual Poetics

In evoking the figures of both Joshua Reynolds and William Hogarth in *Tristram Shandy*, Sterne exploits an ongoing battle, in the world of art theory and practice, between Shaftesbury's followers and their competitors. Ronald Paulson argues in his essay 'English Painting – One School or Two?' that the language John Barrell has described as the discourse of 'civic humanism,' established in Shaftesbury's writings early in the century, encountered resistance right up until the Royal Academy's founding in 1769.[6] Before 1769, Hogarth's theories and practices provided an antiacademic model that influenced painters as varied as Benjamin West and Joseph Wright of Derby. Although Sterne mentions Hogarth explicitly only once in *Tristram Shandy*, in a passing reference to *The Analysis of Beauty* – 'if you have not [read it], I wish you would,' Tristram declares as he begins his description of Dr Slop (1: 121) – the novel remains, at heart, a Hogarthian text. As William V. Holtz has argued, the comic tone of the novel echoes Hogarth's own proclivity for eliciting laughter in the representation of the indecorous; the connection between the two artists emerges even more strikingly, Holtz notes, 'if we compare the radical artistic independence of these men with the more conservative and traditional attitudes, as expressed by Reynolds and his friend Dr. Johnson.'[7]

In 1759, Reynolds was formulating the ideas that would become central to the *Discourses*, which he began writing ten years later. In an *Idler* essay Reynolds promotes the 'Grand Stile' that, as a theoretical principle, follows in the footsteps of Shaftesbury. Attacking the realism of Dutch painting and its English admirers, Reynolds argues that representations of beauty must conform to general, rather than particular, ideas: 'The grand style of painting requires this minute attention to be carefully avoided, and must be kept as separate from it as the style of poetry from that of history ... The Italian attends only to the invariable, the great and general ideas which are fixed and inherent in universal nature.'[8] As we saw in our reading of Reynolds's *Discourses* in chapter 1, the neoclassical aesthetic insists on the refusal of ornament and the particular, focusing instead on the representation of 'great and general ideas' as the standard by which artistic merit can be determined. Reynolds echoes Shaftesbury's dismissal of the 'miniature' in his rejection of the 'minute' details of everyday life that are represented in Dutch painting, looking instead to the 'invariable' and the normative for artistic inspiration.

'Paint her to your own mind': Sterne's Concupiscible Narratives   153

Tristram Shandy refuses such a view, of course, relishing the peculiar and particular as the starting points for an investigation of human psychology. Pursuing the skeptical stance latent in Locke's and Hogarth's empiricism, Sterne challenges the idea of the disinterested spectator that Reynolds assumes as the starting point of aesthetic judgment. In the *Analysis,* Hogarth argues that the spectator who searches for the idea, rather than the substance, of a painting becomes the worst, rather than the best, judge of pictures:

> It is also evident that the painter's eye may not be a bit better fitted to receive these new impressions, who is ... too much captivated with the works of art; for he also is apt to pursue the shadow, and drop the substance ... As a confirmation of this seeming paradox, it has ever been observ'd at all auctions of pictures ... that the very worst painters sit as the most profound judges, and are trusted only, I suppose, on account of their *disinterestedness.*[9]

Hogarth marks ironically the idea of the connoisseur's 'disinterested' engagement with the art object, exposing 'a subtext of ownership, control, and desire' in the connoisseur's posturing at auctions.[10] Abstractions only detract from the experience of creating and appreciating true painting, covering art in 'shadows' and evacuating desire from the spectatorial moment. As we have seen in chapter 1, debates surrounding the idea of disinterested modes of spectatorship invariably form part of a larger gendering of social and aesthetic epistemologies. It is significant, then, that Hogarth's focus on the engaged spectator, presumably male, extends into a consideration of the place of women in the field of vision. Hogarth praises the serpentine '*line of beauty*' found in such objects as the female bustline, and places Venus at the centre of his theoretical speculation:

> There is an elegant degree of plumpness peculiar to the skin of the softer sex, that occasions these delicate dimplings in all their other joints, as well as these of the fingers; which so perfectly distinguishes them from those even of a graceful man; and which, assisted by the more soften'd shapes of the muscles underneath, presents to the eye all the varieties in the whole figure of the body, with gentler and fewer parts more sweetly connected together, and with such a fine simplicity as will always give the turn of the female frame, represented in the Venus, the preference to that of the Apollo.[11]

In celebrating the female body as an ideal visual object, Hogarth makes an explicit connection between sexual desire and aesthetic interest, a connection that is reinforced in the epigraph to the *Analysis* that Hogarth borrows from Book IX of *Paradise Lost*: 'So varied he, and of his tortuous train / Curled many a wanton wreath in sight of Eve, / To lure her eye' (ll.516–18). Satan's serpentine form serves as the primal scene of aesthetic desire (a fact that immediately places Hogarth's celebration of the form within a transgressive moral frame), and his encounter with Eve appears as a seduction, a seduction then reenacted between Adam and Eve. Like the serpent, Milton's Eve has the line of beauty on her side – her hair 'in wanton ringlets waved / As the vine curls her tendrils' (Book IV, ll. 306–7), to which Hogarth calls particular attention in his consideration of the serpentine line: 'The many waving and contrasted turns of naturally intermingling locks ravish the eye with the pleasure of the pursuit ... The poet knows it, as well as the painter, and has described the wanton ringlets waving in the wind.'[12] The centrality of the female form to Hogarth's aesthetic counters all of Shaftesbury's claims concerning the necessary de-eroticization of art and spectatorship, and builds desire into the very structure of beholding. As Paulson observes, 'This conjunction of Eve, Satan, and the Fall ... is the clearest acknowledgment Hogarth makes that his aesthetic, centering on woman and the serpent ... as graceful forms, must focus morally on the scene of man's temptation and fall from another kind of 'grace.'[13]

What both Hogarth's and Paulson's accounts do not include is Eve's, rather than Adam's, status as a spectator in the moment Milton represents. Eve allows herself to be 'lured' away from the idea of goodness in pursuit of the more immediate visual gratifications provided by Satan's form, the wreaths he creates, and the appeal of the apple. While within the confines of the *Analysis* Eve serves, like Venus, as an object, rather than the subject, of Hogarth's gaze, the artist's choice of epigraph presents the figure of the female spectator as the ideal beholder. In his attempt to subvert the neoclassical ideals of a disembodied spectator, Hogarth could not have found a better example of the spectatorial subject feared most by Shaftesbury. As we shall see, *Tristram Shandy* celebrates this figure in its rewriting of Hogarth's aesthetics of desire.

First, however, it is important to note how Sterne establishes the visual aspect of the novel in relation to its central concerns. John A. Dussinger provides an insightful account of Sterne's engagement with Berkeley's theories of vision, noting how Sterne takes up the idea of vision as a discourse of signs as arbitrary and imaginative as language.[14] Sterne

'Paint her to your own mind': Sterne's Concupiscible Narratives 155

consistently links his interest in the visual to his narrative practice, most obviously in the marbled page that stands as the 'motly emblem' of Tristram's work, a typically obfuscating guide to the story Tristram attempts to recount (1:268). The difficulty of interpreting the visual material that Tristram provides for his reader corresponds both to the challenge of narrative and to Tristram's understanding of the human mind as 'wrapt up ... in the dark covering of uncrystallized flesh and blood' (1:83). In this characterization of the mind Sterne mocks Locke's dream of the mind as a space in which objects 'lie so orderly as to be found upon occasion' by the subject of thought.[15] As we saw earlier, Shaftesbury revised Locke's dream in his account of the reader of literature who can use a text as a self-disciplining mirror. The 'peculiar speculative habit' that Shaftesbury hopes will emerge from the reader's encounter with the literary certainly appears in Sterne's novel, but with a Shandean twist:

> If the fixture of *Momus*'s glass, in the human breast, according to the proposed emendation of that arch-critic, had taken place ——— ... nothing more would have been wanting, in order to have taken a man's character, but to have taken a chair and gone softly, as you would to a dioptrical bee-hive, and look'd in, — view'd the soul stark naked ... traced all her maggots from their first engendering to their crawling forth ... then taken your pen and ink and set down nothing but what you had seen, and could have sworn to. (1.82–3)

The ideas of visual penetration and of representing a life in visual terms appear as two of Tristram's obsessions, despite his recognition of the futility of such a dream – 'this is an advantage not to be had by the biographer in this planet' (1:83). Tristram's fantasy reflects the voyeurism of the gaze directed at the man whose 'character' is to be traced, and the desire for possession of the 'soul stark naked' that replaces Shaftesbury's abstract Truth. The embodied subject here reveals in all of its coarse materiality, which appears intimately related to the moment of aesthetic production.

Tristram's obsession leads, not to the establishment of 'one will,' as Shaftesbury would have it, but to prurience and to deviance from any stable notion of either self or narrative. Instead of Reynolds's 'great and general ideas' we are left with the hobby horse. Arguing for its ubiquity in the opening pages of the narrative, Tristram comments on the futility of unseating politicians: 'Were their lordships unhorsed this very night,

——— 'tis ten to one but that many would be worse mounted by one half before to-morrow morning' (1:13). When individuals look inside themselves, they see not a reflection of a self disinterestedly observed, but the workings of desire writ large on a range of objects, including competing selves.

Tristram frequently evokes the workings of vision as the means by which individuals attempt to establish an interpretive community, as in the story of Baussiere and the whiskers: 'There are some trains of ideas which leave prints of themselves about our eyes and eye-brows; and there is a consciousness of it, somewhere about the heart, which serves but to make these etchings the stronger – we see, spell, and put them together without a dictionary' (1:413). Again echoing Locke, Sterne introduces the workings of desire into the workings of the human understanding – only 'some' trains of 'certain' ideas leave prints, and it is primarily licentious narratives that are able to engrave themselves, like an etching, on the mind, creating a nonverbal standard that enables us to understand Tristram's meaning 'without a dictionary.' The creation of these standards draws on particularly gendered expectations. Tristram links the question of knowledge in general to the difficulty of reconciling female and male perspectives in a passage that describes Walter Shandy's idiosyncratic view of the world:

> The truth was, his road lay so very far on one side, from that wherein most men travelled — that every object before him presented a face and section of itself to his eye, altogether different from the plan and elevation of it seen by the rest of mankind — ...
>
> This is the true reason, that my dear *Jenny* and I, as well as all the world besides us, have such eternal squabbles about nothing. — She looks at her outside, — I, at her in — . How is it possible we should agree about her value? (1:456–7)

In tracing Walter Shandy's deviance from conventional paths of understanding, Tristram mocks Locke's belief in the stability of visual evidence as the basis for primary ideas, asserting instead the potential for objects to present alternative 'faces' to the eyes of their beholders. Tristram turns from the subject of his father's understanding to the difficulties that emerge when men and women try to understand each other – Jenny directs a self-critical gaze toward her appearance, while Tristram insists upon the sentimental worth of her heart. The idea of 'value' becomes embedded in the particularity of sexual difference, and the possibility

'Paint her to your own mind': Sterne's Concupiscible Narratives 157

of consensus based on any abstraction appears remote and even undesirable – the difficulty of interpretation constitutes its own form of pleasure.

While both men and women appear invested in the world of Shandean private interests, the women of the novel most powerfully define this world's visual aspect. In particular, the figure of Widow Wadman embodies the ways of seeing that are intimately tied to women's experiences in the novel. The widow first encounters Toby in the privacy of her home – 'the house and all the furniture is her own' (1:665) – a space that allows her a particular form of spectatorial authority:

> There is nothing in it out of doors and in broad day-light, where a woman has a power, physically speaking, of viewing a man in more lights than one — but here, for her soul, she can see him in no light without mixing something of her own goods and chattels along with him ——— till by reiterated acts of such combinations, he gets foisted into her inventory. (2:665)

The private, domestic space that had come to be associated with women by the mid-eighteenth century – here literally owned by a woman – allows Widow Wadman to turn her act of spectatorship into a mode of calculation and consumption that Shaftesbury had complained of earlier in the century, and that Reynolds would warn of in his *Discourses* a few years later. Outside of the social contract that renders wives the property of their husbands, and daughters that of their fathers, the widow draws on her social authority in directing her gaze toward Toby and in rendering him an integral part of her private affairs. 'A daughter of Eve' (1:664), Widow Wadman cannot distinguish morally between objects in a field of vision – Toby resembles the accoutrements that Shaftesbury and Reynolds would banish from the ideal moment of spectatorship. While Widow Wadman is not looking at an art work, her appropriation of Toby as a contribution to her inventory resonates with Shaftesbury's attack on self-indulgent ways of seeing in general, modes of beholding that threaten, in his world view, the integrity of both art and social relations.

Sterne draws, in his portrait of the widow, on Hogarth's witty representations of the relationship between 'rich stuffs' and their owners, and the pleasure of the widow's gaze appears as the yardstick of the novel's visual imperatives.[16] Its connection to a particularly feminine agency manifests itself in its ability to pull male characters of the novel away from their solipsistic pursuits.[17] The widow's eye, as Martha F. Bowden has pointed out, serves as a means of drawing Toby into a marriage plot: 'There never was an eye of them all, so fitted to rob my uncle Toby of his repose, as the very eye, at which he was looking' (2:708).[18] Women's propensity for amorous glances and voyeuristic peeping appears as contagious and ensnaring to the Shaftesburian Walter Shandy, who, ever the staunch misogynist, writes 'the bitterest Philippicks against the eye that ever man wrote' whenever he finds himself under siege (2:709). Elizabeth Shandy's desire to watch the unfolding of Toby's advance upon the widow's house echoes Widow Wadman's interest in discovering the truth of Toby's groin wound: 'I could like, said my mother, to look through the key-hole out of *curiosity*' (2:729). While Elizabeth Shandy's eye, which appears as a 'thin, blue, chill, pellucid chrystal,' betrays no hint of desire in its physical attributes, it remains associated, through the sexualized image of the keyhole, to Widow Wadman's eye, which similarly conceals its aggressive desires: 'Twas an eye full of gentle salutations ——— and soft response –' (2:736, 708). Tristram specifically addresses 'Madam,' who elsewhere typifies the lewd reader, in his consideration of his mother's gaze, and we can place Elizabeth Shandy's eyes in the lineage that Tristram traces from the female reader back 'to those of Venus herself' (2:708).

Within this frame of reference, the female gaze mirrors the voyeurism of the reader that the novel as a whole emphasizes in its repeated turn to the eye as a principle of transgression and desire: 'to look into pupils — is not that dangerous? ... An eye is for all the world exactly like a cannon' (1:326, 2:707). We spend most of our time by one keyhole or another.[19] Although Tristram argues to the contrary, we sense that he may have inherited his 'lewd' tendencies from his mother and her gaze, and Toby believes that looking into a woman's eye is almost 'as bad as talking bawdy' (2:741), despite the widow's ability to keep her sexual appetite hidden behind a sentimental look that momentarily blinds Toby to her real intentions. The novel's desire to talk bawdy modifies its Hogarthian impulse, then, insofar as it locates the origins of its erotic energy in the idea of women as subjects, as well as objects, of the gaze.

Even as the various men in the novel try to ward off the incursions of female agency figured in the amorous glances directed toward them, the narrative makes it clear that women's modes of spectatorship are embedded in the fabric of novel making and novel reading. The interdependence of male and female conceptions of vision appears even at the moment when Tristram wants to assert his masculine aesthetic authority most forcefully. Describing Janatone of Montreuil, Tristram exclaims:

'Paint her to your own mind': Sterne's Concupiscible Narratives 159

'May I never draw more ... if I do not draw her in all her proportions, and with as determin'd a pencil, as if I had her in the wettest drapery' (2:589). Tristram's reference to sculpture's practice of covering its models in wet drapery allows the sketch to turn into a pornographic moment that simultaneously reveals and conceals the female body in a titillating display created, we assume, for the pleasure of the male reader. The female spectator would seem to have no place in this scene, which confines women to the status of objects and structures its bawdy talk around a specifically male sensibility.

But the scene is more complex than this reading suggests. We are introduced to Janatone, not as a passive object, but as a seductive artist who diverts Tristram from his task:

— A slut! in running them over within these five minutes that I have stood looking at her, she has let fall at least a dozen loops in a white thread stocking ——— Yes, yes — I see, you cunning gipsy! — 'tis long, and taper — you need not pin it to your knee — and that 'tis your own — and fits you exactly. ———

——— That Nature should have told this creature a word about a *statue's thumb!* ——— (2.589)

Janatone orchestrates the scene that unfolds around her, and her act of knitting her own 'stocking' corresponds to Tristram's fantasy of the wet drapery sketch – both Tristram and Janatone find sexual pleasure in an artistic objective correlative. The knitting of the stocking, and the dropping of the stitches, qualifies the novel's assertions elsewhere about female desire for the 'real' penis; here Janatone seems willing to use the idea of her artistic mastery – the stocking is her 'own' – as a means of accessing the power of seduction usually attributed to the plots of the male libertine. Tristram's dream of the artistic mastery he will achieve in his drawing is indistinguishable from Janatone's sexual authority, which assumes a prior knowledge of 'a *statue's thumb.*' Far from concerning herself with various artistic theories about the necessary relation of the thumb to the rest of the statue's body, however, Janatone playfully lets the '*thumb*' stand for the whole, mocking simultaneously the idea of the artist's disinterestedness and the phallus's inflated importance as the symbol of masculine power.

Tristram attempts to regain control of the moment by reclaiming the sexual licence that Janatone asserts – 'I have her thumbs and fingers in at the bargain if they can be any guide to me' (2:589) – but the young woman has set the pattern for sexualizing the aesthetic moment: *her* thumb will serve as Tristram's guide. Bemoaning the transitory nature of Janatone's beauty, Tristram exclaims, 'I would not answer for my aunt Dinah, was she alive ——— 'faith, scarce for her picture ——— were it but painted by Reynolds.' The evocation of Reynolds, rather than affirming Tristram's movement toward artistic greatness, reminds him of his incompetence: '— But if I go on with my drawing, after naming that son of Apollo, I'll be shot ———' (2:590). The contrast between the amateur sketcher and the master painter places Tristram in the same artistic league as the knitting Janatone. But Tristram does not even achieve her status as he relinquishes his pencil in defeat. Janatone, meanwhile, continues to produce the stocking that fits her exactly. Female beauty may be transitory in the eyes of men like Tristram, but women remain artists long after the male gaze has directed its attention elsewhere. With or without a Reynolds's representation of her concupiscible body, Aunt Dinah asserts an authority over the family narrative that none of the Shandean men can deny.[20]

The allusion to Reynolds as the son of Apollo marks the distance between the narrative practice in which Tristram is engaged and the high-culture art created by the painter. But far from conceding Reynolds's superiority, the reference subtly appeals to the desire to see Reynolds's high-mindedness challenged, a challenge delivered both by the presence of Dinah, a woman defined by her dangerous sexuality, and by the novel's commitment to Dionysus, the alter ego of Apollo, whose sexual spirit, if not ability, is evoked throughout the novel. Tristram's competition with Janatone defines the shared space they occupy as artists, a space of private performances that seems controlled, to a large extent, by women and their desires. As much as he tries to flee this space, Tristram finds himself inevitably drawn back to it, as if envisioning narrative depended upon, to a certain extent, recognizing women's role in its creation and consumption.[21]

Portraiture and Authorial Self-Fashioning

According to William V. Holtz, Sterne spent some of his time 'dabbling in painting' and once a celebrated writer set about cultivating the friendships of Reynolds, Gainsborough, and Hogarth. Portraiture, in particular, seems to have engaged much of Sterne's attention; he sat not only for Gainsborough and Reynolds, but for other painters as well, and was interested in how his friends were represented in their portraits.[22] A notable example of Sterne's preoccupation with the portraits of those close to him appears in a letter to Eliza Draper:

> I am just returned from our dear Mrs. James's, where I have been talking of thee for three hours. — She has got your picture, and likes it: but Marriott, and some other judges, agree that mine is the better, and expressive of a sweeter character. But what is that to the original? yet I acknowledge that hers is a picture for the world; and mine is calculated only to please a very sincere friend, or sentimental philosopher. — In the one, you are dressed in smiles, with all the advantages of silks, pearls, and ermine; — in the other, simple as a vestal — appearing the good girl nature made you; — which, to me, conveys an idea of more unaffected sweetness, than Mrs. Draper, habited for conquest, in a birthday suit, with her countenance animated, and her dimples visible.[23]

The tension between the two portraits centres around the nature of Eliza's appeal, which for the author resides in her privacy and innocence – in her 'sweetness' – but which for a larger public is signalled by the erotic energy that Mrs James's portrait connotes with its attention to the allure of 'silks, pearls, and ermine.' Sterne's representation of the portrait that appears as 'a picture for the world' echoes the characterization of Restoration portraiture and the women that it represents, like Eliza, 'habited for conquest.' Sterne goes on to point out the theatricality that Eliza brought to her sitting for this 'public' portrait: 'You endeavoured to collect every charm of your person into your face, with more than *common* care, the day you sat for Mrs James. – Your colour too, brightened; and your eyes shone with more than usual brilliancy.' Sterne insinuates a lack of sincerity and an unnatural effort in Eliza's attempt to render herself appealing to a general audience of spectators, and then goes on to deflate Eliza's expectations of admiration: 'You are not handsome, Eliza, nor is yours a face that will please the tenth part of your beholders.' Sterne softens the blow by complimenting Eliza's 'intelligent ... animated ... [and] good' countenance, but uses a language of feeling and responsiveness that separates Eliza from all the women that Sterne has 'saw, read, or heard of,' and prevents her from achieving a general standard of beauty that could grant Eliza the kind of authority other beautiful women might enjoy.[24]

Sterne's comments initially appear to define Eliza's representations in terms of their ability to connote her erotic power and her innocence, but they then take away the power Eliza might choose by refusing the appeal of the eroticized spectacle. Sterne's portrait of Eliza must be the superior representation because it secures the sitter's relation to the world, which is effectively reduced to a sphere that includes, finally, only 'a very sincere friend, or sentimental philosopher.' The radical curtailing of Eliza's authority over the visual field marks Sterne's anxiety about women's place in the public sphere, a fear that I will discuss below. For now I would like to draw attention to another aspect of the description of the portraits, which involves Sterne's positioning of himself as the artist depicting Eliza in the moment of the sitting: 'I then requested you to come simple and unadorned when you sat for me — knowing (as I see with *unprejudiced* eyes) that you could receive no addition from the silk-worm's aid, or jeweller's polish.' Though the portrait in question was painted by Richard Cosway, Sterne effectively places himself in the painter's position, claiming the '*unprejudiced*' eyes of the painter as a means of asserting the validity of the representation he admires. Sterne argues for the possibility of the disinterested spectator that he satirizes in *Tristram Shandy* in order to maintain his claim on Eliza and her affections. A similar, if less anxious, comment appears in a letter to Catherine Fourmantel: 'I shall be out of humour with You, & besides will not paint your Picture in black which best becomes You, unless you accept of a few Bottles of Calcavillo, which I have order'd my Man, to leave at the Dore in my absence.' Here Sterne, as the actual portrait painter, claims his rights as an artist in order to have Fourmantel accept his gift – a gesture that highlights the power of the male artist in relation to his sitter.[25]

Elsewhere in his correspondence Sterne reveals a deep investment in the idea of the portrait as a means of understanding his literary endeavours and their relation to his personal identity. Sterne uses one of the criteria for evaluating portraiture – the idea of likeness – in a letter written just before the publication of the first two volumes of *Tristram Shandy*, in which he insists that his novel must contain 'the air and originality ... which ... resemble the Author.' Here Sterne looks to close the gap between the idea of his 'real' self and the life of his text, a gesture summed up most famously in his characterization of *Tristram Shandy* as a self-portrait: 'Tis ... a picture of myself.'[26] The portrait that Reynolds painted of Sterne (figure 25) would seem to further this pursuit of verisimilitude – the look that the author commands establishes a community of spectators who celebrate Sterne's ironic juxtaposition of his clerical robes and the licentious sense of humour for which, by the time the portrait appeared, he was famous. By conflating fictional and nonfictional worlds in the figure of 'Yorick,' Sterne establishes a form of literary authority that depends on an appreciation of his 'real' self. The spectators who understand Sterne's humour confirm this moment of self-fashioning in their appreciation of the portrait, allowing the painting to replicate its subject's knowingness in the viewers themselves.

This reading confirms Holtz's analysis of Sterne's attachment to the portrait as representative of the author's desire 'to transmute his deeply felt individuality into an image to endure for all time'; the idea of the portrait mirrors *Tristram Shandy*'s more general pictorial aesthetic, Holtz argues, in its desire to achieve a 'static, nontemporal quality of subjective life.'[27] However, upon closer examination, Sterne's investment in portraiture reveals a more complex relationship between the representation and the author, a relationship that also informs the visual dynamics at work in *Tristram Shandy*. Writing to Catherine Fourmantel, Sterne celebrated the circulation of Reynolds's portrait in print form: 'There is a fine print going to be done of me – so I shall make the most of myself, & sell both inside & out.' The idea of a marketable 'inside & out' speaks to Sterne's concern with self-fashioning as a form of self-alienation that allows the writer to sell various aspects of the author 'Sterne.' Sterne's comment also speaks to the author's shrewd calculation of the extent to which the circulation of his image in the form of a print taken from Reynolds's portrait could enhance his marketability and expand the domain of his writing's influence by impressing a visual image of 'Yorick' upon the reading public. Sterne is able to capitalize on the mass marketing techniques of print culture and on the cultural prestige of Reynolds's name, linking himself to high and low culture simultaneously. The print that was made of the original painting allowed Sterne's image to circulate freely, most noticeably as the frontispiece of the sermons with which the print was first published. The idea of selling both 'inside' and 'out' speaks to Sterne's willingness to commodify himself, and it also establishes a double vision of the author as both text and image – two objects that may, but do not necessarily, coincide with one another. Sterne exploits the audience's desire to bridge the gap between the text and the author in their consumption of the author's portrait. In his playful use of 'Yorick' as a name both identical to and divorced from his personal identity, Sterne keeps his audience wanting to know more about the man behind the robes and texts. Here we are reminded of Manley's description of herself in *Rivella*, an image that used the idea of the private individual to further the career of the public author, capitalizing on the public's desire to 'know' the person behind the text, even while refusing, in the moment of self-fashioning, any revelation. Sterne similarly sells himself, but his very awareness of this moment of commodification precludes the possibility that the portrait will reveal an 'authentic' self behind the mask of the texts that the sitter has produced. His self-consciousness also suggests that the comments concerning *Tristram Shandy* as a portrait of himself may have been calculated to establish a way of thinking about the novel among the reading public. Sterne claimed, in 1760, that he 'wrote not [to] be *fed*, but to be *famous*.'[28]

Most importantly, Sterne's desire to sell himself by way of the portrait looks suspiciously like stereotypical accounts of the degraded appetite for female self-promotion that portraits were assumed to feed, a charge with which women novelists also had to struggle. Dr John Hill's scandalous biography of Sterne (first published in 1760 in the *Royal Female Magazine* and reprinted immediately in the *London Chronicle*) recounts the author's description of himself as a prostitute: 'He says he is now just like a fashionable mistress, whom every body solicits, because 'tis the fashion, but who may walk the street a fortnight, and in vain solicit corporal Stare for a dinner.'[29] Sterne's comment declares the conventional association of fame with the feminine, and his own desires to the sale of female sexual favours. The novel, as a genre, enables this propensity for whoring, as does the portrait.

Sterne's investment in portraiture marks a turn away from both Hogarth's and Reynolds's commitment to historical painting as the preeminent genre. Sterne actively embraces the portrait in *Tristram Shandy*, and in doing so, places a feminized aesthetic and mode of beholding at the heart of the novel's enterprise. Many critics have observed the references to the language of painting at work in Tristram's descriptions of various characters, and the pictorial aspect of these verbal portraits was not lost on contemporary painters. Most famously, Hogarth agreed to Sterne's request for a portrait of Trim as he presents his sermon in the second volume of the novel, a narrative moment that makes an explicit reference to Hogarth's 'line of beauty.' In representing the novel's sentimental aspect, other painters turned to descriptions of Maria taken from both *Tristram Shandy* and *A Sentimental Journey*. But the portrait of Maria that appears in *Tristram Shandy* complicates the visual representations of such artists as Joseph Wright of Derby and Angelica Kauffman. Initially, Sterne's description seems to set Maria up as the passive spectacle of victimized virtue – 'She was in a thin white jacket with her hair, all but two tresses, drawn up into a silk net, with a few olive-leaves twisted a little fantastically on one side' – but, as Tom Keymer has shown, the scene is not without its irony, including, impor-

'Paint her to your own mind': Sterne's Concupiscible Narratives 165

tantly, Maria's awareness of the erotic impulse behind Tristram's leap from the carriage to her side: 'MARIA look'd wistfully for some time at me, and then at her goat ——— and then at me ——— and then at her goat again, and so on, alternately ———' (2:783). As Keymer points out, the 'implied comparison' between Tristram and 'a traditional emblem of lust (the misadventure with the sash notwithstanding) is not to Tristram's advantage.'[30] Significantly, Maria's act of looking contributes to the transformation of the scene from a purely sentimental tableau into a mixture of sensibility and satire, a mixture that also appears elsewhere in the narrative whenever the widow interrupts Toby's naïve view of the world. Sterne's portrait of Maria, rather than stabilizing the sentimental moment, opens it up to a paradoxical reading in which two competing accounts of the figure's significance appear. As in the sentimental representations of women's reading that we saw in Reynolds's and Romney's portraits of readers in chapter 1, Sterne's characterization of Maria sustains two accounts of the figure's meaning, as well as granting her a spectatorial agency of her own.

Tristram Shandy's most important portrait allusion appears in the novel's invitation to the reader to draw Widow Wadman.

> Let love therefore be what it will, — my uncle *Toby* fell into it.
> ——— And possibly, gentle reader, with such a temptation — so wouldst thou: For never did thy eyes behold, or thy concupiscence covet any thing in this world, more concupiscible than widow *Wadman*.
> ### CHAP. XXXVIII
> To conceive this right, — call for pen and ink — here's paper ready to your hand. ——— Sit down, Sir, paint her to your own mind ——— as like your mistress as you can ——— as unlike your wife as your conscience will let you — 'tis all one to me ——— please but your fancy in it. (2.565–6)

Like the moment when Tristram encounters Janatone and Maria, this scene initially appears to marginalize both the female figure and the female reader. Widow Wadman disappears completely as Tristram calls upon his reader to paint a portrait of his own object of desire. Whereas the widow's desire for Toby remains attached to his specificity – 'Madam' is not asked to imagine her lover as a means of accessing the truth of Toby – the male reader's desire takes on a generalized aspect, standing in as representative of the imagination's potential to produce images at will. The blank page that Sterne offers his reader for the construction of his fantasy gives back to the male reader an image of his own mind, and in this sense functions as a mirror rather than as a representation of alterity.[31] We are encouraged to imagine men sitting down with their pens in hand, and at the moment we imagine that scene, the alternative – an image of the widow – fades away.

But if the moment's refusal to draw in the details of the widow's face may seem to deprive the female character of her specificity, it also works to open up the visual moment as a larger creative opportunity; as Dennis W. Allen has argued, the blank page suggests that Tristram's 'recounting of his narrative is as much an imaginative as a referential activity.'[32] While the widow might not remain the focus of attention, the idea of an embodied woman, rather than an abstracted or idealized figure of beauty, reminds us of the portrait's connection to the everyday world of private interests, a world in which women, as well as men, draw sketches of themselves and other women. Indeed, sketching was most often identified as an appropriate activity for women secluded in the home, an end in itself – as Tristram's imagined drawing is – rather than prepatory work for a larger project in oil. In the *Polite Lady, or a Course of Female Education* (1769), a mother declares: 'No young lady deserves [an] honourable character without a competent knowledge in the art of drawing,' and Maria Edgeworth, a generation later, confirmed that sketching would 'increase a lady's chance of a prize in the matrimony lottery.'[33] We have already noted Tristram's identification with Janatone as an amateur artist, in contrast to the figure of Reynolds, and the moment of the sketch reinforces the distance of the reader with a sketching pen in his hand from the world of masculine art production and appreciation. We are no longer in the realm of *Tom Jones*, in which Fielding invokes the Venus de Medici to generate a collective male appreciation of Sophia Western's beauty. Rather, we inhabit a moment here that links the male reader to the novel's female characters, who similarly engage in moments of private fantasy and artistic licence.

In foregrounding the figure of the sketcher alone in a private library, Sterne also brings the idea of the novel reader into the picture. The chapter's address to 'Sir' constructs its reader as male, but the interest in the representation of women's faces and bodies in women's magazines of the period indicates that the female reader, as much as 'Sir,' might like to draw Widow Wadman in a demonstration of desire not defined simply by the parameters of the male pornographic imagination. As in Manley's *New Atalantis*, the possible presence of a female beholder at this moment effectively triangulates the gaze, preventing a simple correspondence between a passive female object and an active male spectator.

'Paint her to your own mind': Sterne's Concupiscible Narratives   167

The voyeurism displayed by Elizabeth Shandy resurfaces here as an epistemology of reading, and portrait drawing appears as a version of novel writing – especially the kind of novel writing that relies on the idea of the whimsical and irreverent as heavily as *Tristram Shandy*.[34] This paradigm, I believe, reveals itself to be closely tied to the world conventionally inhabited by women whose imaginations both shape and consume the genres Sterne investigates so thoroughly.

The disappearance of the widow as the subject of representation speaks as much to the novel's refusal to reveal, in its pictorial moments, any stable visual representation as it does to the evacuation of her particular meaning. The complexity of the gender dynamics that appear around the blank page and around the representation of the portrait more generally takes us back to the passage that introduces the marbled page, the 'motly emblem' of Tristram's work. The mention of 'long noses' inspires Tristram to remark:

> ——— Now don't let Satan, my dear girl, in this chapter, take advantage of any one spot of rising-ground to get astride of your imagination, if you can any ways help it; or if he is so nimble as to slip on, ——— let me beg of you, like an unback'd filly, *to frisk it, to squirt it, to jump it, to rear it, to bound it,* ——— *and to kick it, with long kicks and short kicks,* till like *Tickletoby*'s mare, you break a strap or a crupper, and throw his worship into the dirt. ——— You need not kill him.
>
> ——— And pray who was *Tickletoby*'s mare? — 'tis just as discreditable and unscholar-like a question, Sir, as to have asked what year (*ab urb. con.*) the second Punic war broke out. — (1:267)

The passage starts out with the idea of the female reader's penis-fixation (a subject to which I will return below), but quickly complicates this association by transforming the female reader into the figure of the penis itself – i.e., Tickletoby's mare – upon which Satan rides. As in the passage that describes Janatone's stocking, the moment highlights the extent to which women have assumed the powers conventionally granted to men through the imaginative experience afforded by novel reading, just as Clarissa's ambitions as a writer and reader enable her, ultimately, to appropriate the plotting techniques of the libertine that have been used against her. The characterization of 'Sir' in the passage similarly confuses gender boundaries, identifying the male reader with the curious Elizabeth Shandy. 'Sir,' like Elizabeth, is chastized for his prurience, here characterized as a lack of learning by the nagging Tristram: 'Without *much reading*, by which your reverence knows, I mean *much knowledge*, you will no more be able to penetrate the moral of the next marbled page (motly emblem of my work!) than the world with all its sagacity has been able to unravel the many opinions, transactions and truths which still lie mystically hid under the dark veil of the black one' (1:268). Of course, the marbled page will give up no knowledge regardless of the reader's ambitions, but its mixed hue speaks eloquently to the extent to which, in the unfolding of *Tristram Shandy*'s particular form of confusion, gender identities and boundaries are mixed and blurred.

The complicated attribution of desires and abilities within this passage allows us to read the motley marbled page as an emblem of the novel's sexual and visual poetics. So far I have described Sterne's relation to these poetics in largely positive terms, as an attempt to capitalize on the novel's and the portrait's relation to women. But, as many feminist critics have pointed out, the novel also registers a deep distrust of the female reader as a cultural agent, a suspicion that, I believe, extends beyond Tristram's particular neuroses to the figure of Sterne himself, whose anxieties I touched upon in reading his letter to Eliza. A sketch that Sterne drew of his wife (figure 26) reveals a moment of anxiety about gender transgression that is hardly sanguine: in it, she appears as a grotesque figure that combines a female body and hair with a face caricatured by masculine features. The drawing seems to satirize the female appropriation of a male agency, implying that the assumption of male 'character' can only turn a woman into a figure of horror. The caricature, of course, represents the inversion of portraiture's commitment to a faithful likeness, attacking the subject and asserting the primacy of the artist over the subject's desires. The aggression that expresses itself in the intention behind the figure responds to the strength perceived in the female body, which appears large and intimidating underneath the veneer of fashionable clothing. The imposing nose reminds us of Reynolds's celebration of Sterne's own nose, here displayed as a sign of women's appropriation of male sexual potency and the creative powers associated with that potency in the figure of 'Yorick' that Reynolds's portrait of Sterne idealizes.

As J. Paul Hunter has observed, this mixture of fear and loathing colours Tristram's relation to Elizabeth Shandy.[35] It also informs his approach to the female reader as she appears in the character of 'Madam.'[36] The female reader fails to demonstrate, at various moments, an ability to generalize her desire beyond its particular object: 'But was the stranger's nose a true nose, or was it a false one?' asks Madam

(1:325). In contrast to the ideal reader, whose mind can generate a multiplicity of ideas at a given textual moment, Madam remains wholly preoccupied with literal meanings, a preoccupation that translates into a failure of the imagination.[37] Trim defines the female imagination entirely in terms of its sexual longing: 'All womankind ... from the highest to the lowest, an' please your honour, love jokes; the difficulty is to know how they chuse to have them cut; and there is no knowing that, but by trying as we do with our artillery in the field, by raising or letting down their breeches, till we hit the mark ———' (2:753). If Freud is right, however, smutty jokes amuse men at the expense of women, so that Trim's formulation works both to attribute to women an appetite for humour that renders them passive and to fix women's desire to a form of physical expression that the male imagination is able to transcend.[38]

The novel sets up a system of surveillance whereby Madam's reading habits are constantly being watched by Tristram; when Madam fails to detect the word that identifies Tristram's mother as a Protestant, she is held up for scrutiny: 'I wish the male-reader has not pass'd by many a one, as quaint and curious as this one, in which the female-reader has been detected. I wish it may have its effects; — and that all good people, both male and female, from her example, may be taught to think as well as read' (1:66). Madam fails because she cannot look and think simultaneously, remaining fixed to a literalist's understanding of narrative and, more generally, literary interest. Madam's appearances serve as a check on the narrative's investment in women, a constant reminder to the reader of the limits of women's reading experiences.

The denigration of Madam in *Tristram Shandy* necessarily qualifies the novel's overall commitment to an aesthetic that embraces women's agency in relation to the novel and the portrait, and takes us back to Sterne's desire to confine Eliza, as a portrait subject, to the strictly domestic virtues of chastity and 'sweetness.' As Hunter points out, *Tristram Shandy* appears at a cultural moment whose anxiety seems to 'derive from a pervasive male sense that men were holding their place only nominally and that women were beginning to control energy, vitality, and ultimately identity.'[39] While this comment seems so sweeping as to characterize male anxiety at almost any historical moment, its explanatory powers increase when we narrow down the claims to address the relationship between women and the novel in mid-eighteenth-century England. It seems unlikely that Sterne was able to separate himself from the concerns that he so eloquently depicts in his representation of Tristram. For the remainder of this chapter, I will analyse how *A Sentimental Journey* works to close down the access points that *Tristram Shandy* establishes as women's. *A Sentimental Journey*, I will argue, ties the world of image and text making to a singularly male imagination, and in doing so, limits its ability to generate the literary interest so engagingly sustained by *Tristram Shandy*.

'In the background of the piece': Women, Portraits, and the Sentimental Traveller

Commenting on the differences between the visual poetics at work in *A Sentimental Journey* and *Tristram Shandy*, R.F. Brissenden notes that Sterne's final novel has 'a visual coherence, a consistent, though muted, pictorial quality which is one of its unique charms.'[40] In what follows, I would like to pursue the line of investigation that Brissenden's observation invites, and in particular to comment on the significance of this visual coherence for the larger concerns of the novel. I believe that the visual aspect of the novel and its understanding of the portrait speak directly to the debate that has long organized discussions of the *Journey*, namely, whether or not Sterne adopts a critical stance toward the representation of sentimental culture he portrays through his characterization of Yorick.[41] My own position is that while Sterne's novel demonstrates a keen awareness of the limits of sentiment, it ultimately refuses to distance itself from sentimental culture. Where *Tristram Shandy* continually opens itself up to interrogation, even at the risk of undermining Sterne's authority, *A Sentimental Journey* works toward yoking its disparate parts into a unified perspective provided by the knowing author. The visual space that the *Journey* portrays functions not so much as an interpretive opportunity for the author and reader alike, but as a site where Sterne can gain the upper hand. What critics have frequently read as the *Journey*'s solipsistic quality, I would argue, constitutes, in its visual character, part of the novel's determination to maintain an authorial hold on the reader.[42]

'Yorick's pursuit of the naked heart is fundamentally an experiment with vision,' claims John A. Dussinger.[43] That the ideal of the naked heart – a phrase that comes up in reference to the knowledge of women – should stand as a central icon for the text, as opposed to 'the uncrystalized flesh and blood' that dominates *Tristram Shandy*'s canvas, signals the difference between the engagements with vision that each of Sterne's novels represents. While maintaining an interest in the language of aesthetics and art practices, the *Journey*, as Brissenden has observed, provides no metacommentary on this language, allowing the pictorial to

'Paint her to your own mind': Sterne's Concupiscible Narratives   171

stand, instead, as a sign of verbal transparency. The one visual icon that illustrates the narrative demonstrates this point; the drawing of the starling on the crest works ironically only insofar as it comments on the bird's use as a tool for social advancement at the same time as it epitomizes the sentimental protest of oppression. The drawing, as a drawing, does not attempt to create an interpretive moment out of this ambiguity. Instead, we are invited to recognize Sterne's own signature in the figure of the bird, the author's hand as the guarantor of the sign's stability, even within a framework that allows both ironic and nonironic understandings of the figure to appear. The interpretive paradox, in other words, is sustained less by the reader's double vision than by the assertion of authorial wit. It is this quality, whereby the complexity of the text is rendered an element of authorial virtuosity, that gives the narrative its solipsistic aspect: 'Was I in a desert,' Yorick exclaims, 'I would find out wherewith in it to call forth my affections — If I could not do better, I would fasten them upon some sweet myrtle, or seek some melancholy cypress to connect myself to — ... I would cut my name upon them.'[44] Yorick's domination of the spaces he inhabits appears here as a sentimental impulse that cannot be checked. The author writes his signature across the world as he finds it, rendering the objects passive underneath his incisions. In the narrative, the trace of the reader becomes less and less visible.

The narrative's controlling impulse, which appears even in its most playful and pleasurable moments, has particular consequences for the female characters who populate the text and, by extension, for the female reader. Various critics have commented on the degree to which class relations allow Yorick to manipulate the women he encounters: 'When the woman is only a *fille de chambre* he can use his class superiority to invite her attention and then reject it,' Dussinger notes, and Eve Kosofsky Sedgwick makes a similar claim: 'The only question between Yorick and lower-class women appears to be whether *he* will succumb to temptation.'[45] The *fille de chambre* listens to Yorick with 'submissive attention,' an attitude that characterizes the lower-class women's relation to the narrator (65). The aristocratic women facilitate Yorick's fantasies of social and sexual desirability, and rarely take on any kind of embodied features. Significantly, the figure of the widow, who appears early in the narrative, has little impact on the narrative, functioning only, through the conventional iconography of a widow's sexual availability, to establish the parameters of Yorick's courtship rituals, which abstract women according to the type of relationship Yorick can establish with them:

'That she was a widow, and wore a character of distress – I went no further; I got ground enough for the situation which pleased me – and had she remained close beside my elbow till midnight, I should have held true to my system, and considered her only under that general idea' (23). The 'general idea' – signalling simultaneously an innocent and licentious reading of Yorick's interest in the widow – takes precedence, in both its sentimental and erotic frameworks, over the actual experience an encounter with the widow might create, allowing the novel to sustain, from start to finish, its particular brand of humour. Brissenden has noted that 'the *Journey* may be a much less bawdy work than *Tristram Shandy*, but it is in some ways much more deliberately and provocatively sexual.'[46] If we remember that for Toby, looking into a woman's eye is akin to 'talking bawdy,' Brissenden's astute comment takes on both a visual and a gendered dimension, for while *Tristram Shandy* places sexuality in the realm of an ongoing conversation between men and women, *A Sentimental Journey* isolates it within a male pornographic imagination that looks inward, rather than into a woman's gaze. Hence we find less variety in the type of sexual humour governing the narrative, and less opportunity for readerly response.

Women in the *Journey* fail to demonstrate the kind of visual agency possessed by Widow Wadman and Elizabeth Shandy, instead appearing as part of the landscape that unfolds around Yorick. When Monsieur Le Count asks about his interest in French women, Yorick claims:

> I could wish ... to spy the *nakedness* of their hearts, and through the different disguises of customs, climates, and religion, find out what is good in them, to fashion my own by – and therefore am I come.
> ... I conceive every fair being as a temple, and would rather enter in, and see the original drawings and loose sketches hung up in it, than the transfiguration of Raphael itself. (84)

In his attempt to claim the innocence of his interest in French women, Yorick takes up the metaphor of the spy, capable of stripping away the trappings of culture to witness the sentimental truths of French women's hearts, a witnessing that will aid Yorick's self-improvement project. Here he indulges in a fantasy that Tristram explicitly refuses in his narrative, of obtaining the status of the disinterested observer of the human soul. The erotic impulse behind the desire is submerged in the trope of the art gallery that appears in the paragraph that follows, where Yorick fashions himself as a connoisseur of the sentimental. He imagines the women as buildings in which are hung 'original drawings and loose sketches' that render more accurately the ideals of human sentiment than the religious art of Raphael. These images presumably depict the true character of the women whose mysteries Yorick wants to delve into, standing as transparent portraits of their interior landscapes.

It is unclear who has drawn the pictures Yorick enjoys, but the possibility that the women themselves have drawn self-portraits seems improbable, given the static quality that they take on in the passage in their figuration both as a space through which Yorick moves and as objects of representation. It seems more likely that men like Yorick have drawn the images, men who, despite their amateur status, capably define the contours of female identity. Unlike Tristram, whose encounters with visual objects typically reveal less than they conceal, Yorick insists on the availability of the images he desires to see. The reader's imagination does not factor into this account of image making; nor does the idea of sexual difference, and the barrier it creates in the attempt to fashion the self after the other in *Tristram Shandy*, pose any obstacle to Yorick's quest. We have no sense that the objects themselves may prove impervious to interpretation, or that the representations of the French women may resist easy consumption by the male beholder. Yorick's voyeurism remains uncomplicated in its libertine attitude and finds no challenge to its authority. In other words, the task of looking, a task of befuddling complexity in *Tristram Shandy*, now takes on the status of a *fait accompli*.

The reference to the loose sketches and drawings, and the inference that these pictures are portraits, takes us back to the blank page in *Tristram Shandy*, as well as to Tristram's attempts to sketch Janatone. Unlike the passage that invites the reader to draw a version of Widow Wadman in *Tristram Shandy*, here the narrative focuses on the process of discovering representations that are already complete, rather than uncovering the reveries that the imagination uses as its starting point for the creation of art. In its insistence on the gap between men as subjects and women as objects of the gaze, this scene forecloses any possibility of the female beholder and artist. Whereas *Tristram Shandy* repeatedly acknowledges women's place in the realm of the amateur artist it depicts, the *Journey* seals the space off for Yorick.

This dichotomization of the field of vision into separate spheres grants Sterne authorial control, even at moments when the parodic elements of the text seem most pronounced. The description of Maria's visual aspect highlights the difference between the two novels. In *Tristram Shandy*, Maria's eyes signal an awareness of Tristram and his connection to the world of male intrigue and desire, but in the *Journey*, they appear only as templates open to Yorick's interpretation: 'I look'd in Maria's eyes, and saw she was thinking more of her father than of her lover or her little goat' (114). The eyes that render Tristram self-conscious of the sexual appetite that men bring to their experience of Maria now become passive objects available for Yorick's touch: 'I sat down close by her; and Maria let me wipe [the tears] away as they fell with my handkerchief. – I then steep'd it in my own – and then in hers – and then in mine – and then I wip'd hers again – and as I did it, I felt such undescribable emotions within me, as I am sure could not be accounted for from any combinations of matter and motion' (114). Yorick's sentimental impulse, as always, grants him a sexual gratification, one that appears masturbatory in its total exclusion of Maria as a desiring agent. As Tom Keymer has observed of this passage, 'It is hard to miss Sterne's implication. Yorick is shopping for sentimental pleasure, for erotic titillation, and in the end for some comfortable affirmation of his own benevolence and immortality ... It is this, not Maria, that is his interest.'[47] Whereas the inclusion of the erotic in *Tristram Shandy* almost always opens up the text to a female beholder and reader, challenging the sentimental innocence of figures like Toby and heightening Tristram's self-consciousness, here it only confirms Yorick's – and by extension, Sterne's – command over the moment, a command that the eye-wiping gesture figures as both bodily and rhetorical.

As in *Tristram Shandy*, the portrait appears as the place where the novel's engagement with questions of vision and gender find their most focused articulation. Various allusions to portraits appear in the text, but the most sustained account describes, significantly, Yorick's encounter with the widow in the opening pages of the narrative:

> I had not yet seen her face — 'twas not material; for the drawing was instantly set about, and long before we had got to the door of the Remise, *Fancy* had finished the whole head, and pleased herself as much with its fitting her goddess, as if she had dived into the TIBER for it — but thou art a seduced, and a seducing slut; and albeit thou cheatest us seven times a day with thy pictures and images, yet with so many charms dost thou do it, and thou deckest out thy pictures in the shapes of so many angels of light, 'tis a shame to break with thee. (17)

The passage grants portrait-painting powers to Fancy rather than to empirical observation, in much the same way that *Tristram Shandy* calls on the reader to 'please but your own fancy in it.' But while Tristram's invocation to Fancy serves to open up the moment to the possibility of other women inhabiting the position of Widow Wadman as the ideal object of desire, Yorick's invocation renders any particular woman irrelevant to the moment of imagining: the widow's actual face is not 'material' to the moment of desire, whereas, for Tristram, each man must imagine a real woman that he desires in order to 'picture' Widow Wadman. Yorick alludes to his fancy's ability to create representations reminiscent of art objects discovered in the Tiber, to sustain illusions that resemble 'so many angels of light.' Fancy, like Janatone, appears as the 'seducing slut,' but she is lodged firmly within the artist's mind, never tempting him toward an intersubjective aesthetic or embodied moment. The passage stresses the portrait's relation to an educated male imagination that can draw upon a large number of images from an artistic tradition, rather than to the world of a private imagination governed by actual embodied figures. We are taken back, at this moment, to the inflated, if ironic, language surrounding Fielding's evocation of the Venus de Medici in his description of Sophia Western, so that the portrait effectively becomes part of an elite, rather than popular, cultural imagination in terms of its imagined representation and the sentiment it generates. The stress on the instantaneous process by which the representation appears – 'the drawing was instantly set about' – further distances the moment from the illumination of the portrait's significance as a genre that draws attention to the materiality of its production.

If the opening paragraph relies on abstraction to define the portrait's role in Yorick's imagination, the lines that follow move in the opposite direction, toward a literal pictorialism that anchors the portrait into place:

> When we had got to the door of the Remise, she withdrew her hand from across her forehead, and let me see the original — it was a face of about six and twenty — of a clear transparent brown, simply set off without rouge or powder — it was not critically handsome, but there was that in it, which in the frame of mind I was in, attached me much more to it — it was interesting; I fancied it wore the characters of a widow'd look. (17)

The move from the abstract images of Fancy to the very literal description of the woman provided by Yorick establishes the twin poles of the portrait aesthetic as grounded in both the real person of the sitter and the imagination of the painter. But whereas the earlier novels we have analysed used the portrait's status as an object determined both by the real and by the artist's aesthetic desires as a means of opening up the interpretive moment to the reader, here the narrative replaces the idea of Fancy with the literal description of the 'original,' eradicating one element of the portrait-making process. The passage narrows the hermeneutical horizon by insisting on the simplicity of the image, and in doing so echoes Sterne's analysis of Eliza Draper's portraits. Sterne's insistence on his superior understanding of Eliza's true nature – an interpretation that demands that Eliza relinquish claims to a more general desirability – here resurfaces in Yorick's obsession with the widow's simplicity and transparency. As in Sterne's letter, Yorick sets the widow's face off from a public conception of beauty – 'it was not critically handsome' – in order to establish the authority of his own interpretation of the face: 'I fancied it wore the characters of a widow'd look.' The portrait retreats as a place where an interpretive opportunity might appear, insisting rather that the reader vicariously enjoy Yorick's consumption of the widow's character.

In moving from a rarefied abstraction to a literalist particularity, Sterne empties the portrait of its ability to establish a reciprocal relationship between author and reader, and between men and women. The idea of double vision that I have traced in *Tristram Shandy* and in earlier novels depends on the placement of the portrait in a space between the two poles that Sterne erects in this passage. Put another way, the idea of double vision is not the same as the double entendre that figures so largely in *A Sentimental Journey*. In this scene with the portrait, the double entendre that appears in Yorick's response to the idea of widowhood only confirms what we already know about the narrator – that sentimental and erotic gratification are coterminous, if not identical. The double vision that characterizes responses to the idea of the portrait in *Tristram Shandy*, in contrast, allows the reader to construct competing readings that do not necessarily dovetail, as they do in this passage. The portrait opens up the text's engagement with the idea of sexual difference in *Tristram Shandy*, while in *A Sentimental Journey* it functions to confirm the logic of the same, to use Luce Irigaray's terminology. Dussinger uses another psychoanalytical discourse, that provided by R.D. Laing, to describe Yorick's relationship to the idea of alterity: 'By keeping an existential detachment from all things around him the "encroaching evil" in otherness (which includes the reader's mind) is held in check.'[48] This 'existential detachment,' I believe, appears in the field of vision as a refusal to encounter women as anything more than objects upon which Yorick can inscribe his signature.

In hearkening back to the male bravado that characterizes *Tom Jones*, Sterne looks to assert male authority over the sentimental culture, and the private interests it sustained as its focus, with which women had come to be aligned by 1767. Sterne's investment in the discourse of sentiment undoubtedly guaranteed his success as an author, especially given many of his readers' refusal to read the vein of irony built into both *Tristram Shandy* and *A Sentimental Journey*.[49] Janet Todd has traced the degree to which, in the novels of the 1760s and 1770s, 'the most sentimental situation is certainly woman's,' and this situation does not simply discipline women as domestic subjects.[50] That women writers were gaining increasing prominence, a development that would be sealed, ten years later, by the sudden fame granted to Frances Burney upon the publication of *Evelina*, meant that authors like Sterne must have developed a keen sense of competition for the reading public's attention, as well as an anxiety about the stability of their own authority as writers of cultural artifacts and scripts. As we shall see, the 1790s provided men with the opportunity to claim sentimental discourses and representations as their own; in this context, women writers, especially those espousing feminist principles, found themselves on the defensive.

Chapter Six

Portraits of the Woman Artist: Kauffman, Wollstonecraft, and Inchbald

But, alas! in the exercise of the arts, industry scarce bears the name of merit.[1]

By the late eighteenth century, both the portrait and the novel had established themselves as dominant modes of cultural expression in England, to the extent that figures like Sterne and Reynolds could both revise and profit from preconceived notions about the form and function of the genres that secured their reputations. That the portrait and the novel remained as susceptible to attack during the last decades of the century as they had been earlier did not hinder authors or painters from capitalizing on their immense popularity. The novel's and the portrait's success at ensconcing themselves in the public's cultural imagination – over the objections of critics – was facilitated by the entrenchment of private interests in the language of public life.[2] By the 1790s, the idea of private interests came to support, for many, a political rhetoric that opposed the revolutionary moment initiated by France.

In her analysis of English cultural responses to the French Revolution, Claudia L. Johnson has traced how, after 1789, 'sentimentality entailed ... the "masculinization" of formerly feminine gender traits ... The affective practices associated with it are valued *not* because they are understood as feminine, but precisely and only insofar as they have been recoded as masculine.'[3] This appropriation had significant consequences for the gendered aspect of the language of private interests. On the one hand, it signalled the intensification of the connection between the domestic and the private – a connection 'private interests' did not, as we have seen, always foster earlier in the century; on the other hand, it posited women's private interests, understood as the articulation of a feminine sensibility, as potentially pathological. As Candace Ward has observed, by the 1790s, 'female sensibility had ... become suspect, increasingly viewed as a sign of self-indulgent emotionalism rather than virtue.'[4] If we look to the world of the portrait and the novel in the 1790s, we see a similar recoding of the genres and their association with the world of private interests. Increasingly the novel and the portrait appear as appropriate, if not necessarily ideal, modes of expression for male writers and painters. Earlier in the century, Fielding and Richardson had engaged in a struggle to legitimize the works they were writing, a competition that, to a certain extent, placed them on a continuum with the women writers of the period. In the last decade of the century, the legitimacy of the novel, as well as that of the portrait, was more widely accepted, making it easier for male authors and painters to achieve critical acclaim as practitioners of these genres, in part because 'private interests,' for men, came to signify not only their economic and political activities but also the extension of male sensibility into the arena of public affairs. At the same time, because of the restrictions increasingly placed on the idea of women's 'private interests' as a form of public self-expression, the woman artist's status as a public figure became a more rather than less vexed issue – women's work could easily be read as an inherently illicit activity.

This chapter will analyse works by Angelica Kauffman, Mary Wollstonecraft, and Elizabeth Inchbald in order to consider three responses that speak to this issue and to each other. The relationship between Wollstonecraft and Inchbald has been defined in the context of these women's Jacobin ideals, but each of the novels I will be examining predates an explicit articulation of this political commitment; the connection I will explore depends on a more general consideration of their understanding, as authors with an astute awareness of the confines of women's social position, of the novel, an assessment that is figured, in both Wollstonecraft's *Mary, a Fiction* and Inchbald's *A Simple Story*, through the trope of the portrait.[5] I will introduce these writers by way of Angelica Kauffman's self-portraits, which appeared in the period linking Sterne to Wollstonecraft and Inchbald. In her self-portraits, I will argue, Kauffman provides a way of reconfiguring the idea of portraiture so as to increase women's access to the public world of art making and art selling. In Wollstonecraft's handling of the portrait trope, I will then suggest, we see a novel that founders in its desire to escape the vicissitudes of women's private interests and their proximity to the woman writer altogether. The second half of the chapter will turn to Elizabeth Inchbald's first novel as a return to the principles governing Kauffman's portrai-

180   Private Interests

ture, one that enables the figure of the woman writer to appear even at the moment of female incarceration in narratives governed by a domestic ideology. *A Simple Story*, I will argue, allows a critical discourse to emerge in its representation of both the novel form and women's relation to the world of private interests, without, as in the case of Wollstonecraft, pathologizing the feminine.

Angelica Kauffman and the Reframing of Portraiture

Much of the feminist commentary on Angelica Kauffman and her work has focused on Kauffman's achievement as a history painter, an achievement remarkable both for the quality of work the painter produced and for her ability to create a space for herself in a field defined in explicitly masculine terms. In discussing Kauffman's commitment to history painting, Wendy Wassyng Roworth places Kauffman in the tradition of 'great male painters,' emphasizing her connection to such painters as Poussin and Carracci, and her distance from a culture of femininity associated with more minor women artists.[6] Within this critical framework, Kauffman's portraiture necessarily takes on a secondary role to her historical works. Germaine Greer voices a common refrain when she writes that 'Angelica Kauffmann [sic] painted portraits when perhaps she would rather have been developing her history paintings.'[7] As there is no evidence to suggest that Kauffman resented painting portraits, Greer's comment indicates the extent to which twentieth-century critics, like their eighteenth-century counterparts, are apt to ignore the significance of portraiture as a genre. In what follows I will explore the extent to which some of Kauffman's most radical statements about the status of women artists appear in the painter's self-portraits, works that highlight issues surrounding women's relation to the genre of portraiture.

It is perhaps less surprising than we imagine that Kauffman was able to achieve such great success as a history painter in late eighteenth-century England. In the absence of a sustained tradition of history painting, critics proved extremely grateful for the appearance of any historical works, regardless of the artist's sex. In the two dozen or so commentaries on Kauffman's work that appear in reviews of the Royal Academy exhibitions that began after 1769, only a few mention Kauffman's gender, and even in these few the point of the observation is more often than not to berate England's male painters for their inadequacy, as in this *London Chronicle* review of 1778: 'MISS KAUFFMAN still maintains her character as one of the first history-painters of the age; and so strong is the turn of her genius to this sublime branch of the art, that while most of the male pencils in the kingdom are employed on portraits, landscapes, &c. she gives us, every succeeding year, fresh proofs of the vigour of her mind by producing something excellent in the historical way.'[8] In none of these reviews is Kauffman censured for presuming to embark on a career of history painting.[9] Richard Polwhele's 1798 attack on Kauffman in 'The Unsex'd Females' came almost twenty years after the painter had left England, and the satire on her use of a language of civic humanism – 'While classic Kauffman her Priapus drew' – can be viewed as part of a 1790s backlash against the French Revolution's use of that discourse, as well as a more general turn against the woman artist as a public figure.[10]

In the context of the art world in which Kauffman worked, it was far more damaging for her to paint portraits than to paint historical works. In particular, self-portraits invited the charges levelled against the '*smiling belle*' we encountered in chapter 1, the woman who insisted on displaying herself next to her portrait in order 'to exhibit the *original*, as well as the *semblance.*'[11] The issues that we have examined so far in relation to the portrait become magnified in the figure of the self-portrait painted by a woman. Self-portraits could not escape the connotation of self-promotion, and for women such an association immediately linked the representations to the world of prostitution. Concerns about the theatricality of representation and its possible duplicity, about the effect of the image on the beholder rendered passive by the artist's gaze, and about the painting's status as an object that can be circulated by the artist and others, also crystallized around the self-portrait. But rather than move toward the 'grand style' of portrait painting that Reynolds adopted in order to overcome the problems associated with portraiture by placing it in an alternative visual register, Kauffman moved in the opposite direction, insisting on the realm of the personal and self-interested as the key terms governing her artistic expression in portraiture, abandoning, in the moment of the portrait, the civic humanist discourse governing her historical works.

In a self-portrait painted in the early 1770s (figure 27), Kauffman appears with her sketchbook and crayon holder, items that draw attention both to the sitter's profession and to the moment of the painting's creation. At the same time as she emphasizes the idea of her labour, Kauffman focuses on her gender in the modest gesture of holding the drapery over her breasts and in the detail afforded to the curls of her hair. The painting as a whole celebrates Kauffman's beauty, which was often remarked upon. Kauffman does not become a passive spectacle in this moment, however, for as Roworth has observed, the hand that holds the drapery at the breast also points toward the painter, suggesting Kauffman's awareness of the theatrical element of the portrait and her own mastery over its conventions.[12] The simultaneous foregrounding of both her work and her femininity sets up a continuum between the private identity Kauffman inhabits as a woman and the public role she plays as a painter, a continuum that works in both directions: the feminine beauty she represents in the painting is both integral to her personal identity, but also alienated from it as the occasion for the aesthetic moment that Kauffman is trained to create.

Kauffman's direct gaze confronts the beholder, acknowledging the paradoxical elements of this configuration of gender and profession. In addressing the beholder, Kauffman seeks to please, both in her particular appeal to a male beholder, and in a more general fashion to the audience that will commission future works from her. Kauffman's appeal insists on the social aspect of portraiture, but defines that social element in very practical terms, as part of a professional culture in which her ability to gratify her sitters will ensure her success as a painter. Rather than attempting to move into a realm of abstraction untainted by the particularity of her circumstances, Kauffman emphasizes her status as a woman and portraiture's attachment to the private as the source of its affect.

When Kauffman moves into a more abstract mode, she does so by incorporating an allegorical aspect into the self-referential representation. In the representation of Kauffman as the character of painting, listening to the inspiration of poetry (figure 28), the shift into the allegorical mode creates two quite different effects. First, the allegorical reference enables Kauffman to demonstrate her education – in this case, her understanding of aesthetic theory – an education that, as a woman, she has necessarily undertaken privately. Kauffman's education allows her entry into the domain of public knowledge and intellectual conversation, but this entry is the result of the singularity of her ability – what one critic called her 'peculiar turn' – rather than her identification with the culture of male privilege.[13]

The second significant aspect of the allegorical mode that Kauffman adopts concerns its association with the conventions of female portraiture, which Marcia Pointon has defined in *Strategies for Showing: Women, Possession, and Representation in English Visual Culture, 1665–1800*. As Pointon argues, the introduction of an allegorical element into a portrait has the effect of forcing the beholder to read at two levels simultaneously.[14] In images like the portrait of the artist as the character of painting, Kauffman uses the dialectical mode that allegory establishes to blur the boundaries between the public domain to which the allegorical representation belongs and the private realm she inhabits as a woman. By placing an allegorical woman next to herself in the painting, Kauffman allows the terms of reference to slide from portrait to allegory, from private to public, and back again. Henry Fuseli noted a tendency for this slippage to occur even in Kauffman's history paintings, claiming that 'her heroines are herself,'[15] and while this practice, of placing the artist in tableaux not identified as self-portraits, is hardly novel, Fuseli's comment suggests that in the case of the woman painter, this self-promotion counters conventional understandings of women's relation to heroism and historical painting. In the case of Painting's representation, Kauffman reminds her beholder of her presence at the same moment that she formulates an aesthetic principle, as if to insist always on the presence of the painter in the canvas we behold. The imperatives of self-portraiture, in other words, take precedence over the idea that painting should remain at the level of moral or historical abstraction.

Kauffman uses the doubleness produced by allegorical portraiture in a more aggressive fashion in her most famous self-portrait, *Angelica Kauffman Hesitating between the Arts of Music and Painting* (figure 29). As several critics have noted, the painting most immediately alludes to the classical story of Hercules's choice between vice and virtue.[16] In the context of eighteenth-century English art criticism, Shaftesbury's comments about the suitability of the Hercules motif as a subject of history painting formed the backbone of civic humanist aesthetic theory and its relation to painting practices. Kauffman's painting immediately complicates Shaftesbury's paradigm by introducing a portrait subject into the representation of the Hercules story. The story turns to the biographical, rather than the historical, as its frame of reference, highlighting the circumstances of Kauffman's development as a woman artist. Those circumstances involved Kauffman's education, as a young girl, in the arts of music and painting, both considered appropriate activities for a young woman to undertake within the privacy of the home. Kauffman's painting marks her turn away from the idea that female accomplishment serves only as an embellishment to a domestic identity. By actively choosing one art over another, Kauffman announces her intention to take up painting as a public and professional engagement. In her reference to the choice of Hercules, Kauffman signals her command of the history of painting, and of paintings such as Poussin's and Carracci's representations of the classical story.

Kauffman's reference to earlier and contemporary versions of the

Hercules story does not simply establish a commitment to the values of the male painting tradition in which her version appears, however. The reconfiguration of the scene with a woman at the centre of the triangle immediately alters the meaning of the tableau. Most immediately, it transforms the gender dynamic in its removal of the erotic tension that conventional representations of the scene establish between Hercules and the figure of Vice. The triangular relation of two women competing for the attention of a man is replaced with an alternative scene, in which the central figure becomes part of a continuum of possible configurations of femininity. The connection between the three women is marked by Kauffman's affiliation with the figure of Painting and fondness for the figure of Music, the object of Kauffman's apologetic look and affectionate touch. In the Poussin and Carracci versions of the scene, Hercules appears absorbed and withdrawn from the women who accost him, an absorption that highlights the philosophical principle governing the painting, as we imagine the mental work required of Hercules in his decision making, rather than focusing our attention on the women who flank him. Indeed, the attentiveness that marks the women's regard for Hercules serves as a guide to the beholder, who is asked to identify with the moment he inhabits. Kauffman's representation allows each woman a significance that is defined in relation to the others, with Kauffman standing out from the others by virtue of her contemporary dress – by virtue, in other words, of the particularity of the portrait aesthetic. Kauffman emphasizes her own importance in the painting not by highlighting the moral significance of the narrative, but rather by stressing the narrative as it relates to the choices that have made her career possible.

Various critics have commented on the effect that Kauffman's representation of herself with two other female figures has on the viewing experience that the painting creates. Griselda Pollock and Rozsika Parker argue that the presence of three female figures together in the tableau 'obscures the necessary distinction between the different status of the allegorical figures ... and the artist.'[17] Parker and Pollock claim that the possible flattening of distinction transforms Kauffman into a passive spectacle – a representation of a beautiful woman created to appeal to a male audience – and they particularly object to the allusion to the Three Graces that Kauffman creates by placing the three female figures together, an allusion that, they argue, further undermines the portrait's ability to claim a particular significance for the figure of Kauffman as a painter. Roworth claims, less negatively, that Kauffman may have been drawing on the title of 'Paintress of the Graces' given to her by De Rossi in 1785, and that the 'heroic' and 'masculine' identification of Kauffman with Hercules counters any negative associations of the feminine that the idea of the Graces might sustain.[18] Angela Rosenthal takes a different approach to the presence of the Graces in the portrait, arguing that the allusion softens the social criticism implicit in Kauffman's claims for herself as a woman artist: 'The balance between the pictorial themes of Hercules and the Three Graces is effected so as to make palatable what on first sight seems inappropriate for her as a female protagonist.'[19] Rosenthal views the inclusion of the Graces allusion as a canny move on Kauffman's part to deflect charges that she might be assuming a masculine role in her commitment to the ideals of history painting.

These accounts view the idea of the Graces as antithetical to the portrait's claims for the independence of the woman artist. But what if Kauffman were using the Graces to reinforce the claims that she establishes in her replacement of the Hercules figure with her own self-representation? I would like to argue that Kauffman's introduction of a second level of allegorical reading invites the beholder to add another dimension to the conceptualization of femininity that is initiated by the display of the three female figures together. Most immediately, the idea of the Graces heightens the sense of female intimacy that the painting already signals in Kauffman's attachment to both Painting and Music. Kauffman's three women are united by their closeness, rather than appearing as three isolated entities. In this sense, even while Kauffman marks her departure from the idea of female artistic accomplishment as an ornamental aspect of a domestic identity in the painting, she also points to the interrelatedness of the arts and their mutual fostering of one another. The individualism marked by Kauffman's career is thus set against a backdrop of female education and a larger community of women who train in music and painting within the privacy of their homes. The Graces' association with Athena, goddess of women's work and of intellectual activity, strengthens the painting's pull toward the private and away from the male civic virtue that traditional representations of the Hercules narrative promote. Most importantly, the possibility that female interest in the arts might exceed social prescription appears in the painting's representation of the women's intense preoccupation with each other, which seems to block, at least partially, the beholder's gaze.

The idea that the women are not simply represented as passive spectacles of female beauty introduces the question of the portrait's erotic content, a content that at first seems to have disappeared in the image's evolution from its classical treatment, in which Hercules finds himself torn between two women. But it reappears in the portrait through Kauffman's allusion to the three Graces and their connections to Aphrodite, Venus, and, most dangerously, the Maenads. As Pointon has noted in her discussion of Reynolds's use of the Graces as a trope in his female portraits, the Graces define a pleasure principle that is not wholly contained by their association with beauty, gentleness, and friendship: 'While they may at one level symbolize harmony, [they] also threaten disorder, pose choice, incite sexual envy and desire for gratification.'[20] This reference not only serves as a counterpoint to the Hercules narrative, but actively turns the painting's manifest content inside out. The possibility of autoeroticism, with the three women representing different versions of Kauffman's self, intensifies the feeling of distance that the painting achieves from the classical story upon which it draws. The script of Kauffman as the accidentally female artist occupying the space of the universal subject, man, is rewritten as the narrative of a woman who succeeds precisely because of her willingness to align the figure of the public artist with a range of possible female identities, both decorous and illicit.

Wollstonecraft's *Mary* and the 'Reverence for mental excellence'

Kauffman never allowed the public to forget that she worked extremely hard to make a living, keeping her body as a source of aesthetic delight and material production at the forefront of her audience's mind, even as women were increasingly aligned with the principles of retirement and passivity by the discourse of private interests toward the end of the century. In her insistence on linking women's private interests to the public sphere, and on the potential for private interests to reveal indecorous subjects, Kauffman resists the idea of virtuous merit as a status conferred on women by a society willing to reward its dutiful daughters, defining merit, instead, as an aesthetic achievement made possible by women's labour and commitment to art. Kauffman's self-portraits, I believe, provide a useful bridge to the literary world in which women writers crafted narratives that allowed them a similar degree of freedom to pursue alternative configurations of female identity. Both Wollstonecraft's *Mary, a Fiction* and Elizabeth Inchbald's *A Simple Story* are often read as autobiographical narratives, and in what follows, I would like to think about their female heroines in relation to the authors' meditations on the novel and its ability, or lack thereof, to theorize private interests that resist association with male privilege while interrogating their alignment, for women, with either a pathologized femininity or domestic retirement. In each novel, I will suggest, these meditations find their most articulate expressions around the figure of the portrait.

As writers, Wollstonecraft and Inchbald were both concerned to distance themselves from 'bad' novel writing, which they both attacked in their literary reviews. Wollstonecraft was particularly virulent in her disparagement of the 'typical' female reader, as well as of the female authors of pulp fiction. In her essays written for the *Analytical Review*, she attacks hackneyed romances again and again. Mitzi Myers views these attacks as part of Wollstonecraft's self-conscious attempt to write herself into an alternative female identity: 'demystifying the contemporary feminine specialty – the novel of sensibility so often "told in letters and written by A Lady" – was instrumental in enabling her to evolve her own distinctive voice, making for an aesthetic at once feminist and romantic.'[21] Wollstonecraft's review of Charlotte Smith's *Emmeline* focuses its attention on the dangers of inflated novelistic sentiment: 'Few of the numerous productions termed novels,' Wollstonecraft writes, 'claim any attention; and while we distinguish this one, we cannot help lamenting that it has the same tendency as the generality, whose preposterous sentiments our young females imbibe with such avidity. Vanity thus fostered, takes deep root in the forming mind, and affectation banishes natural graces, or at least obscures them.' Wollstonecraft's comments assume that the bad novel reader is a female reader, one who cannot read a text without having its inflated rhetoric inform her understanding of herself. 'Affectation' introduces the idea of the theatrical into the reading moment; ideally, reading should confirm the 'natural graces' of the reader in an unmediated fashion. Inchbald follows in a similar vein, satirizing the undisciplined female reader: 'She requires transport, bliss, extatic joy, in the common occurrences of every day.' For Inchbald, the reality principle is undermined by bad novels, and both Inchbald and Wollstonecraft imagine an alternative configuration of novel reading made possible by works from which the readers, 'if they are wise ... will know how to profit' in their everyday lives.[22] But, as we shall see, Wollstonecraft and Inchbald responded in quite different ways to the idea of novel writing when they crafted their first works.

Wollstonecraft opens *Mary* with an Advertisement that defines her novel as a composition governed by the working of its author's soul, rather than by the example of its literary predecessors. Rather than identifying with authors, in particular women authors, who have gone before, Wollstonecraft insists on the tie between the work's originality as a piece of fiction, and the character it is able to describe in its heroine: 'In an artless tale, without episodes, the mind of a woman, who has thinking powers is displayed ... Without arguing physically about *possibilities* – in a fiction, such a being may be allowed to exist.'[23] As Johnson has argued, Wollstonecraft's insistence on the fictionality of the text creates a double bind for the author and for the narrative as a whole, for even as it points with one hand to the possibility of the woman it describes, it takes away the possibility with the other by allowing that 'the status of the fantasy is subjunctive at best and figmentary at worst.'[24] This problem, I believe, extends to Wollstonecraft's attempts to distance herself from the idea of the novel altogether, for if Wollstonecraft's attacks on the form in part constitute social criticism, they also reveal a personal anxiety about the author's relation, as a woman, to the world of novel writing and reading. As Myers has noted of Wollstonecraft's novels as a whole, the works inevitably reveal a disjunction between theory and practice, for they cannot, without collapsing as texts that aim to engage their readers, sustain the sarcastic and superior tone of Wollstonecraft's criticism with regard to the form upon which they depend.[25] In separating herself from other women writers, Wollstonecraft effectively isolates herself, and this isolation finds its fullest expression in the singularity of the heroine of *Mary*, who repeatedly is set against the 'real' women populating the novel.

In the narrative's opening pages, the corruption of femininity is linked closely to the influence of novel reading. Mary's self-absorbed mother spends her time looking at herself in the mirror – fashioning, in effect, her own self-portraits – and reading novels, and the two activities are figured as different versions of narcissism. Novels appear as 'those most delightful substitutes for bodily dissipation,' as part of a process of degeneration that has its roots in the female body's essentially pathological sensibility (2). The mother is granted only a 'bodily, or ... animal soul' as a result of her affection for activities such as novel reading and socializing, entertainments which 'are all equally addressed to the senses' (2).[26] The mother's focus on the surface of things renders her, ultimately, 'a mere nothing' a cipher capable of bearing no meaning if only because, to use Pope's misogynist formulation, she is 'matter too soft a lasting mark to bear.'[27]

The novel that Mary singles out as an example of her mother's debauched taste centres around, significantly, a portrait narrative. Mary recounts the plot of *The Platonic Marriage*: 'The picture that was found on a bramble-bush, the new sensitive-plant, or tree, which caught the swain by the upper-garment, and presented to his ravished eyes a portrait. – Fatal image! – It planted a thorn in a till then insensible heart, and sent a new kind of a knight-errant into the world' (2). The portrait appears lodged in a discourse of sensuality and sexual intrigue, the swain appearing 'ravished' the moment the portrait imparts its 'fatal image.' The narrative's focus on the immediacy of the portrait's effect and on its seductive powers echoes the charges laid against the portrait in the art criticism we examined in chapter 1, and in Wollstonecraft's attack on the luxuriant pleasure afforded by the portrait narrative we hear echoes of Shaftesbury's denigration of sensuality in the moment of beholding. The reference to the 'knight-errant' ties the language of the visual arts back into the world of novels, particularly bad novels. Predictably, the mother who reads the portrait narrative is seduced, like the characters described in the work, by the emotion it creates, and she plants, 'in imitation of those susceptible souls, a rose bush' (3). The portrait, like the novel, encourages the reader to relinquish her intellectual powers, creating pleasure in the absence, rather than the presence, of a critical language.[28]

Mary attempts to escape the claustrophobia of feminine culture that the portrait and the novel signal by adopting the language of the sublime, which, as Gary Kelly has observed, connects Mary to the world of masculine power and intelligence.[29] 'Sublime ideas filled her young mind,' we discover, and Mary is contrasted with her intimate friend Ann by way of the sublime/beautiful opposition: 'In every thing it was not the great, but the beautiful, or the pretty, that caught [Ann's] attention. And in composition, the polish of style, and harmony of numbers, interested her much more than the flights of genius, or abstracted speculations' (5, 13). Throughout the narrative, Mary's affinity for the sublime aligns her perspective with an omniscient power, as when, while at sea, she experiences a storm that makes the sailors despair. Mary responds to the storm's danger by thinking of music suitable to the occasion: 'Some of Handel's sublime compositions occurred to her, and she sung them to the grand accompaniment. The Lord God Omnipotent reigned, and would reign for ever, and ever!' (46). Mary's attachment to sublime experiences grants her a commanding intellectual gaze that in turn establishes an ontological disjuncture between the daughter and her 'vegetating' mother (6).

When Mary responds to the events unfolding around her, her bodily experiences always appear as part of a larger moment of intellectual engagement. Her eyes, for example, are 'frequently moistened' by 'the sweet tears of benevolence ... [They] would never have been observed if her soul had not animated them' (10). These eyes are compared to those of the debauched, whose eyes 'look like polished diamonds, and dart from every superfice, giving more light to the beholders than they receive themselves' (10). In a language reminiscent of the political discourse of Manley's *The New Atalantis*, Wollstonecraft opposes the integrity of depth and inward-looking perception to the pleasure of the superficial eye, which looks but does not see, and which cannot communicate gesturally as part of an emotional exchange. Mary's eyes never threaten to draw attention to themselves outside of a sentimental framework, unlike the glances of those in her mother's social circle, who practise their seductive arts on all they encounter. The invisibility of Mary's eyes contributes to a larger program of self-abnegation that finds its fullest expression in the pathologization of the body, which is repeatedly disavowed as a means of allowing Mary access to power: 'She practised the most rigid œconomy, and had such power over her appetites and whims, that without any great effort she conquered them so entirely, that when her understanding or affections had an object, she almost forgot she had a body which required nourishment' (12). The fantasy Wollstonecraft sustains throughout the novel creates an ideal of sensibility expressed in the body (as a way of signalling the integrity of feeling) without the body possibly taking on an agency of its own. Mary muses, '"Sensibility is the most exquisite feeling of which the human soul is susceptible: when it pervades us, we feel happy; and could it last *unmixed*, we might form some conjecture of the bliss of those paradisiacal days, when the obedient passions were under the dominion of reason, and the impulses of the heart did not need correction"' (53, emphasis added). It is the problem of mixing the body with feelings, at the risk of the body mediating those feelings, that the novel repeatedly attempts to overcome.

Wollstonecraft marks the transcendence of the body as the sign of her heroine's escape from the debilitating confines of a life lived as a 'typical' woman.[30] During her sojourn in Portugal, Mary encounters a group of women who, like her mother, serve as a foil to the heroine. The contrast between the foibles of femininity and Mary's rational selfhood appears most strongly marked in a moment when the portrait appears again:

> When the weather began to clear up, Mary sometimes rode out alone, purposely to view the ruins that still remained of the earthquake: or she would ride to the banks of the Tagus, to feast her eyes with the sight of that

magnificent river. At other times she would visit the churches, as she was particularly fond of seeing historical paintings.

One of these visits gave rise to the subject, and the whole party descanted on it; but as the ladies could not handle it well, they soon adverted to portraits; and talked of the attitudes and characters in which they should wish to be drawn. Mary did not fix on one – when Henry, with more apparent warmth than usual, said, 'I would give the world for your picture, with the expression I have seen in your face, when you have been supporting your friend.'

This delicate compliment did not gratify her vanity, but it reached her heart. She then recollected that she had once sat for her picture – for whom was it designed? For a boy! Her cheeks flushed with indignation, so strongly did she feel an emotion of contempt at having been thrown away – given in with an estate. (28)

The opening paragraph of the scene aligns Mary's interest in the sublime with her taste for historical paintings, a taste that the narrator elsewhere confirms in her condemnation of Portuguese ornamental excess: 'Gothic finery, and unnatural decorations, which they term ornaments, are conspicuous in their churches and dress. Reverence for mental excellence is only to be found in a polished nation' (30). In contrast to Mary, the women staying at the hotel reveal their intellectual vacuity in their inability to appreciate the value of historical painting, a subject that they avoid because it escapes their limited range of education, as well as their own depraved taste, which is summed up in the idea of the portrait. In representing their desire to have themselves represented in 'attitudes and characters,' the text links the women to a particularly feminine form of portraiture, since the allegorical portrait was almost uniquely women's domain of representation when *Mary* was written. The women's desire to appear in a guise other than their own links them to the malleable superficiality associated with Mary's mother early in the narrative, to a female propensity for a world of fantasy and seduction far removed from any rational or properly sensible reality. Indeed, by wanting portraits of themselves to express an alternative reality by means of an allegorical representation, the women signal their desire to blur the boundaries between fact and fiction. Wollstonecraft suspects the women of feminine theatricality, attacking precisely the aesthetic that Kauffman celebrates in her self-portraits. Instead of drawing attention to the novel's own theatricality, which stages the representation of a woman that Wollstonecraft has introduced, in her preface, as a purely fictional being, the narrative backs away from its association with women who readily claim their interest in the world of fantasy and performance.

An alternative account of the portrait appears in Henry's desire to have Mary represented at the moment when she is most 'herself' – a moment defined by her altruism and sympathy for another. In contrast to the selfish narcissism Wollstonecraft associates with the women who enjoy picturing themselves, here Henry describes the idealized image of a selfless woman whose absorbed posture turns her away from the spectator's gaze. While the other women long for the theatrical and the fantasies it can inspire, Mary longs for nothing – at least, her desires are projected onto Henry, who appears as the ideal artist and beholder, wishing only for a moment of sentiment untainted by voyeuristic, erotic desires. Appropriately, Henry's comment circumvents the self-love that the common portrait is viewed as inspiring, eliciting only a sympathetic response in Mary, speaking to her heart rather than to her vanity. The ideal portrait, then, aligns the beholder's gaze and the sitter's body with the mental operations of a cultivated sensibility, becoming, like a historical painting, part of a world of rational thought and abstraction, rather than the world of excited bodies.

Mary's past experience with portraiture stands in sharp relief to Henry's account of the ideal representation. She conflates the story of her own portrait's status as a painting commissioned by and for a male patron with her circulation on the marriage market as an object traded by her father. Unlike the women who grant themselves a degree of agency in their imaginary constructions of the portrait tableaux, Mary thinks of her own portrait only as a version of her alienated self, a commodity rendered passive by law and property rights, 'given in with an estate.' Her version of the portrait reformulates the emptiness that characterizes her mother's existence, for the representation has effectively evacuated, through its participation in the arranged marriage plot, any version of the self that Mary recognizes as her own.

Mary's objection to finding herself part of a chain of substitutions that include her representation speaks not only to the specific circumstances of her oppression at the hands of her father, but also to her fears of any kind of self-division, including that of the mind and body. The portrait's bodiliness and possible excess makes Henry's desire for Mary's image, and his attachment to Mary more generally, somewhat dubious, part of a larger sexual narrative that Mary must refuse. As Johnson points out, Mary 'is revolted by the primal scene towards which the Henry plot is leading her.'[31] The portrait signals the body's corporeality, its inevitable presence even at the moments defined most clearly in sentimental terms. Henry's idealized image of the portrait only leads Mary to respond to her own image with disgust, a revulsion articulated in the ejaculation, 'For a boy!' Mary's husband appears as a figure of maleness uncultivated as an adult mind, a man defined, in other words, only by his sex – and by extension, his male sexuality, adolescent and precocious. Mary's comment betrays the fear that her portrait will be viewed with sexual desire and will encourage its beholder to view her body as an erotic object, a fear that finds its fullest expression in the final pages of the narrative: 'When her husband would take her hand, or mention any thing like love, she would instantly feel a sickness, a faintness at her heart, and wish, involuntarily, that the earth would open and swallow her' (67).

While Kauffman makes use of the portrait's doubleness – its ability to signal both a body and a mind capable of controlling, as well as absorbing, the beholder's gaze – in her representations, Wollstonecraft refuses the possibility of a female agency figured through the thinking body. Instead, she gestures toward her heroine's imminent demise as a release from the world of self-division and alienation: 'She thought she was hastening to that world *where there is neither marrying*, nor giving in marriage' (68, emphasis in text). In Wollstonecraft's epistemological framework, Mary's death signals the death of representation and the chain of possible substitutions it implies. Rather than manipulating, as Samuel Richardson does in *Clarissa*, the potential for duality lodged in the portrait, both in life and death, Wollstonecraft presents the portrait narrative and her heroine's life more generally only in terms of its ability to render a woman passive in relation to the forces of patriarchal customs and discourses. In turn, the conflation of embodiment and enslavement in the fictional form most closely associated with women establishes, in *Mary*, the contours of a narrative dilemma with which Wollstonecraft would grapple for the rest of her writing life. It also creates, in relation to the portrait and the novel, the impossibility of women inhabiting these genres in positive terms. The body that laboured to write *Mary* is necessarily denied in the terms established by the novel, which instead celebrates, in its preface, the 'soul of the author' ([i]) freed from history and example.

The strain of Wollstonecraft's attempts to distance herself from the novel's and the portrait's associations with a degraded femininity appears in the novel's degeneration, in its final pages, into the very mode of sentimental fiction that Wollstonecraft despised. Her later repudiation of *Mary*, recorded in a letter to her sister in 1797, speaks to her awareness of the novel's failure, which was also commented upon by a review that appeared two years after the novel was first published:

> The fiction is of that cast which is called moral; that is, good principles and a love of virtue are inculcated throughout: but we very much doubt whether these tender and pathetic moral tales ever do, in fact, contribute to promote virtue and morality in the world. They are too apt to enervate young minds; to cherish propensities which are better checked; to make them affect what they do not feel; to give them false and romantic notions of life; to teach them to expect incidents and characters which are rarely, if ever, to be found; to disgust and put them out of humour with such as actually occur.[32]

This language, of course, echoes precisely the claims that Wollstonecraft made against other women's novels of the period, and indicates the extent to which *Mary*'s attempts to move beyond the confines of a feminine sensibility inadvertently bring the novel face to face with the most extreme manifestations of female hysteria and narcissism. As Johnson eloquently states, '*Mary*, its heroine, and its plot fall exhausted before categories of sex and gender.'[33]

Wollstonecraft's vexed relation to the cultural forms associated with the feminine can be read a number of ways. Marilyn Butler suggests that Wollstonecraft's novels reflect 'two traditions' that confronted women writers at the end of the eighteenth century: 'They retain the introverted intensity that went with the heroine of sensibility, while also demonstrating that a social novel in which the protagonist is a woman deals, perforce, with a drearily narrow view of society, a frustrating, repetitive type of social experience.'[34] Susan Gubar takes a more negative view of the dynamic that Wollstonecraft's attack on the feminine initiates. Describing the 'odd juxtapositions' that appear between *A Vindication of the Rights of Woman* and Wollstonecraft's novels, Gubar argues that 'the misogynist portrait of the feminine penned by the feminist may, in fact, represent Wollstonecraft's efforts to negotiate the distance between desire and dread, what she thought she should have been and what she feared herself to be.'[35] Wollstonecraft could not imagine, it appears, a woman writer whose success did not depend on her evacuation of the personal and the particular – of the world of private interests – from the authorial persona. *Mary* effectively cuts the ground out from under the figure of the embodied female subject, and in doing so forced the author into a self-defeating posture by refusing to acknowledge the conditions of the novel's production by a woman. Elizabeth Inchbald, as we shall see, saved her narrative and her own authorial persona from a similar fate by focusing, like Kauffman, on the work involved in the creation of art.

The Return of the Repressed: Inchbald's *A Simple Story*

A Simple Story was widely praised when it first appeared in 1791, and Inchbald was heralded as a preeminent novelist: 'Mrs Inchbald has discovered the true path which she ought to pursue,' wrote the *Critical Review*.[36] The *General Magazine*'s review commented: 'The work will always give satisfaction to an intelligent and feeling reader, because it treats of no concern but those of the heart, and delineates no scenes but those of a domestic nature, in which every parent, every child, and every friend, are interested, as they are all more or less liable to be called upon to act a part.'[37] The idea of the novel's ability to expand the range of the domestic to include everyone suggests the power of private interests to speak a universalizing language, the language of the heart, a language recognized by 1791 as finding its most palpable and legitimate expression in the novel. Inchbald demonstrates her acumen by aptly representing this sphere of human experience – 'our authoress manifests an accurate knowledge of the human heart' – with exceptional force: 'to those who delight in tracing the struggles and the bursts of passion, we announce a degree of pleasure, which seems to be the greater because the power of communicating it is uncommon.'[38] Nowhere (with the exception of Wollstonecraft's review of the novel, to which I will return below) do the critics condemn the illicit conduct of the novel's heroine, Miss Milner.[39] Rather, the novel appears as a safe repository of emotional excess, a place where, as Catherine Gallagher has so insightfully argued, women readers might exercise their emotions in order to better regulate their feelings in 'real' life: 'Such a deliberate creation of emotional discontinuity allows for a separate dimension of affective life, one in which emotions were only "practiced" ... such emotional "practice" would have been especially important for women in an age when the new affective demands of family life came into conflict with the still prevalent belief that women were not to love before they were beloved.'[40] Gallagher makes this comment in her discussion of Charlotte Lennox's *Female Quixote*, a novel whose dénouement bears a striking resemblance to that of *A Simple Story* in its representation of a young woman's entrance into a marriage with a man whom she has not yet learned to love.

If critical commentary appears comfortable with the various excesses displayed in *A Simple Story*, it reveals a level of dissatisfaction with the formal structure of the text.[41] I will return to this critical dissatisfaction as I discuss the textual moments around which it appears. For now, I would like to suggest that these narrative irruptions highlight the novel's latent resistance to the very terms that guaranteed its success. Inchbald's insistence on her public status as an author finds expression in the structural fissures of the text, narrative moments that find their thematic counterpart in the novel's representation of women's relation to visual culture in general and the portrait in particular. Like Kauffman, Inchbald opens up the text to reveal the body of the artist as a source of both resistance and autonomy.

The portrait that Inchbald presents of herself in the novel's prefatory remarks defines a rhetorical mode that the novel employs throughout its narrative: 'The writer frankly avows, that during the time she has been writing it, she has suffered every quality and degree of weariness and lassitude, into which no other employment could have betrayed her ... But, alas! in the exercise of the arts, industry scarce bears the name of merit. – What then is to be substitute in the place of genius? GOOD FORTUNE.'[42] Many eighteenth-century critics observed the singularity of these remarks as a form of self-introduction: 'The mind is enamoured with the repeated discoveries of its own powers, and congratulates itself while it contemplates its beauteous offspring. Let Mrs. Inchbald reflect how often she has experienced such delight, such rapture, and forbear to complain of the labour by which it was preceded.'[43] Like Kauffman, Inchbald draws attention to the work involved in creating the narrative that absorbs her readers; 'I was ten months, unceasingly, finishing my novel,' she recounted later.[44] 'Weariness and lassitude' replace the idea of genius, foregrounding the physical toll that the writing has taken on the author rather than entertaining the idea that to write is to become absorbed into the narrative's imaginary landscape. Inchbald refuses the fantasy that authors inhabit the worlds in an unmediated fashion, a fiction upheld by Wollstonecraft in her 'Advertisement' to *Mary*: 'Lost in a pleasing enthusiasm, they live in the scenes they represent' ([i]). While Wollstonecraft imagines herself as her novel's ideal reader, Inchbald identifies her writing as a form of labour motivated by necessity – in other words, as a sign of her status as a professional woman, rather than as a woman enjoying leisure time filled with novel reading.

A similar reluctance to enter into socially sanctioned habits of reading and learning characterizes the attitude of the heroine in *A Simple Story*'s first two volumes. Like her predecessor, Miss Betsy Thoughtless, Miss Milner appears impervious to pedagogy. The blankness that characterizes Miss Milner, like that of Betsy Thoughtless, does not constitute her as a *tabula rasa*, as it does in such characters as the young Lord Elmwood and Miss Fenton: 'Lord Elmwood had discovered all that beauty in Miss Fenton which every common observer could not but see – the charms of her mind and her fortune had been pointed out to him by his Tutor; and the utility of their marriage in perfect submission to his precepts, his lordship never permitted himself to question' (38). When her guardian, Dorriforth, insists on the importance '"of reflection; of reading; of thoughts for a future state,"' Miss Milner responds with equivocation: 'She sometimes put on the looks and gesture of assent, and sometimes even spoke the language of conviction; but this, the first call of dissipation would change to ill-timed raillery' (18). The language that describes Miss Milner's resistance focuses on the potential for the visual to register an intent that does not, in fact, exist in the bearer of the look. In his analysis of the slipperiness of promises in *A Simple Story*, Ian Balfour comments on this narrative element, describing the novel's preoccupation 'with correlating the visual and the verbal or the visual (in the sense of what appears to be the case) and the realm of action, with attention to discrepancies between one's words and one's looks.'[45] As in Haywood's novel, the visual domain becomes the space of resistance to the social demands that various guardian figures would like to place on the heroine. Miss Milner enjoys her power as a spectacle and the freedom to which she is entitled as an unmarried woman: 'She was beautiful, she had been too frequently told the high value of that beauty, and thought those moments passed in wasteful idleness during which she was not gaining some new conquest' (15).

Even while insisting on her beauty, the narrative's focus on Miss Milner's visual aspect tends to obscure rather than clarify her relation to the world, introducing an interpretive problem that stands in contrast to the figure Dorriforth: 'On his countenance you beheld the feelings of his heart ... On this countenance his thoughts were pictured' (8). The different relation Miss Milner and Dorriforth bear to the visual defines their conflicting understanding of the self's necessary subordination to social demands, with Miss Milner ready to manipulate the world of appearances in order to maintain what little power she has. For Dorriforth, the fit between the world of appearances and his internal reality confirms his authority; for Miss Milner, such a fit would involve self-abnegation. Indeed, at one of the few moments when Miss Milner takes to heart a critical view of her conduct, she experiences 'an inward nothingness,' a feeling that confirms the sense that for women to internalize social dictates is to relinquish any claim to agency (40).[46]

The most notable instance of Miss Milner's ability to manipulate the world of visual appearances occurs when she dresses for the masquerade. Terry Castle has defined the transgressive elements of the masquerade, noticing, in particular, the significance of Miss Milner's costume, which appears as markedly ambiguous.[47] Inchbald writes that 'although it was the representative of the goddess of Chastity, yet from the buskins, and the petticoat made to festoon far above the ankle, it had, on the first glance, the appearance of a female much less virtuous' (155). This costume takes us back to Kauffman's self-portraits, and the double vision they use to establish both the visual interest of the representation and the authority of the artist in relation to the aesthetic experience created by the painting. Indeed, Miss Milner's appearance in the masquerade costume transforms her into a *tableau vivant*, of the kind that Pointon has discussed in her analysis of Emma Hamilton, the mistress of Charles Grenville, wife of William Hamilton, and lover of Lord Nelson. Emma Hamilton was frequently the subject of allegorical portraits, and she took her popularity as an image on canvas one step farther, actually performing the poses in which she had been painted as a series of 'attitudes:' 'Emma Hamilton (and her promoter) offered her body as a picture to an audience ... as a representation which bridged the gap between actuality (performance) and fantasy (representation).'[48] Emma's enactments of the themes governing her portraits allowed the real body to be present in the moment of creating the allegorical allusion, making it seem more readily accessible to the sexual fantasies generated by the representation even while heightening the sensationalism of that body by 'staging' it. The allegorical allusion that Miss Milner creates in her masquerade costume has a similar effect, intensifying the erotic charge already connected to her body through the convergence of the classical language governing the representation of Diana and the language of eighteenth-century sexual transgression, summed up in the idea of the prostitute. Inchbald's use of the double vision focuses on the issue of self-representation as a form of self-governance implicit in both Diana's and the prostitute's identities and enacted in Miss Milner's refusal to obey Dorriforth's injunction concerning the masquerade.

The kind of epistemological confusion created by this mixing of the real and the representational appears, in the case of Miss Milner, as a confusion both of the boundaries separating licit and illicit female conduct, and as a blurring of gender categories. When interrogated about Miss Milner's costume, the servants respond equivocally: '"She was in men's cloaths,"' declares one; '"She went in her own dress, my lord ... a woman's dress to be sure,"' replies another (159). Castle observes that 'The ambiguity here is related to the fact that the heroine impersonates Diana, the most androgynous and sexually elusive of classical goddesses.'[49] There is also the sense that in self-consciously manipulating the costume to make it appear more dangerous, Miss Milner has taken on a kind of agency that appears perverse in its intention, and that the mere assumption of the right to perform this masquerade creates confusion in the eyes of her beholders. Pointon notes that similar confusion appears when Emma Hamilton's 'art' is likened to that of the Apollo Belvedere.[50] The act of performance, in both Emma's and Miss Milner's cases, provides access to the male realm of experience, granting the women a form of authority that nonetheless relies on the spectacle of the female body, as when Miss Milner appears at the masquerade ball: 'she perceived she was the first object of admiration in the place' (161).

Miss Milner's moment of self-fashioning necessarily disrupts the marriage plot the heroine inhabits, for it assumes that female self-transformation can be tied to an agenda other than the one established by the exchange relations of the marriage market. Just as Miss Milner's character proves impervious to pedagogical imprinting, so too her theatrical impulse resists a form of role-playing restricted to the conventions of domestic femininity. Even in the moment of marriage, Miss Milner's behaviour remains partially indecipherable. When Dorriforth asks if she will be the dutiful wife that she has not been as a lover, she does not articulate a response, but rather allows 'the expression of her face, the tears with which she bathed his hands' to speak for her (192). The visualization of the body, far from confirming the integrity of sentiment, only heightens the difficulty of interpreting Miss Milner's acts.

The scene that follows the marriage ceremony abruptly concludes the narrative sustained by the novel's first two volumes: 'We left Lady Elmwood in the last volume at the summit of human happiness; a loving and beloved bride. – We begin this volume, and find her upon her death bed' (195). Miss Milner's death marks the moment when the visual collapses into a pedagogical framework, as the narrative offers up the spectacle of the dying woman as a lesson to the reader: 'In a large gloomy apartment of this solitary habitation ... was laid upon her death-bed, the once lovely Lady Elmwood – pale, half-suffocated with the loss of breath' (199). Miss Milner has been transformed into a passive figure whose meaning only points toward a death that results directly from a moral transgression: 'The beautiful, the beloved Miss Milner – she is no longer beautiful – no longer beloved – no longer – tremble while you read it! – no longer – virtuous' (194). The reader is encouraged to establish a cause and effect relation between Miss Milner's fall from grace and her descent into the grave, and to imagine the spectacle of death as part of a large moral paradigm. The abjection of this spectacle is reinforced by the transformation of Miss Milner's own modes of beholding, which likewise serve a disciplinary function in the final moments of the heroine's life: 'Her dying eyes darted a ray of brightness – but her failing voice endeavoured, in vain, to articulate – At length, her eyes fixing upon her daughter as their last dear object, she was just understood to utter the word "Father"' (200–1).

Critics for both *The Monthly Review* and *The Critical Review* objected to the abrupt ending of Miss Milner's story, and the roughness of the transition to her daughter's narrative: 'This same haste, and apparent desire of finishing the production *out of hand*, to speak in the workman's phrase, have also been the cause of Mrs. Inchbald's carrying us, too precipitately, from the events of Lady Elmwood's life, and her last scenes of it, to those of her daughter, many years afterward.'[51] Another commentary returns to the terms governing the *Critical Review*'s objections to the novel's preface, complaining that Inchbald's refusal to disavow the labour of writing carries into the narrative structure of her work, reducing the novel's artistic achievement. The critic's discomfort with the heavy-handedness of the transition highlights what is often overlooked in the transitional moment between the two narratives – the extent to which the rupture exposes the potential for violence to emerge out of the marriage plot and its pedagogical imperatives. As Jo Alyson Parker observes, 'The very disunity of the text enables Inchbald to make a unified argument about women's limited options.'[52] Indeed, the violence required to bring Miss Milner's agency as both a subject and object of vision into line with a moral lesson effectively calls that lesson into question, revealing the extent to which marriage guarantees only loss for women in a social world governed by dictatorial patriarchs such as Lord Elmwood. The *General Magazine* commented on the arbitrary nature of Miss Milner's fall, refusing to believe in the novel's attempts to attribute her disgrace to a faulty education:

> Much stress, by our fair authoress, is every where put on the wrong education of Miss Milner. This her father regrets on his death-bed, and this is seriously impressed on the reader as the great lesson to which the whole relation refers: but, in the conduct of this lady, it is no where specified, or even very apparent, except in that criminality which we conceive an absurdity, as justified, indicated, or countenanced in the least degree by any feature in her character.[53]

Portraits of the Woman Artist 201

In its defence of Miss Milner, the review reveals the extent to which education has not informed Miss Milner's character at all, and points toward the fact that the only exception to this rule appears to have occurred with Miss Milner's transformation into Lady Elmwood, a transformation that leads immediately, in narrative time, to the heroine's death. This critical, and, I believe, textual awareness of the extent to which Miss Milner's death appears more closely connected to the effects of marriage than to the effects of the character's flaws allows us to reflect on the extent to which the alignment of the mother's eye with the imperative 'Father' may function less as an endorsement than as a critique of the parental dictates governing the concluding volumes of the novel.

Most critics today read the concluding volumes of *A Simple Story* in light of the defeatist tone that they hear in the transitional moment bridging Miss Milner's story to her daughter's. Jane Spencer articulates a commonly held view in stating that 'all the troubling questions raised by Miss Milner are laid to rest by Lady Matilda, a submissive and properly feminine father's daughter.'[54] Castle provides an alternative perspective, however, claiming that 'Matilda's story not only resembles her mother's, it is a displaced recapitulation.'[55] In what follows, I would like to pursue Castle's line of investigation in order to suggest how Inchbald was able to craft a novel that avoids the traps encountered by *Mary*, even while occupying, to a certain extent, what Johnson calls the 'hyperfeminine' space that increasingly was assigned to women writers at the end of the eighteenth century.[56] In particular, I will trace how the portrait narrative that evolves in the last two volumes of the novel intensifies, rather than disperses, the transgressive elements of Miss Milner's performance as a *tableau vivant* in the masquerade scene, an intensification that brings the novel even closer to the practices of Angelica Kauffman examined earlier in this chapter.

As Castle points out, the structure of the novel's second half bears a striking resemblance to the first, and the thematic concern with the visual informs this connection. Matilda represents, first and foremost, the renewed threat of the visual and its capacity to disrupt familial law. Dorriforth, now Lord Elmwood, issues strict injunctions against seeing his daughter after she comes into his protection: 'But, if, whether by design or by accident, I ever see or hear from her; that moment my compliance to her mother's supplication ceases, and I abandon her once more' (213). The taboo associated with the presence of the daughter's body in the field of vision heightens the erotic frisson waiting to find expression between the father and the daughter, and establishes the law of the father that the narrative longs to violate. The narrative's description of Matilda takes us back to the ambiguity surrounding the figure of Miss Milner in her masquerade costume; significantly, this description appears as Matilda meditates on a portrait of her father:

> In the features of her father she was proud to discern the exact moulds in which her own appeared to have been modelled; yet Matilda's person, shape, and complection [sic] were so extremely like what her mother's once were, that at the first glance she appeared to have a still greater resemblance of her, than of her father – but her mind and manners were all Lord Elmwood's. (220)

I will return to the significance of the portrait trope below. For now, I would like to stress the extent to which the description equivocates as to which parent Matilda most resembles, suggesting first her father, then mother, then father again. In reading this passage, it becomes impossible to decide – Matilda seems able to shape-shift in the moment she is beheld. The narrative first grants us Matilda's perspective on her resemblance to her father, but then offers its own assessment of her resemblance to her mother and father, associating her body with Miss Milner and her 'mind and manners' with Lord Elmwood. Rather than confirming the female body as the site of irrational desire, this configuration creates the possibility of a body that will serve as the agent of a consciously recognized desire for the presence of the father in the daughter who sees herself in him: 'The consanguineous relationship between the viewer and subject here adds a narcissistic as well as incestuous element to Matilda's fascination with the painting.'[57] In the moment of beholding she describes here, Inchbald brings together the rational and irrational into a configuration that echoes Kauffman's blending of features commonly opposed as irreconcilably masculine and feminine.

In the gender confusion surrounding Matilda's description, we recall Miss Milner's cross-gendered masquerade costume and its ability to elicit conflicting reports concerning its appearance. Castle notes how the masquerade space of the first half of the novel reappears in the very domestic space inhabited by Lord Elmwood and his daughter, and I would add, further, that Matilda is defined by the fact that she inhabits the masquerade costume of gender transgression in her very person. For it is not only in her appearance that Matilda demonstrates a curious blurring of gender boundaries: 'Matilda was moved, but she possessed too much of the manly resentment of her father, to discover what she felt for the first few minutes' (259).

Matilda repeatedly attempts to wield the power possessed by her father, exercising her authority, in particular, over the feminized character of her cousin, Rushbrook.[58] Matilda measures her relation to her father, not by the distance he maintains from her, but by her desire to come as close to him as possible, both in her own attitudes and in her desire to close the gap between them. Matilda's desire for her father fills her fantasy life: '"She would lay hold of his hands, clasp his knees, provoke him to spurn her, which would be joy in comparison to this cruel indifference"' (244). She is prone to kissing hands that have shaken his and shows an active fixation on the objects he has touched: 'a hat, lying on one of the tables, gave her a sensation beyond any other she experienced on this occasion – in that trifling article of his dress, she thought she saw himself, and held it in her hand with pious reverence' (246). George E. Haggerty claims that 'Lady Matilda fetishizes these leavings and plays with his pen because patriarchy itself has made any other relation to power utterly pointless,' but I would draw attention to the extent to which Matilda also entertains the fantasy not only of having her father, but of *being* him and assuming his authority.[59] Rushbrook would also like to be a version of Lord Elmwood, but only so as to become the object of Matilda's desire; Matilda wants the power associated with her father's position.

Matilda's imaginative visualization of her father finds its objective correlative in the portrait upon which she is free to gaze:

> There was one object, however, among all she saw, which attracted her attention above the rest, and she would stand for hours to look at it – This was a full length portrait of Lord Elmwood, esteemed a very capital picture, and a great likeness – to this picture she would sigh and weep; though when it was first pointed out to her, she shrunk back with fear, and it was some time before she dared venture to cast her eyes completely upon it. (220)

Matilda's response to the portrait mimics her touching of her father's objects, whereby the object stands in a synechdochic relation to the body itself. Here the portrait first strikes fear into Matilda because of the daughter's awareness of the father's law, which forbids her entrance into his visual space. But the portrait's status as a substitution for the father, rather than consolidating Elmwood's hold over Matilda, inadvertently allows her to practise transgressing that law, granting her the power of the spectator, a power that, in this moment of beholding, seems to render the father passive, a screen upon which the daughter projects all of her longing. As in Betsy Thoughtless's handling of Trueworth's miniature, the female gaze here seems capable of rendering the male body it perceives malleable and open to new interpretations, to the extent that, as we saw above, Matilda reads the portrait as a version of self-portraiture. The portrait's gaze – and its authority over the family's visual space – disappears in this scene, allowing Matilda to appropriate, momentarily, the position of power enjoyed by her father in her assumption of spectatorial control.

Matilda assumes a conventionally feminine posture before the portrait, weeping and sighing, but reveals a stubborn tenacity in her willingness to stand for hours in front of the painting, as if to become a version of the painting itself. In this combination of masculine and feminine traits, Matilda produces a paradoxically aggressive masochism that aims at the father's seduction. While Matilda's worship and mimicry of her father's postures renders her in part complicitous with her own oppression, rebellion against his law emerges simultaneously in the unregulated body that Matilda has inherited from her mother. The famous staircase scene represents the realization of Matilda's desire:

> When she had descended a few stairs, she heard a footstep walking slowly up; and, (from what emotion she could not tell,) she stopt [*sic*] short, half resolved to return back. – She hesitated a single instant which to do – then went a few steps farther till she came to the second landing place; when, by the sudden winding of the staircase, – Lord Elmwood was immediately before her!
>
> She had felt something like affright before she saw him – but her reason told her she had nothing to fear, as he was far away. – But now the appearance of a stranger whom she had never before seen; an air of authority in his looks as well as in the sound of his steps; a resemblance to the portrait she had seen of him; a start of astonishment which he gave on beholding her; but above all – her *fears* confirmed her it was him. – She gave a scream of terror – put out her trembling hands to catch the balustrades on the stairs for support – missed them – and fell motionless into her father's arms.
>
> He caught her, as by that impulse he would have caught any other person falling for want of aid. – Yet when he found her in his arms, he still held her there – gazed on her attentively – and once pressed her to his bosom.

At length, trying to escape the snare into which he had been led, he was going to leave her on the spot where she fell, when her eyes opened and she uttered, 'Save me.' – Her voice unmanned him. His long-restrained tears now burst forth – and seeing her relapsing into the swoon again, he cried out eagerly to recall her. – Her name did not however come to his recollection – nor any name but this – 'Miss Milner – Dear Miss Milner.' (273–4)

I quote this passage at length because it retraces the terrain laid out by the portrait motif earlier in Matilda's narrative. Matilda desires her father more than she fears him, and is willing to break the family taboos that separate her from him in her descent down the stairs. The response of fear that coming face to face with her father provokes in Matilda facilitates, rather than hinders, the reunion, allowing the body to express Matilda's desire in its collapse into the father's arms – just as the fear that Matilda experiences when she views the portrait for the first time leads not to her avoiding, but rather to her obsessive beholding of, the image of the patriarch. When Lord Elmwood makes signs of relinquishing his daughter's body, Matilda recovers long enough to beg, '"Save me."' As Nora Nachumi notes, 'The eloquence of Matilda's body – and its ability to affect Elmwood emotionally – ... earn her a limited form of autonomy.'[60] Matilda renders the figure of masculine authority passive once more, seeming to trigger a castration anxiety in her father – 'Her voice unmanned him' – which in turn allows for the release of his repressed feelings. Lord Elmwood's breakdown enables both the realization of Matilda's fantasy – he relinquishes his posture of 'cruel indifference' – and the resurrection of her mother; in his embrace with his daughter, Elmwood's youthful passion is revived. It is Matilda's body that now provokes Lord Elmwood to cry, '"Miss Milner – Dear Miss Milner."' Matilda reduces her father to a hapless lover once more, placing him in the only powerless position he has ever known – that of Miss Milner's fiancé.

Like Miss Milner's trip to the masquerade, Matilda's moment of transgression necessarily provokes an immediate backlash. Lord Elmwood orders his servant to separate him from his child, refusing to touch Matilda's hand: 'And seizing her hand, [Giffard] pulled it with violence – it fell – and her father went away' (274). At this point Matilda takes up the role of hysteric, becoming a sentimental heroine weak and sick with distress. But the agency she assumes in relation to her father's portrait does not disappear entirely; rather, it becomes part of the visual landscape of the Gothic narrative that Matilda's banishment from

Elmwood Castle initiates. Wollstonecraft objected to Matilda's transfiguration into a Gothic heroine, claiming that,

> educated in adversity she should have learned (to prove that a cultivated mind is a real advantage) how to bear, nay, rise above her misfortunes, instead of suffering her health to be undermined by the trials of her patience, which ought to have strengthened her understanding. Why do all female writers, even when they display their abilities, always give a sanction to the libertine reveries of men?[61]

Wollstonecraft's comments are revealing in that they expose the sexual content latent in the narrative of Matilda's decline, a content that the criticism attributes to Inchbald's need to gratify her male readers. But in fact, the libertine aspect of the narrative focuses its attention on the breakdown of the laws that have kept Matilda apart from her father, a disintegration that begins to occur as men rush to and from the spectacle of her wasting body. Rushbrook returns from a visit to Matilda 'heated' and 'disordered,' only to find himself struck by the connection between father and daughter: 'There was yet that which engaged his attention, beyond any circumstance relating to himself – the features of Lord Elmwood – of which his daughter's, whom he had just beheld, had the most striking resemblance' (313). The portrait motif, and the danger it contains, begins to include more participants in its visual field as the Gothic tension of the narrative is heightened.

The increasingly surreal aspect of the narrative allows Inchbald to return more explicitly to the topoi of transgression and desire that organized Miss Milner's story in the first two volumes of the novel. As Marilyn Butler has observed, the discourse of the Gothic in Ann Radcliffe provides access to 'a sphere which is not special to women, but in which women may have more awareness and more articulateness – reduction to the inmost core of being, the point at which rage, inadequacy, and threatened identity become felt as sufficiently real to blot out external reality.' In particular, Butler notes how the Gothic is able to comment upon 'a topic virtually taboo for middle-class women authors, the heroine's sexuality.'[62] Matilda's pitiful condition mirrors the state of abjection that brought her father to her once before, and her victimization inspires his return once again, albeit on different terms. As the predatory Viscount Margrave steals Matilda away from her home, it is the spectacle of her body and her screams that initiate her reunion with Lord Elmwood. A local farmer, 'being informed Lady Matilda was her whom he had

Portraits of the Woman Artist 207

beheld, this intelligence, joined to the powerful effect her screams had on him, made him resolve to take horse immediately, and with some friends, follow the carriage till they should trace the place to which she was conveyed' (321). The threat of violation to his daughter's body immediately brings Lord Elmwood to the rescue and allows the father and daughter to be united as a family group that is defined in opposition to the desires of the interloper: 'That moment her father entered – and with the unrestrained fondness of a parent, folded her in his arms ... These were the happiest moments she had ever known – perhaps the happiest *he* had ever known' (328–9).

Here the narrative seems to close the gap, as it did in the pages joining the two halves of the novel, between the world of visual pleasure and the law of the father; Matilda responds to her father's words 'with a look of love and duty; her tongue could not utter a sentence' (329). At this point we know that Matilda's intentions and looks are aligned within a matrix of daughterly desire now properly domesticated. It is precisely the possibility of this occurrence that Jane Gallop warns against in *The Daughter's Seduction*: 'The father's law has so restructured the daughter and her desires that it is hard, well nigh impossible, to differentiate the Father (that is to say, the Law) from the male sexed body.'[63] Thus when Lord Elmwood directs her to marry Rushbrook, it seems that Matilda agrees to do so, although she has previously revealed no interest in Rushbrook as a lover: 'The idea of love never once came to her thoughts; and she would sport with Rushbrook like the most harmless child' (334). The earlier transgressions, which depended on a separation of the father's body from his law, are now superceded by Matilda's willingness to obey Lord Elmwood *because* of her desire – a disappointing trajectory, to say the least.

It seems that eighteenth-century critics were also disappointed in the ending. 'We think also, that the total change in Lord *Elmwood*'s sentiments, and the subsequent events, constituting the *denouement* and conclusion of the work, rush on the mind with too much hurry and confusion,' wrote *The Monthly Review*.[64] 'Never was an impatience to conclude more manifest in this novel: and we are persuaded that it was under the latent influence of those feelings of impatience, and of the bad effects of them on her denouement, that Mrs. Inchbald wrote her preface,' agreed *The Critical Review*.[65] The idea that the conclusion might be linked to Inchbald's authorial fatigue provides a way of reading against the grain of the novel's ostensibly pat conclusion. For the critical uneasiness with the conclusion suggests that the marriage plot does not, in this instance, satisfy the expectations that have been set up by the text. Like the rough transition between volumes two and three, the heavy-handedness of the conclusion reveals certain truths about the moment it describes.

The forced quality of the novel's closing moments reminds us of the withering comment that appeared in the *Monthly Review*'s assessment of *The Portrait* (1783): 'Novels *must* end happily.'[66] The narrator's response to Rushbrook's proposal of marriage registers the ambivalence of the moment: 'Whether the heart of Matilda, such as it has been described, *could* sentence him to misery, the reader is left to surmise' (337). The reader remembers, indeed, that Matilda's heart has formed a deep attachment to one man – but that man is not Rushbrook. Inchbald does not naturalize the marriage plot by having Matilda fall in love with Rushbrook, and Matilda's unconsciousness of even the possibility that she might be united with her cousin makes the marriage appear arranged. The narrative commits its heroine to a marriage plot at almost exactly the same moment that it describes her passion for her father, a coincidence that heightens the strangeness of the novel's conclusion. By highlighting the sisterly nature of Matilda's feelings for Rushbrook, Inchbald continues the incest narrative, suggesting its centrality in the workings of the exchange relations governing the family, while simultaneously producing a queasy feeling in the reader vis-à-vis Rushbrook's and Matilda's marriage.[67] The marriage plot thus sustains the Gothic tone that has coloured all of Matilda's story, undermining its final insistence on the benefits of 'A PROPER EDUCATION' by drawing our attention to plot contrivances that appear more fanciful than pedagogical.

The double vision we experience at the novel's conclusion, whereby Matilda appears in two very different roles simultaneously, takes us back to the split picture provided by Miss Milner in her masquerade costume, and to the undecidability of Matilda's countenance that appeared in relation to her father's portrait. The very rhetorical structure of the novel's description of Matilda's entrance into marriage – 'Whether the heart of Matilda ... *could* sentence him to misery' – invites us to contemplate a perverse twist instead of the pat resolution we are offered. We wonder about the author's intention, and as we do, the figure of Elizabeth Inchbald labouring over her novel's conclusion appears. Anna Lott describes a similar rhetorical moment in her account of Inchbald's response to George Colman the Younger's attack on her essays. Inchbald writes, 'The judgment on which I placed my reliance on this occasion was – that many readers might be amused and informed, whilst no one dramatist could possibly be offended, by the cursory remarks of a female observer'; as Lott notes, this comment is 'powerfully duplicitous. By taking a self-consciously deferential stance, claiming that a woman's words should not be offensive – should not, in fact, even be taken seriously – Inchbald effectively diffuses and deflects Colman's criticism and any further criticism before it can occur'[68] In the rhetorical space of *A Simple Story*, a space in which appearances and realities are often misaligned, a similarly crafty epistemology appears, one that acknowledges the woman author's ability to appear invested in the pedagogical imperatives of sentimental fiction even as it flouts those imperatives.

In her own comments on novel writing, Inchbald celebrated the liberty it affords the author: 'The Novelist is a free agent.'[69] *A Simple Story* demonstrates this point in the freedom it takes both with its narrative structure and its subject matter. Like Angelica Kauffman, and like Delarivier Manley writing three generations before her, Inchbald molds the exigencies of women's private lives to accord her female characters more, rather than less, agency, and models this configuration of agency after the figure of the woman writer. Rather than pathologizing femininity, like Wollstonecraft, Inchbald turns it inside out, allowing her novel to articulate a vantage point from which to recognize the potential for feminine culture, and the world of private interests it sustains, to provide a point of access to the world of public debate. As Spencer argues, 'The novel has a feminist interest, not because it shares the contemporary advocacy of a rational education for women, but because it reveals what was repressed in order to make that case.'[70] Kauffman's self-portraits, in their careful manipulation of the codes of desire and decorum surrounding late-eighteenth-century understandings of femininity, provide a visual correlative to Inchbald's textual work, and together, the two provide us with an alternative account to the one provided by Wollstonecraft's despairing vision. They also suggest how women artists found ways to resist the appropriation of the sensibility and private interests by male writers and painters in order to maintain their hold on the imaginations of readers and viewers alike.

Afterword

The story I have told about the eighteenth-century novel's encounter with portraiture could have followed several different plot lines. I could have started with the Restoration's encounter with Catholicism and the problem of icons, reading eighteenth-century Protestantism's concerns about the portrait through the lens of its theological debates about images. Or I could have meditated on the disjunction between critical reception histories and practice, in order to think about why the terms governing discussions of the novel and the portrait seem not to have changed while the genres underwent various formal transformations over the course of the long eighteenth century. The book could have undertaken an interdisciplinary study of the different constraints governing novel writing and portrait painting, or have provided a description of the various kinds of relationships formed between writers and painters. And finally, the study could have compared audience responses to particular texts and paintings from a sociological perspective.

Each of these approaches would encounter – sooner rather than later, I believe – the question of women's relation to the novel and the portrait: Protestant attacks on Catholicism's images invoked the Whore of Babylon's corrupt body, rendering the difference between the portrait and the religious painting difficult to sustain in, for example, the contemplation of Restoration courtesan portraits or even in Reynolds's use of saints in his allegorical portraits of women. Novel and portrait criticism could not find ways to articulate the genres' investment in women as consumers and practitioners until the boundaries governing those activities had been sufficiently privatized to safeguard the male prerogative for such activities in the public sphere. Disciplinary boundaries and interdisciplinary relationships between artists were organized around notions of sexual difference and homosocial relations, with men increasingly consolidating their power both in opposition to and alliance with other male artists, and women seeking support from their male colleagues. Audience responses reconfigured gender relations in England's public and private spaces.

Novels represent the act of beholding and of being beheld in order to comment on their own activities as narratives, and my investigation of the sexual poetics of reading and seeing has used the novel's interest in portraiture to explain this habit of self-reflection. By engaging in extensive close reading of key novels of the period, I have wanted my reader to experience the texts as intensively as I conceive the eighteenth-century reader to have done. My desire to create a phenomenology of novel reading challenges the accounts of discipline and the novel, surveillance and the workings of the gaze that have appeared in the wake of Foucault's influential studies of European eighteenth-century culture. I have stressed the enormous pleasure that the novel provides in its intellectual pursuits, pleasure that should not be read simply as a voluntary internalization of ideology. While the novel may incorporate models for living into itself, the experience of novel reading is less about models and more about living, a distinction that Foucault's paradigms, when applied to the novel, tend to collapse. When *Clarissa*, for example, represents the internalization of Christian virtue, Christian virtue turns into something quite different from what contemporary moral tracts might describe; *Betsy Thoughtless* articulates a pedagogical program that no reader other than a blatant misogynist, whom the novel represents and discredits, could wish upon the novel's heroine; *A Simple Story* presents us with two marriage narratives so insistently bizarre that they cast a perverse light on the trajectory most often assumed to constitute the modern novel's *raison d'être*. In other words, I have insisted on the novel's ability to comment on and resist the culture that produced it, to seek pleasure in and around the laws governing social relations.

I have framed my close readings, then, in opposition to the critical narrative that describes the novel's evolution in terms of a mid-century paradigm shift that coincides with a consolidation of middle-class authority. Instead, I have developed a set of key words that link early and later novels, keeping the boundaries between the traditions of scandal narratives and later fiction, as well as between satiric and sentimental discourses, as fluid as possible. 'Private interests,' 'the aesthetics of excess,' and 'the theatricality of beholding' have stood as abstractions to which the study returns repeatedly. Each of these carries a particular weight in relation to the workings of vision I have described, and the relationship between them is worth considering here. I have used the term 'private interests' to challenge the idea that 'domestic ideology' sufficiently describes the novel's engagement with interiority, both physical and psychological, and with women's cultural status in eighteenth-century England; this idea is both sociological and formal in its resistance to the idea that novels incarcerate or teach women in their narrative structures and representations.[1] 'The aesthetics of excess' links 'private interests' to a moment – the Restoration – which stands both as a historical point of reference and as an attitude that the mid- and late eighteenth-century novel incorporates into its epistemological framework. The Restoration's conception of visual culture, such as Manley and other scandal writers understood it, informed the eighteenth-century novel's and portrait's ability to sustain multiple versions of themselves and their subjects simultaneously. In particular, the idea of beholding and of novel reading as theatrical moments takes us back to the Restoration's commitment to public display, which the novel and the portrait refigure by imagining the private subjects as part of a larger public, one that I have described, using Stanley Fish's term, as an interpretive community.

In my final chapter, I suggested that the last decade of the eighteenth century witnessed a terminus of sorts, creating a moment when the novel and the portrait were well enough established to render their representations less culturally threatening, and when 'private interests' could be contained more readily than in previous decades, both by domestic and capitalist ideologies. But the terror of Matthew Lewis's *The Monk* and the abjection of Mary Hays's *The Memoirs of Emma Courtney*, to name only two 1790s narratives that resist this move toward closure, remind us of the portrait's ability to keep the novel near the edge of scandal's delightful – and commercially profitable – abyss. If some of the issues surrounding the novel and the portrait appeared less fraught by the beginning of the nineteenth century, the memory of each genre's ability to signify an illicit, rather than a moral, reading of sentiment remained a feature of the portrait trope right through the nineteenth century.

As a way of demonstrating this point, I would like to end with Jane Austen, who, for many historians of the novel, epitomizes the novelist's successful rise to cultural preeminence and the ascendence of the marriage plot to an aesthetic principle of sentimental victory (for better or for worse). In *Pride and Prejudice* Elizabeth Bennet encounters a portrait of Darcy at his estate at Pemberley. Having listened to the family housekeeper sing the praises of her master, Elizabeth considers Darcy's countenance in a new light: 'She thought of his regard with a deeper sentiment of gratitude than it had ever raised before.' What appears as a sentimental awakening of love in the heroine cannot be extricated from the context in which it appears. The portrait stands as a material representative of the wealth and power that its sitter possesses as the owner of the estate, and Elizabeth is excited by the knowledge that Darcy's haughty 'regard' has come down from its aristocratic and Olympian height to view her as a lover. The commentary on his character provided by Mrs. Reynolds, whose name surely represents a sly reference to Sir Joshua, gratifies Elizabeth, but serves only as a source of humour for another listener – Mr Gardiner finds himself 'highly amused by the kind of family prejudice, to which he attributed her excessive commendation of her master.' Mr Gardiner's common-sensical and bourgeois refusal to entertain Mrs Reynolds's admiration – and by extension the aesthetic excess that the aristocratic portrait signals – bespeaks an attitude previously assumed by Elizabeth. But now her private interests govern the moment of beholding, and Elizabeth's tongue-in-cheek admission, later in the narrative, that her love for Darcy can be dated to her 'first seeing his beautiful grounds at Pemberley,' can be taken at face value in light of the portrait's role in transforming her feelings from contempt to admiration.[2] Austen leaves the reader on the hook, allowing the portrait to stand both as the guarantor of genuine affection experienced by her heroine and as the symbol of all that Elizabeth has to gain as the mistress of Darcy's estate; Elizabeth appears both as a sentimental heroine and an eroticized gold-digger.

Jane Austen translates the tensions surrounding the trope of the portrait in eighteenth-century novels forward into the new aesthetics of social realism, allowing irony to subsume some of the interpretive problems the portrait creates in earlier narratives.[3] Indeed, the trope of the portrait established the parameters of a discussion of gender and vision that was sustained, in various guises, until the end of the nineteenth century – for example, in George Eliot's *Middlemarch* and Oscar Wilde's *Picture of Dorian Gray*. To show how eighteenth-century habits of thinking inform novels and their confrontations with the visual throughout the Romantic and Victorian eras is the work of another study. For now, it is enough to point to the durability of the relationship between the portrait and the novel, and to how this long relationship keeps open the space in which the novel can image conceptions of the self and private interests, the complexity of power but also the subtle dynamism of pleasure.

Notes

Introduction

1 Ian Watt, *The Rise of the Novel: Studies in Defoe, Richardson and Fielding* (Berkeley and Los Angeles: University of California Press, 1957), p. 173.
2 My argument about the competing definitions concerning the significance of private interests draws upon Albert O. Hirschman's study, *The Passions and the Interests: Political Arguments for Capitalism before Its Triumph* (Princeton: Princeton University Press, 1977).
3 Rousseau, *The Social Contract* in *The Social Contract and Other Later Political Writings*, ed. and trans. Victor Gourevitch (Cambridge: Cambridge University Press, 1997), p. 91.
4 Michel Foucault, *Discipline and Punish: The Birth of the Prison*, trans. Alan Sheridan (London: Allen Lane/Penguin, 1977); see especially, 'The Spectacle of the Scaffold,' pp. 33–69, and 'Panopticism,' pp. 195–228. For 'fabricates' and 'sensual proximity' see pp. 217, 216.
5 Nancy Armstrong, *Desire and Domestic Fiction: A Political History of the Novel* (Oxford: Oxford University Press, 1987), p. 278 n. 42.
6 John Bender, *Imagining the Penitentiary: Fiction and the Architecture of Mind in Eighteenth-Century England* (Chicago and London: University of Chicago Press, 1987), p. 11.
7 Bender, 'Impersonal Violence: The Penetrating Gaze and the Field of Narration in *Caleb Williams*,' *Vision and Textuality*, ed. Stephen Melville and Bill Readings (Durham, NC: Duke University Press, 1995), pp. 256–81; quote is on p. 264.
8 For the best treatment of Foucault's understanding of vision, see Martin Jay, *Downcast Eyes: The Denigration of Vision in Twentieth-Century French Thought* (Berkeley and London: University of California Press, 1993), chapter 7,

'From the Empire of the Gaze to the Society of the Spectacle: Foucault and Debord,' pp. 381–434.
9 One example of this critical tendency appears in the recent work of Jones DeRitter, who evokes Foucault in his discussion of the tension between the worlds of the novel and the theatre in eighteenth-century England, claiming that 'the authoritarian voice of the bourgeois culture of this era does seem to be interested in devaluing the human body as such.' For DeRitter, the novel serves as the mouthpiece for this authoritarian voice, aggressively disciplining the physical in its attempts to 'write the body out of existence,' in part through the creation and maintenance of 'an increasingly rigid specular economy.' These claims appear, at least to this reader, excessive, serving only to narrow our view of the novel and its sophisticated and nuanced understanding of the body. See Jones DeRitter, *The Embodiment of Characters: The Representation of Physical Experience on Stage and in Print, 1728–1749* (Philadelphia: University of Pennsylvania Press, 1994), pp. 147, 21, 73.
10 Mary Poovey, *The Proper Lady and the Woman Writer: Ideology as Style in the Works of Mary Wollstonecraft, Mary Shelley, and Jane Austen* (Chicago and London: University of Chicago Press, 1984).
11 Third Earl of Shaftesbury [Anthony Ashley Cooper], *Characteristics of Men, Manners, Opinions, Times*, ed. John M. Robertson (Indianapolis and New York: Bobbs-Merrill, 1964), p. 128. Richard Rorty describes this habit of self-surveillance as the invention of Lockean epistemology: 'The novelty was the notion of a single inner space in which bodily and perceptual sensations ... were objects of quasi-observation.' *Philosophy and the Mirror of Nature* (Princeton: Princeton University Press, 1979), p. 50.
12 Catherine Gallagher defines with great precision the pedagogical imperative of the novel in *Nobody's Story: The Vanishing Acts of Women Writers in the Marketplace, 1670–1820* (Berkeley and Los Angeles: University of California, 1994).
13 [Miss Elliot], *The Portrait*, 2 vols. (London, 1783), 2: 192–3.
14 Leo Bersani, 'Representation and Its Discontents,' *Allegory and Representation: Selected Papers from the English Institute*, ed. Stephen J. Greenblatt (Baltimore and London: Johns Hopkins University Press, 1981), pp. 145–62; quote is on p. 150.
15 Here I am following the thesis of David Marshall's *The Surprising Effects of Sympathy: Marivaux, Diderot, Rousseau, and Mary Shelley* (Chicago and London: University of Chicago Press, 1988). My study as a whole works closely with Marshall's observation that 'theatricality and sympathy are closely related problems' (p. 2).

16 Roland Barthes, *Camera Lucida: Reflections on Photography*, Trans. Richard Howard (New York: Hill and Wang, 1981), pp. 27, 26.
17 In her engaging study of the epistolary novel in France and England, April Alliston reads the figure of the portrait's disruptive force through its proximity to the framing devices associated with systems of patrilineal inheritance, which women writers negotiated and subverted through their literary correspondences; Alliston maintains that these correspondences resist the normative specularity of the portrait-as-example: 'The frame becomes a readable frame rather than a specular one, an open, fragmentary, and multiplicitous one rather than a closed or normative one, when it becomes an epistolary frame.' *Virtue's Faults: Correspondences in Eighteenth-Century British and French Women's Fiction* (Stanford: Stanford University Press, 1996), p. 16.
18 Harriet Guest, 'A Double Lustre: Femininity and Sociable Commerce, 1730–1760,' in *The Politics of Difference*, ed. Felicity Nussbaum, special issue of *Eighteenth-Century Studies* 23.4 (Summer 1990): p. 483.
19 Armstrong, *Desire and Domestic Fiction*, p. 18.
20 Joseph Addison and Richard Steele, *The Spectator*, 5 vols., ed. Donald F. Bond (Oxford and New York: Clarendon, 1987), Addison no. 15, 1: 66–7; Steele no. 79, 1: 341.
21 John Hughes quoted in *The Spectator*, Steele no. 33, 1:140.
22 *The Spectator*, Addison no. 10, 1:147 and no. 57, 1:242.
23 John Hughes quoted in *The Spectator*, Steele no. 33, 1:140.
24 *The Spectator*, Addison no. 98, 1:413.
25 John Hughes quoted in *The Spectator*, Steele no. 104, 1:435.
26 In his analysis of Mr Spectator's dream of visual mastery, Scott Paul Gordon has identified the anxiety surrounding the 'aggressive spectacle' that appears in the pages of Addison's journal, and he defines the spectatorial regime that Addison creates in response as a fantasy 'which must always struggle to sustain itself.' 'Voyeuristic Dreams: Mr. Spectator and the Power of Spectacle,' *The Eighteenth Century* 36.1 (Spring 1995): p. 19.
27 In a more general assessment of the Restoration and eighteenth-century novel's visuality, William Beatty Warner has recently noted that 'the very diffuseness of novelistic spectacle made its effects uncertain, and its control nearly impossible.' *Licensing Entertainment: The Elevation of Novel Reading in Britain, 1684–1750* (Berkeley and Los Angeles: University of California Press, 1998), p. 129.
28 This aspect of my argument echoes Ronald Paulson's claims in the Preface to *The Beautiful, Novel, and Strange: Aesthetics and Heterodoxy* (Baltimore: Johns Hopkins University Press, 1996). In studying the novel and the

portrait I am pursuing Paulson's analysis of the 'popular' as having 'a crucial relevance to those who contributed to the high-cultural pursuit of philosophical goals' in the eighteenth century (p. xix). My focus on the ways that domestic ideology was challenged by the literary imperatives of earlier forms of fiction is an expressly aesthetic concern; for an interrogation of the idea that domestic ideology organized women's social engagements with the public sphere, see Amanda Vickery, *The Gentleman's Daughter: Women's Lives in Georgian England* (New Haven and London: Yale University Press, 1998). 'In so far as the language of domesticity became more powerful and pervasive [in the eighteenth century], then genteel women became increasingly adept at manipulating it to pursue a range of activities and assume a set of responsibilities outside the home,' Vickery argues (293–4).

29 This claim follows the logic of Peter Brooks's assertion, in his analysis of eighteenth-century French prose fiction, that even after Richardson and Rousseau, 'there are repeated instances of a basic allegiance to the enterprise of the novel of worldliness.' *The Novel of Worldliness: Crébillon, Marivaux, Laclos, Stendhal* (Princeton: Princeton University Press, 1969), p. 170. I will return to the idea of 'the novel of worldliness' in chapter 2.

30 Here my understanding of the eighteenth-century novel's development as a genre dovetails with Deidre Shauna Lynch's argument concerning the evolution of the relationship between fashionable commodities and the novel's understanding of 'character' in *The Economy of Character: Novels, Market Culture, and the Business of Inner Meaning* (Chicago and London: University of Chicago Press, 1998). I will return to Lynch's astute study in my discussion of the miniature portrait in chapter 4.

31 In focusing my attention on the novel's engagement with visual aesthetics, I am following the lead of two generations of critics who have explored the interrelations between the visual arts and literature in the eighteenth century. This exploration has been governed, in part, by an interest in the eighteenth century's frequent and forceful return to Horace's claim, *Ut pictura poesis* (as a picture, so a poem), a claim that, as many critics have noted, took on a greater significance as a critical exhortation in the neo-classical moment than in its original context. Some of the most notable critical works of this tradition include John Barrell, *The Birth of Pandora and the Division of Knowledge* (Philadelphia: University of Pennsylvania Press, 1992); Morris R. Brownell, *Alexander Pope and the Arts of Georgian England* (Oxford: Clarendon, 1978); Jean H. Hagstrum, *The Sister Arts: The Tradition of Literary Pictorialism and English Poetry from Dryden to Gray* (Chicago: University of Chicago Press, 1958); Lawrence Lipking, *The Ordering of the Arts in*

Eighteenth-Century England (Princeton: Princeton University Press, 1970); Ronald Paulson, *Hogarth*, vol. 1: *The 'Modern Moral Subject,' 1697–1732*, vol. 2: *High Art and Low, 1732–1750*, vol. 3: *Art and Politics, 1750–1764* (New Brunswick, NJ: Rutgers University Press, 1991–3); *Popular and Polite Art in the Age of Hogarth and Fielding* (Notre Dame and London: University of Notre Dame Press, 1979); Richard Wendorf, *The Elements of Life: Biography and Portrait-Painting in Stuart and Georgian England* (Oxford and New York: Clarendon, 1990); James Anderson Winn, *'When Beauty Fires the Blood': Love and the Arts in the Age of Dryden* (Ann Arbor: University of Michigan Press, 1992).

32 In positing 'private interests' as the term governing the portrait-novel connection, I am promoting what Wendy Steiner calls a 'three-term relation' of comparative studies. The problem with this model, she notes, is that the mean can end up splitting 'into two discrete entities,' so that, in this case, 'private interests' would come to mean something quite different in the world of the novel than it does in the world of portraiture. However, the particular dialectic governing both the portrait's and the novel's interest in women's relation to private interests would seem to guarantee, at least partially, the stability of the term as a terrain shared by the two genres. See Steiner, *The Colors of Rhetoric: Problems in the Relation between Modern Literature and Painting* (Chicago and London: University of Chicago Press, 1982), pp. 3–5.

33 Wendorf, *The Elements of Life: Biography and Portrait-Painting in Stuart and Georgian England* (Oxford and New York: Clarendon, 1990).

34 In *The True Story of the Novel*, Margaret Anne Doody comments on the novel's abiding interest in *ekphrasis:* 'Prose fiction in every era carries a large interest in *ekphrasis*, an interest that it has never seen any theoretical need to abandon' (New Brunswick, NJ: Rutgers University Press, 1996), p. 504. In an art historical context, Wayne E. Franits looks at the way that ekphrastic literature helps us to understand the aesthetics of seventeenth-century Dutch realist painting: 'Ekphrastic poetry ... offers one methodological model for our investigation of seventeenth-century images of domesticity. It admonishes us that we must pay heightened attention to the realistic qualities of these paintings, because it was precisely their visual properties – versus an elaborate program of concealed symbols – that communicated meaning for contemporaries.' *Paragons of Virtue: Women and Domesticity in Seventeenth-Century Dutch Art* (Cambridge and New York: Cambridge University Press, 1993), p. 13. These observations apply equally, I believe, to a consideration of eighteenth-century English portraiture.

35 James Grantham Turner has observed how different disciplines define alternative ideas about vision: 'For the art historian sight is always potentially delightful, whereas for the literary historian language is always potentially heroic while sight leads to the foul practices of the voyeur and the overseer.' 'Introduction: A History of Sexuality?' in *Sexuality and Gender in Early Modern Europe: Institutions, Texts, Images*, ed. James Grantham Turner (Cambridge and New York: Cambridge University Press, 1993), p. 6.
36 Martin Jay, *Downcast Eyes: The Denigration of Vision in Twentieth-Century French Thought* (Berkeley and London: University of California Press, 1993), p. 14.

1: The Novel and the Portrait in Eighteenth-Century England

1 Taylor, *Early Opposition to the English Novel: The Popular Reaction from 1760 to 1830* (Morningside Heights, NY: King's Crown Press, 1943).
2 For a discussion of eighteenth-century art criticism and art practices, see also Iain Pears, *The Discovery of Painting: The Growth of Interest in the Arts in England, 1680–1768* (New Haven: Published for the Paul Mellon Centre for Studies in British Art by Yale University, 1988).
3 Barrell, *The Political Theory of Painting from Reynolds to Hazlitt: 'The Body of the Public'* (New Haven and London: Yale University Press, 1986); Ellis Waterhouse, *Painting in Britain, 1530 to 1790* (London: Penguin, 1969), p. 187.
4 Third Earl of Shaftesbury [Anthony Ashley Cooper], *Characteristics of Men, Manners, Opinions, Times*, ed. John M. Robertson (Indianapolis and New York: Bobbs-Merrill, 1964), p. 96; James Barry, 'Lecture II: On Design,' in *The Works of James Barry, Esq., Historical Painter; Lectures on Painting, Delivered at the Royal Academy*, 2 vols. (London, 1809), 1: 389.
5 John Dryden, 'To Sir Godfrey Kneller,' in *John Dryden*, ed. Keith Walker (Oxford and New York: Oxford University Press, 1987), p. 460, ll. 156–7; p. 461, l. 165.
6 Shaftesbury, *Second Characters or The Language of Forms*, ed. Benjamin Rand (Bristol, Eng.: Thoemmes Press, 1995), p. 135. In separating portraiture from history painting within this discourse, Shaftesbury is practising a form of historical revisionism for, strictly speaking, history painting also ought to be excluded from the liberal arts since it was executed, in classical times, by slaves. But Shaftesbury wants to advocate the usefulness of history painting in the creation of a modern civic attitude, an attitude that portraiture, he argues, could never maintain. For a full analysis of Shaftesbury's understanding of history painting as part of a 'civic humanist' theory of painting, see 'Introduction: A Republic of Taste,' pp. 1–68 in Barrell, *Political Theory of Painting from Reynolds to Hazlitt*.

7 *London Chronicle* 41, 24–6 April 1777, p. 396. Most of the critical commentary surrounding the portrait appears in reviews of the Royal Academy's exhibitions and so much of the criticism I will be examining here was formulated after 1769, when the Academy was established. The critical attacks on portraiture take their cue from earlier theorists such as Roger de Piles and Shaftesbury, but it is interesting to note that by the time these critics were writing, novel criticism was established as a practice, and much of the language initially used by literary critics in their discussions of the novel reappeared in the art criticism of the later eighteenth century.
8 By 'the aesthetic' I mean to suggest the eighteenth-century's understanding of an interpretive experience that is universally communicable and socially useful, one that imparts artistic and moral principles simultaneously.
9 Samuel Johnson, 'The Vanity of Human Wishes,' in *The Works of Samuel Johnson*, vol. 6: *Poems*, ed. E.L. McAdam, Jr, with George Milne (New Haven and London: Yale University Press, 1964), p. 95, ll. 83–6.
10 *London Chronicle* 43, 25–8 April 1777, p. 405.
11 Joshua Reynolds, 'Discourse IV, Dec. 10, 1771,' in *Discourses on Art*, ed. Robert R. Wark (San Marino, CA: Huntington Library, 1959), p. 70.
12 Terry Castle analyses the social anxiety surrounding the masquerade in the first chapter of *Masquerade and Civilization: The Carnivalesque in Eighteenth-Century English Culture and Fiction* (Stanford: Stanford University Press, 1986).
13 Shaftesbury, *Second Characters*, p. 61.
14 Reynolds, 'Discourse III, Dec. 14, 1770,' in *Discourses on Art*, p. 50.
15 J.G.A. Pocock, *Virtue, Commerce, and History. Essays on Political Thought and History, Chiefly in the Eighteenth Century* (Cambridge: Cambridge University Press, 1985), pp. 99, 235. John Barrell notes the way that women were excluded from history painting's interpretive community in *The Political Theory of Painting*, pp. 66–8. One of the reasons for the tendency for critics to associate women with portraiture may have been the fact that women were 'the most predictable and consistent group of buyers' from at least one eighteenth-century portrait painter, according to Louise Lippincott. See Lippincott, *Selling Art in Georgian London: The Rise of Arthur Pond* (New Haven and London: Published for the Paul Mellon Centre for Studies in British Art by Yale University Press, 1983), p. 68. Portraiture shared the gendered terms of its denigration with other eighteenth-century art practices. Patricia Crown has documented the hostility expressed toward the rococo as it be-gan to influence English painting practices: 'The detractors of the Rococo in England and France complained that it did not follow any order, that it was lawless, unstable, that it seduced the ignorant. Worse, it appealed to women, who were ignorant; it was effeminate in

subject as well as form, and like women it was little and licentious.' See 'British Rococo as Social and Political Style,' *Eighteenth-Century Studies* 23.3 (Spring 1990): p. 281. What is clear from these attacks is the extent to which the insistent disinterestedness that frames the aesthetic theories of Shaftesbury and later Reynolds inevitably leads to a gendered hierarchy of taste, in which women find themselves below men as subjects. Elizabeth A. Bohls has linked aesthetic and political theories and their denigration of women in her excellent essay 'Disinterestedness and Denial of the Particular: Locke, Adam Smith, and the Subject of Aesthetics,' in *Eighteenth-Century Aesthetics and the Reconstruction of Art*, ed. Paul Mattick (Cambridge and New York: Cambridge University Press, 1993), pp. 16–51.

16 Roger de Piles, *Cours de Peinture par Principes* (Paris: Jacques Estienne, 1708), pp. 297–8. Translations are mine, with thanks to Robert Barsky.

17 Shaftesbury, *Second Characters*, p. 131. Interestingly, the logic of this kind of critique implies that the man who can spend a huge amount of money on a history painting escapes the taint of commercialism; grand spending and the 'grand style' contribute to civic virtue, while women's limited purchasing power and the portrait undermine it.

18 Pope, 'Epistle II. To a Lady. Of the Characters of Women,' in *Epistles to Several Persons (Moral Essays)*, ed. F.W. Bateson, Twickenham Edition of the Poems of Alexander Pope, vol. 3.2 (London: Methuen; New Haven: Yale University Press, 1951), p. 47, ll. 5–10.

19 Piles, *Cours de Peinture par Principes*, p. 6. Jacqueline Lichtenstein argues that the transgression of the ideal 'conversation' is built into Piles' theory, that the image necessarily 'seduces and unsettles the spectator' ('Making Up Representation: The Risks of Femininity,' in *Misogyny, Misandry, and Misanthropy*, ed. R. Howard Bloch and Frances Ferguson [Berkeley: University of California Press, 1989], p. 84). I disagree, insofar as Piles and the English theorists who follow him work hard to conceptualize a rhetorical and disembodied spectatorial moment.

20 For comprehensive accounts of novel criticism, see Taylor, *Early Opposition to the English Novel*; Joseph F. Bartolomeo, *A New Species of Criticism: Eighteenth-Century Discourse on the Novel* (Newark: University of Delaware Press; London and Toronto: Associated University Presses, 1994); Ioan Williams, ed. *Novel and Romance, 1700–1800: A Documentary Record* (New York: Barnes and Noble, 1970) and *The Idea of the Novel in Europe, 1600–1800* (London: Macmillan, 1979); William B. Warner, *Licensing Entertainment: The Elevation of Novel Reading in Britain, 1684–1750* (Berkeley: University of California Press, 1998). Laura L. Runge's 1995 article 'Gendered Strategies in the Criticism of Early Fiction' details the extent to

which the novel's reception history participated in a larger struggle around the gendering of the eighteenth-century's literary hierarchy. *Eighteenth-Century Studies* 28.4 (Summer 1995): 363–78.
21 John Moore, *The Works of Tobias Smollett, M.D. With Memoirs of His Life; To which is Prefixed a View of the Commencement and Progress of Romance, by John Moore, M.D.* 8 vols.(London, 1797), 1: xcii.
22 Warner, *Licensing Entertainment*, p. 9.
23 Mackenzie, *The Lounger* 20 (18 June 1785): 79; *Analytical Review* 3 (Feb. 1789): 222.
24 Elizabeth Montagu, Dialogue XXVIII, in George Lyttleton, *Dialogues of the Dead*, 2nd ed. (London: 1760; reprint, New York: Garland, 1970), p. 314.
25 *Gentleman's Magazine* 37 (Dec. 1767): 580.
26 Warner, *Licensing Entertainment*, p. 11.
27 *Gentleman's Magazine* 37 (Dec. 1767): 580; *Monthly Review* 23 (Dec. 1760): 523.
28 Henry Fielding, *The History of Tom Jones, A Foundling*, 2 vols. ed. Martin C. Battestin and Fredson Bowers (Oxford: Oxford University Press, 1975), 1:487.
29 Chesterfield, Philip Dormer Stanhope, Earl of, *Letters Written by the Late Right Honourable Philip Dormer Stanhope, Earl of Chesterfield, to his Son, Philip Stanhope*, 2 vols. (London, 1774), Letter 52, 1:129 (French) and 131 (English trans.); Vicesimus Knox, 'On Novel Reading,' No. XVIII, *Essays Moral and Literary*, 2 vols. 2nd ed. (London 1779; reprint, New York: Garland, 1972), 2: 191–2; Ruffhead, *Monthly Review* 29 (May 1761): 415.
30 Goldsmith, written in the character of Lien Chi Altangi, in *The Citizen of the World*, Letter LXXXIII. *Collected Works of Oliver Goldsmith*. 5 vols. Ed. Arthur Friedman (Oxford: Clarendon, 1966), 2: 341. Friedman notes that 'the whole passage ... is drawn with very little change from [Jean Baptiste] Du Halde, n.1, 2, p. 340.'
31 Berenger, *The World* 79 (4 July 1754): 474. J[ohn] and A[nna] L[aetitia] Aikin, 'An Enquiry into Those Kinds of Distress Which Excite Agreeable Sensations,' from *Miscellaneous Pieces, in Prose* (London, 1773), p. 212.
32 Henry Mackenzie, *The Lounger* 20 (18 June 1785); Berenger, *The World* 79 (4 July 1754).
33 Montagu, 'Dialogue XXVIII,' *Dialogues of the Dead*, p. 316; Hurd, 'Dissertation, On the Idea of Universal Poetry,' in *The Works of Richard Hurd, D.D. Lord Bishop of Worcester*, 8 vols. (London: T. Cadall and W. Davies, 1811), 2: 20.
34 Automathes [Richard Griffith], *Something New*, 2 vols. (London, 1772), 1: 205.

224   Notes to pages 24–8

35 J. Paul Hunter observes that 'from the beginning the novel involved itself with forbidden, repressed, or secret arenas of human activity.' *Before Novels: The Cultural Contexts of Eighteenth-Century English Fiction* (New York and London: Norton, 1990), p. 35. Lennard J. Davis presents a brief but suggestive discussion of eroticism and early eighteenth-century fiction in *Factual Fictions: The Origins of the English Novel* (New York: Columbia University Press, 1983), pp. 116–120.
36 Shaftesbury, *Characteristics of Men*, p. 132.
37 Ibid.
38 Vicesimus Knox, 'On Novel Reading,' 2: 189–90.
39 James Beattie, 'On Fable and Romance,' *Dissertations Moral and Critical* (London 1783; reprint, New York: Garland, 1971), p. 574; *London Magazine and Monthly Chronologer* 12 (Jan. 1743): 330.
40 On women and novel reading, see Warner, *Licensing Entertainment*, pp. 140–2, and Taylor, 'Women and Fiction,' in *Early Opposition to the English Novel*, pp. 52–86.
41 Henry James Pye, *A Commentary Illustrating the Poetic of Aristotle* (London, 1792; reprint, New York: Garland, 1971), p. 145.
42 Letter entitled, 'Sentiments of eminent Writers in Honour of the Female Sex,' *Gentleman's Magazine* 58, pt. 2 (Nov. 1788): 960.
43 Laura L. Runge, 'Gendered Strategies,' p. 364.
44 One could argue that Reynolds's attempts to lift portraiture through his promotion of the 'grand style,' but the fact remains that Reynolds never bestowed the status of great art to the genre in his writings.
45 For an analysis of Richardson's contribution to the development of a British painting tradition, see John Brewer, *The Pleasures of the Imagination: English Culture in the Eighteenth Century* (London: HarperCollins; New York: Farrar, Straus, and Giroux, 1997), pp. 215–18.
46 Jonathan Richardson, Sr, *An Essay on the Theory of Painting* (London, 1715), pp. 15–16.
47 Claudio Tolomei as quoted in Richard Brilliant, *Portraiture* (Cambridge, MA: Harvard University Press, 1991), p. 129.
48 Richardson, *An Essay*, p. 18.
49 Richardson, *An Essay*, p. 14. Wendorf has defined the relationship between biography and portraiture in *The Elements of Life: Biography and Portrait-Painting in Stuart and Georgian England* (Oxford and New York: Clarendon, 1990).
50 Richardson, *An Essay*, p. 24.
51 Ibid., pp. 15–16; Samuel Johnson, *Idler* 45 (24 Feb. 1759), *The Works of*

Samuel Johnson, vol. 2: *The Idler and the Adventurer*, ed. J. Bate, John M. Bullit, and L.F. Powell (New Haven and London: Yale University Press, 1963), p. 140.
52 Jonathan Richardson, Sr, 'An Essay on the Whole Art of Criticism As It Relates to Painting,' *Two Discourses* (London, 1725; reprint, Bristol, Eng. and Sterling, VA: Thoemmes Press, 1998), p. 68.
53 Marcia Pointon, *Strategies for Showing: Women, Possession, and Representation in English Visual Culture, 1665–1800* (Oxford and New York: Oxford University Press, 1997), p. 45.
54 Laurence Sterne, *Letters of Laurence Sterne*, ed. Lewis Perry Curtis (Oxford: Clarendon, 1935), p. 412.
55 Edmund A. Burke, 'Letter to a Noble Lord,' *The Works of the Right Honourable Edmund Burke*, 6 vols. Ed. William Willis and Frank Walter Raffety (London: Oxford University Press, 1925–1930), 6: 75.
56 Lawrence Lipking discusses Burke's use of Reynolds's portrait in *The Ordering of the Arts in Eighteenth-Century England* (Princeton: Princeton University Press, 1970), pp. 174–5.
57 Manley, *The Secret History of Queen Zarah and the Zararians*, in *Popular Fiction by Women 1660–1730*, ed. Paula R. Backscheider and John J. Richetti (Oxford, Clarendon Press, 1996), p. 47.
58 *Monthly Review* 5 (Dec. 1751): 512; *Monthly Review* 29 (May 1761): 415.
59 Samuel Richardson, Preface, *Pamela or, Virtue Rewarded*, ed. T.C. Duncan Eaves and Ben D. Kimpel (Boston: Houghton Mifflin, 1971), p. 3. Italics in original.
60 Review of *The Adventures of Peregrine Pickle, in which are intended the Memoirs of a Lady of Quality, Monthly Review* 4 (March 1751): 356.
61 *Gentleman's Magazine* 40 (Oct. 1770): 455.
62 Edgeworth quoted in James Boaden, *The Memoirs of Mrs. Inchbald*, 2 vols. (London, 1833), 2: 152–3.
63 Clara Reeve, Preface, *The Old English Baron: A Gothic Story. A New Edition* (London, 1782), pp. vi–vii.
64 Automathes, *Something New*, 1: 203–4; *London Magazine and Monthly Chronologer* 12 (Jan. 1743): 33; Knox, 'On Novel Reading,' 2: 188–9.
65 My reading of eighteenth-century female portraiture confirms the arguments made by Marcia Pointon in *Hanging the Head: Portraiture and Social Formation in Eighteenth-Century England* (New Haven and London: Published for the Paul Mellon Centre for Studies in British Art by Yale University Press, 1993) and in *Strategies for Showing*, especially chapter 5, 'Portraiture, Excess, and Mythology: Mary Hale, Emma Hamilton, and Others ... "in

Bacchante,"' pp. 173–227). Pointon is one of very few critics to bring the insights of feminist, Foucaultian, and psychoanalytical theories to bear on the study of portraiture.
66 Nancy Armstrong, *Desire and Domestic Fiction: A Political History of the Novel* (Oxford and New York: Oxford University Press, 1987), p. 77.
67 Addison, *The Spectator*, ed. Donald F. Bond, 5 vols. (Oxford and New York: Clarendon, 1987), no. 15, 1: 69.
68 *Morning Herald*, 9 May 1786.
69 'Fresnoy,' letter in *Middlesex Journal* (1769); quoted in Whitley, *Artists and Their Friends in England, 1700–1799*, 2 vols. (New York and London: Benjamin Blom, 1968), 1: 252.
70 Johann Wilhelm von Archenholz, *A Picture of England Containing a Description of the Laws, Customs, and Manners of England. Interspersed with Curious and nteresting Anecdotes of Many Eminent Persons* (London, 1797), p. 305.
71 Pointon, 'Intriguing Jewellery: Royal Bodies and Luxurious Consumption,' in *Luxurious Sexualities: Effeminacy, Consumption, and the Body Politic in Eighteenth-Century Representation*, ed. Mary Peace and Vincent Quinn, special issue of *Textual Practice* 11. 3 (Winter 1997): 493–516; p. 507.
72 Simon Trusty, *An ODD LETTER, on a Most interesting Subject, to Miss K - - F - h-r. Recommended to the Perusal of the LADIES of GREAT BRITAIN.* (London, 1760), pp. 12–13.
73 Pointon notes that 'while the library was the responsibility of the husband, pictures and "curious cabinet pieces" should be "under the custody" of the wife' (*Strategies for Showing*, p. 44).
74 J.G.A. Pocock, *Virtue, Commerce, and History*, p. 118.
75 Nicholas Penny, *Reynolds*, ed. Nicholas Penny (New York: Harry N. Abrams, 1986), p. 212.
76 Penny provides some evidence that Sir Charles Bingham, later Lord Lucan, commissioned the Cleopatra portrait of Fisher, but the *London Chronicle* advertisement suggests otherwise. See Penny, 'Miss Kitty Fisher in the Character of Cleopatra,' *Reynolds*, p. 196.
77 Diana Donald, '"Characters and Caricatures": The Satirical View,' in *Reynolds*, ed. Nicholas Penny, p. 357.
78 Quoted in Desmond Shawe-Taylor, *The Georgians: Eighteenth-Century Portraiture and Society* (London: Barrie and Jenkins, 1990), p. 20.
79 'Anthony Pasquin' (John Williams), *Memoirs of the Royal Academicians; Being an Attempt to Improve the National Taste* (London, 1796), as quoted by Wendorf, *Sir Joshua Reynolds, the Painter in Society* (Cambridge, MA: Harvard University Press, 1996), p. 61.

80 'Rigdum Funidos,' *Kitty's Stream: or, the Noblemen Turned Fisher-men. A Comic Satire. Addressed to the Gentlemen in the Interest of the Celebrated Miss K – – F – – r* (London, 1759), pp. 4–5, 9.
81 Alexander Pope, *An Essay on Criticism, Pastoral Poetry and An Essay on Criticism*, ed. E. Audra and Aubrey Williams, Twickenham Edition of the Poems of Alexander Pope, vol. 1 (London: Methuen; New Haven: Yale University Press, 1961), p. 298, l. 538.
82 'Trusty,' *An ODD LETTER*, pp. 27–8.
83 *Morning Chronicle and London Advertiser*, 25 April 1778.
84 *Public Advertiser*, 2 May 1782.
85 James Grantham Turner, 'Sex and Consequence,' *Review* 11 (1989): p. 163; Pointon, *Strategies for Showing*, pp. 178, 199–202.
86 Pointon makes this claim about Reynolds's female portraiture, arguing that various portraits 'invite viewers, while beholding fashionable ladies, to glimpse Graces, which while they may at one level symbolize harmony, also threaten disorder, pose choice, incite sexual envy and desire for gratification' (*Strategies for Showing*, p. 178).
87 The connections between eighteenth-century visual culture and the world of the novel can be traced in a variety of ways; one obvious occasion of mutual interest can be found in Joseph Highmore's famous depictions of scenes from *Pamela*. For an excellent discussion of how *Pamela* was received by a 'spectacle-crazed society,' see James Grantham Turner, 'Novel Panic: Picture and Performance in the Reception of Richardson's *Pamela*,' *Representations* 48 (Fall 1994): 76.
88 In a recent article, William Beatty Warner analyses portraits and genre paintings that represent readers, contrasting the sober representations of readers as virtuous with the excesses of rococo depictions of readers as sexually licentious. Warner follows Michael Fried in associating the former with the aesthetics of absorption, the latter with those of theatricality. Because he does not consider the critical reception surrounding portraiture in England, the images he considers 'safe' – for example, Reynolds's portrait of Theophila Palmer – appear removed from the controversies surrounding the novel that Warner so astutely describes, and whose visual correlative he locates in examples of erotically charged European art. In fact, as my discussion of English portraits will suggest, there was no way to separate a reader like the young girl Reynolds represents from the susceptible young women critics so often evoked in their attacks on the novel: a painter as socially observant as Reynolds would not have missed the connection between his sitter and a larger reading public. See Warner,

'Staging Readers Reading,' in *Reconsidering the Rise of the Novel*, ed. David Blewett, special issue of *Eighteenth-Century Fiction* 12.2–3 (Jan.–April 2000): 391–416.
89 In his assessment of Georgian portraiture, Desmond Shawe-Taylor claims that 'reading is for women connected with tender sympathies. It is assumed that they will read romances.' *The Georgians: Eighteenth-Century Portraiture and Society* (London: Barrie and Jenkins, 1990), p. 122. While there is no evidence in most eighteenth-century portraits to support this claim, Shawe-Taylor accurately describes the period's conception of women as inveterate novel readers, to which the portraits of women holding anonymous books may well be referring. Tillyard writes that Emily, the Countess of Kildare (figure 8), 'had a standing order with the London bookseller Mrs Dunoyer for "all the new books,"' and quotes a letter in which Emily writes, 'I love to see everything new that comes out, either pretty or foolish.' *Aristocrats, Caroline, Emily, Louisa, and Sarah Lennox, 1740–1832* (London: Chatto and Windus; New York: Farrar, Straus, and Giroux, 1994), p. 48.
90 For an analysis of women's participation in the arts and the consumer culture to which novels and portraits belonged in eighteenth-century England, see Brewer, *The Pleasures of the Imagination, English Culture in the Eighteenth Century* (London: HarperCollins; New York: Farrar, Straus, and Giroux, 1997), pp. 56–122.
91 Fried, *Absorption and Theatricality: Painting and Beholder in the Age of Diderot* (Berkeley: University of California Press, 1980), pp. 31, 104; emphasis Fried's.
92 Fried attaches this moral seriousness to an anti-Rococo movement in French painting. See Fried, *Absorption and Theatricality*, p. 35.
93 Richardson defined the aesthetic agenda of *Clarissa* in his postscript to the novel.
94 Although the sitter for this portrait is often identified as Honora Sneyd, Arthur B. Chamberlain presents irrefutable evidence that the sitter is not Sneyd. See Chamberlain, *George Romney*, (New York: Books for Libraries Press, 1910; reprint 1971), pp. 123, 386–9.
95 Gallagher, *Nobody's Story: The Vanishing Acts of Women Writers in the Marketplace, 1670–1820* (Berkeley and Los Angeles: University of California Press, 1994), pp. xvii–xviii.
96 Judy Egerton, *Wright of Derby* (London: The Tate Gallery; New York: Metropolitan Museum of Art, 1990), p. 49.
97 Unfortunately, I was unable to obtain permission to reproduce this painting.
98 Nicholas Penny, 'Miss Kitty Fisher,' *Reynolds*, p. 193.
99 Ibid.

100 For a discussion of this portrait's engagement with 'Patriot' ideology, see David Bindman, *Hogarth and His Times: Serious Comedy* (London: For the Trustees of the British Museum by British Museum Press in association with the Parnassus Foundation, 1997), pp. 46–8.
101 For a full account of Mary Edwards's story, and of her patronage of Hogarth, see Ronald Paulson, *Hogarth: His Life, Art, and Times* 2 vols. (New Haven and London: Published for the Paul Mellon Centre for Studies in British Art by Yale University Press, 1971), 1: 333–7; more recently, Nadia Tscherny has investigated Edwards's and Hogarth's relationship – and its significance to our understanding of this portrait – in 'An Un-Married Woman: Mary Edwards, William Hogarth, and a Case of Eighteenth-Century British Patronage,' in *Women and Art in Early Modern Europe: Patrons, Collectors, and Connoisseurs*, ed. Cynthia Lawrence (University Park: Penn. State University Press, 1997), pp. 237–54.
102 Ronald Paulson provides a reading of Elizabeth I's relation to Hogarth's aesthetic theory in his Introduction to *The Analysis of Beauty*; in particular, he focuses on the extent to which Hogarth's interest in placing the image of the female body at the centre of his discourse leads him to the idea of blazonry and the figure of Elizabeth as 'the erotic version of the Body Politic' (New Haven: Published for the Paul Mellon Centre for Studies in British Art by Yale University Press, 1997), p. xlii.
103 For the best articulation of how visual culture became part of the critical context of the eighteenth century's most famous novel, Richardson's *Pamela*, see Turner, 'Novel Panic.'

2: Envisioning Literary Interest: Manley's *The New Atalantis*

1 Delarivier Manley, *The New Atalantis*, ed. Rosalind Ballaster (London: Penguin, 1992), p. 35. All future references are to this edition and will be cited parenthetically.
2 Peter Brooks, *The Novel of Worldliness: Crébillon, Marivaux, Laclos, Stendhal* (Princeton: Princeton University Press, 1969), p. 169.
3 Recent critics of Manley's work have highlighted the extent to which the *chronique scandaleuse* serves as a foil to later eighteenth-century novels. In defining the gap between Manley's amatory narratives and the sentimental fiction that emerged in the mid-eighteenth century, critics reconfirm a rift that eighteenth-century novelists writing after Manley were eager to claim. These accounts confirm the trajectory that Nancy Armstrong defines in 'The Rise of the Domestic Woman' toward the creation, in eighteenth-

century literary and cultural discourses, of a modern female subject 'capable of regulating desire.' See *Desire and Domestic Fiction, A Political History of the Novel* (New York and Oxford: Oxford University Press, 1987), p. 95. See also Gallagher, *Nobody's Story; The Vanishing Acts of Women Writers in the Marketplace, 1670–1820* (Berkeley and Los Angeles: University of California Press, 1994); Jane Spencer, *The Rise of the Woman Novelist: From Aphra Behn to Jane Austen* (NewYork: Basil Blackwell, 1986); Ros Ballaster, *Seductive Forms: Women's Amatory Fiction from 1684 to 1740. With Particular Reference to Aphra Behn, Delarivier Manley, and Eliza Haywood* (Oxford: Clarendon; New York: Oxford University Press, 1992); William Beatty Warner, *Licensing Entertainment: The Elevation of Novel Reading in Britain, 1684–1750* (Berkeley: University of California Press, 1998).
4 Brooks, *The Novel of Worldliness*, p. 16; Alliston, *Virtue's Faults: Correspondences in Eighteenth-Century British and French Women's Fiction* (Stanford: Stanford University Press, 1996), p. 14.
5 While I agree with William Beatty Warner's criticism that feminist analyses of Manley have overlooked the extent to which her fiction 'exploits the pleasures of cross-gender identification' in their attention to the figure of the female reader, I am more inclined than he to stress the urgency of Manley's attention to the issues that, as a woman writer, she must address in order to claim authority for herself. See *Licensing Entertainment*, p. 92.
6 Ronald Paulson, *Satire and the Novel in Eighteenth-Century England* (New Haven and London: Yale University Press, 1967), p. 222.
7 Gallagher reads Manley's interest in the personal attractions of public figures as a feature of women's writing of the period: '[The] shift in the political meaning of male beauty from its ability to overawe the male observer to its power to create longing in the female viewer signals the new relevance in the hero of personal traits that were designated as outside official political culture and associated with femininity and chastened passions' (*Nobody's Story*, p. 113).
8 Ballaster, *Seductive Forms*, pp. 115–16.
9 For an excellent account of Manley's political intrigues and acumen, see 'Political Crimes and Fictional Alibis: The Case of Delarivier Manley,' in Gallagher's *Nobody's Story*, pp. 88–144.
10 Cynthia Richards, '"The Pleasures of Complicity": Sympathetic Identification and the Female Reader in Early Eighteenth-Century Women's Amatory Fiction,' *The Eighteenth Century* 36.3 (Autumn 1995): 232.
11 Here Manley establishes an image of political corruption that Swift would later use in *Gulliver's Travels*. In Book One, the Lilliputian government announces its intention to blind Gulliver, claiming that it will be sufficient

for him 'to see by the Eyes of the Ministers, since the greatest Princes do no more.' *Gulliver's Travels*, ed. Colin McKelvie (London, 1726; reprint, Delmar, NY: Scholars' Facsimiles and Reprints, 1976), p. 123.
12 For a definition of the development of civic and civil humanist discourses in eighteenth-century England, see J.G.A. Pocock, *Virtue, Commerce, and History: Essays on Political Thought and History, Chiefly in the Eighteenth Century* (Cambridge: Cambridge University Press, 1985). Recently, Gallagher has demonstrated how 'the writing woman in Manley's works tends to wander the borderland between civic and civil humanism, continually crossing from one side to the other, picking up permissions and impediments from both sides'(*Nobody's Story*, p. 118).
13 Here I am following the line of argument advanced by John Barrell in *The Political Theory of Painting from Reynolds to Hazlitt: 'The Body of the Public'* (New Haven and London: Yale University Press, 1986).
14 Barrell, *The Political Theory of Painting*, p. 31.
15 Ibid., p. 33.
16 For a detailed discussion of how the king's body has been understood, historically, as a representation, see Louis Marin, *Portrait of the King*, trans. Martha M. Houle (Minneapolis: University of Minnesota Press, 1988), and Ernst H. Kantorowicz, *The King's Two Bodies: A Study in Mediaeval Political Theology* (Princeton: Princeton University Press, 1957).
17 Cynthia Richards, 'The Pleasures of Complicity,' p. 221.
18 John J. Richetti, *Popular Fiction Before Richardson: Narrative Patterns, 1700–1739* (Oxford: Clarendon; New York: Oxford University Press, 1992), p. 138.
19 Janet Todd, 'Life After Sex: The Fictional Autobiography of Delariv[i]er Manley,' *Women's Studies* 15.1–3 (1988): 52.
20 Paulson, *Satire and the Novel*, p. 222. I would not go so far as Warner, who suggests that amatory fiction supports 'a licentious ethical nihilism' (*Licensing Entertainment*, p. 92); rather, I think an alternative moral economy linked to the negotiation of women's private interests appears in the novel.
21 Mary Ann Doane has analysed the figure of the hieroglyph as a particular sign of female subjectivity in her reading of Freud; the hieroglyph, she argues, both stands as the sign of 'a mystery, an inaccessible though desirable otherness' and represents 'the lack of a distance or gap between sign and referent.' Doane uses the hieroglyph as a means of exposing Freud's limitations on the subject of femininity, but we can also posit its aesthetic as one that allows for an economy of signs not necessarily defined by a dominant order. See Doane, 'Film and the Masquerade: Theorizing the

Female Spectator,' in *Femmes Fatales, Feminism, Film Theory, Psychoanalysis* (New York and London: Routledge, 1991), pp. 18–19.
22 Addison, *The Spectator*, 5 vols., ed. Donald F. Bond (Oxford: Clarendon, 1987), no. 412, 3:541.
23 Thirty-five years later, Burke would reiterate the pleasures of the visual in his aesthetic theory. Describing the experience of looking at a beautiful woman's upper torso, Burke writes that it is like a 'deceitful maze, through which the unsteady eye glides giddily, without knowing where to fix, or whither it is carried,' eroticizing – as Manley does – Addison's idea that we 'find our Thoughts a little agitated and relieved at the sight of such Objects as are ever in Motion, sliding away from beneath the Eye of the Beholder.' Pt. 3, Section 15, 'Gradual Variations,' *A Philosophical Enquiry, into the Origin of Our Ideas of the Sublime and Beautiful*, ed. James T. Boulton (Notre Dame and London: University of Notre Dame Press, 1968), p. 115; *Spectator* no. 412, 3:542.
24 Manley, *The Adventures of Rivella*, ed. Katherine Zelinsky (Peterborough, Ontario: Broadview Literary Texts, 1999), pp. 47, 48.
25 Ruth Perry, *Women, Letters, and the Novel* (New York: AMS, 1980), p. 157.
26 Paula R. Backscheider, *Spectacular Politics: Theatrical Power and Mass Culture in Early Modern England* (Baltimore and London: The Johns Hopkins University Press, 1993), pp. 143, 145.
27 Samuel Pepys, *The Diary of Samuel Pepys*, 11 vols., ed. Robert Latham and William Matthews (Berkeley and Los Angeles: University of California Press, 1972), 7: 393.
28 'The portrait of the king as absolute monarch ... signifies and shows this place of transit between the name, where the body has become signifier, and the narrative, the story, through which law has become body.' Marin, *Portrait of the King*, p. 14.
29 Ellis Waterhouse, *Painting in Britain, 1530 to 1790* (London: Penguin, 1969), p. 62.
30 In order to avoid confusion, I will refer to this portrait as that of Nell Gwyn, since it is labelled as such in the Denys Eyre Bower collection at Chiddingstone Castle, where it now resides. For an account of the debate over the figure the painting represents, see Oliver Millar, *Sir Peter Lely, 1618–80: Exhibition at 15 Carlton House Terrace, London SW1* (London: National Portrait Gallery, 1978), p. 62.
31 Millar, *Sir Peter Lely*, pp. 12, 20.
32 Millar comments on the 'richly atmospheric' representation of landscape that appears in Lely's early portraits (*Sir Peter Lely*, p. 12). I would suggest that this landscape aesthetic was a central aspect of Lely's portraits throughout the painter's career.

33 Alexander Pope, 'The First Epistle of the Second Book of Horace,' *The Poems of Alexander Pope. Imitations of Horace: With An Epistle to Dr. Arbuthnot and The Epilogue to the Satires*, ed. John Butt, Twickenham Edition of the Poems of Alexander Pope, vol. 4 (London: Methuen, 1939), pp. 207, ll. 139–40; 209, ll. 149–52.
34 John Dryden, 'Preface to Sylvae, or the Second Part of Poetical Miscellanies, 1685,' *The Poems of John Dryden*, ed. John Sargeaunt (London: Oxford University Press, 1925), p. 384.
35 Ann Rose Plogsterth, 'The Institution of the Royal Mistress and the Iconography of Nude Portraiture in Sixteenth-Century France' (PhD diss., Columbia University, 1991), p. 222.
36 Theodore Reff on Manet's *Olympia* as quoted by Michael Fried in *Absorption and Theatricality: Painting and Beholder in the Age of Diderot* (Berkeley: University of California Press, 1980), p. 182, n. 11.
37 Michael Fried, *Absorption and Theatricality*, p. 4; Fried, 'Manet's Sources: Aspects of his Art, 1859–65,' *Artforum* 7.7 (March 1969): 69 n. 27.
38 Janet Todd, 'Life After Sex,' p. 48.
39 Ballaster, *Seductive Forms*, p. 127.
40 Patricia Köster's edition of *The New Atalantis* grants Charlot even more control over this scene. The punctuation of the text, as it appears in this edition, links the consciousness of desire to Charlot, rather than to the duke: 'The Duke aw'd and trembling with his Passsion, approach'd her as a Goddess; conscious of his and her own desires, the mantling Blood wou'd smile upon her Cheeks, sometimes glowing with delight, then afterwards, by a feeble recollection of Virtue, sink apace, to make room for a guilty succeeding Paleness.' *The Novels of Mary DelaRiviere Manley*, ed. Patricia Köster (Gainesville, FL: Scholars' Facsimiles and Reprints, 1971), 1: 68.
41 Manley, *The Adventures of Rivella*, p. 113.
42 Teresa de Lauretis, *Alice Doesn't: Feminism, Semiotics, Cinema* (Bloomington: Indiana University Press, 1984), pp. 142–3.
43 As Gallagher has observed, 'It would be difficult to place Manley squarely inside the Scriblerian milieu we associate with Swift, Pope, and Arbuthnot, for in their discourse the idea of woman often functions in ways that Manley's texts could not consistently accommodate' (*Nobody's Story*, p. 108).
44 Warner brilliantly reads this episode in terms of the competing modes of reading it represents. See *Licensing Entertainment*, pp. 100–10.
45 I am not persuaded by Ros Ballaster's reading of the cabal as a 'utopian framework that is, generally, endorsed' (*Seductive Forms*, p. 140).
46 Gallagher, *Nobody's Story*, p. 141.
47 James Grantham Turner notes that during the Restoration period, 'the threat to mutilate the alleged whore or her male accomplice, to deface

the defamer of one's honour and "mark" the sexual transgressor, was still relatively common in the domestic and political arena.' *Libertines and Radicals in Early Modern London: Sexuality, Politics, and Literary Culture, 1630–1685* (Cambridge University Press, forthcoming).
48 Gallagher, *Nobody's Story*, p. 141.
49 Ballaster, *Seductive Forms*, p. 139. This reading of the narrative's remarks fits into Ballaster's larger thesis concerning the cabal's importance as a utopic trope within *The New Atalantis*, one that enables Manley to represent her desire for 'the masculine purchase on representation' (p. 152).
50 Mary Wortley Montagu, *Letters from the Levant during the Embassy to Constatinople, 1716–1718* (London, 1838; reprint, New York: Arno, 1971), p. 127.
51 In this sense Manley takes as her cue Aphra Behn's mode of self-fashioning, which Catherine Gallagher has astutely delineated in her analysis of Behn's identification with both prostitute and actress: 'Her relationship to the actress is like the prostitute's relationship to her own body: the mask that hides the face signals the availability of the body but also implies the impenetrability of the controlling mind' (*Nobody's Story*, p. 34).
52 Susan Sniader Lanser, *Fictions of Authority: Women Writers and Narrative Voice* (Ithaca and London: Cornell University Press, 1992), pp. 26–7.

3: 'Ravished Sight': Picturing *Clarissa*

1 Samuel Richardson, *Clarissa, or the History of a Young Lady*, ed. Angus Ross (London: Viking Penguin, 1985), pp. 543, 1099. All future references are to this edition and will be cited parenthetically.
2 Recently Jerry C. Beasley has argued that 'Richardson was more indebted to the women who preceded him than he cared to acknowledge' ('*Clarissa* and Early Female Fiction,' in *Clarissa and Her Readers: New Essays for The 'Clarissa' Project*, ed. Carol Houlihan Flynn and Edward Copeland [New York: AMS, 1999], 69). The critical consensus remains committed, however, to the idea that Richardson marks a singular rejection of his female predecessors. See, for example, William B. Warner's *Licensing Entertainment: The Elevation of Novel Reading in Britain, 1684–1750* (Berkeley: University of California Press, 1998).
3 Scott Paul Gordon, 'Disinterested Selves, *Clarissa* and the Tactics of Sentiment,' *ELH* 64.2 (Summer 1997): 473–502; 477.
4 Ibid., p. 495.
5 Samuel Johnson quoted in Hester Lynch Piozzi, *Anecdotes of the Late Samuel*

Johnson, L.L. During the Last Twenty Years of His Life 4th ed. (London, 1786), p. 221.
6 Leopold Damrosch, Jr, *God's Plot and Man's Stories: Studies in the Fictional Imagination from Milton to Fielding* (Chicago and London: University of Chicago Press, 1985), p. 233.
7 William Beatty Warner, *Reading 'Clarissa': The Struggles of Interpretation* (New Haven and London: Yale University Press, 1979), p. xii; Margaret Anne Doody, *A Natural Passion: A Study of the Novels of Samuel Richardson* (Oxford: Clarendon, 1974), pp. 239–40. See also: Tassie Gwilliam, *Samuel Richardson's Fictions of Gender* (Stanford: Stanford University Press, 1993); John Mullan, *Sentiment and Sociability: The Language of Feeling in the Eighteenth Century* (Oxford: Clarendon., 1988); Brenda Bean Tooley, 'Actaeon as Spectator: Intrusive Vision and Configurations of Femininity in Rochester, Swift, and Richardson' (PhD diss., University of Notre Dame, 1991).
8 Leo Braudy, 'Penetration and Impenetrability in *Clarissa*,' *New Approaches to English Literature: Selected Papers from the English Institute*, ed. Phillip Harth (New York and London: Columbia University Press, 1974), p. 194.
9 Gordon D. Fulton has observed how the two visual systems upheld by Belford and Lovelace come to resemble each other: 'While Lovelace's construction of woman as erotic object contrasts Belford's construction of woman as object of sentimental pathos, both men nonetheless *project* onto Clarissa.' Fulton claims that Richardson's heroine responds to her visual objectification by exhausting her body, 'emptying it in fulfilling a divine purpose'– a trajectory that other critics have also defined as the *telos* governing *Clarissa*. This chapter will provide a different account of the novel's response to the oppressive scopic regimes it describes. See Fulton, 'Why Look at Clarissa?' *Eighteenth-Century Life* 20.2 (May 1996): pp. 29, 30.
10 In her will we discover that Clarissa owns three portraits of herself; the Vandyke-style portrait I will discuss in this section is the only portrait to appear in the early part of the narrative. The only sustained critical attention that this portrait has received appears in Janet E. Aikins, 'Richardson's "Speaking Pictures,"' in *Samuel Richardson: Tercentenary Essays*, Margaret Anne Doody and Peter Sabor (Cambridge and New York: Cambridge University Press, 1989), pp. 146–66. Aikins's essay provides an excellent overview of Richardson's interest in the visual arts and the idea of *ekphrasis*, moving through each of his three novels. I hope to add more detail to Aikins's observations concerning *Clarissa*, and in particular, to explore her comment that 'Richardson's fiction is centrally concerned with the complexity of being a "spectator" of both art and life' (p. 148).

11 Janet Aikins, "Richardson's "Speaking Pictures,'" p. 163.
12 Clarissa's belief in the integrity of the aristocracy represents a Tory idealism that Margaret Anne Doody has defined in 'Richardson's Politics,' *Eighteenth-Century Fiction* 2.2 (January 1990): 113–26. In the tragic world of *Clarissa*, this idealism only serves to render Clarissa more vulnerable to Lovelace.
13 Here James and Clarissa represent two features that April Alliston has identified as central to the circulation of portraits: James stresses the portrait's value 'as movable property' while Clarissa confers on it the 'legitimacy of descent,' despite the Harlowes' recent entry into England's upper class. See Alliston, *Virtue's Faults: Correspondences in Eighteenth-Century British and French Women's Fiction* (Stanford: Stanford University Press, 1996), p. 36. The novel's preoccupation with the Harlowes' investment in the aristocracy speaks to its identification of the interests that the *nouveau riche* and the established order share. As Daniel P. Gunn points out, 'the novel's surface action depicts a conflict within the ruling class – a disagreement between rival predators – rather than a conflict between representatives of different classes' ('Is *Clarissa* Bourgeois Art?' *Eighteenth-Century Fiction* 10.1 [October 1997]: 8). I disagree with Gunn's larger claim, that Richardson's novel upholds the interests of this ruling class in its representation of female virtue as the source of moral authority. Clarissa's virtue sustains a more radical social commentary than such a reading of the novel's politics implies.
14 Margaret Anne Doody, *A Natural Passion*, p. 232.
15 Male portraiture, by contrast, represents men throughout their lives, defining them at various points of their careers in the public world. Aileen Ribeiro, *The Art of Dress: Fashion in England and France 1750 to 1820* (New Haven and London: Yale University Press, 1995), p. 7. Ribeiro provides a taxonomy of the Vandyke style in female portraiture in her 1975 doctoral thesis for the University of London, reprinted by Garland: *The Dress Worn at Masquerades in England, 1730 to 1790, and Its Relation to Fancy Dress in Portraiture* (New York and London: Garland, 1984), pp. 158–86.
16 Aileen Ribeiro, *The Art of Dress*, pp. 203–4.
17 Ibid., p. 163
18 Terry Castle, *Masquerade and Civilization: The Carnivalesque in Eighteenth-Century English Culture and Fiction* (Stanford: Stanford University Press, 1986), p. 68; Ribeiro, *The Art of Dress*, p. 163; Castle, *Masquerade and Civilization*, p. 57.
19 Wayne E. Franits observes that in seventeenth-century Dutch genre painting and portraiture, 'the connection between needlework and the virtue of diligence was stressed at every possible occasion.' *Paragons of*

Virtue: Women and Domesticity in Seventeenth-Century Dutch Art (Cambridge and New York: Cambridge University Press, 1993), p. 27.
20 James Grantham Turner links this struggle between Clarissa and her father over the patterns to Lovelace's obsession with imposing a 'prefabricated character' on Richardson's heroine. See 'Lovelace and the Paradoxes of Libertinism,' *Samuel Richardson: Tercentenary Essays*, eds. Doody and Sabor, p. 86.
21 Karen Jackson Ford, *Gender and the Poetics of Excess: Moments of Brocade* (Jackson: University of Mississippi Press, 1997), p. 7.
22 William Beatty Warner, *Licensing Entertainment*, p. 92.
23 Eve Kosofsky Sedgwick, *Between Men: English Literature and Male Homosocial Desire* (New York: Columbia University Press, 1985), p. 50. Sedgwick draws on Lévi-Strauss in her reading of male homosocial relation and the traffic in women in Wycherley's *The Country Wife*.
24 Thomas C. Duncan Eaves and Ben D. Kimpel note that Highmore evidently painted this portrait of Clarissa before the novel was printed, and that the portrait 'has been lost, or at any rate is unidentifiable.' Eaves and Kimpel, *Samuel Richardson: A Biography*, (Oxford: Clarendon, 1971), p. 189. Alison Lewis, in an unpublished catalogue raisonné of Highmore's works, also lists the portrait among Highmore's lost paintings. 'Joseph Highmore: 1692–1780,' PhD diss., Harvard, 1975, 1: 552–61 and 2: 562–99.
25 Barbauld, *The Correspondence of Samuel Richardson*, ed. Anna Laetitia Barbauld, 6 vols. (London: R. Phillips, 1804; reprint, New York: AMS Press, 1966), 4: 249.
26 Paradoxically, Lovelace shares this sentiment with Clarissa. Lovelace knows that he has the power of class position and wealth to maintain the reputation he desires, whereas Clarissa depends on her spiritual status to achieve public acclaim.
27 James Grantham Turner, 'Lovelace and the Paradoxes of Libertinism,' *Samuel Richardson: Tercentenary Essays*, p. 84.
28 Third Earl of Shaftesbury [Anthony Ashley Cooper], *Second Characters, or The Language of Forms*, ed. Benjamin Rand (Bristol, Eng.: Thoemmes Press, 1995), p. 61.
29 Aikins, 'Richardson's "Speaking Pictures,"' pp. 159–61.
30 Ford, *Gender and the Poetics of Excess*, p. 18.
31 Braudy, 'Penetration and Impenetrability in *Clarissa*,' p. 199.
32 Terry Castle, *Clarissa's Ciphers: Meaning and Disruption in Richardson's 'Clarissa'* (Ithaca and London: Cornell University Press, 1982), p. 102.
33 Dorothy Van Ghent made this point many years ago: 'we begin to feel that the optical tactic [at work in *Clarissa*] must be "working" in a somewhat

complex strategic way ... One effect of this strategy is to make of the reader a Peeping Tom, to make him share in the dubious delights of voyeurism.' *The English Novel: Form and Function* (New York: Rinehart, 1953), p. 49. More recently, Warner has defined the way in which the text encourages us to view Clarissa through Lovelace's eyes, concluding that, ultimately, we want to penetrate her as much as Lovelace does. In other words, Lovelace's hermeneutic violence vis-à-vis Clarissa is identical to our own: 'What is perhaps finally most dishonest of all is the humanists' timid disinclination to acknowledge the pleasures they've enjoyed in interpreting *Clarissa.*' *Reading 'Clarissa': The Struggles of Interpretation*, p. 258.

34 T.C. Duncan Eaves and Ben D. Kimpel, 'An Unpublished Pamphlet by Samuel Richardson,' p. 403.
35 Tom Keymer has documented the support Richardson received in his defence of this scene from Jane Collier. See 'Jane Collier, Reader of Richardson, and the Fire Scene in *Clarissa*,' in *New Essays on Samuel Richardson*, ed. Albert J. Rivero (New York: St. Martin's, 1996), pp. 141–62.
36 Richardson, *Selected Letters of Samuel Richardson*, ed. John Carroll (Oxford: Clarendon, 1964), p. 107.
37 Here the novel aligns the fates of the fetishized virgin and the loathed whore. As Jocelyn Harris has provocatively argued, 'Clarissa ... resembles the virtuous and victimized courtesan who would eventually supersede her in the history of the erotic novel. She is Lucretia to Mrs. Sinclair's Messalina,' ('Grotesque, Classical and Pornographic Bodies in *Clarissa*,' in *New Essays on Samuel Richardson*, ed. Albert J. Rivero, p. 113).
38 From this perspective, Mark Kinkead-Weekes's definition of Clarissa's rape as a public event takes on a rather sinister cast:

> The rape is a public trial in the strict sense; the first stage in proving a hypothesis about the true nature of Woman. If we want an analogy we should think of a scientific experiment carried out in front of an expert audience. It is the most extraordinary climax of any novel in English. Yet it is not for any desire to shock, let alone titillate, by the *outré*. It is because, for Richardson, the rape of his heroine enables him to expose her innermost nature (*Samuel Richardson, Dramatic Novelist* [Ithaca: Cornell University Press, 1973], p. 231).

In witnessing the rape, Kinkead-Weekes argues, even as it is mediated by the epistolary form, we attend the moment that will allow Clarissa's truth to appear. Of course, Sinclair and the prostitutes also witness the rape, and it is unclear that they find it an uplifting experience. But they, unlike the readers Kinkead-Weekes evokes, do not constitute an 'expert audience.' Or do they? Kinkead-Weekes's logic breaks down if we acknowledge that the prostitutes probably do know more about the mechanics of rape, and the psychological effects which attend it, than do most of Richardson's readers. The idea that the 'expert audience' will not be vulnerable to titillation avoids the inescapable alignment of our gaze with that of the prostitutes who, as Tassie Gwilliam notes, 'stand in for [Lovelace] as voyeur' while he rapes Clarissa (*Samuel Richardson's Fictions of Gender*, p. 97). To attempt such a foreclosure of the rape scene as Kinkead-Weekes performs is to deny the more serious challenge that the text poses for us.

39 Warner, *Reading 'Clarissa': the Struggles of Interpretation*, p. 50.
40 Warner, 'Reading Rape: Marxist-Feminist Figurations of the Literal,' *Diacritics: A Review of Contemporary Criticism* 13.4 (Winter 1983): 32.
41 Margaret Anne Doody analyses the Elizabethan style of this monument in her chapter, 'The Visual Image in *Clarissa*,' pp. 216–40 in *A Natural Passion: A Study of the Novels of Samuel Richardson*.
42 This baroque visual movement finds its aesthetic equivalent in the macabre tableau that appears in Clarissa's first dream of Lovelace: 'He stabbed me to the heart, and then tumbled me into a deep grave ready dug, among two or three half-dissolved carcases; throwing in the dirt and earth upon me with his hands, and trampling it down with his feet' (342–3).
43 Doody, *A Natural Passion*, p. 228.
44 Another factor complicates Belford's praises; as Brenda Bean argues, 'Belford's objective status [as spectator] is constantly endangered, as he is himself conscious, by the equivocal relation he has had to Clarissa's persecution' 'Sight and Self-Disclosure: Richardson's Revision of Swift's "The Lady's Dressing Room,"' *Eighteenth-Century Life* 14.1 (February 1990): 14. This observation ties into my argument concerning the complicity of the reader in the process of Clarissa's reification.
45 Braudy, 'Penetration and Impenetrability in *Clarissa*,' p. 194.
46 Preston, *The Created Self: The Reader's Role in Eighteenth-Century Fiction* (London: Heinemann, 1970), p. 89.
47 Preston highlights the importance of eyes and visual signs in the brothel, and contrasts this system of meaning with Clarissa's epistemology, arguing that Lovelace's manipulation of vision represents 'the violation ... of the language that she believes in against all the weight of the book, the silent language of feeling and of reality' (*The Created Self*, p. 91). What Preston does not identify is the cross-over that occurs between Richardson's and Lovelace's modes of seeing, which I will discuss below as a way of complicating the idea that *Clarissa* celebrates its heroine's ways of seeing.
48 John Mullan, *Sentiment and Sociability*, pp. 76–7.
49 Gwilliam, *Samuel Richardson's Fictions of Gender*, p. 94.

50 Isobel Grundy has recently documented Clarissa's commitment to the rhetoric of law, which she uses to oppose Lovelace's use of force. See 'Seduction Pursued by Other Means? The Rape in *Clarissa*.' *Clarissa and Her Readers*, ed. Flynn and Copeland, pp. 255–67.
51 As Jocelyn Harris notes, 'Richardson appropriates pornography, exploiting its devices to show the reader another way.' 'Grotesque, Classical and Pornographic Bodies in *Clarissa*,' p. 114.
52 I will be arguing against a thesis commonly advanced – that the novel's conclusion celebrates Clarissa's visual transparency and sincerity. For a recent articulation of this reading of the novel, see Juliet McMaster, 'Reading the Body in *Clarissa*,' *Clarissa and Her Readers*, pp. 189–212.
53 Frances Ferguson analyses the implications of Clarissa's assumption of this body in 'Rape and the Rise of the Novel,' *Representations* 20 (Fall 1987): 88–112. Recently, Sandra MacPherson has returned to the question of consent in *Clarissa* that Ferguson first raised, arguing that Richardson's novel represents 'a central document in the movement from intentionalism to consequentialism in English jurisprudence and public-policy.' 'Lovelace, Ltd.,' *ELH* 65.1 (Spring 1998): 117.
54 Gwilliam, *Samuel Richardson's Fictions of Gender*, p. 103.
55 Ian Watt, *The Rise of the Novel: Studies in Defoe, Richardson and Fielding* (Berkeley and Los Angeles: University of California Press, 1957), p. 218.
56 Castle, *Clarissa's Ciphers*, p. 141. David Marshall has also astutely commented on the uncanniness of Clarissa's coffin, and on the ambiguity of the spectacle Clarissa's corpse creates more generally. See 'Fatal Letters: *Clarissa* and the Death of Julie,' *Clarissa and Her Readers*, pp. 213–53.
57 Jacques Derrida describes 'trace' as 'the enigmatic relationship of the living to its other and of an inside to an outside,' in *Of Grammatology*, trans. Gayatri Chakravorty Spivak (Baltimore and London: The Johns Hopkins University Press, 1976), p. 70.
58 In Clarissa's abhorrence of the body's potential to betray her in this way, we see a larger hatred of the body at work, one that John Allen Stevenson has insightfully linked to the novel's gnostic habits of mind. 'In the eyes of the world,' Stevenson notes, '[Clarissa] is her body, and her only chance to deny that insistence and assert her own sense of herself is to escape both her body and the world' ('"Alien Spirits": The Unity of Lovelace and Clarissa,' *New Essays on Samuel Richardson*, ed. Albert J. Rivero, p. 91). Clarissa puts the body to use, however, in planning her escape; in this sense, her death-drive marks a more, rather than less, embodied self.
59 The idea that Clarissa could have conceived while being raped brings up the difficult questions raised by eighteenth-century medical discourse.

In *Making Sex, Body and Gender from the Greeks to Freud* (Cambridge and London: Harvard University Press, 1990), Thomas Laqueur argues that for the most part the eighteenth-century medical community believed that women could not conceive without having an orgasm, and that having an orgasm implied a consent on the part of the woman to the sexual act that elicited this physical response. However, Laqueur also claims that this model was frequently contested by various examples, including the one which he cites in the opening pages of the book: A young woman, presumed dead, is raped by a necrophilic monk; the next day she revives, having only been in a coma, and discovers herself pregnant. Furthermore, Laqueur points out that a new discourse of sex was beginning to circulate by the second half of the eighteenth century, one that severed conception and pleasure from each other. According to this new model of reproductive physiology, 'the ovarian system ... could work not only without the influence of the conscious self but without any phenomenal sign' (*Making Sex*, p. 163).

60 Richardson, *Selected Letters of Samuel Richardson*, p. 110.
61 Brian McCrea reads the politics of pregnancy in *Clarissa* through the novel's interrogation of patriarchal authority as it is abused by the Harlowe men and Lovelace. 'Were she to admit herself to be with child, she would vindicate Lovelace's replacement of the biological father with the name-father; she would become his accomplice in declaring the superannuation of James Harlowe, Sr and Lord M.' 'Clarissa's Pregnancy and the Fate of Patriarchal Power' *Eighteenth-Century Fiction* 9.2 (January 1997): 147.
62 Even after discovering that Clarissa will not adopt his line of thinking after he has raped her, Lovelace maintains a devotion to the idea of his transformative powers: 'Thou hadst the two letters in thy hand,' he writes to Belford, 'Had they been in mine, the seal would have yielded to the touch of my warm finger ... and the folds, as other plications have done, opened of themselves to oblige my curiosity' (1085).
63 Toni Bowers's insightful analysis of maternity in *Clarissa* reveals the terrible and terrifying example Charlotte Harlowe has set her daughter: 'By representing a mother who by her very abjection helps to perpetuate tyranny, *Clarissa* exposes the fiction that affective maternal sentiment has significance apart from practical, discursive empowerment.' *The Politics of Motherhood: British Writing and Culture, 1680–1760* (Cambridge and New York: Cambridge University Press, 1996), p. 203.
64 Jonathan Loesberg, 'Allegory and Narrative in *Clarissa*,' *Novel* 15.1 (Fall 1981): 51; Toni Bowers, *Politics of Motherhood*, p. 221.
65 Here my reading departs from the more pessimistic account of Clarissa's

body as non-representable provided by Joy Kyunghae Lee, who argues that within the patriarchal economy that structures Clarissa's life, the heroine 'only remains an empty cipher ... Outside of patriarchal systems ... the female body doesn't signify.' 'The Commodification of Virtue: Chastity and the Virginal Body in Richardson's *Clarissa*,' *The Eighteenth Century: Theory and Interpretation* 36.1 (Spring 1995): 52.

66 Clarissa's acuity on this point should make us question Kinkead-Weekes's celebration of the rape scene as a moment of scientific revelation.

67 David Marshall, 'Fatal Letters,' p. 216.

68 Here I am reading against April London's view of the will as the ultimate displacement of Clarissa's body and energy. The conjunction of women and property in history and the novel that London's study as a whole so amply demonstrates is, in *Clarissa*, I believe, never resolved, even in the conciliatory character of Belford. *Women and Property in the Eighteenth-Century English Novel* (Cambridge and New York: Cambridge University Press, 1999).

69 David Marshall has made a similar point about Clarissa's posthumous rhetorical gestures; her address to Lovelace, he suggests, represents 'a Gothic or even a Jacobean scenario of revenge in which she seems to rise from the dead or appear as a ghost to admonish Lovelace.' 'Fatal Letters,' p. 216.

70 Paul de Man, 'Autobiography as De-Facement,' *The Rhetoric of Romanticism* (New York: Columbia University Press, 1984) pp. 76, 78.

71 Aikins, 'Richardson's "Speaking Pictures,"' p. 163.

72 Daryl S. Ogden reads Clarissa's gift to Anna as the sign of 'Sapphist (scopic) desire.' 'Richardson's Narrative Space-Off: Freud, Vision and the (Heterosexual) Problem of Reading *Clarissa*,' *Literature and Psychology* 42.4 (1996): 50.

73 Terry Eagleton, *The Rape of Clarissa: Writing, Sexuality, and Class Struggle in Samuel Richardson* (Minneapolis: University of Minnesota Press, 1982), pp. 76–7.

74 Isobel Grundy, 'Seduction Pursued by Other Means? The Rape in *Clarissa*,' p. 265.

75 James Boswell, *The Journal of a Tour to the Hebrides with Samuel Johnson, LL.D.*, ed. R.W. Chapman (London: Oxford University Press, 1961), p. 306.

4: Refiguring Virtue: *The History of Miss Betsy Thoughtless* and *Amelia*

1 Mary Granville (Pendarves) Delany, in a letter to Mrs Dewes, 18 January 1752, *Henry Fielding, the Critical Heritage*, ed. Ronald Paulson and Thomas

Lockwood (London: Routledge and Kegan Paul; New York: Barnes and Noble, 1969), p. 313.

2 Deborah J. Nestor has described *Betsy Thoughtless* as a critical success; however, her assessment depends on a review of the novel that appeared thirty-five years later, when the novel form was more firmly established as a legitimate genre, and Haywood's novel could appear less culpable in its description of female transgression. The one contemporary review of the novel – that of the *Monthly Review* in 1751 – denigrates the novel in terms that I explore below. See Nestor, 'Virtue Rarely Rewarded: Ideological Subversion and Narrative Form in Haywood's Later Fiction,' *Studies in English Literature 1500–1900* 34.3 (Summer 1994): 579–98, especially p. 595 n. 5.

3 In her reading of *Amelia*, Jill Campbell observes that Fielding's heroine steps into the position of 'domestic "angel," which we often think of as really materializing in the Victorian era and only beginning to take shape at the end of the eighteenth century.' *Natural Masques: Gender and Identity in Fielding's Plays and Novels* (Stanford: Stanford University Press, 1995), p. 206.

4 Both Fielding and Haywood are indebted to Mme de Lafayette's *La Princesse de Clèves* (1678) for their narratives of portrait theft. I will return to Haywood's allusions to Lafayette below.

5 Deidre Shauna Lynch, *The Economy of Character: Novels, Market Culture, and the Business of Inner Meaning* (Chicago and London: University of Chicago Press, 1998), p. 4.

6 Ibid., p. 118.

7 Steven J. Gores, 'The Miniature as Reduction and Talisman in Fielding's *Amelia*,' *Studies in English Literature 1500–1900* 37.3 (Summer 1997), p. 589; Susan Stewart, *On Longing, Narratives of the Miniature, the Gigantic, the Souvenir, the Collection* (Durham and London: Duke University Press, 1993), p. 69.

8 Richard Wendorf, *The Elements of Life: Biography and Portrait-Painting in Stuart and Georgian England* (Oxford and New York: Clarendon, 1990), pp. 130, 133.

9 Steven J. Gores estimates that a miniature could cost as little as one-fifth the price of a full-length portrait. Gores, 'The Miniature as Reduction and Talisman,' p. 591 n. 2.

10 John Ingamells and Robert Raines have suggested that this image does not represent Peg Woffington at all, but is rather a subject painting. That it could be a subject painting rather than a portrait highlights the importance of the woman-miniature motif as a subject of cultural interest. See Ingamells and Raines, 'A Catalogue of the Paintings, Drawings, and Etchings

of Philip Mercier,' *The Forty-Sixth Volume of the Walpole Society 1976–1978* (London: Printed for the Walpole Society [by] Pitman Press, 1978), p. 49.

11 Wendorf, *The Elements of Life*, p. 130.

12 As several historians of sexuality have observed, this spectacle was also associated with the body of the homosexual man. For one insightful account of eighteenth-century understandings of the transgressive male body as spectacle, see Cameron McFarlane's *The Sodomite in Fiction and Satire, 1660–1750* (New York: Columbia University Press, 1997).

13 There is almost nothing written on *Betsy Thoughtless*; more frequently critics direct their attention to Haywood's early works, which link Haywood to Behn and Manley both thematically and historically. The best instance of this type of criticism appears in Ballaster's *Seductive Forms: Women's Amatory Fiction from 1684 to 1740. With Particular Reference to Aphra Behn, Delarivier Manley, and Eliza Haywood* (Oxford: Clarendon, 1992). Another instance of criticism dealing with Haywood's early career appears in John J. Richetti's *Popular Fiction before Richardson: Narrative Patterns 1700–1739* (Oxford: Clarendon, 1969), in which Richetti describes Haywood as 'the most important producer of popular fiction before *Pamela*' (p. 179). For the most comprehensive evaluation of Haywood, see Christine Blouch's 1991 unpublished doctoral dissertation, 'Eliza Haywood: Questions in the Life and Works' (University of Michigan, 1991). Mary Anne Schofield also writes on Haywood, although most of her work is general and descriptive, rather than critical; see '"Descending Angels:" Salubrious Sluts and Pretty Prostitutes in Haywood's Fiction,' in *Fetter'd or Free? British Women Novelists, 1670–1815*, ed. Mary Anne Schofield and Cecilia Macheski (Athens, OH and London: Ohio University Press, 1986), pp. 186–200. Schofield, *Eliza Haywood* (Boston: Twayne, 1985); Schofield, 'Exposé of the Popular Heroine: The Female Protagonists of Eliza Haywood,' *Studies in Eighteenth-Century Culture* 12 (1983): 93–103. Deborah J. Nestor provides a lucid and cogent account of Haywood's response to mid-eighteenth-century domestic ideology in 'Virtue Rarely Rewarded: Ideological Subversion and Narrative Form in Haywood's Later Fiction.' See also Beth Fowkes Tobin's Introduction to the recent Oxford edition of *Betsy Thoughtless. The History of Miss Betsy Thoughtless* (Oxford and New York: Oxford University Press, 1997), pp. ix–xxxv, Jane Spencer, *The Rise of the Woman Novelist: From Aphra Behn to Jane Austen* (Oxford and New York: Basil Blackwell, 1986), pp. 147–53; and Janet Todd, *The Sign of Angellica: Women, Writing and Fiction, 1660–1800* (New York: Columbia University Press, 1989), pp. 147–51.

14 'Amatory pulp fiction like Haywood's identifies the heights of emotional

inexpressibility as the defining, essentially female moment, not just for the women it represents but for the female narrator herself as the originating and certifying imaginative experience behind her writing,' John J. Richetti argues. 'Voice and Gender in Eighteenth-Century Fiction: Haywood to Burney,' in *Women and Early Fiction*, ed. Jerry C. Beasley, special issue of *Studies in the Novel* 19.3 (Fall 1987): 267.

15 Janet Todd, *The Sign of Angellica*, p. 148.
16 *Monthly Review* 5 (October 1751): 394.
17 Eliza Haywood, *The History of Miss Betsy Thoughtless*, ed. Beth Fowkes Tobin (Oxford and New York: Oxford University Press, 1997), p. 9. Future references will be to this edition and will be cited parenthetically. I agree with Susan Sniader Lanser's sense of the moralizing narrator's misogyny: 'Such a narrator reinscribes her identity as masculine in spirit if not in name.' *Fictions of Authority: Women Writers and Narrative Voice* (Ithaca and London: Cornell University Press, 1992), p. 49.
18 *The Female Spectator* (London, 1748), Vol. I, p. 2. Interestingly, Haywood does not attempt to assume the disembodied spectatorial position of Addison's persona. Instead she theorizes the production of *The Female Spectator* as a collective effort amongst several female 'spies': 'they are to be considered ... as several members of one body, of which I am the mouth' (vol. I, p. 5). In fact, Haywood's female contributors, who meet twice a week to discuss the news they have retrieved, appear more like a gossip network than anything else, especially given the nature of the stories they recount. Haywood's journalistic model seems closer to Manley's scandal-mongering than to Addison's 'disinterested' paradigm, finally, despite her attempt to sell her journalism as a reformative program: 'the gratification [the reader] should receive from being made acquainted with other people's affairs, should at the same time teach every one to regulate their own' (vol. I, p. 3).
19 Haywood's rewriting of Lafayette begins with the reversal of roles in the story of the miniature's theft. In *La Princesse de Clèves* the male lover steals the miniature of the novel's heroine. Where April Alliston looks to the conventions of epistolarity as the means by which the knots of Lafayette's gender politics are partially untied, I believe Haywood effectively rewrites the spectatorial dynamic the miniature creates from Betsy's perspective. For Alliston's reading of Lafayette, see *Virtue's Faults*, pp. 33–76.
20 Margaret Anne Doody, 'Deserts, Ruins and Troubled Waters: Female Dreams in Fiction and the Development of the Gothic Novel,' *Genre* 10.4 (Winter 1977) 538.
21 Samuel Richardson, *Clarissa, or, The History of a Young Lady*, ed. Angus Ross (London: Viking Penguin, 1985), p. 970.

22 My reading of this scene counters Deidre Shauna Lynch's reading of *Betsy Thoughtless* as a novel that reveals 'the fact that women's bodies are not really their own.' *The Economy of Character*, p. 102. That Betsy becomes a widow – a figure of economic independence – shortly after this scene reinforces my sense that the novel is about how women might reclaim their bodies.

23 Here again Haywood rewrites Lafayette's narrative, which represents the princess gazing on her lover as he appears in a historical painting; unbeknownst to her, the subject of her look is a witness to her private moment of beholding: 'She sat down and gazed with rapt attention at his picture as if overwhelmed by the love this picture inspired. At this moment it would have been impossible to describe Monsieur de Nemours' feelings.' *The Princess of Clèves*, Walter J. Cobb, trans. New York: Meridian, 1989, p. 133. Haywood intensifies this dynamic by having Trueworth's discovery of Betsy's passion coincide with the revelation of her earlier theft of the miniature. The tragic vision that Lafayette's narrative sustains more closely resembles *Clarissa* than it does Haywood's novel, which isolates Trueworth from the more general social commentary on masculinity that it sustains, rendering his gaze not only harmless but enabling for Betsy. On the implications of Lafayette's representation of male narcissism and the gaze, see Naomi Schor, 'The Portrait of a Gentleman: Representing Men in (French) Women's Writing,' in *Misogyny, Misandry, and Misanthropy*, ed. R. Howard Bloch and Frances Ferguson (Berkeley: University of California Press, 1989), pp. 113–33.

24 *The Female Spectator*, vol. I, p. 206. Haywood does not explicitly include portraits in her praise of painting, singling out instead 'history, landscape, and sea-pieces' as the most useful genres. The scene that unfolds around Trueworth's portrait indicates why portraiture may not have made the list, and why it functions so usefully as a novelistic device.

25 Ballaster, *Seductive Forms*, p. 169.

26 I am not convinced by Angela J. Smallwood's argument that Amelia's characterization is a product of 'rationalist-feminist thinking.' *Fielding and the Woman Question: The Novels of Henry Fielding and Feminist Debate 1700–1750* (New York: St Martin's Press, 1989), p. 126.

27 J. Paul Hunter, *Occasional Form: Henry Fielding and the Chains of Circumstance* (Baltimore and London: Johns Hopkins University Press, 1975), p. 196. Jill Campbell, *Natural Masques*, p. 212.

28 My reading of Richardson sustains a similar impulse, but I believe that Richardson is a more sophisticated reader of gender and sexuality than Fielding, and as such is interested in explicitly entertaining radical ideas of

female identity, whatever the cost to his commitment to the imperatives of virtue.
29 Henry Fielding, *Amelia*, ed. Martin C. Battestin (Middletown, CT: Wesleyan University Press, 1984), p. 66. Future references will be to this edition and will be cited parenthetically.
30 Frederic T. Blanchard, *Fielding the Novelist: a Study in Historical Criticism* (New York: Russell and Russell, 1966), pp. 84, 95. More recently, Jill Campbell has noted the confusion surrounding the significance of Amelia's nose, which allows 'the very mark of a new ideal of exemplary female selflessness and strength ... [to] collapse back into a sign either of woman's absurdly inadequate impersonation of male identity or of her own threatening qualities of unruliness and passion within an older model of female nature.' *Natural Masques*, p. 211. For Johnson's assessment of *Amelia*, see Ronald Paulson and Thomas Lockwood, eds., *Henry Fielding: The Critical Heritage*, p. 445, and Hester Lynch Piozzi, *Anecdotes of the Late Samuel Johnson, L.L.D. During the Last Twenty Years of His Life*, 4th ed. (London, 1786), p. 221.
31 Henry Fielding, *Covent-Garden Journal* no. 8 (28 January 1752): *The Covent-Garden Journal and A Plan of the Universal Register Office*, ed. Bertrand A. Goldgar (Middletown, CT: Wesleyan University Press, 1988), p. 65.
32 A.R. Towers, '*Amelia* and the State of Matrimony,' *Review of English Studies* 5.18 (April 1954): 157; George Sherburn, 'Fielding's *Amelia*: An Interpretation,' in *Fielding: A Collection of Critical Essays*, ed. Ronald Paulson (Englewood Cliffs, NJ: Prentice-Hall, 1962), p. 149; Allan Wendt, 'The Naked Virtue of *Amelia*,' *Journal of English Literary History* 27.2 (June 1960): 131.
33 Patricia Meyer Spacks, 'Female Changelessness; or, What Do Women Want?' *Studies in the Novel* 19 (1987): 273, 280. See also April London, 'Controlling the Text: Women in *Tom Jones*,' *Women and Early* Fiction, ed. Jerry C. Beasley, special issue of *Studies in the Novel* 19.3 (Fall 1987): 323-33.
34 Campbell, *Natural Masques*, p. 241.
35 Kermode identifies the 'Good Heart' as the basis of Fielding's moral criteria, which assume 'a supposedly instinctive understanding on the part of both reader and writer of Right and Wrong.' 'Richardson and Fielding,' *Cambridge Journal* 4.2 (1950): 109.
36 As J. Paul Hunter and others have pointed out, the moral tone of *Amelia* is far more severe and strict than in Fielding's other novels. This rigidity seems proportionate to the potential for moral relativism apparent in the novel, a relativism which, as in this scene, seems to force the reader to choose between the knowingness of evil and the ignorance of innocence.

At other points in the narrative, Fielding's judicial voice defines a third option, that of moral laws which stand above the quagmire of experience.

37 See Wendt, 'The Naked Virtue of Amelia,' pp. 131–48. For an interesting account of Fielding's ambivalence toward prostitutes in general, see Bertrand A. Goldgar, 'Fielding and the Whores of London,' *Philological Quarterly* (Spring 1985): 265–73.
38 Brian McCrea, 'Politics and Narrative Technique in Fielding's *Amelia*,' *Journal of Narrative Technique* 13.3 (Fall 1983): 137.
39 George E. Haggerty, 'Amelia's Nose; or, Sensibility and Its Symptoms,' *The Eighteenth Century: Theory and Interpretation* 36.2 (Summer 1995): 152.
40 Samuel Richardson, *Selected Letters of Samuel Richardson*, ed. John Carroll (Oxford: Clarendon, 1964), p. 197.
41 George E. Haggerty provides a very insightful reading of the autobiographical impulse in *Amelia* in 'Fielding's Novel of Atonement: Confessional Form in *Amelia*,' *Eighteenth-Century Fiction* 8.3 (April 1996): 383–400.
42 Terry Castle, *Masquerade and Civilization: The Carnivalisque in Eighteenth-Century English Culture and Fiction* (Stanford: Stanford University Press, 1986), p. 179.
43 Lennard J. Davis argues that Fielding's refusal to repair Amelia's nose upsets the 'imposed binary of good/bad, beautiful/deformed, in the regulation of female bodies.' See Davis, 'Dr. Johnson, Amelia, and the Eighteenth Century,' *'Defects': Engendering the Modern Body*, ed. Helen Deutsch and Felicity Nussbaum (Ann Arbor, MI: Univ. of Michigan Press, 2000), p. 69. However, the eighteenth century's debates about the meaning of female beauty – upon which Fielding's representations of the prostitutes' 'ingaging qualities' (47) draw – suggest that this opposition was not as characteristic of the period as Davis claims. I would argue, further, that Amelia's scar never jeopardizes the heroine's beauty, and that Fielding wanted, by keeping the scar in the narrative, to idealize this beauty's uniqueness.
44 See Fielding *The History of Tom Jones: A Foundling*, 2 vols. ed. Martin C. Battestin (Middleton, CT: Wesleyan University Press, 1975), Book VI, chap. 2, 1:155–7. That Fielding's account of Sophia is both highly literary and even ironic does not, I believe, detract from its erotic potential. The accumulation of descriptive detail fixes the reader's gaze on Sophia's imaginary body, and exerts a powerful ekphrastic force, so that even if Sophia is only *like* the famous paintings and statues to which Fielding compares her, she is equally represented as an aesthetic object.
45 John Hughes quoted in *The Spectator*, Steele no. 33, 1: 140–1.
46 Castle, *Masquerade and Civilization*, p. 180.
47 Wendorf, *The Elements of Life*, p. 127.

48 Wendorf describes this enlargement effect as a formal property of the miniature: 'The constriction in size, with its more intense scrutiny of the human face (often viewed at close quarters), actually suggests an augmented importance on behalf of its subject.' *The Elements of Life*, p. 133.
49 'In Fielding's attack on the decadent aristocracy in *Amelia*, social obligation has become explicitly financial, transformed into a kind of social capital deployed to oppress the lower classes,' James Thompson argues. 'Patterns of Property and Possession in Fielding's Fiction,' *Eighteenth-Century Fiction* 3.1 (October 1990): 40.
50 As Thompson argues, 'Fielding's obsession with prostitution in *Amelia* is connected with capitalization, as in the central contrast between the good wife, Amelia, who protects her virtue at all cost, and Mrs. Trent' ('Patterns of Property and Possession,' p. 40 n. 40). Money's invisibility is guaranteed by the secrecy of the illicit transactions which govern William Booth's attempts to escape debt.
51 Hunter, *Occasional Form*, p. 195.
52 See Battestin, ed., *Amelia*, Appendix VI, p. 569, no. 184, ll. 24–6.
53 There are enough allusions to high culture (from which Fielding believed women to be rightly excluded) to warrant the claim that Fielding is addressing a male audience in *Amelia*, despite his attempt to inject a domestic ethos into the novel.
54 Cynthia Griffin Wolff, 'Fielding's *Amelia*: Private Virtue and Public Good,' *Texas Studies in Literature and Language* 10.1 (Spring 1968): 54.
55 This difference, however pronounced, should not lead us to set up an easy anti-feminist/feminist opposition between Fielding and Richardson. Smallwood makes this point convincingly in the Introduction to *Fielding and the Woman Question*, pp. 5–6.
56 Henry Fielding, *The Covent-Garden Journal* no. 5 (18 January 1752), *The Convent-Garden Journal and a Plan of the Universal Register Office*, ed. Bertrand A. Goldgar, p. 44.
57 Castle, *Masquerade and Civilization*, p. 241. Castle also suggests, and I agree, that 'however stylized, [this scene] is probably the most sympathetic, least ironic representation of female desire in all of Fielding's fiction' (p. 241).
58 Frederick G. Ribble has observed that Amelia 'seems to have two constitutions, or a constitution with very puzzling, contradictory properties, a constitution both delicate and resilient.' 'The Constitution of the Mind and the Concept of Emotion in Fielding's *Amelia*,' *Philological Quarterly* 56.1 (Winter 1977): 116. The miniature's casing of jewels here exemplifies the interpretive dilemma that Patricia Fumerton analyses in her reading of Renaissance miniatures: 'The "rooms" of artifice of a Hilliard miniature ...

never finally open to reveal fully the self. The layers of self-revealing, self-concealing ornament extend indefinitely.' 'Secret Arts': Elizabethan Miniatures and Sonnets, *Representations* 15 (Summer 1986): 70–1.
59 Gores, 'The Miniature as Reduction and Talisman,' p. 590.
60 Patricia Meyer Spacks, 'Female Changelessness,' p. 280.

5: 'Paint her to your own mind': Sterne's Concupiscible Narratives

1 Laurence Sterne to Mrs Daniel Draper (Eliza), [March 1767], *Letters of Laurence Sterne*, ed. Lewis Perry Curtis (Oxford: Clarendon, 1965), p. 312.
2 For a full account of Sterne's use of these authors, see Melvyn New's introduction to Laurence Sterne, *The Life and Opinions of Tristram Shandy, Gentleman: The Text*, 3 vols., ed. Melvyn New and Joan New, Florida Edition of the Works of Laurence Sterne (Gainesville: University of Florida Press, 1984), 3:1–31. Future references to *Tristram Shandy* will be to this edition and will be cited parenthetically in the text.
3 This paper follows Dennis W. Allen's 'Sexuality/Textuality in *Tristram Shandy*' in its representation of Sterne's linguistic play as a means of opening up the text to complex gender identifications. Allen focuses on phallic and vaginal metaphors, while I analyse the representation of vision, but my conclusions support his claim that 'the goal of imaginative play with language is, finally, not power but pleasure.' *Studies in English Literature, 1500–1900* 25.3 (Summer 1985): 670.
4 *Tristram Shandy*'s investment in the visual arts has long engaged Sterne critics, who argue that Sterne found the theories and practices of eighteenth-century pictorial aesthetics a particularly rich source for his innovative novelistic agenda, enabling him to develop what R.F. Brissenden has described as a 'satiric rococo'(a term Joseph Burke used to define Hogarth's aesthetic) in a literary medium. The most sustained examination of Sterne's interest in the visual appears in William V. Holtz's book-length study of *Tristram Shandy*, in which Holtz eloquently investigates the biographical and literary impulses that motivated Sterne to craft his innovative style. Holtz argues that 'the pictorial aesthetic sanction[ed] his radical effort to transcend the apparent limits of language and of narrative' (pp. 115–16), and claims that the visual aspect of *Tristram Shandy* derives its power from Sterne's 'system of thought in which *to think* and *to see* are virtually synonymous, an aesthetic in which *to paint* and *to write* are equally close' (p. 150). Holtz suggests that we should understand Sterne's incorporation of the visual into his narrative as a means of establishing the permanence of identity against the flux of time: 'we can see Tristram's

nontemporal, spatial narrative mode not only as an evasion of the threat of death, the ultimate problem of time, but also, in a positive and affirmative light, as the assertion of his personality, in all its integrity and variety, against this threat' (p. 138). See William V. Holtz, *Image and Immortality: A Study of 'Tristram Shandy'* (Providence, RI: Brown University Press, 1970); Holtz more recently returned to the subject of *Tristram Shandy*'s visual poetics in 'The Journey and the Picture: the Art of Sterne and Hogarth,' *A History of Book Illustration: 29 Points of View*, ed. Bill Katz (Metuchen, NJ and London: Scarecrow Press, 1994), pp. 315–32. See also Ronald Paulson, *Hogarth*, vol. 3: *Art and Politics*; 1750–1764 (New Brunswick, NJ: Rutgers University Press, 1993); R.F. Brissenden, 'Sterne and Painting,' *Of Books and Humankind: Essays and Poems Presented to Bonamy Dobrée* (London: Routledge and Kegan Paul, 1964), pp. 93–108; Melvyn New, 'William Hogarth and John Baldessari: Ornamenting Sterne's *Tristram Shandy*,' *Word and Image* 11.2 (April–June 1995): 182–95. Christopher Fanning raises the issue of the novel's visual dynamics in relation to the text's typographical concerns in 'On Sterne's Page: Spatial Layout, Spatial Form, and Social Spaces in *Tristram Shandy*,' *Eighteenth-Century Fiction* 10.4 (July 1998): 429–50.

5 In the past ten years, feminist critics have levelled a series of indictments against *Tristram Shandy*. Ruth Perry states the negative critical consensus most precisely when she claims that Sterne's novel is 'a man's book if ever there was one.' 'Words for Sex: The Verbal-Sexual Continuum in *Tristram Shandy*,' *Studies in the Novel* (Spring 1988) 20.1: 29. See also, Barbara M. Benedict, '"Dear Madam,": Rhetoric, Cultural Politics and the Female Reader in Sterne's *Tristram Shandy*,' *Studies in Philology* 89.4 (Fall 1992): esp. p. 490. Howard Anderson also has argued for the misogyny of Sterne's construction of the female reader in 'Structure, Language, Experience in the Novels of Laurence Sterne,' *The First English Novelists: Essays in Understanding*, ed. J.M. Armistead (Knoxville: University of Tennessee Press, 1985), pp. 185–223. Susan Noakes makes a similar argument about *Tristram Shandy* as part of a larger thesis concerning traditional representations of female readers. See 'On the Superficiality of Women,' *The Comparative Perspective on Literature: Approaches to Theory and Practice*, ed. Clayton Koelb and Susan Noakes (Ithaca and London: Cornell University Press, 1988), pp. 339–55. On the pedagogical double-bind that *Tristram Shandy* produces for the feminist reader, see Elizabeth W. Harries, 'The Sorrows and Confessions of a Cross-Eyed "Female-Reader" of Sterne,' in *Approaches to Teaching Sterne's 'Tristram Shandy*,' ed. Melvyn New (New York: MLA, 1989), esp. pp. 114–15. Against such criticism, as well as against earlier accounts of the novel that ignore the female characters in *Tristram Shandy*, an alternative feminist tradition has emerged to recuperate Sterne's representation of

women. Urging a reconsideration of the novel, Juliet McMaster claims that 'ced*Tristram Shandy* is *about* misogyny, and against it.' 'Walter Shandy, Sterne, and Gender: A Feminist Foray,' *English Studies in Canada* 15.4 (December 1989): 456. See also Ruth Marie Faurot, 'Mrs. Shandy Observed,' *Studies in English Literature 1500–1900* 10.3 (Summer 1970): 579–89; Leigh A. Ehlers, 'Mrs. Shandy's "Lint and Basilicon": The Importance of Women in *Tristram Shandy*,' *South Atlantic Review* 46.1 (January 1981): 61–75; Juliet McMaster, '"Uncrystalized Flesh and Blood": The Body in *Tristram Shandy*,' *Eighteenth-Century Fiction* 2.3 (April 1990): 197–214; Paula Loscocco, 'Can't Live Without 'Em: Walter Shandy and the Woman Within,' *The Eighteenth Century: Theory and Interpretation* 32.2 (Summer 1991): 166–79; Martha F. Bowden, 'The Interdependence of Women in *Tristram Shandy*: A Chapter of Eyes, Sausages and Sciatica,' *English Language Notes* 31.4 (June 1994): 40–7. William E. Rivers vindicates the figure of dear Jenny in his essay, 'The Importance of Tristram's "Dear, Dear Jenny,"' *Interpretations* 13.1 (Fall 1981): 1–9. My own critical standpoint tends to rest with the more positive vision of *Tristram Shandy*, although I would not attribute the novel's investment in women as a protofeminist stance on Sterne's part. Rather, I would read Sterne's desire to represent women as cultural agents as a necessary part of *Tristram Shandy*'s larger agenda; as I will argue in my discussion of *A Sentimental Journey* at the end of the chapter, Sterne went on to restructure this agenda from a strictly masculinist vantage point.

6 Ronald Paulson, 'Review Essay: English Painting – One School or Two?' *Eighteenth-Century Life* 17.3 (November 1993): 104–19. I take the examples that follow and my analysis of Hogarth's relation to civic humanist discourses directly from Paulson's article.

7 Holtz, *Image and Immortality*, p. 35. Brissenden makes a similar observation: 'Sterne became a friend of Reynolds, but he remained fundamentally unsympathetic to the "grand style"; and he was too much of a natural heretic, and too interested in the variety and unpredictability of human behaviour, to subscribe to the neo-classical credo.' 'Sterne and Painting,' p. 103.

8 Reynolds, 'Grand Stile of Painting,' *The Idler*, no. 79, *The Works of Samuel Johnson, LL.D.*, vol.2: *The Idler and The Adventurer*, ed. W.J. Bate, John M. Bullit, and L.F. Powell (New Haven and London: Yale University Press, 1963), p. 247.

9 Hogarth, *The Analysis of Beauty*, ed. Ronald Paulson (New Haven and London: Published for the Paul Mellon Centre for Studies in British Art by Yale University Press, 1997), p. 19.

10 Paulson, Introduction, *The Analysis of Beauty*, p. xxiv. For Hogarth, true

disinterestedness 'is not moral judgment but understanding – and the artist's function is not to enforce morality but to analyse it as another object with its own formal properties' (Paulson, Introduction, p. xxxiii).

11 Hogarth, *The Analysis of Beauty*, pp. 51, 58–9; Paulson notes in 'Review Essay: English Painting' that Venus's appearance in the first illustration of the *Analysis* further strengthens her position in Hogarth's aesthetic: 'Hogarth may have taken a hint from Spence, but he keeps his focus on Venus, substitutes for Mars an Apollo and for Vulcan a Hercules, suggesting that she is always going to be the center of *some* romantic triangle, and in no sense devalues her' (p. 108).

12 Milton, *Paradise Lost: An Authoritative Text, Background and Sources, Criticism*, ed. Scott Elledge (New York: Norton, 1975), pp. 196, 86; Hogarth, *The Analysis of Beauty*, pp. 34–5.

13 Ronald Paulson, *Breaking and Remaking: Aesthetic Practice in England, 1700–1820* (New Brunswick, NJ and London: Rutgers University Press, 1989), pp. 195–6.

14 John A. Dussinger, *The Discourse of the Mind in Eighteenth-Century Fiction* (The Hague and Paris: Mouton, 1974), pp. 178–80.

15 John Locke, *An Essay Concerning Human Understanding*, ed. Peter Nidditch (Oxford: Clarendon, 1975), pp. 162–3. Sterne also may be thinking of the reformulation of Locke's idea in David Hume's representation of the mind as 'a kind of theatre, where several perceptions successively make their appearance.' 'Of Personal Identity,' *A Treatise of Human Nature*. 2nd ed., ed. L.A. Selby-Bigge and Peter H. Nidditch (Oxford: Clarendon, 1978), p. 253.

16 For the full text of Shaftesbury's objection to a spectatorial appreciation of 'rich stuffs,' see chapter 1. For an analysis of Hogarth's relation to the commodities he represented in his paintings, see Paulson, 'Review Essay: English Painting,' pp. 105–7. Melvyn New argues that Widow Wadman stands as a figure for Sterne's imagination, claiming that 'the persistent reduction of human love to its physical manifestations is the weapon Sterne brings to bear against the sentimental view of man which Toby embodies.' *Laurence Sterne as Satirist: A Reading of 'Tristram Shandy'* (Gainesville: University of Florida Press, 1969), p. 195. New's comment draws our attention to the importance of the Widow to Sterne's narrative project as a whole, an importance that G.S. Rousseau also stresses in the analysis of the Widow's representation that appears in 'Threshold and Explanation: The Social Anthropologist and the Critic of Eighteenth-Century Literature,' *The Eighteenth Century: Theory and Interpretation* 22.2 (Spring 1981): 127–52. These observations indicate that women serve as more than 'rhetorical opportunities' (Benedict, '"Dear Madam,"' p. 497) in Sterne's novel. In

placing the widow at the heart of the novel's libidinous impulses, I am modifying J. Paul Hunter's claim that Elizabeth Shandy 'is finally the figure of the novel's subversive creative imagination.' My interest in the visual dimension of the widow's agency encourages me to give her priority in the list of the novel's female characters. See Hunter, 'Clocks, Calendars, and Names: The Troubles of Tristram and the Aesthetics of Uncertainty,' *Rhetorics of Order/Ordering Rhetorics in English Neoclassical Literature*, ed. J. Douglas Canfield and J. Paul Hunter (Newark: University of Delaware Press; London and Toronto: Associated University Presses, 1989), p. 196.

17 Indeed, Melvyn New has argued that Toby's failure to connect with Widow Wadman represents 'a critical commentary on the solipsistic failure of sentimentalism.' The Widow stands for 'a promise and a responsibility' that Sterne celebrates in the novel as a whole. New, 'William Hogarth and John Baldessari: Ornamenting Sterne's *Tristram Shandy*,' pp. 194, 195.

18 Bowden traces the representation of the eye in *Tristram Shandy* to Robert Burton. See 'The Interdependence of Women in *Tristram Shandy*,' pp. 40–7.

19 In his reading of an early scene of book 5, Jacques Berthoud notes that the text works 'less to condemn social prurience than to provoke it.' 'Shandeism and Sexuality,' *Laurence Sterne: Riddles and Mysteries*, ed. Valerie Grosvenor Myer, (London: Vision; Totowa, NJ: Barnes and Noble, 1984), p. 25.

20 I would not go so far as Dennis W. Allen in pursuing this line of argument. Allen claims that the novel sustains a 'vaginal view' of artistic production. 'Sexuality/Textuality in *Tristram Shandy*,' p. 670.

21 J. Paul Hunter's comments regarding Tristram's obsession with lineage provide insight into the larger gender dynamic operating in Sterne's novel: 'The Shandy family myth tries desperately to hold the male line. It is a mark of the times and of Sterne's generic insight into the times that the line will not hold nor the narrative order contain.' 'Clocks, Calendars, and Names,' p. 196.

22 Holtz, *Image and Immortality*, pp. 4–5.

23 Sterne to Eliza, [March 1767], *The Letters of Laurence Sterne*, ed. Lewis Perry Curtis (Oxford: Clarendon, 1935), p. 312.

24 Ibid., pp. 312, 313.

25 Ibid., p. 312; Sterne to Catherine Fourmantel [1759], p. 81. In a note to the letter to Fourmantel, Lewis Perry Curtis quotes John Croft's comments regarding Sterne's activities as a painter: '"He wou'd take up the Pencil and paint Pictures. He chiefly copied Portraits. He had a good Idea of Drawing, but not the least of mixing his colours. There are several Pictures of his painting at York, such as they are"' (*Letters*, p. 82, n. 2).

26 Sterne, [Summer 1759], *Letters*, p. 76; Sterne to David Garrick 27
January 1760, *Letters*, p. 87.
27 Holtz, *Image and Immortality*, pp. 154, 116.
28 Sterne to Catherine Fourmantel, [April 1760?], *Letters*, p. 105; Sterne,
30 January 1760, *Letters*, p. 90.
29 *London Chronicle* 7, 3–6 May 1760, p. 435.
30 Tom Keymer, 'Marvell, Thomas Hollis, and Sterne's Maria: Parody in
A Sentimental Journey,' *The Shandean* 5 (November 1993): 9–31; p. 12.
31 Benedict makes a related point when she suggests that Tristram's conception of his mother defines her as 'a cipher, even a hole or blank like the Widow's portrait who serves merely to draw out the characters of the Shandy men' ('"Dear Madam,"' p. 498). The widow's portrait does not draw out the Shandy men, however, so much as the Shandy reader.
32 Allen, 'Sexuality/Textuality in *Tristram Shandy*,' p. 666.
33 *The Polite Lady; or a Course of Female Education. In a Series of Letters, from a Mother to Her Daughter*, 2nd ed., corr. (London, 1769), pp. 16–17; Maria and R.L. Edgeworth, *Practical Education*, 3 vols. (London, 1801): 3.6.
34 James Grantham Turner links Sterne's representation of voyeurism in the blank portrait scene to the debates that surrounded *Pamela*'s publication a generation earlier. See 'Novel Panic: Picture and Performance in the Reception of Richardson's *Pamela*,' *Representations* 48 (Fall 1994): 80.
35 Hunter, 'Clocks, Calendars, and Names,' p. 196.
36 My argument here follows Barbara M. Benedict's in '"Dear Madam,"' pp. 485–98.
37 Ruth Perry makes a related point in 'Words for Sex;' The Verbal-Sexual Continuum in *Tristram Shandy*,' p. 31.
38 For an analysis of the homosocial structure of indecent jokes, see Sigmund Freud's *Jokes and their Relation to the Unconscious*, ed. and trans. James Strachey (New York: Norton, 1963), pp. 100–1.
39 Hunter, 'Clocks, Calendars, and Names,' p. 194.
40 Brissenden, 'Sterne and Painting,' p. 95.
41 Some of the most important contributions to this debate appear in the following: R. F. Brissenden, *Virtue in Distress: Studies in the Novel of Sentiment from Richardson to Sade* (London: Macmillan; New York: Barnes and Noble, 1974); John K. Sheriff, *The Good-Natured Man: The Evolution of a Moral Ideal, 1660–1800* (University, AL: University of Alabama Press, 1982); Arthur Hill Cash, *Sterne's Comedy of Moral Sentiments: The Ethical Dimension of the 'Journey'* (Pittsburgh: Duquesne University Press; Louvain, Belgium: Éditions E. Nauwelaert, 1966); John A. Dussinger, *The Discourse of the Mind in Eighteenth-Century Fiction* (The Hague and Paris: Mouton, 1974); Gardner D. Stout, Jr,

'Yorick's *Sentimental Journey*: A Comic "Pilgrim's Progress" for the Man of Feeling,' *Journal of English Literary History* 30.4 (December 1963): 395–412; Tom Keymer, 'Marvell, Thomas Hollis, and Sterne's Maria: Parody in *A Sentimental Journey*,' *The Shandean* 5 (November 1993): 9–31; Robert Markley, 'Sentimentality as Performance: Shaftesbury, Sterne, and the Theatrics of Virtue,' *The New Eighteenth Century: Theory, Politics, English Literature*, ed. Laura Brown and Felicity Nussbaum (New York: Methuen, 1987), pp. 210–30.

42 'What may look like an invitation to share moral agency with the author is in fact more likely to be a tactical immobilization of the reader's resistance to what is being proposed.' Jonathan Lamb, 'Sterne and Irregular Oratory,' *The Cambridge Companion to the Eighteenth-Century Novel*, ed. John J. Richetti (Cambridge: Cambridge University Press, 1996), 154. Lamb makes this claim in relation to both *Tristram Shandy* and *A Sentimental Journey*, but I believe it is more applicable to the later novel.

43 John A. Dussinger, *The Discourse of the Mind in Eighteenth-Century Fiction*, p. 177.

44 Laurence Sterne, *A Sentimental Journey through France and Italy by Mr. Yorick* (with *The Journal to Eliza* and *A Political Romance*), ed. Ian Jack (Oxford: Oxford University Press, 1984), p. 28. Future references will be to this edition and will be cited parenthetically.

45 Dussinger, *The Discourse of the Mind in Eighteenth-Century Fiction*, p. 194; Eve Kosofsky Sedgwick, *Between Men: English Literature and Male Homosocial Desire* (New York: Columbia University Press, 1985), p. 78.

46 Brissenden, *Virtue in Distress: Studies in the Novel of Sentiment from Richardson to Sade*, p. 224.

47 Keymer, 'Marvell, Thomas Hollis, and Sterne's Maria,' p. 14.

48 Dussinger, *The Discourse of the Mind in Eighteenth-Century Fiction*, p. 177; see also pp. 182–200.

49 Tom Keymer's wonderful analysis of the parodic elements at work in the representation of Maria includes a summary of her consumption as 'a veritable icon of sentimental distress.' See 'Marvell, Thomas Hollis, and Sterne's Maria,' p. 11.

50 Janet Todd, *The Sign of Angellica: Women, Writing and Fiction, 1660–1800* (New York: Columbia University Press, 1989), p. 141.

6: Portraits of the Woman Artist: Kauffman, Wollstonecraft, and Inchbald

1 Elizabeth Inchbald, Preface, *A Simple Story*, ed. J.M.S. Tompkins (Oxford: Oxford University Press, 1988), p. 1.

2 Albert O. Hirschman argues that the publication of Smith's *Wealth of Nations* in 1776 marks the end of the conflict between the idea of passions and interests; according to Smith, Hirschman suggests, 'the material welfare of "the whole society" is advanced when everyone is allowed to follow his own private interest.' *The Passions and the Interests: Political Arguments for Capitalism before Its Triumph* (Princeton: Princeton University Press, 1977), p. 111.
3 Claudia L. Johnson, *Equivocal Beings: Politics, Gender, and Sentimentality in the 1790s: Wollstonecraft, Radcliffe, Burney, Austen* (Chicago and London: University of Chicago Press, 1995), p. 14.
4 Candace Ward, 'Inordinate Desire: Schooling the Senses in Elizabeth Inchbald's *A Simple Story*,' *Studies in the Novel* 31.1 (Spring 1999): 2.
5 For an analysis of the relationship between Wollstonecraft and Inchbald as Jacobin writers, see Eleanor Ty, *The Unsex'd Revolutionaries: Five Women Novelists of the 1790s* (Toronto: University of Toronto Press, 1993); Gary Kelly, *Women, Writing, and Revolution, 1790–1827* (Oxford: Clarendon, 1993), and Kelly, *The English Jacobin Novel: 1780–1805* (Oxford: Clarendon, 1976).
6 Wendy Wassyng Roworth, 'Biography, Criticism, Art History: Angelica Kauffman in Context,' *Eighteenth-Century Women and the Arts*, ed. Frederick M. Keener and Susan E. Lorsch (New York and Westport, CT: Greenwood Press, under the auspices of Hofstra University, 1988), p. 219.
7 Germaine Greer, *The Obstacle Race: The Fortunes of Women Painters and Their Work* (London: Secker and Warburg; New York: Farrar, Straus, and Giroux, 1979), p. 277.
8 *London Chronicle* 43, 30 April–2 May 1778, p. 421.
9 I disagree with the emphasis that Wendy Wassyng Roworth places on the comments made about Kauffman's gender in the Royal Academy exhibition reviews, if only because these statements are simply outnumbered by the other comments that appear during the period, which stress many other characteristics of Kauffman's work. See Roworth, 'Kauffman and the Art of Painting in England,' in *Angelica Kauffman: A Continental Artist in Georgian England*, ed. Wendy Wassyng Roworth (London: Reaktion Books, in association with Brighton's Royal Pavilion, Art Gallery and Museums, 1992) esp. p. 86.
10 Richard Polewhele [sic], 'The Unsex'd Females; a Poem, Addressed to the Author of the Pursuits of Literature' (New York: Wm. Cobbett, 1800), p. 26.
11 *Morning Herald*, 6 May 1786.
12 Roworth, 'Kauffman and the Art of Painting in England,' p. 38.

13 *Middlesex Journal,* 25–8 April 1772.
14 For Marcia Pointon's discussion of female portraiture and allegory, see chapters 2 (pp. 59–88) and 5 (pp. 174–227) of *Strategies for Showing: Women, Possession, and Representation in English Visual Culture, 1665–1800* (Oxford and New York: Oxford University Press, 1997).
15 Fuseli quoted in Greer, *The Obstacle Race,* p. 82.
16 Some aspects of my argument about this painting follow the fine work of Wendy Wassyng Roworth and Angela Rosenthal. See Roworth, 'Biography, Criticism, Art History: Angelica Kauffman in Context,' *Eighteenth-Century Women and the Arts,* eds. Frederick M. Keener and Susan E. Lorsch, pp. 209–223, esp. pp. 218–221; Rosenthal, 'Angelica Kauffman Ma(s)king Claims,' *Art History* 15.1 (March 1992): 38–59, esp. pp. 46–9.
17 Rozsika Parker and Griselda Pollock, *Old Mistresses: Women, Art and Ideology* (New York: Pantheon, 1981), p. 91
18 Roworth, 'Biography, Criticism, Art History,' p. 221.
19 Rosenthal, 'Angelica Kauffman Ma(s)king Claims,' p. 47.
20 Pointon, *Strategies for Showing,* p. 178.
21 Mitzi Myers, 'Sensibility and the "Walk of Reason": Mary Wollstonecraft's Literary Reviews as Cultural Critique,' *Sensibility in Transformation: Creative Resistance to Sentiment from the Augustans to the Romantics: Essays in Honor of Jean H. Hagstrum,* ed. Syndy McMillen Conger (London and Toronto: Associated University Presses, 1990), p. 123.
22 Wollstonecraft, *Analytical Review* 1 (May–August 1788): 333; Elizabeth Inchbald, *The Artist* 1 (1810): 13, 16. For an excellent analysis of Wollstonecraft's and Inchbald's literary criticism in relation to Romanticism, see Anne K. Mellor, 'A Criticism of Their Own: Romantic Women Literary Critics,' *Questioning Romanticism,* ed. John Beer (Baltimore and London: Johns Hopkins University Press, 1995), pp. 29–48.
23 Mary Wollstonecraft, *Mary, a Fiction,* in *Mary, a Fiction and The Wrongs of Woman,* ed. Gary Kelly (Oxford: Oxford University Press, 1976), p. [i]. All future references will be to this edition and will be cited parenthetically.
24 Johnson, *Equivocal Beings,* pp. 49–50.
25 Myers views the contradiction that appears in Wollstonecraft's *œuvre* in a more positive light: 'Although Wollstonecraft's creative work cannot wholly escape from literary conventions, her critical practice demonstrates a surer mastery of these codes.' 'Sensibility and the "Walk of Reason,"' p. 134.
26 Johnson observes the relentless attacks launched at the female body throughout Wollstonecraft's works in chapter 2 of *Equivocal Beings,* pp. 47–69; Syndy McMillen Conger more specifically focuses on the representation of the mother in *Mary* as a figure for the corrupt sentimental heroine of

the novels Wollstonecraft's text satirizes. See Conger, *Mary Wollstonecraft and the Language of Sensibility* (London and Toronto: Associated University Presses, 1994), pp. 35–60.

27 Pope, 'Epistle II. To a Lady. Of the Characters of Women,' *Epistles to Several Persons (Moral Essays)*, ed. F.W. Bateson, Twickenham Edition of the Poems of Alexander Pope, vol. 3.2 (London: Methuen; New Haven: Yale University Press, 1951), p. 45, l. 3.

28 Interestingly, this description of the mother's revery sounds much like the idealized picture of literary interest that Wollstonecraft presents in her 'Advertisement': 'Those compositions only have power to delight, and carry us willing captives, where the soul of the author is exhibited, and animates the hidden springs. Lost in a pleasing enthusiasm, they live in the scenes they represent; and do not measure their steps in a beaten track, solicitous to gather expected flowers, and bind them in a wreath, according to the prescribed rules of art' ([i]). I will return to this seemingly paradoxical correlation below.

29 See Gary Kelly, *Revolutionary Feminism: The Mind and Career of Mary Wollstonecraft* (New York: St Martin's Press, 1992), p. 50.

30 I am conflating the narrator's voice with Mary's because I believe, especially by the end of the narrative, that the novel makes little, if any, distinction between the two voices. As Mitzi Myers points out, 'Initially more in control and more fully aware than Mary herself, "the Author" who composes the book's "Advertisement," the "I" who instructs the "Gentle Reader" how to discriminate among varieties of heroism, eventually merges with Mary herself.' 'Pedagogy as Self-Expression in Mary Wollstonecraft: Exorcising the Past, Finding a Voice,' *The Private Self: Theory and Practice of Women's Autobiographical Writings*, ed. Shari Benstock (Chapel Hill: University of North Carolina Press, 1988), p. 200. For an analysis of the narrator/author/character relationship in *Mary*, see also Kelly, *Revolutionary Feminism*, pp. 51–4, and Conger, *Mary Wollstonecraft and the Language of Sensibility*, pp. 55–60.

31 Johnson, *Equivocal Beings*, p. 57.

32 *Monthly Review*, 2nd ser., 2 (May–August 1790): 353.

33 Johnson, *Equivocal Beings*, p. 58.

34 Marilyn Butler, 'The Woman at the Window: Ann Radcliffe in the Novels of Mary Wollstonecraft and Jane Austen,' *Gender and Literary Voice*, ed. Janet Todd (New York and London: Holmes and Meier, 1980), p. 144.

35 Susan Gubar, 'Feminist Misogyny: Mary Wollstonecraft and the Paradox of "It Takes One to Know One,"' *Feminist Studies* 20.3 (Fall 1994): 461.

36 *The Critical Review; or Annals of Literature*, 2nd ser., 1 (February 1791): 207.

37 *General Magazine* (February 1791): 71.
38 *Lady's Magazine* (February 1791): 59; *Critical Review*, 2nd ser., 1 (February 1791): 213.
39 Eighteen years later, Maria Edgeworth linked the novel's emotional intensity to its success as a narrative: 'I cried my eyes almost out before I came to the end of the story: I think it the most pathetic and the most powerfully interesting tale I ever read.' Edgeworth to her cousin, Miss Sophy Ruxton, Dec. 1809. *The Life and Letters of Maria Edgeworth*, 2 vols., ed. Augustus J.C. Hare (Freeport, NY: Books for Libraries Press, 1971), 1:177–8.
40 Catherine Gallagher, *Nobody's Story: The Vanishing Acts of Women Writers in the Marketplace, 1670–1820* (Berkeley and Los Angeles: University of California Press, 1994), p. 192.
41 Michael Boardman does not consider this critical reception history when he argues that Inchbald was 'motivated by elements of thought that ... did not seem to disturb her own contemporaries.' The eighteenth-century critical uneasiness with the formal properties of Inchbald's narrative calls into question the argument Boardman advances in his dismissive attack on feminist readings of *A Simple Story*: that when we look at the novel in terms of its structural principles, ideological considerations drop away. 'Inchbald's *A Simple Story*: An Anti-Ideological Reading,' *The Eighteenth Century: Theory and Interpretation* 37.3 (Fall 1996): 281.
42 Elizabeth Inchbald, Preface, *A Simple Story*, ed. J.M.S. Tompkins (Oxford and New York: Oxford University Press, 1988), p. 1. All future references will be to this edition and will be cited parenthetically.
43 *Critical Review*, 2nd ser., 1 (February 1791): 207.
44 Inchbald quoted in J.M.S. Tompkins, ed., Introduction, *A Simple Story* (London: Oxford University Press, 1967), p. xi.
45 Ian Balfour, 'Promises, Promises: Social and Other Contracts in the English Jacobins (Godwin/Inchbald),' *The New Romanticisms: Theory and Critical Practice*, ed. David. L. Clark and Donald C. Goellnicht, (Toronto: University of Toronto Press, 1994), p. 250 n. 36.
46 On this subject, see George E. Haggerty, 'Female Abjection in Inchbald's *A Simple Story*,' *Studies in English Literature 1500–1900* 36.3 (Summer 1996): 655–71.
47 Terry Castle, *Masquerade and Civilization: The Carnivalesque in Eighteenth-Century Culture and Fiction* (Stanford: Stanford University Press, 1986), pp. 310–33.
48 Marcia Pointon, *Strategies for Showing*, pp. 201–2.
49 Terry Castle, *Masquerade and Civilization*, p. 312.
50 Pointon, *Strategies for Showing*, pp. 200–1.

51 *Monthly Review*, 2nd ser., 4 (January–April, 1791): 437.
52 Jo Alyson Parker, 'Complicating *A Simple Story*: Inchbald's Two Versions of Female Power,' *Eighteenth-Century Studies* 30.3 (Spring 1997): p. 267.
53 *General Magazine* (February 1791): 70.
54 Jane Spencer, Introduction, *A Simple Story*, ed. J.M.S. Tomkins (Oxford and New York: Oxford University Press, 1988), p. xx. For other articulations of this view, see also, Eleanor Ty, 'Disruption and Containment: The Mother and Daughter in *A Simple Story*,' in *Unsex'd Revolutionaries*, pp. 85–100; Katharine M. Rogers, 'Inhibitions on Eighteenth-Century Women Novelists: Elizabeth Inchbald and Charlotte Smith,' *Eighteenth-Century Studies* 11.1 (Fall 1977): 63–78; Susan Allen Ford, '"A name more dear": Daughters, Fathers, and Desire in *A Simple Story*, *The False Friend*, and *Mathilda*,' *Re-Visioning Romanticism: British Women Writers, 1776–1837*, ed. Carol Shiner Wilson and Joel Haefner (Philadelphia: University of Pennsylvania Press, 1994), pp. 51–71.
55 Castle, *Masquerade and Civilization*, p. 323. Haggerty argues along similar lines: 'Lady Matilda offers Inchbald the opportunity to extend her tale of quasi-Gothic horror and to redirect its force.' 'Female Abjection in *A Simple Story*,' p. 664.
56 Johnson, *Equivocal Beings*, p. 12.
57 Ward, 'Inordinate Desire,' p. 13.
58 Rushbrook's status as a feminized figure links him to the other female characters in the novel; the young man seems, indeed, to act out Miss Milner's narrative in a more explicit fashion than does Matilda: his desire for an illicit object who cannot be named links him to Miss Milner, as does his tendency to equivocate when confronted, and it is his repeated references to Lady Elmwood that prevents her from disappearing from the manifest content of the narrative altogether.
59 Haggerty, 'Female Abjection in Inchbald's *A Simple Story*,' p. 666.
60 Nora Nachumi, '"Those Simple Signs": The Performance of Emotion in Elizabeth Inchbald's *A Simple Story*,' *Eighteenth-Century Fiction* 11.3 (April 1999): p. 332.
61 Wollstonecraft, *Analytical Review* 10 (May–August 1791): 101–2.
62 Butler, 'The Woman at the Window,' pp. 140–1.
63 Jane Gallop, *The Daughter's Seduction: Feminism and Psychoanalysis* (Ithaca: Cornell University Press, 1982), p. 78.
64 *Monthly Review*, 2nd ser., 4 (January–April 1791): 437–8.
65 *Critical Review*, 2nd ser. (February 1791): 208.
66 *Monthly Review* 69 (November 1783): 439.
67 Parker makes a similar observation: 'Matilda's final fate – disposal in

marriage to her cousin Rushbrook – is itself somewhat troubling with its suggestion of incest, inbreeding, and a family turning in on itself rather than forging new social ties' ('Complicating *A Simple Story*,' p. 267). Haggerty suggests that the marriage plot 'seems so much less important than the paternal resolution ... that Inchbald feels that it is better to hint at it as a possibility than to claim it as a fact' ('Female Abjection in Inchbald's *A Simple Story*,' p. 669).
68 Inchbald quoted by Anna Lott, 'Sexual Politics in Elizabeth Inchbald,' *Studies in English Literature, 1500–1900* 34.3 (Summer 1994): 637.
69 Inchbald, *The Artist* 1, no. 14 (June 13, 1807): 16.
70 Jane Spencer, Introduction, *A Simple Story*, ed. J.M.S. Tompkins (Oxford and New York: Oxford University Press, 1988), p. xiv.

Afterword

1 Imagining novel readers of a later generation, Joyce Appleby asks, 'What were all those young women in the early nineteenth century doing when they eagerly consumed the literature of romance? They were seeking pleasure, learning about the world, finding models and exerting their own desires in the face of a clerical offensive against the reading of novels. Fashions set norms, but like statements, fashions point the way to their subversion.' 'Consumption in Early Modern Social Thought,' *Consumption and the World of Goods*, eds. John Brewer and Roy Porter (London and New York: Routledge, 1993), p. 172.
2 Jane Austen, *Pride and Prejudice*, ed. James Kinsley and Frank W. Bradbrook (London: Oxford University Press, 1970), pp. 220, 219, 332. Austen's *Emma* also uses the trope of the portrait to highlight the novel's interest in the subjectivism inherent in the act of beholding – and, by extension, of reading.
3 I am hesitant, even within the rhetoric of conclusion, to situate Jane Austen as a figure of closure. D.A. Miller's brilliant readings of Austen note the way that her novels 'are directed toward a state of absolute propriety: proper understanding expressed in proper erotic objects and proper social arrangements. Yet her narratives are generated precisely by an underlying instability of desire, language, and society, and as such, they are inevitably felt to threaten the very possibility of this definitive, "finalizing" state of affairs.' *Narrative and Its Discontents, Problems of Closure in the Traditional Novel* (Princeton, NJ: Princeton University Press, 1981), p. x. The formal principle governing my reading of the novel has been recently defined by J. Paul Hunter: 'Readers of narratives are like readers of other texts in

caring about the how more than the what, in finding process more important than outcome, texture than ending, desire than the stilling of desire.' 'Serious Reflections on Farther Adventures: Resistances to Closure in Eighteenth-Century English Novels,' *Augustan Subjects: Essays in Honor of Martin C. Battestin*, ed. Albert J. Rivero (Newark: University of Delaware; London: Associated Univ. Presses, 1997), p. 291.

Bibliography

Primary Sources

PERIODICALS

Analytical Review
The Artist
Critical Review
General Magazine
Gentleman's Magazine
Lady's Magazine
London Chronicle
London Magazine and Monthly Chronologer
The Lounger
Middlesex Journal
Monthly Review
Morning Chronicle and London Advertiser
Morning Herald
Morning Post
Morning Star
Public Advertiser
Public Ledger
St. James Chronicle
The World

PUBLISHED WORKS

Primary Sources

Addison, Joseph, and Richard Steele. *The Guardian*. Ed. John Calhoun Stephens. Lexington: University Press of Kentucky, 1982.

- *The Spectator.* 5 vols. Ed. Donald F. Bond. Oxford and New York: Clarendon, 1987.
Aikin, John, and Anna Laetitia Aikin. 'An Enquiry into Those Kinds of Distress Which Excite Agreeable Sensations.' In *Miscellaneous Pieces, in Prose.* London: J. Johnson, 1773.
Archenholz, Johann Wilhelm von. *A Picture of England: Containing a Description of the Laws, Customs, and Manners of England. Interspersed with Curious and Interesting Anecdotes of Many Eminent Persons.* London, 1797.
Austen, Jane. *Pride and Prejudice.* Ed. Frank W. Bradbrook and James Kinsley. London: Oxford University Press, 1970.
Automathes [Richard Griffith]. *Something New.* 2 vols. London: E. and D. Dilly, 1772.
Barbauld, Anna Laetitia, ed. *The Correspondence of Samuel Richardson.* 6 vols. London: R. Phillips, 1804.
Barry, James. *The Works of James Barry Esq., Historical Painter; Lectures on Painting, Delivered at the Royal Academy.* 2 vols. London: T. Cadell and W. Davies, 1809.
Beattie, James. 'On Fable and Romance.' In *Dissertations Moral and Critical.* London: Bernhard Fabian, 1783; reprint, New York: Garland, 1971.
Behn, Aphra. *The Works of Aphra Behn.* Ed. Montague Summers. New York: B. Blom, 1967.
Boaden, James, ed. *Memoirs of Mrs. Inchbald: Including Her Familiar Correspondence with the Most Distinguished Persons of Her Time.* 2 vols. London: R. Bentley, 1833.
Boswell, James. *The Journal of a Tour to the Hebrides with Samuel Johnson, LL.D.* Ed. R.W. Chapman. London: Oxford University Press, 1961.
Burke, Edmund. 'A Letter to a Noble Lord.' In *The Works of the Right Honourable Edmund Burke.* 6 vols. Ed. William Willis and Frank Walter Raffety. London: Oxford University Press, 1925–30.
- *A Philosophical Enquiry into the Origin of Our Ideas of the Sublime and Beautiful.* Ed. James T. Boulton. Notre Dame, IN, and London: University of Notre Dame Press, 1968.
Chesterfield, Earl of [Philip Dormer Stanhope]. *Letters Written by the Late Right Honourable Philip Dormer Stanhope, Earl of Chesterfield, to His Son, Philip Stanhope.* 2 vols. London: F. Newbery, 1774.
Dennis, John. *The Critical Works of John Dennis.* 2 vols. Ed. Edward Niles Hooker. Baltimore: Johns Hopkins University Press, 1939–43.
Dryden, John. *John Dryden.* Ed. Keith Walker. Oxford and New York: Oxford University Press, 1987.

- *The Poems of John Dryden.* Ed. John Sargeaunt. London: Oxford University Press, 1925.
- *The Works of John Dryden.* Ed. Edward Niles Hooker and H.T. Swedenberg, Jr. Berkeley: University of California Press, 1956.

Edgeworth, Maria. *The Life and Letters of Maria Edgeworth.* 2 vols. Ed. Augustus J.C. Hare. Boston and New York: Houghton Mifflin, 1894; reprint, Freeport, NY: Books for Libraries Press, 1971.

Edgeworth, Maria, and Richard Lovell Edgeworth. *Practical Education.* 2nd ed. 3 vols. London: Printed for J. Johnson by J. Crowder, 1801.

[Elliott, Miss]. *The Portrait, a Novel.* 2 vols. London: T. Hookham, 1783.

Fielding, Henry. *Amelia.* Ed. Martin C. Battestin. Middletown, CT: Wesleyan University Press, 1983.

- *The Covent-Garden Journal and A Plan of the Universal Register Office.* Ed. Bertrand A. Goldgar. Middletown, CT: Wesleyan University Press, 1988.
- *The History of the Adventures of Joseph Andrews and of His Friend Mr. Abraham Adams and An Apology for the Life of Mrs. Shamela Andrews.* Ed. Douglas Brooks-Davies. Oxford: Oxford University Press, 1990.
- *The History of Tom Jones, A Foundling.* 2 vols. Ed. Martin C. Battestin and Fredson Bowers. Oxford: Oxford University Press, 1975.

Fielding, Sarah. *Remarks on Clarissa (1749).* London: J. Robinson, 1749; reprint, Los Angeles: William Andrews Clark Memorial Library, University of California, 1985.

Freud, Sigmund. *Jokes and Their Relation to the Unconscious.* Ed. and trans. James Strachey. New York: Norton, 1963.

Funidos, Rigdum [pseud.]. *Kitty's Stream; or, the Noblemen turned Fisher-men. A comic satire. Addressed to the Gentlemen in the interest of the celebrated Miss K—y F—r.* London: A. Moore, 1759.

Haywood, Eliza. *The Female Spectator.* 4 vols. London: T. Gardner, 1748.

- *The History of Miss Betsy Thoughtless.* Ed. Beth Fowkes Tobin. Oxford and New York: Oxford University Press, 1997.

Hogarth, William. *The Analysis of Beauty.* Ed. Ronald Paulson. New Haven and London: Published for the Paul Mellon Centre for Studies in British Art by Yale University Press, 1997.

Horace. 'Ars Poetica.' In *Horace's Satires and Epistles.* Trans. Jacob Fuchs. New York: Norton, 1977.

Hume, David. *A Treatise of Human Nature.* 2nd ed. Ed. L.A. Selby-Bigge and Peter H. Nidditch. Oxford: Clarendon, 1978.

Hurd, Richard. *The Works of Richard Hurd, D.D. Lord Bishop of Worcester.* 8 vols. London: T. Cadell and W. Davies, 1811.

Inchbald, Elizabeth. *A Simple Story.* Ed. J.M.S. Tompkins. Oxford and New York: Oxford University Press, 1988.
Johnson, Samuel. *The Idler and The Adventurer.* Vol. 2 of *The Works of Samuel Johnson LL.D.* New Haven and London: Yale University Press, 1963.
– *Poems.* Vol. 6 of *The Works of Samuel Johnson LL.D.* New Haven and London: Yale University Press, 1964.
Knox, Vicesimus. 'On Novel Reading.' In *Essays Moral and Literary.* 2nd ed. 2 vols. London: Edward and Charles Dilly, 1779; reprint, New York: Garland, 1972.
La Fayette, Madame de [Marie-Madeleine Pioche de La Vergne]. *The Princess of Clèves.* Trans. Walter J. Cobb. New York: Meridian, 1989.
Locke, John. *An Essay Concerning Human Understanding.* Ed. Peter H. Nidditch. Oxford: Clarendon, 1975.
Manley, Delarivier. *The Adventures of Rivella.* Ed. Katherine Zelinsky. Peterborough, Ontario: Broadview Literary Texts, 1999.
– *The New Atalantis.* Ed. Rosalind Ballaster. Harmondsworth: Penguin, 1992.
– *The Secret History of Queen Zarah and the Zararians: Being a looking-glass for ——— —— In the Kingdom of Albigion. Popular Fiction by Women 1660–1730. An Anthology.* Ed. Paula R. Backscheider and John J. Richetti, pp. 45–80. Oxford: Clarendon, 1996.
Milton, John. *Paradise Lost: An Authoritative Text, Backgrounds and Sources, Criticism.* Ed. Scott Elledge. New York: Norton, 1975.
Montagu, Elizabeth. 'Dialogue XXVIII.' In *Dialogues of the Dead,* by George Lyttleton. 2nd ed. London, 1760; reprint, New York: Garland, 1970.
Montagu, Mary Wortley. *Letters from the Levant during the Embassy to Constantinople, 1716–18.* London: Joseph Rickerby, 1838; reprint, New York: Arno, 1971.
Moore, John. *The Works of Tobias Smollett, M.D. With Memoirs of His Life; To Which is Prefixed a View of the Commencement and Progress of Romance, by John Moore, M.D.* London: B. Law, et al., 1797.
Pepys, Samuel. *The Diary of Samuel Pepys.* 11 vols. Ed. Robert Latham and William Matthews. Berkeley and Los Angeles: University of California Press, 1972.
Piles, Roger de. *Cours de Peinture par Principes.* Paris: Jacques Estienne, 1708.
Piozzi, Hester Lynch. *Anecdotes of the Late Samuel Johnson, LL.D. During the Last Twenty Years of His Life.* 4th ed. London: T. Cadell, 1786.
Polite Lady; or A Course of Female Education, The. In a Series of Letters, from a Mother to Her Daughter. 2nd ed., corr. London, 1769.
Polwhele, Richard. 'The Unsex'd Females: A Poem, Addressed to the Author of the Pursuits of Literature.' New York: Wm. Cobbett, 1800.

Pope, Alexander. *Epistles to Several Persons (Moral Essays)*. Ed. F.W. Bateson. Twickenham Edition of the Poems of Alexander Pope, vol. 3.2. London: Methuen; New Haven: Yale University Press, 1951.
- *Imitations of Horace with An Epistle to Dr Arbuthnot and The Epilogue to the Satires.* Ed. John Butt. Twickenham Edition of the Poems of Alexander Pope, vol. 4. London: Methuen, 1939.
- *Pastoral Poetry and An Essay on Criticism.* Ed. E. Audra and Aubrey Williams. Twickenham Edition of the Poems of Alexander Pope, vol. 1. London: Methuen; New Haven: Yale University Press, 1961.

Pye, Henry James. *A Commentary Illustrating the Poetic of Aristotle.* London: John Stockdale, 1792; reprint, New York: Garland, 1971.

[Reeve, Clara]. *The Old English Baron: A Gothic Story. A New Edition.* London: Charles Dilly, 1782.

Reynolds, Joshua. *Discourses on Art.* Ed. Robert R. Wark. San Marino, CA: Huntington Library, 1959.

Richardson, Jonathan, Sr. *An Essay on the Theory of Painting.* London, 1715.
- *Two Discourses.* London, 1725; reprint, Bristol, and Sterling, VA: Thoemmes Press, 1998.

Richardson, Samuel. *Clarissa, or, The History of a Young Lady.* Ed. Angus Ross. Hammondsworth: Viking Penguin, 1985.
- *Pamela or, Virtue Rewarded.* Ed. T.C. Duncan Eaves and Ben D. Kimpel. Boston: Houghton Mifflin, 1971.
- *Selected Letters of Samuel Richardson.* Ed. John Carroll. Oxford: Clarendon, 1964.

Rousseau, Jean-Jacques. *The Social Contract and Other Later Political Writings.* Ed. and trans. by Victor Gourevitch. Cambridge: Cambridge University Press, 1997.

Shaftesbury, Third Earl of [Anthony Ashley Cooper]. *Characteristics of Men, Manners, Opinions, Times.* Ed. John M. Robertson. Indianapolis, IN, and New York: Bobbs-Merrill, 1964.
- *Second Characters or The Language of Forms.* Ed. Benjamin Rand. Bristol: Thoemmes Press, 1995.

Smollett, Tobias. *The Adventures of Ferdinand Count Fathom.* Ed. Jerry C. Beasley and O. M. Brack. Athens: University of Georgia Press, 1988.

Sterne, Laurence. *Letters of Laurence Sterne.* Ed. Lewis Perry Curtis. Oxford: Clarendon, 1965.
- *The Life and Opinions of Tristram Shandy, Gentleman: The Text.* Ed. Melvyn New and Joan New. Florida Edition of the Works of Laurence Sterne, vols. 1–3. Gainesville: University Presses of Florida, 1984.
- *A Sentimental Journey Through France and Italy by Mr. Yorick with The Journal to*

Eliza and A Political Romance. Ed. Ian Jack. Oxford: Oxford University Press, 1984.
Swift, Jonathan. *Gulliver's Travels.* Ed. Colvin McKelvie. London, 1726; reprint, Delmar, NY: Scholars' Facsimiles and Reprints, 1976.
Trusty, Simon [pseud.]. *An ODD LETTER, On a Most interesting Subject, To Miss K— F–h-r. Recommended to the Perusal of the LADIES of GREAT BRITAIN.* London: Printed for C.B. and sold by J. Williams, 1760.
Walpole, Horace. *Anecdotes of Painting in England 1760–1795.* New Haven: Yale University Press, 1937.
Wollstonecraft, Mary. *Mary, a Fiction and The Wrongs of Woman.* Ed. Gary Kelly. London: Oxford University Press, 1976.

Secondary Sources

Aikins, Janet E. 'Richardson's "Speaking Pictures."' In *Samuel Richardson: Tercentenary Essays,* ed. Margaret Anne Doody and Peter Sabor, 146–66. Cambridge and New York: Cambridge University Press, 1989.
Allen, Dennis W. 'Sexuality/Textuality in *Tristram Shandy.*' *Studies in English Literature 1500–1900* 25, 3 (Summer 1985): 651–70.
Alliston, April. *Virtue's Faults: Correspondences in Eighteenth-Century British and French Women's Fiction.* Stanford: Stanford University Press, 1996.
Armistead, J.M., ed. *The First English Novelists: Essays in Understanding.* Knoxville: University of Tennessee Press, 1985.
Armstrong, Nancy. *Desire and Domestic Fiction: A Political History of the Novel.* Oxford and New York: Oxford University Press, 1987.
Avedon, Richard. *Portraits.* London: Thames and Hudson; New York: Farrar, Straus and Giroux, 1976.
Backscheider, Paula R. *Spectacular Politics: Theatrical Power and Mass Culture in Early Modern England.* Baltimore and London: Johns Hopkins University Press, 1993.
Ballaster, Ros. *Seductive Forms: Women's Amatory Fiction from 1684 to 1740. With Particular Reference to Aphra Behn, Delarivier Manley, and Eliza Haywood.* Oxford: Clarendon; New York: Oxford University Press, 1992.
Barrell, John. *The Birth of Pandora and the Division of Knowledge.* London: Macmillan; Philadelphia: University of Pennsylvania Press, 1992.
– *English Literature in History, 1730–80: An Equal, Wide Survey.* London: Hutchinson; New York: St Martin's Press, 1983.
– *The Political Theory of Painting from Reynolds to Hazlitt: 'The Body of the Public.'* New Haven and London: Yale University Press, 1986.

Barrell, John, ed. *Painting and the Politics of Culture: New Essays on British Art 1700–1850.* Oxford and New York: Oxford University Press, 1992.
Barthes, Roland. *Camera Lucida: Reflections on Photography.* Trans. Richard Howard. New York: Hill and Wang, 1981.
– *S/Z.* Trans. Richard Miller. New York: Hill and Wang, 1974.
Bartolomeo, Joseph F. *A New Species of Criticism: Eighteenth-Century Discourse on the Novel.* Newark: University of Delaware Press; London and Toronto: Associated University Presses, 1994.
Bean, Brenda. 'Sight and Self-Disclosure: Richardson's Revision of Swift's "The Lady's Dressing Room."' *Eighteenth-Century Life,* n.s., 14, 1 (February 1990): 1–23.
Beasley, Jerry C. *Novels of the 1740s.* Athens: University of Georgia Press, 1982.
Beer, John, ed. *Questioning Romanticism.* Baltimore and London: Johns Hopkins University Press, 1995.
Bender, John. *Imagining the Penitentiary: Fiction and the Architecture of Mind in Eighteenth-Century England.* Chicago and London: University of Chicago Press, 1987.
– 'Impersonal Violence: The Penetrating Gaze and the Field of Narration in *Caleb Williams.*' In *Vision and Textuality,* ed. Stephen Melville and Bill Readings, 256–81. Durham, NC: Duke University Press, 1995.
Benedict, Barbara M. '"Dear Madam": Rhetoric, Cultural Politics and the Female Reader in Sterne's *Tristram Shandy.*' *Studies in Philology* 89, 4 (Fall 1992): 485–98.
Bersani, Leo. 'Representation and Its Discontents.' In *Allegory and Representation: Selected Papers from the English Institute,* ed. Stephen J. Greenblatt, 145–62. Baltimore and London: Johns Hopkins University Press, 1981.
Bindman, David. *Hogarth and His Times: Serious Comedy.* London: British Museum; Berkeley and Los Angeles: University of California Press, 1997.
Blanchard, Frederic T. *Fielding the Novelist: A Study in Historical Criticism.* New York: Russell and Russell, 1966.
Bloch, R. Howard, and Frances Ferguson, eds. *Misogyny, Misandry, and Misanthropy.* Berkeley: University of California Press, 1989.
Bloom, Edward A., and Lillian D. Bloom. *Joseph Addison's Sociable Animal: In the Marketplace, on the Hustings, in the Pulpit.* Providence, RI: Brown University Press, 1971.
Blouch, Christine. 'Eliza Haywood: Questions in the Life and Works.' PhD Diss., University of Michigan, 1991.
– 'Eliza Haywood and the Romance of Obscurity.' *Studies in English Literature 1500–1900* 31, 3 (summer 1991): 535–51.

Boardman, Michael. 'Inchbald's *A Simple Story*: An Anti-Ideological Reading.' *The Eighteenth Century: Theory and Interpretation* 37, 3 (Fall 1996): 271–84.
Bohls, Elizabeth A. 'Disinterestedness and Denial of the Particular: Locke, Adam Smith, and the Subject of Aesthetics.' In *Eighteenth-Century Aesthetics and the Reconstruction of Art*, ed. Paul Mattick, 16–51. Cambridge and New York: Cambridge University Press, 1993.
Bolla, Peter de. *The Discourse of the Sublime: Readings in History, Aesthetics, and the Subject*. Oxford and New York: Basil Blackwell, 1989.
Booth, Wayne C. *The Rhetoric of Fiction*. 2nd ed. Chicago and London: University of Chicago Press, 1983.
Bowden, Martha F. 'The Interdependence of Women in *Tristram Shandy*: A Chapter of Eyes, Sausages and Sciatica.' *English Language Notes* 31, 4 (June 1994): 40–7.
Bowers, Toni. *The Politics of Motherhood: British Writing and Culture, 1680–1760*. Cambridge and New York: Cambridge University Press, 1996.
Braudy, Leo. 'Penetration and Impenetrability in *Clarissa*.' In *New Approaches to Eighteenth-Century Literature: Selected Papers from the English Institute*, ed. Phillip Harth, 177–206. New York and London: Columbia University Press, 1974.
Brewer, John. *The Pleasures of the Imagination: English Culture in the Eighteenth Century*. London: HarperCollins; New York: Farrar, Straus and Giroux, 1997.
Brewer, John, and Roy Porter, eds. *Consumption and the World of Goods*. London and New York: Routledge, 1993.
Brilliant, Richard. *Portraiture*. Cambridge, MA: Harvard University Press, 1991.
Brissenden, R.F. 'Sterne and Painting.' In *Of Books and Humankind: Essays and Poems Presented to Bonamy Dobrée*, ed. John Butt, 93–108. London, Routledge and Kegan Paul, 1964.
– *Virtue in Distress: Studies in the Novel of Sentiment from Richardson to Sade*. London: Macmillan; New York: Barnes and Noble, 1974.
British Council. *British Painting in the Eighteenth Century: An Exhibition under the Gracious Patronage of Her Majesty the Queen [Shown at] The Montreal Museum of Fine Arts, The National Gallery of Canada, The Art Gallery of Toronto, [and] The Toledo Museum of Art, 1957–1958 in Collaboration with the British Council*. London: Montreal Museum of Fine Arts et al., 1957.
Brooks, Peter. *The Novel of Worldliness: Crébillon, Marivaux, Laclos, Stendhal*. Princeton: Princeton University Press, 1969.
Brownell, Morris R. *Alexander Pope and the Arts of Georgian England*. Oxford: Clarendon, 1978.
Bryson, Norman. *Vision and Painting: The Logic of the Gaze*. New Haven and London: Yale University Press, 1983.
Bryson, Norman, Michael Ann Holly, and Keith Moxey, eds. *Visual Theory: Painting and Interpretation*. Cambridge: Polity Press, 1991.

Butt, John, ed. *Of Books and Humankind: Essays and Poems Presented to Bonamy Dobrée.* London: Routledge and Kegan Paul, 1964.
Campbell, Jill. *Natural Masques: Gender and Identity in Fielding's Plays and Novels.* Stanford: Stanford University Press, 1995.
Canfield, J. Douglas, and J. Paul Hunter, eds. *Rhetorics of Order/Ordering Rhetorics in English Neoclassical Literature.* Newark: University of Delaware Press; London and Toronto: Associated University Presses, 1989.
Carretta, Vincent. *The Snarling Muse: Verbal and Visual Political Satire from Pope to Churchill.* Philadelphia: University of Pennsylvania Press, 1983.
Cash, Arthur Hill. *Sterne's Comedy of Moral Sentiments: The Ethical Dimension of the Journey.* Pittsburgh, PA: Duquesne University Press; Louvain, Belgium: Éditions E. Nauwelaerts, 1966.
Castle, Terry. *Clarissa's Ciphers: Meaning and Disruption in Richardson's 'Clarissa.'* Ithaca and London: Cornell University Press, 1982.
– *Masquerade and Civilization: The Carnivalesque in Eighteenth-Century English Culture and Fiction.* Stanford: Stanford University Press, 1986.
Chamberlain, Arthur B. *George Romney.* New York: Books for Libraries Press, 1910; reprint 1971.
Clark, David L., and Donald C. Goellnicht, eds. *The New Romanticisms: Theory and Critical Practice.* Toronto and Buffalo: University of Toronto Press, 1994.
Conger, Syndy McMillen. *Mary Wollstonecraft and the Language of Sensibility.* Madison, NJ: Fairleigh Dickinson University Press; London and Toronto: Associated University Presses, 1994.
Conger, Syndy McMillan, ed. *Sensibility in Transformation: Creative Resistance to Sentiment from the Augustans to the Romantics: Essays in Honor of Jean H. Hagstrum.* Madison, NJ: Fairleigh Dickinson University Press; London and Toronto: Associated University Presses, 1990.
Crown, Patricia. 'British Rococo as Social and Political Style.' *Eighteenth-Century Studies* 23, 3 (Spring 1990): 269–82.
Damrosch, Leopold, Jr. *God's Plot and Man's Stories: Studies in the Fictional Imagination from Milton to Fielding.* Chicago and London: University of Chicago Press, 1985.
Davis, Lennard J. *Factual Fictions: The Origins of the English Novel.* New York: Columbia University Press, 1983.
De Lauretis, Teresa. *Alice Doesn't: Feminism, Semiotics, Cinema.* Bloomington: Indiana University Press, 1984.
de Man, Paul. *The Rhetoric of Romanticism.* New York: Columbia University Press, 1984.
DeRitter, Jones. *The Embodiment of Characters: The Representation of Physical Experience on Stage and in Print, 1728–1749.* Philadelphia: University of Pennsylvania Press, 1994.

Derrida, Jacques. *Of Grammatology.* Trans. Gayatri Spivak. Baltimore and London: The Johns Hopkins University Press, 1976.
Doane, Mary Ann. *Femmes Fatales: Feminism, Film Theory, Psychoanalysis.* New York and London: Routledge, 1991.
Doody, Margaret Anne. 'Deserts, Ruins and Troubled Waters: Female Dreams in Fiction and the Development of the Gothic Novel.' *Genre* 10, 4 (Winter 1977): 529–72.
– *A Natural Passion: A Study of the Novels of Samuel Richardson.* Oxford: Clarendon, 1974.
– 'Richardson's Politics.' *Eighteenth-Century Fiction* 2, 2 (January 1990): 113–26.
– *The True Story of the Novel.* New Brunswick, NJ: Rutgers University Press, 1996.
Doody, Margaret Anne, and Peter Sabor, eds. *Samuel Richardson: Tercentenary Essays.* Cambridge and New York: Cambridge University Press, 1989.
Dussinger, John A. *The Discourse of the Mind in Eighteenth-Century Fiction.* The Hague and Paris: Mouton, 1974.
Eagleton, Terry. *The Rape of Clarissa: Writing, Sexuality and Class Struggle in Samuel Richardson.* Minneapolis: University of Minnesota Press, 1982.
Eaves, T.C. Duncan, and Ben D. Kimpel. *Samuel Richardson: A Biography.* Oxford: Clarendon, 1971.
– 'An Unpublished Pamphlet by Samuel Richardson.' *Philological Quarterly* 63, 3 (Summer 1984): 401–9.
Egerton, Judy. *Wright of Derby.* London: Tate Gallery; New York: Metropolitan Museum of Art, 1990.
Ehlers, Leigh A. 'Mrs. Shandy's "Lint and Basilicon": The Importance of Women in *Tristram Shandy.*' *South Atlantic Review* 46, 1 (January 1981): 61–75.
Einberg, Elizabeth, et al. *Manners and Morals: Hogarth and British Painting, 1700–1760.* London: Tate Gallery, 1987.
Fanning, Christopher. 'On Sterne's Page: Spatial Layout, Spatial Form, and Social Spaces in *Tristram Shandy.*' *Eighteenth-Century Fiction* 10, 4 (July 1998): 429–50.
Faurot, Ruth Marie. 'Mrs. Shandy Observed.' *Studies in English Literature 1500–1900* 10, 3 (Summer 1970): 579–89.
Ferguson, Frances. 'Rape and the Rise of the Novel.' *Representations* 20 (Fall 1987): 88–112.
Flynn, Carol Houlihan, and Edward Copeland, eds. *Clarissa and Her Readers: New Essays for The 'Clarissa' Project.* New York: AMS, 1999.
Ford, Karen Jackson. *Gender and the Poetics of Excess: Moments of Brocade.* Jackson: University Press of Mississippi, 1997.
Foucault, Michel. *Discipline and Punish: The Birth of the Prison.* Trans. Alan Sheridan. Harmondsworth: Penguin, 1977.

Franits, Wayne E. *Paragons of Virtue: Women and Domesticity in Seventeenth-Century Dutch Art.* Cambridge and New York: Cambridge University Press, 1993.
Fried, Michael. *Absorption and Theatricality: Painting and Beholder in the Age of Diderot.* Berkeley and Los Angeles: University of California Press, 1980.
– 'Manet's Sources: Aspects of His Art, 1859–65.' *Artforum* 7, 7 (March 1969): 28–82.
Fulton, Gordon D. 'Why Look at Clarissa?' *Eighteenth-Century Life*, n.s., 20, 2 (May 1996): 21–32.
Fumerton, Patricia. '"Secret Arts": Elizabethan Miniatures and Sonnets.' *Representations* 15 (Summer 1986): 57–97.
Gallagher, Catherine. *Nobody's Story: The Vanishing Acts of Women Writers in the Marketplace, 1670–1820.* Berkeley and Los Angeles: University of California Press, 1994.
Gallop, Jane. *The Daughter's Seduction: Feminism and Psychoanalysis.* Ithaca: Cornell University Press, 1982.
Goldgar, Bertrand A. 'Fielding and the Whores of London.' *Philological Quarterly* 64, 2 (Spring 1985): 265–73.
Gordon, Scott Paul. 'Disinterested Selves: *Clarissa* and the Tactics of Sentiment.' *ELH: A Journal of English Literary History* 64, 2 (Summer 1997): 473–502.
– 'Voyeuristic Dreams: Mr. Spectator and the Power of Spectacle.' *The Eighteenth Century* 36, 1 (Spring 1995): 3–23.
Gores, Steven J. 'The Miniature as Reduction and Talisman in Fielding's *Amelia.*' *Studies in English Literature 1500–1900* 37, 3 (Summer 1997): 573–93.
Greer, Germaine. *The Obstacle Race: The Fortunes of Women Painters and Their Work.* London: Secker and Warburg; New York: Farrar, Straus and Giroux, 1979.
Grundy, Isobel. 'Seduction Pursued by Other Means? The Rape in *Clarissa.*' In *Clarissa and Her Readers*, ed. Carol Houlihan Flynn and Edward Copeland, 255–67.
Gubar, Susan. 'Feminist Misogyny: Mary Wollstonecraft and the Paradox of "It Takes One to Know One."' *Feminist Studies* 20, 3 (Fall 1994): 453–73.
Guest, Harriet. 'A Double Lustre: Femininity and Sociable Commerce, 1730–60.' In *The Politics of Difference*, ed. Felicity Nussbaum. Special issue of *Eighteenth-Century Studies* 23, 4 (Summer 1990): 479–501.
Gunn, Daniel P. 'Is *Clarissa* Bourgeois Art?' *Eighteenth-Century Fiction* 10, 1 (October 1997): 1–14.
Gwilliam, Tassie. *Samuel Richardson's Fictions of Gender.* Stanford: Stanford University Press, 1993.
Haggerty, George E. 'Amelia's Nose: Or, Sensibility and Its Symptoms.' *The Eighteenth Century: Theory and Interpretation* 36, 2 (Summer 1995): 139–56.

- 'Female Abjection in Inchbald's *A Simple Story*.' *Studies in English Literature 1500–1900* 36, 3 (Summer 1996): 655–71.
- 'Fielding's Novel of Atonement: Confessional Form in *Amelia*.' *Eighteenth-Century Fiction* 8, 3 (April 1996): 383–400.

Hagstrum, Jean H. *The Sister Arts: The Tradition of Literary Pictorialism and English Poetry from Dryden to Gray*. Chicago and London: University of Chicago Press, 1958.

Harris, Jocelyn. 'Grotesque, Classical and Pornographic Bodies in *Clarissa*.' In *New Essays on Samuel Richardson*, ed. Albert J. Rivero, 101–16.

Harth, Phillip, ed. *New Approaches to Eighteenth-Century Literature: Selected Papers from the English Institute*. New York and London: Columbia University Press, 1974.

Hirschman, Albert O. *The Passions and the Interests: Political Arguments for Capitalism before Its Triumph*. Princeton: Princeton University Press, 1977.

Holtz, William V. *Image and Immortality: A Study of Tristram Shandy*. Providence, RI: Brown University Press, 1970.

- 'The Journey and the Picture: The Art of Sterne and Hogarth.' In *A History of Book Illustrations: 29 Points of View*, ed. Bill Katz, 315–32. Metuchen, NJ, and London: Scarecrow Press, 1994.

Hunter, J. Paul. *Before Novels: The Cultural Contexts of Eighteenth-Century English Fiction*. New York and London: Norton, 1990.

- *Occasional Form: Henry Fielding and the Chains of Circumstance*. Baltimore and London: Johns Hopkins University Press, 1975.
- 'Serious Reflections on Farther Adventures: Resistances to Closure in Eighteenth-Century English Novels.' In *Augustan Subjects: Essays in Honor of Martin C. Battestin*, ed. Albert J. Rivero, 276–94. Newark: University of Delaware Press; London: Associated University Presses, 1997.

Ingamells, John, and Robert Raines. 'A Catalogue of Paintings, Drawings and Etchings of Philip Mercier.' In *The Forty-Sixth Volume of the Walpole Society 1976–1978*. London: Printed for the Walpole Society [by] Pitman Press, 1978.

Jay, Martin. *Downcast Eyes: The Denigration of Vision in Twentieth-Century French Thought*. Berkeley, Los Angeles, and London: University of California Press, 1993.

Johnson, Claudia L. *Equivocal Beings: Politics, Gender, and Sentimentality in the 1790s: Wollstonecraft, Radcliffe, Burney, Austen*. Chicago and London: University of Chicago Press, 1995.

Kantorowicz, Ernst H. *The King's Two Bodies: A Study in Mediaeval Political Theology*. Princeton: Princeton University Press, 1957.

Katz, Bill, ed. *A History of Book Illustration: 29 Points of View*. Metuchen, NJ, and London: Scarecrow Press, 1994.

Keener, Frederick M., and Susan E. Lorsch, eds. *Eighteenth-Century Women and the Arts*. New York and Westport, CT: Greenwood Press, under the auspices of Hofstra University, 1988.
Kelly, Gary. *The English Jacobin Novel, 1780–1805*. Oxford: Clarendon, 1976.
– *Revolutionary Feminism: The Mind and Career of Mary Wollstonecraft*. New York: St. Martin's; London: Macmillan, 1992.
– *Women, Writing, and Revolution, 1790–1827*. Oxford: Clarendon, 1993.
Kermode, Frank. 'Richardson and Fielding.' *Cambridge Journal* 4, 2 (1950): 106–14.
Keymer, Tom. 'Marvell, Thomas Hollis, and Sterne's Maria: Parody in *A Sentimental Journey*.' *The Shandean* 5 (November 1993): 9–31.
Kinkead-Weekes, Mark. *Samuel Richardson: Dramatic Novelist*. Ithaca: Cornell University Press, 1973.
Koelb, Clayton, and Susan Noakes, eds. *The Comparative Perspective on Literature: Approaches to Theory and Practice*. Ithaca and London: Cornell University Press, 1988.
Lanser, Susan Sniader. *Fictions of Authority: Women Writers and Narrative Voice*. Ithaca and London: Cornell University Press, 1992.
Laqueur, Thomas. *Making Sex: Body and Gender from the Greeks to Freud*. Cambridge, MA, and London: Harvard University Press, 1990.
Lawrence, Cynthia, ed. *Women and Art in Early Modern Europe: Patrons, Collectors, and Connoisseurs*. University Park: Pennsylvania State University Press, 1997.
Lee, Joy Kyunghae. 'The Commodification of Virtue: Chastity and the Virginal Body in Richardson's *Clarissa*.' *The Eighteenth Century: Theory and Interpretation* 36, 1 (Spring 1995): 38–54.
Lewis, Alison. 'Joseph Highmore, 1692–1780.' PhD Diss., Harvard University, 1975.
Lipking, Lawrence. *The Ordering of the Arts in Eighteenth-Century England*. Princeton: Princeton University Press, 1970.
Lippincott, Louise. *Selling Art in Georgian London: The Rise of Arthur Pond*. New Haven and London: Published for the Paul Mellon Centre for Studies in British Art by Yale University Press, 1983.
Loesburg, Jonathan. 'Allegory and Narrative in *Clarissa*.' *Novel* 15, 1 (Fall 1981): 39–59.
London, April. 'Controlling the Text: Women in *Tom Jones*.' In *Women and Early Fiction*, ed. Jerry C. Beasley. Special issue of *Studies in the Novel* 19, 3 (Fall 1987): 323–33.
– *Women and Property in the Eighteenth-Century English Novel*. Cambridge and New York: Cambridge University Press, 1999.

Loscocco, Paula. 'Can't Live Without 'Em: Walter Shandy and the Woman Within.' *The Eighteenth Century: Theory and Interpretation* 32, 2 (Summer 1991): 166–79.
Lott, Anna. 'Sexual Politics in Elizabeth Inchbald.' *Studies in English Literature 1500–1900* 34, 3 (Summer 1994): 635–48.
Lynch, Deidre Shauna. *The Economy of Character: Novels, Market Culture, and the Business of Inner Meaning.* Chicago and London: University of Chicago Press, 1998.
MacPherson, Sandra. 'Lovelace, Ltd.' *ELH: A Journal of English Literary History* 65, 1 (Spring 1998): 99–121.
Marin, Louis. *Portrait of the King.* Trans. Martha M. Houle. Minneapolis: University of Minnesota Press, 1988.
Marshall, David. 'Fatal Letters: *Clarissa* and the Death of Julie.' In *Clarissa and Her Readers*, ed. Carol Houlihan Flynn and Edward Copeland, 213–53.
– *The Surprising Effects of Sympathy: Marivaux, Diderot, Rousseau, and Mary Shelley.* Chicago and London: University of Chicago Press, 1988.
Mattick, Paul, ed. *Eighteenth-Century Aesthetics and the Reconstruction of Art.* Cambridge and New York: Cambridge University Press, 1993.
McCrea, Brian. 'Clarissa's Pregnancy and the Fate of Patriarchal Power.' *Eighteenth-Century Fiction* 9, 2 (January 1997): 125–48.
– 'Politics and Narrative Technique in Fielding's *Amelia.*' *Journal of Narrative Technique* 13, 3 (Fall 1983): 131–40.
McFarlane, Cameron. *The Sodomite in Fiction and Satire, 1660–1750.* New York: Columbia University Press, 1997.
McMaster, Juliet. 'Reading the Body in *Clarissa.*' In *Clarissa and Her Readers*, ed. Carol Houlihan Flynn and Edward Copeland, 189–212.
– '"Uncrystalized Flesh and Blood": The Body in *Tristram Shandy.*' *Eighteenth-Century Fiction* 2, 3 (April 1990): 197–214.
– 'Walter Shandy, Sterne, and Gender: A Feminist Foray.' *English Studies in Canada* 15, 4 (December 1989): 441–58.
Millar, Oliver. *Sir Peter Lely, 1618–80: Exhibition at 15 Carlton House Terrace, London SW1.* London: National Portrait Gallery, 1978.
Miller, D.A. *Narrative and Its Discontents: Problems of Closure in the Traditional Novel.* Princeton: Princeton University Press, 1981.
Mullan, John. *Sentiment and Sociability: The Language of Feeling in the Eighteenth Century.* Oxford: Clarendon, 1988.
Myer, Valerie Grosvenor, ed. *Laurence Sterne: Riddles and Mysteries.* London: Vision; Totowa, NJ: Barnes and Noble, 1984.
Myers, Mitzi. 'Pedagogy as Self-Expression in Mary Wollstonecraft: Exorcising the Past, Finding a Voice.' In *The Private Self: Theory and Practice of Women's*

Autobiographical Writings, ed. Shari Benstock, 192–210. Chapel Hill and London: University of North Carolina Press, 1988.

Nachumi, Nora. '"Those Simple Signs": The Performance of Emotion in Elizabeth Inchbald's *A Simple Story*.' *Eighteenth-Century Fiction* 11, 3 (April 1999): 317–38.

Nestor, Deborah J. 'Virtue Rarely Rewarded: Ideological Subversion and Narrative Form in Haywood's Later Fiction.' *Studies in English Literature 1500–1900* 34, 3 (Summer 1994): 579–98.

New, Melvyn. *Laurence Sterne as Satirist: A Reading of 'Tristram Shandy.'* Gainesville: University of Florida Presses, 1969.

– 'William Hogarth and John Baldessari: Ornamenting Sterne's *Tristram Shandy*.' *Word and Image* 11, 2 (April–June 1995): 182–95.

New, Melvyn, ed. *Approaches to Teaching Sterne's 'Tristram Shandy.'* New York: MLA, 1989.

Nussbaum, Felicity, and Laura Brown, eds. *The New Eighteenth Century: Theory, Politics, English Literature.* New York: Methuen, 1987.

Ogden, Daryl S. 'Richardson's Narrative Space-Off: Freud, Vision and the (Heterosexual) Problem of Reading *Clarissa*.' *Literature and Psychology* 42, 4 (1996): 37–52.

Parker, Jo Alyson. 'Complicating *A Simple Story*: Inchbald's Two Versions of Female Power.' *Eighteenth-Century Studies* 30, 3 (Spring 1997): 255–70.

Parker, Rozsika, and Griselda Pollock. *Old Mistresses: Women, Art and Ideology.* New York: Pantheon, 1981.

Paulson, Ronald. *The Beautiful, Novel, and Strange: Aesthetics and Heterodoxy.* Baltimore and London: Johns Hopkins University Press, 1996.

– *Breaking and Remaking: Aesthetic Practice in England, 1700–1820.* New Brunswick, NJ and London: Rutgers University Press, 1989.

– *Hogarth.* 3 vols. New Brunswick, NJ: Rutgers University Press, 1991–3.

– *Hogarth: His Life, Art, and Times.* 2 vols. New Haven and London: Published for the Paul Mellon Centre for Studies in British Art by Yale University Press, 1971.

– 'Introduction.' *The Analysis of Beauty*, by William Hogarth. New Haven: Published for the Paul Mellon Centre for Studies in British Art by Yale University Press, 1997. xvii–lxiii.

– *Popular and Polite Art in the Age of Hogarth and Fielding.* Notre Dame, IN, and London: University of Notre Dame Press, 1979.

– 'Review Essay: English Painting – One School or Two?' *Eighteenth-Century Life*, n.s., 17, 3 (November 1993): 104–19.

– *Satire and the Novel in Eighteenth-Century England.* New Haven and London: Yale University Press, 1967.

Paulson, Ronald, ed. *Fielding: A Collection of Critical Essays.* Englewood Cliffs, NJ: Prentice-Hall, 1962.
Paulson, Ronald, and Thomas Lockwood, eds. *Henry Fielding: The Critical Heritage.* London: Routledge and Kegan Paul; New York: Barnes and Noble, 1969.
Pears, Iain. *The Discovery of Painting: The Growth of Interest in the Arts in England, 1680–1768.* New Haven and London: Published for the Paul Mellon Centre for Studies in British Art by Yale University Press, 1988.
Penny, Nicholas, ed. *Reynolds.* New York: Harry N. Abrams, 1986.
Perry, Ruth. *Women, Letters, and the Novel.* New York: AMS, 1980.
– 'Words for Sex: The Verbal-Sexual Continuum in *Tristram Shandy.*' *Studies in the Novel* 20, 1 (Spring 1988): 27–42.
Plogsterth, Ann Rose. 'The Institution of the Royal Mistress and the Iconography of Nude Portraiture in Sixteenth-Century France.' PhD Diss., Columbia University, 1991.
Pocock, J.G.A. *Virtue, Commerce, and History: Essays on Political Thought and History, Chiefly in the Eighteenth Century.* Cambridge: Cambridge University Press, 1985.
Pointon, Marcia. *Hanging the Head: Portraiture and Social Formation in Eighteenth-Century England.* New Haven and London: Published for the Paul Mellon Centre for Studies in British Art by Yale University Press, 1993.
– 'Intriguing Jewellery: Royal Bodies and Luxurious Consumption.' In *Luxurious Sensualities: Effeminacy, Consumption, and the Body Politic in Eighteenth-Century Representation,* ed. Mary Pearce and Vincent Quinn. Special issue of *Textual Practice* 11, 3 (Winter 1997): 493–516.
– *Strategies for Showing: Women, Possession, and Representation in English Visual Culture, 1665–1800.* Oxford and New York: Oxford University Press, 1997.
Poovey, Mary. *The Proper Lady and the Woman Writer: Ideology as Style in the Works of Mary Wollstonecraft, Mary Shelley, and Jane Austen.* Chicago and London: University of Chicago Press, 1984.
Preston, John. *The Created Self: The Reader's Role in Eighteenth-Century Fiction.* London: Heinemann, 1970.
Ribble, Frederick G. 'The Constitution of the Mind and the Concept of Emotion in Fielding's *Amelia.*' *Philological Quarterly* 56, 1 (Winter 1977): 104–22.
Ribeiro, Aileen. *The Art of Dress: Fashion in England and France 1750 to 1820.* New Haven and London: Yale University Press, 1995.
– *The Dress Worn at Masquerades in England, 1730 to 1790, and Its Relation to Fancy Dress in Portraiture.* New York and London: Garland, 1984.
Richards, Cynthia. '"The Pleasures of Complicity": Sympathetic Identification

and the Female Reader in Early Eighteenth-Century Women's Amatory Fiction.' *The Eighteenth Century* 36, 3 (Autumn 1995): 220–33.

Richetti, John J. *The English Novel in History, 1700–1780.* London: Routledge, 1999.

– *Popular Fiction before Richardson: Narrative Patterns, 1700–1739.* Oxford: Clarendon; New York: Oxford University Press, 1992.

– 'Voice and Gender in Eighteenth-Century Fiction: Haywood to Burney.' In *Women and Early Fiction*, ed. Jerry C. Beasley. Special Issue of *Studies in the Novel* 19, 3 (Fall 1987): 263–72.

Richetti, John J., *The Cambridge Companion to the Eighteenth-Century Novel.* Cambridge and New York: Cambridge University Press, 1996.

Rivero, Albert J., ed. *Augustan Subjects: Essays in Honor of Martin C. Battestin.* Newark: University of Delaware Press; London: Associated University Presses, 1997.

– *New Essays on Samuel Richardson.* New York: St Martin's Press, 1996.

Rivers, William E. 'The Importance of Tristram's "Dear, Dear Jenny."' *Interpretations* 13, 1 (Fall 1981): 1–9.

Rogers, Katharine M. 'Inhibitions on Eighteenth-Century Women Novelists: Elizabeth Inchbald and Charlotte Smith.' *Eighteenth-Century Studies* 11, 1 (Fall 1977): 63–78.

Rorty, Richard. *Philosophy and the Mirror of Nature.* Princeton: Princeton University Press, 1979.

Rosenthal, Angela. 'Angelica Kauffman Ma(s)king Claims.' *Art History* 15, 1 (March 1992): 38–59.

Rousseau, G.S. 'Threshold and Explanation: The Social Anthropologist and the Critic of Eighteenth-Century Literature.' *The Eighteenth Century: Theory and Interpretation* 22, 2 (Spring 1981): 127–52.

Roworth, Wendy Wassyng. 'Biography, Criticism, Art History: Angelica Kauffman in Context.' In *Eighteenth-Century Women and the Arts*, ed. Frederick M. Keener and Susan E. Lorsch, 209–33. New York and Westport, CT: Greenwood Press, under the auspices of Hofstra University, 1988.

Roworth, Wendy Wassyng, ed. *Angelica Kauffman: A Continental Artist in Georgian England.* London: Reaktion Books, in association with Brighton's Royal Pavilion, Art Gallery and Museums, 1992.

Runge, Laura L. 'Gendered Strategies in the Criticism of Early Fiction.' *Eighteenth-Century Studies* 28, 4 (Summer 1995): 363–78.

Schofield, Mary Anne. *Eliza Haywood.* Boston: Twayne, 1985.

– 'Exposé of the Popular Heroine: The Female Protagonists of Eliza Haywood.' *Studies in Eighteenth-Century Culture* 12 (1983): 93–103.

Schofield, Mary Anne, and Cecilia Macheski, eds. *Fetter'd or Free? British Women Novelists, 1670–1815.* Athens and London: Ohio University Press, 1986.
Sedgwick, Eve Kosofsky. *Between Men: English Literature and Male Homosocial Desire.* New York: Columbia University Press, 1985.
Shawe-Taylor, Desmond. *The Georgians: Eighteenth-Century Portraiture and Society.* London: Barrie and Jenkins, 1990.
Sheriff, John K. *The Good-Natured Man: The Evolution of a Moral Ideal, 1660–1800.* University: University of Alabama Press, 1982.
Smallwood Angela J. *Fielding and the Woman Question: The Novels of Henry Fielding and Feminist Debate 1700–1750.* New York: St Martin's Press, 1989.
Spacks, Patricia Meyer. 'Female Changelessness; or, What Do Women Want?' *Studies in the Novel* 19, 3 (Fall 1987): 273–83.
Spencer, Jane. *The Rise of the Woman Novelist: From Aphra Behn to Jane Austen.* Oxford and New York: Basil Blackwell, 1986.
Steiner, Wendy. *The Colors of Rhetoric: Problems in the Relation between Modern Literature and Painting.* Chicago and London: University of Chicago Press, 1982.
– *Exact Resemblance to Exact Resemblance: The Literary Portraiture of Gertrude Stein.* New Haven: Yale University Press, 1978.
Steiner, Wendy, ed. *Image and Code.* Ann Arbor, MI: Horace H. Rackham School of Graduate Studies, 1981.
Stevenson, John Allen. '"Alien Spirits": The Unity of Lovelace and Clarissa.' In *New Essays on Samuel Richardson,* ed. Albert J. Rivero, 85–99.
Stewart, Susan. *On Longing: Narratives of the Miniature, the Gigantic, the Souvenir, the Collection.* Durham, NC, and London: Duke University Press, 1993.
Stout, Gardner D., Jr. 'Yorick's *Sentimental Journey*: A Comic "Pilgrim's Progress" for the Man of Feeling.' *ELH: A Journal of English Literary History* 30, 4 (December 1963): 395–412.
Straub, Kristina. 'Reconstructing the Gaze: Voyeurism in Richardson's *Pamela.*' *Studies in Eighteenth-Century Culture* 18 (1988): 419–31.
– *Sexual Suspects: Eighteenth-Century Players and Sexual Ideology.* Princeton: Princeton University Press, 1992.
Strong, Roy. *The English Icon: Elizabethan and Jacobean Portraiture.* London: Paul Mellon Foundation for British Art, in association with Routledge and Kegan Paul; New York: Pantheon, 1969.
Strong, Roy, ed. *The British Portrait, 1660–1960.* Woodbridge, Suffolk: Antique Collectors' Club, 1991.
Taylor, John Tinnon. *Early Opposition to the English Novel: The Popular Reaction from 1760 to 1830.* Morningside Heights, NY: King's Crown Press, 1943.
Thompson, James. 'Patterns of Property and Possession in Fielding's Fiction.' *Eighteenth-Century Fiction* 3, 1 (October 1990): 21–42.

Tillyard, Stella. *Aristocrats: Caroline, Emily, Louisa, and Sarah Lennox, 1740–1832.* London: Chatto and Windus; New York: Farrar, Straus and Giroux, 1994.

Todd, Janet. 'Life After Sex: The Fictional Autobiography of Delariv[i]er Manley.' In *Last Laughs: Perspectives on Women and Comedy*, ed. Regina Barreca. Special Issue of *Women's Studies* 15, 1–3 (1988): 43–55.

– *The Sign of Angellica: Women, Writing and Fiction, 1660–1800.* New York: Columbia University Press; London: Virago, 1989.

Todd, Janet. ed. *Gender and Literary Voice.* New York and London: Holmes and Meier, 1980.

Tompkins, J.M.S. Introduction to *A Simple Story*, by Elizabeth Inchbald. London: Oxford University Press, 1967.

Tooley, Brenda Bean. 'Actaeon as Spectator: Intrusive Vision and Configurations of Femininity in Rochester, Swift, and Richardson.' PhD Diss., University of Notre Dame, 1991.

Towers, A.R. '*Amelia* and the State of Matrimony.' *Review of English Studies*, n.s., 5, 18 (April 1954): 144–57.

Townsend, Dabney. 'Shaftesbury's Aesthetic Theory.' *Journal of Aesthetics and Art Criticism.* 41, 2 (Winter 1982): 205–14.

Traugott, John. '*Clarissa*'s Richardson: An Essay to Find the Reader.' In *English Literature in the Age of Disguise*, ed. Maximillian E. Novak, 157–203. Berkeley: University of California Press, 1977.

– 'Molesting *Clarissa*.' *Novel* 15, 2 (Winter 1982): 163–70.

Turner, James Grantham. 'Introduction: A History of Sexuality?' In *Sexuality and Gender in Early Modern Europe: Institutions, Texts, Images*, ed. James Grantham Turner, 1–9. Cambridge and New York: Cambridge University Press, 1993.

– 'Lovelace and the Paradoxes of Libertinism.' In *Samuel Richardson: Tercentenary Essays*, ed. Margaret Anne Doody and Peter Sabor, 70–88. Cambridge and New York: Cambridge University Press, 1989.

– 'Novel Panic: Picture and Performance in the Reception of Richardson's *Pamela*.' *Representations* 48 (Fall 1994): 70–96.

– 'Sex and Consequence.' *Review* 11 (1989): 133–77.

Tuveson, Ernest. 'The Importance of Shaftesbury.' *ELH: A Journal of English Literary History* 20 (1953): 267–99.

Ty, Eleanor. *Unsex'd Revolutionaries: Five Women Novelists of the 1790s.* Toronto and Buffalo: University of Toronto Press, 1993.

Uphaus, Robert W. *The Impossible Observer: Reason and the Reader in Eighteenth-Century Prose.* Lexington: University Press of Kentucky, 1979.

Van Ghent, Dorothy. *The English Novel, Form and Function.* New York: Rinehart, 1953.

Vickery, Amanda. *The Gentleman's Daughter: Women's Lives in Georgian England.*
    New Haven and London: Yale University Press, 1998.
Ward, Candace. 'Inordinate Desire: Schooling the Senses in Elizabeth
    Inchbald's *A Simple Story.*' *Studies in the Novel* 31, 1 (Spring 1999): 1-18.
Warner, William Beatty. *Licensing Entertainment: The Elevation of Novel Reading in
    Britain, 1684–1750.* Berkeley: University of California Press, 1998.
- *Reading 'Clarissa': The Struggles of Interpretation.* New Haven and London: Yale
    University Press, 1979.
- 'Reading Rape: Marxist-Feminist Figurations of the Literal.' *Diacritics:
    A Review of Contemporary Criticism* 13, 4 (Winter 1983): 12-32.
- 'Staging Readers Reading.' In *Reconsidering the Rise of the Novel*, ed. David
    Blewett. Special Issue of *Eighteenth-Century Fiction* 12, 2-3 (January–April
    2000): 391-416.
Wasserman, Earl R. 'Nature Moralized: The Divine Analogy in the Eighteenth
    Century.' *ELH: A Journal of English Literary History* 20 (1953): 39-76.
Waterhouse, Ellis. *Painting in Britain, 1530–1790.* 3rd ed. Harmondsworth:
    Penguin, 1969.
Watt, Ian. *The Rise of the Novel: Studies in Defoe, Richardson and Fielding.* Berkeley
    and Los Angeles: University of California Press, 1957.
Wendorf, Richard. *The Elements of Life: Biography and Portrait-Painting in Stuart
    and Georgian England.* Oxford and New York: Clarendon, 1990.
- *Sir Joshua Reynolds: The Painter in Society.* Cambridge, MA: Harvard University
    Press, 1996.
Wendorf, Richard, ed. *Articulate Images: The Sister Arts from Hogarth to Tennyson.*
    Minneapolis: University of Minnesota Press, 1983.
Wendt, Allan. 'Clarissa's Coffin.' *Philological Quarterly* 39 (1960): 481-95.
- 'The Naked Virtue of *Amelia.*' *ELH: A Journal of English Literary History* 27, 2
    (June 1960): 131-48.
West, Shearer. 'Patronage and Power: The Role of the Portrait in Eighteenth-
    Century England.' In *Culture, Politics, and Society in Britain, 1660–1800*, ed.
    Jeremy Black and Jeremy Gregory, 131-53. Manchester and New York:
    Manchester University Press, 1991.
Whitley, William T. *Artists and Their Friends in England, 1700–1799.* 2 vols. New
    York and London: Benjamin Blom, 1968.
Williams, Ioan. *The Idea of the Novel in Europe, 1600–1800.* London: Macmillan;
    New York: New York University Press, 1979.
Williams, Ioan, ed. *Novel and Romance, 1700–1800: A Documentary Record.* New
    York: Barnes and Noble, 1970.
Wilson, Carol Shiner, and Joel Haefner, eds. *Re-Visioning Romanticism: British*

Women Writers, 1776–1837. Philadelphia: University of Pennsylvania Press, 1994.
Wilt, Judith. 'He Could Go No Farther: A Modest Proposal about Lovelace and Clarissa.' *PMLA* 92, 1 (January 1977): 19–32.
Wind, Edgar. *Hume and the Heroic Portrait: Studies in Eighteenth-Century Imagery*. Ed. Jaynie Anderson. Oxford: Clarendon, 1986.
Winn, James Anderson. *'When Beauty Fires the Blood': Love and the Arts in the Age of Dryden*. Ann Arbor: University of Michigan Press, 1992.
Wolff, Cynthia Griffin. 'Fielding's *Amelia*: Private Virtue and Public Good.' *Texas Studies in Literature and Language* 10, 1 (Spring 1968): 37–55.

Index

Italic type refers to figure numbers. Figures are found following p. 132.

Addison, Joseph, *The Spectator,* 7–9, 21, 34, 38, 58, 76, 123, 141; and Steele, 8, 9
Aikin, John, and Anna Laetitia, 23–4
Aikins, Janet, 83, 91, 111, 235n10
allegory, 33, 62, 100, 108–9, 110. *See also* portraits, allegorical
Allen, Dennis W., 166, 250n3, 254n20
Alliston, April, 51, 217n17, 236n13, 245n19
amatory fiction, 15, 22, 53, 68, 78, 79, 115, 133, 135, 145, 229n3. *See also* scandal narrative
Analytical Review, 22
Appleby, Joyce, 262n1
Armstrong, Nancy, 4, 7, 34
Austen, Jane, *Pride and Prejudice,* 212–13; *Emma,* 262n2

Backscheider, Paula, 59
Balfour, Ian, 197
Ballaster, Ros, 52, 63, 76, 135, 233n45, 234n49
baroque, aesthetics of, 61, 87, 97, 109, 239n42

Barrell, John, 16, 55, 152, 220n6, 221n15
Barthes, Roland, 7, 10, 59
Bean, Brenda, 239n44
Beasley, Jerry C., 234n2
Beaufort, Duke of, 55–6
Behn, Aphra, 10, 15, 78
beholding, 3, 10, 11, 33, 51, 55, 64, 65–6, 73, 75, 118, 133, 151, 157, 189, 200, 202, 204; and absorption, 43, 44, 45, 184; and reading, 14, 262n2; theatricality of, 45–6, 211. *See also* Fried, Michael; spectatorship
Bender, John, 5, 215n6
Benedict, Barbara M., 255nn31, 36
Berenger, Richard, 23
Berkeley, George, 154
Bersani, Leo, 6
Berthoud, Jacques, 254n19
Bindman, David, 229n100
Blanchard, Frederic T., 136
Boardman, Michael, 260n41
body, female, 10, 34, 37–8, 94, 109; male, 55–7, 98, 119, 230n7, 244n12;

monarchical, 51, 55, 60, 61, 119, 232n28. *See also* spectacle
Bohls, Elizabeth, 221-2n15
Boswell, James, 114
Bowden, Martha F., 157, 254n18
Bowers, Toni, 108, 241n63
Bradshaigh, Lady, *21*, 89, 95, 106
Braudy, Leo, 81, 92, 99
Brewer, John, 228n90
Brissenden, R.F., 170, 172, 250n4, 252n7
Brooks, Peter, 50-1, 218n29
Browne, Alice, 41
Burke, Edmund, 29, 31, 232n23
Burney, Frances, *Evelina*, 44, 177
Butler, Marilyn, 194, 206

Campbell, Jill, 136, 137, 243n3, 247n30
Carracci, Annibale, 183-4
Castle, Terry, 85-6, 93, 105, 140, 141, 147, 197, 198, 201, 202, 221n12, 249n57
Castlemaine, Lady (Barbara Villiers), 60
Chamberlain, Arthur B., 228n94
Charles II, King, 60-1
Chesterfield, Earl of, 23
Cleland, John, 30, 135
Colman, George, 208
Conger, Syndy McMillen, 258n26, 259n30
Cosway, Richard, 162
courtesans, 34, 47, 48, 60-2, 77, 210, 238n37. *See also* Kitty Fisher
Critical Review, 195, 200, 207
Croft, John, 254n25
Crown, Patricia, 221n15

Damrosch Jr, Leopold, 80
Davis, Lennard J., 224n35, 248n43

Delany, Mary, 115, 135
De Lauretis, Teresa, 64
de Man, Paul, 111
DeRitter, Jones, 216n9
Derrida, Jacques, 240n57
Doane, Mary Ann, 231n21
domestic ideology, 4, 7, 12, 116-17, 119, 180, 195, 212
Doody, Margaret Anne, 80, 83, 97, 127, 219n34, 236n12, 239n41
Draper, Eliza, 161-2, 176
Dryden, John, 'To Sir Godfrey Kneller,' 16; 'Preface to Sylvae,' 61
Dussinger, John A., 154, 170, 171, 176

Eagleton, Terry, 113
Eaves, Thomas C. Duncan, and Ben D. Kimpel, 237n24
Edgeworth, Maria, 31, 166, 260n39
Edwards, Mary, 47-8. *See also* Hogarth
ekphrasis, 12, 219n34
Eliot, George, *Middlemarch*, 213
Elliot, Grace Dalrymple, 40-1
excess, aesthetics of, 87, 211, 212,

Ferguson, Frances, 240n53
Fielding, Henry, 11, 15, 22, 145, 179; *Amelia*, 11, 30, 115-17, 118-19, 135-49; *Tom Jones*, 23, 138, 141, 151, 166, 175, 177; *Shamela*, 137
Fish, Stanley, 212
Fisher, Kitty, 35-40, 41, 47, 52
Ford, Karen Jackson, 87, 92
Foucault, Michel, 4, 5, 211, 215n4; *Discipline and Punish*, 4
Fourmantel, Catherine, 162, 163
Franits, Wayne, 219n34, 236n19
Fresnoy (pseud.), 35-6
Freud, Sigmund, 169, 255n38
Fried, Michael, 43, 62, 228n92
Fulton, Gordon D., 235n9

Fumerton, Patricia, 249n58
Funidos, Rigdum (pseud.), *Kitty's Stream: or, the Noblemen Turned Fisher-men*, 39–40
Fuseli, Henry, 183

Gainsborough, Thomas, 160; *Grace Dalrymple Elliot, 2*, 40; *Grace Dalrymple Elliot, 3*, 41; *Lady with a Spaniel, 7*, 42; *Mary 'Perdita' Robinson, 24*, 118
Gallagher, Catherine, 44, 72, 74, 195, 216n12, 230n7, 231n12, 233n43, 234n51
Gallop, Jane, 207
Garrick, David, 118
General Magazine, 195, 200
Gentleman's Magazine, 22, 25
Gothic fiction, 206
Goldsmith, Oliver, 23
Gordon, Scott Paul, 79–80, 217n26
Gores, Stephen J., 117, 148
Greer, Germaine, 180
Grundy, Isobel, 113, 240n50
Gubar, Susan, 194
Guest, Harriet, 7
Gunn, Daniel P., 236n13
Gwilliam, Tassie, 100, 104
Gwyn, Nell, *17*, 60, 61, 62

Haggerty, George E., 140, 203, 248n41, 261n55, 261–2n67
Hamilton, Emma (née Emma Hart), 41, 198–9
Harris, Jocelyn, 238n37, 240n51
Hays, Mary, *Memoirs of Emma Courtney*, 212
Haytley, Edward, *Miss E. Wandesford, 20*, 84; *Sir Roger and Lady Bradsheigh, 21*, 84–5
Haywood, Eliza, 10, 15, 78, 139; *The History of Miss Betsy Thoughtless*, 11, 115–17, 118–35, 136, 142–3, 145, 148, 149, 151, 196–7, 211; *The Female Spectator*, 123, 124, 132, 245n18, 246n24
hieroglyphics, 58, 84, 102, 105, 114, 231n21
Highmore, Joseph, *Elizabeth Harris, 4*, 42, 88–9
Hill, John, 164
Hirschman, Albert O., 215n2, 257n2
history painting, 16–19, 28, 38, 52, 180, 191
Hogarth, William, 157, 160, 164; *Miss Mary Edwards, 15*, 47–8, 142; *The Analysis of Beauty*, 151–4
Holtz, William V., 152, 160, 163, 250n4
Hudson, Thomas, *Anne Bouverie, 22*, 85; *Mary, Lady Wray, 5*, 42
Hughes, John, 8
Hume, David, *A Treatise of Human Nature*, 253n15
Hunter, J. Paul, 136, 144, 168, 169, 224n35, 247n36, 253–4n16, 254n21, 262n3
Hurd, Richard, 24

Inchbald, Elizabeth, 11, 187, 208–9; *A Simple Story*, 31, 179–80, 186, 194, 195–209, 211
Ingamells, John, and Robert Raines, 243n10
Irigaray, Luce, 176

Jay, Martin, 13, 215n8
Johnson, Claudia L., 178, 188, 192, 201, 258n26
Johnson, Samuel, 80, 114, 136, 152; *Idler*, 28; 'The Vanity of Human Wishes,' 17, 18

Kantorowicz, Ernst H., 231n16
Kauffman, Angelica, 164, 179, 180–6, 191, 193, 194, 196, 198, 201, 202, 209; *Self-Portrait*, 27, 181; *Self-Portrait in the Character of Painting Embraced by Poetry*, 28, 182–3; *Self-Portrait Hesitating between the Arts of Music and Painting*, 29, 183–6
Kelly, Gary, 189, 259n30
Kermode, Frank, 247n35
Keymer, Tom, 164–5, 174, 238n35, 256n49
Kinkead-Weekes, Mark, 238n38
Kneller, Sir Godfrey, 8, 9, 16
Knox, Vicesimus, 23, 25, 32

Laclos, Choderlos, *Dangerous Liaisons*, 44
La Fayette, Madame de [Marie-Madeleine Pioche de La Vergne], 243n4, 245n19, 246n23
Laing, R.D., 176
Lamb, Jonathan, 256n42
Lanser, Susan Sniader, 77, 245n17
Laqueur, Thomas, 240–1n59
Lawrence, Thomas, 39
Lely, Peter, 48, 60–2, 63, 69; *Nell Gwyn*, 17, 60; *Portrait of Louise de Kéroualle, Duchess of Portsmouth*, 16, 60
Lennox, Charlotte, *The Female Quixote*, 195
lesbianism, 70–5
letters, 42, 45–9
Lewis, Matthew, *The Monk*, 212
libertinism, 12, 67, 69, 70, 74, 80, 81, 91–101, 105, 110, 112
Lichtenstein, Jacqueline, 222n19
Lippincott, Louise, 221n15
literary interest, 3, 50, 57

Locke, John, 153, 155, 156
Loesberg, Jonathan, 107, 108
London, April, 242n68
London Chronicle, 16, 18, 39, 180
London Magazine and Monthly Chronologer, 25
Lott, Anna, 208–9
Lynch, Deidre Shauna, 116–17, 218n30, 246n22

Mackenzie, Henry, 22, 24
Mandeville, Bernard, 79
Manet, Edouard, *Olympia*, 62
Manley, Delarivier, 10, 11, 15, 45, 77, 78, 115, 117, 136, 190, 209, 212; as 'Delia,' 56–7, 65; *Adventures of Rivella*, 58, 63, 163; *New Atalantis*, 10, 50–77, 79, 81, 83, 84, 87, 101–2, 114, 118, 151, 166, 190, 233n40; *Secret History of Queen Zarah*, 30
Marin, Louis, 60, 231n16, 232n28
marriage, 84, 95, 97, 199, 201, 208, 212
Marshall, David, 110, 216n15, 240n56, 242n69
McCrea, Brian, 139, 241n61
McFarlane, Cameron, 244n12
McMaster, Juliet, 240n52
Mellor, Anne K., 258n22
Mercier, Philip, *Peg Woffington*, 23, 118
Millar, Oliver, 61, 232n32
Miller, D.A., 262n3
Milton, John, *Paradise Lost*, 141, 154
Montagu, Elizabeth, 22
Montagu, Lady Mary Wortley, 76
Monthly Review, 23, 30, 120, 200, 207, 208
Moore, John, 22

Morning Chronicle and London Advertiser, 18, 21
Morning Herald, 20, 34–5
Morning Post, 17
Morning Star, 17, 18
Mullan, John, 99
Myers, Mitzi, 187, 188, 258n25, 259n30

Nachumi, Nora, 205
Nestor, Deborah J., 243n2
New, Melvyn, 253n16
novels, 50, 79, 115, 150, 177, 179, 210–14; critical reception, history of, 14, 22–6, 29–33, 150, 187; reading of, 3, 14, 22, 25, 41, 51, 158, 188, 196, 211, 212; writing of, 3, 41, 51, 158, 209; and vision, 5–6

Ogden, Daryl S., 242n72

Parker, Jo Alyson, 200, 261n67
Parker, Rozsika, 184
Paulson, Ronald, 57, 152, 154, 217n28, 229nn101, 102, 252n6, 253n11
Pears, Iain, 220n2
Penny, Nicholas, 47, 226n76
Pepys, Samuel, 60
Perry, Ruth, 59, 255n37
Peters, Matthew William, 21
Piles, Roger de, *Cours de Peinture par Principes*, 19–20
Plogsterth, Ann, 62
Pocock, J.G.A., 19, 38, 231n12
Pointon, Marcia, 28, 37, 41, 182–3, 186, 198, 199, 225n65, 226n73, 227n86, 258n14
Polite Lady, or a Course of Female Education, 166

Pollock, Griselda, 184
Polwhele, Richard, 'The Unsex'd Females,' 181
Poovey, Mary, 5, 216n10
Pope, Alexander, 'Epistle to a Lady,' 20, 188; *An Essay on Criticism*, 40; 'The First Epistle of the Second Book of Horace,' 61–2
pornography, 67–8, 94, 133, 159, 166, 172
The Portrait, a Novel [Miss Elliot], 6, 208
portrait moral, 51
portraits, 6–7, 12, 41, 76, 179, 210, 211; allegorical, 182–8, 191; and authorial self-fashioning, 160–70; critical reception, history of, 14, 16–22, 26–9, 210; erotic, 64, 65, 133; female, 33–49, 52, 57, 60–2, 191; and the female reader, 33, 42–9; male, 47, 52, 119, 236n15; miniature, 67–9, 112, 116–19 (*see also* Haywood, Eliza, *The History of Betsy Thoughtless*; Fielding, Henry, *Amelia*); portrait narrative, 10–11; Restoration, 48, 60–3, 161; self-portraits, 100, 111, 204 (*see also* Kauffman, Angelica)
Portsmouth, Duchess of (Louise de Keroualle), 60, 62. *See also* Lely, Peter
Poussin, Nicolas, 183–4
pregnancy, 105–8
Preston, John, 99, 239n47
private interests, 3–4, 7, 14–15, 17, 31, 33, 41, 47, 66, 75, 79–80, 90, 103, 116, 137, 151, 157, 177, 178–9, 186, 194, 195, 209, 211–12, 219n32, 257n2
prostitution, 21, 33–4, 35, 36, 37, 39,

40, 41, 48, 52, 96, 99, 100, 138–9, 143, 146, 148, 164, 181, 198. *See also* courtesans

Public Advertiser, 21, 33

Pye, Henry James, 25

Radcliffe, Ann, 206

realism, literary, 94, 109; psychological, 115, 147; social, 129, 149, 213

Reeve, Clara, 31, 32

Restoration, 10, 15, 32, 34, 40, 60, 77, 98, 119, 210, 212

Reynolds, Joshua, 15, 16, 26, 28, 33, 34, 152–3, 155, 160, 164–6, 168, 178, 181, 186, 210, 213; *Discourses,* 18, 19, 26, 157; *Emily, Countess of Kildare,* 8, 43; *A Girl Reading,* 10, 43, 46; and Kitty Fisher, 35–40, 43, 47; *Kitty Fisher,* 14, 47, 48; *Kitty Fisher as Cleopatra Dissolving the Pearl,* 1, 36–8, 48, 51; *Laurence Sterne,* 25, 162–3

Ribble, Frederick G., 249n58

Ribeiro, Aileen, 83–4, 85

Richards, Cynthia, 53, 56

Richardson Sr, Jonathan, 31; *An Essay on the Theory of Painting,* 26–8

Richardson, Samuel, 15, 22, 140, 179; *Pamela,* 3, 4, 30–1, 136; *Clarissa,* 10, 11, 31, 33, 43, 44, 78–114, 115, 116, 117, 120, 125, 128, 129, 135, 136, 141, 144–5, 149, 151, 193, 211

Richetti, John, 57, 119

Robinson, Mary, 118

Romney, George, 165; *Lady McLeod,* 6, 42; *Serena,* 11, 44

Rorty, Richard, 216n11

Rosenthal, Angela, 185, 258n16

Rousseau, G.S., 253n16

Rousseau, Jean-Jacques, *The Social Contract,* 3, 4

Roworth, Wendy Wassyng, 180, 182, 184–5, 257n9, 258n16

Royal Academy, 20, 21, 34, 35, 40, 180, 221n7

Ruffhead, Owen, 23

Runge, Laura L., 25–6, 222n20

Russell, John, *Miss Chambers,* 9, 43

St. James Chronicle, 17

satire, 150, 211; political, 52–7, 59

scandal narrative, 22, 50, 58, 66, 78, 79, 121, 124, 211, 229n3. *See also* amatory fiction

Schor, Naomi, 246n23

Sedgwick, Eve Kosofsky, 87, 171, 237n23

seduction plot, 57, 62, 118, 159. *See also* amatory fiction

sentiment, 4, 69, 79, 81, 109, 174, 211, 212; sentimental aesthetics, 56, 135, 150; sentimental culture, 170, 177; sentimental novel, 24, 25, 43, 80, 193, 209, 229n3

Shaftesbury, Third Earl of, 5, 6, 23, 25, 31, 55, 59, 117, 120, 152, 154, 155, 157, 183, 189, 220n6; 'Advice to an Author,' 24; *Characteristics of Men, Manners, Opinions, Times,* 16, 220n4; *Second Characters,* 16, 19, 20, 222n17

Shawe-Taylor, Desmond, 228n89

Smallwood, Angela J., 246n26, 249n55

Smith, Charlotte, 187

Spacks, Patricia Meyer, 137, 149

spectacle, 3, 4, 6, 7, 9, 34, 47, 63, 64, 66, 69, 76, 100–1, 109, 120–1, 130, 132–4, 139, 199; portrait as, 6, 10, 148

spectatorship, 4, 7, 33, 43, 55, 63, 67,

73, 116, 135, 141, 153–4, 157, 158; sympathetic, 5, 6, 11, 101, 118, 148. *See also* beholding
Spencer, Jane, 201, 209
Steiner, Wendy, 219n32
Sterne, Laurence, 11, 25, 29, 31, 164, 178, 179; caricature of his wife, *26*; *Sentimental Journey*, 151, 164, 170–7; *Tristram Shandy*, 11, 150–70, 172, 173, 174–5
Stevenson, John Allen, 240n58
Stewart, Susan, 117
sublime, 189
Swift, Jonathan, 53, 143, 230n11
sympathy, 89, 103; and portraits, 28, 29, 31, 33

Taylor, John Tinnon, 15, 220n1
Thompson, James, 249nn49, 50
Tiepolo, Giovanni Battista, 36
Tillyard, Stella, 228n89
Todd, Janet, 63, 120, 177
Tolomei, Claudio, 27
Trevisani, Francesco, 36
Trusty, Simon (pseud.), *An ODD LETTER ... to Miss K– – F—h-r*, 37, 40
Tscherny, Nadia, 229n101
Turner, James Grantham, 41, 91, 220n35, 227n87, 233n47, 237n20, 255n34

van Dyck, Anthony, 27
Vandyke style, 10, 82–6, 102, 111, 112–14
Van Ghent, Dorothy, 237n33
Vickery, Amanda, 217–18n28

vision, 4, 10, 13, 99, 190, 213
visual culture, 11–12, 15
voyeurism, 6, 11, 33, 45–6, 51, 57, 76, 81, 92, 102, 118, 131, 133, 148, 155, 158, 166, 173

Ward, Candace, 179
Warner, William Beatty, 22, 23, 80, 87, 96, 217n27, 227n88, 230nn3, 5, 231n20
Waterhouse, Ellis, 60
Watt, Ian, 3, 104
Wendorf, Richard, 12, 117, 119, 142, 224n49
Wendt, Allan, 139
West, Benjamin, 152
Wilde, Oscar, *Picture of Dorian Gray*, 213
Williams, Ioan, 22
Woffington, Peg, *19*, 78, 118. *See also* Mercier, Philip
Wolff, Cynthia Griffin, 144
Wollstonecraft, Mary, 11, 209; *Analytical Review*, 187, 206; *Mary, a Fiction*, 179–80, 186–94, 196, 259n28; *Vindication*, 194
women, as artists, 181, 209; and authorship, 3, 10, 48, 52, 56, 64, 65, 78, 178–80, 208–9; and portraiture, 33–49; and reading, 33, 42–3, 45–6, 48–9, 78, 171, 188–9
Wright of Derby, Joseph, 45–6, 47, 152, 164; *A Girl Reading a Letter by Candlelight, with an Old Man ...*, *13*, 45–6; *A Girl Reading a Letter by Candlelight, with a Young Man ...*, *12*, 45

www.ingramcontent.com/pod-product-compliance
Lightning Source LLC
Chambersburg PA
CBHW030304080526
44584CB00012B/431